Henry William Wolff

People's banks

A record of social and economic success. Second Edition

Henry William Wolff

People's banks
A record of social and economic success. Second Edition

ISBN/EAN: 9783337107819

Printed in Europe, USA, Canada, Australia, Japan

Cover: Foto ©Suzi / pixelio.de

More available books at **www.hansebooks.com**

PEOPLE'S BANKS:

A RECORD OF SOCIAL AND ECONOMIC SUCCESS

BY

HENRY W. WOLFF.

"If some one had told me a few years ago what progress co-operation was about to make, I should have said that he was talking of a vision of Utopia."—Mr GLADSTONE.

"Le plus grand banquier du monde est celui qui dispose de l'obole du prolétaire."—JULES SIMON.

Second Edition.

REVISED AND ENLARGED.

LONDON:
P. S. KING & SON,
12 AND 14, KING STREET, WESTMINSTER.
1896.

All rights reserved.

TO

THE HON. L. LUZZATTI,

Councillor of State; late Italian Minister of the Treasury and Finance;

THE FOUNDER OF THE ITALIAN BANCHE **POPOLARI,**

HIS COUNTRY'S BENEFACTOR,

THIS VOLUME IS

DEDICATED

IN TOKEN OF WARM PERSONAL **AFFECTION**

AND UNALTERED ESTEEM.

CONTENTS.

	PAGE
PREFACE	xiii
PREFACE TO THE FIRST EDITION	xv
PUBLICATIONS BY THE SAME AUTHOR ON THE SAME AND ALLIED SUBJECTS	xvii
LIST OF AUTHORITIES . . .	xix

CHAPTER I.

INTRODUCTION 1

Social Importance of the Subject—Its Bearing on the Labour Question—Its Bearing on the Land Question—Capital and Labour are not necessarily antagonistic—The Working-man "his own Capitalist"—Want of Employment remedied by Increase of Production—Two Californias—Success of People's Banks—A System based upon Self-help—Mr Gladstone on Thrift—Self-help made Productive as well as Provident—What People's Banks may do—In Towns—Working-men their own Employers—In the Country—"A New World"—"Co-operation has done it all"—Moral Results superior even to Economic—Appreciation by the Poor—Simplicity of the **System**—Its Security—Our past Indifference to the Subject—"**Aidez-à-faire.**"

CHAPTER II.

THE GENERAL IDEA 15

The general Idea is not new—Difficulties of its Application—Efficacy of Credit—Only small Funds required at starting—Early Co-operation in Spain and Portugal—The Problem to be solved—Sir R. Morier's Opinion: Labour can be Mortgaged—"The Capitalisation of Honesty"—The Working-man to work out his own Salvation—Wastefulness of Charities as compared with Self-help—Instances quoted from France—Difficulties of inducing the Honest Poor to borrow—Security is not obtainable otherwise than by Self-help — Self-help has succeeded where Charity has failed—Instances quoted from Alsace, Italy, and

CHAPTER II.—*continued.*

Germany—Frankenheim—The Lesson to be drawn—The Poor Man is the most scrupulous Repayer—Sir R. Morier's Cardinal Rules—"Democratised Credit"—In England Credit is still the Monopoly of the Rich—"Aspirare a discendere."

CHAPTER III.

THE TWO PROBLEMS 30

The Task is two-fold—Its Economic Aspect—People's Banks as Savings Banks—"Collecting Banks"—People's Banks as fixing Savings in their own Localities—The first economic Object is cheap Credit—The Question is not one of Money but of Security—Lord Salisbury on "Money"—Scotch Cash Credit—Two Foundations for Security—Agricultural and Industrial Credit—The Point of Divergence—Characteristic Requirements in Dense Populations—In Sparse—The two kinds of Credit are not antagonistic, but complementary.

CHAPTER IV.

THE TWO ASPECTS OF THE QUESTION . . 41

"Mutualism" and "Co-operation"—Advantages of purely Economic Co-operation—Interest stronger than mere Sense of Duty—How this applies to Co-operative Banking—"L'esprit de lucre domine tout"—It is nevertheless useful—Altruistic Co-operation—It is genuinely Co-operative—And based upon Self-help—Its Effects—Recriminations between Partisans of the two Types.

CHAPTER V.

CREDIT TO AGRICULTURE 49

Why Agriculture must be classed as a "Poor" Calling—Agriculture has become a "Business" without the Resources of a "Business"—Its Need of Money—Instances of the Utility of Money: Woolwich—Fresnes—Dippoltshausen—The Need is furthermore attested by the Report of the Royal Agricultural Commission—"Tant vaut l'homme, tant vaut la terre"—The Small Cultivator's Needs—Profitableness of Small Holdings—A Case quoted from Germany—The Forest of Montello—The Case of the Larger Farmer—Where Money may help—How Credit helped in the Drought of 1893—An Example from France—M. Giraud in the Nièvre—Similar Cases occurring in Germany and Austria—A Sussex Landlord's Application of the Lesson—What Credit the Farmer has now—Landlord's Credit—Dealer's Credit—Banker's Credit—Scotch Cash Credit—Usurer's Credit—Why Ordinary Banks cannot provide what is wanted—Opinion of the President of the German Imperial Bank—"L'échéance agricole n'est que nominale"—Necessity of creating a marketable Personal Security.

CHAPTER VI.

THE "CREDIT ASSOCIATIONS" OF SCHULZE-DELITZSCH   71

The Germans the first Organisers of Co-operative Credit—Schulze-Delitzsch—The first "Credit Association"—Dr Bernhardi improves the System—Schulze's peculiar Aptitude—His Difficulties—Government Persecutions—Schulze's Problem stated by himself—Unlimited Liability—It is not indispensable—The real "Keystone of the System"—"Compulsory Savings Banks"—Schulze's System described—The Success of the System—Extended beyond Germany—Smallness of Losses—Practical Success assured in some measure by Departures from Theoretical Rules—Agricultural Credit—Its large Amount—The Credit Associations of Augsburg—Insterburg—Gotha—A small Bank: Walldorf—Cosel—Defects in the Schulze-Delitzsch Organisation—Salutary effect of a Compulsory Audit—In spite of all the Schulze-Delitzsch System has done inestimable good—Statistics.

CHAPTER VII.

THE RAIFFEISEN "LOAN BANKS"   115

The Origin of Raiffeisen "Loan Banks"—Their Founder—The "Jews"—Their Usurious Practices—Excessive Distress calls forth a Remedy—A Co-operative Bakery—Co-operative Purchase of Stock—The First "Loan Bank"—Triumph of the Movement—Never a Penny lost—Raiffeisen's Aim—His System—Safeguards adopted—Simplicity of the Method—How the Loan Banks are trusted—Federation of the Banks—The Central Council—The Central Bank—Its Services—Co-operative Supply—Further Developments—Benefits of the Loan Bank System—The Causes of Success Analysed—Instance of Mülheim—"A Happy Combination of Business and Philanthropy."

CHAPTER VIII.

OFFSHOOTS AND CONGENERS   152

Spread of Co-operative Banking—Offshoots in Germany—Of the Schulze-Delitzsch Type—Of the Raiffeisen Type—"Particularist" Secessions—The Haas Associations—The "Peasants' Associations"—Political Banks—"Co-operative Law"—Belgian "Peasants' Associations"—Austria and Hungary—Co-operative Banking among various Races—Slav Associations—Communal Loan Banks—German Credit Associations—Instances—Credit Associations in Galicia—Schulze-Delitzsch Banks in Hungary—Army and Navy Loan Associations—Raiffeisen Banks—An Official Inquiry—The Result—An Austrian Raiffeisen Bank—Slav Raiffeisen Banks—Transylvania—Hybrid Banks in the County of Pesth—Co-operative Banking in Scandinavia—In the Netherlands—In Russia—In Servia—In Roumania—In Spain and Portugal—The Spanish Positos—Modern Co-operative Banking in Spain—India: The "Nidhis"—China—Japan.

CHAPTER IX.

THE "BANCHE POPOLARI" OF ITALY . 195

PAGE

Past Attempts to create Popular Credit—The Italian Savings Banks—Luigi Luzzatti—Departing in some features from Schulze's System, he creates a New Type of Bank—He limits Liability—Reduces the Value of Shares and the Time allowed for Payment—How Honesty is "Capitalised"—Wholly Democratic Administration—The Results are: Admirable Management, a large Inflow of Deposits, Safety of Transactions—Bankers Support the Movement—The Friendly Societies—History of the Movement—The Pioneer Bank of Milan—Its Troubles and its Triumph—The Causes of Success—Representation of Classes in the Banks—Organisation—Comitato di Sconto—Comitato dei Rischi—Variety of the Banks' Operations—Short Terms and Small Loans Preferred—The Supply of Funds—The Consiglio—The Sindaci—The Probiviri—The Reserve Fund—Merits and Defects of the System—The "Loan of Honour"—Credit to Agriculture—The Law of 1869—Cartelle Agrarie—The Law of 1887—Cartelle a scadenza fissa—M. Sani's Method—Spread and Growth of the Movement—Present Position of the Banks—Scarcely touched by the Crisis—Unsound Banks—Instances of Sound Ones—Agricultural and Urban—A Working-men's Bank—"Catholic" Banks—M. Luzzatti, "the Benefactor of his Country."

CHAPTER X.

THE "CASSE RURALI" OF ITALY . 260

Need of Small Village Banks—Common Features in Rural Italy and Rural England—Instances of Oppression—Usury common before the Banks were created—The Earliest Propaganda—Dr Leone Wollemborg—His first Cassa Rurale—Its Organisation—A Slight Departure from Raiffeisen Methods—Increase of the Casse—Their Success—The Village Bank of Loreggia—Its Work Explained—Object-lessons—Corazza—The Good which Village Banks generally have done—Testimonials to their Work—Village Banks employed as Succursales to great Savings Banks—Parma—"Catholic" Village Banks—Don Luigi Cerutti—The Work of such Banks—Advantages of and Objections to the Enlistment of the Denominational Principle—The Casse as a Factor of National Regeneration.

CHAPTER XI.

THE BELGIAN "BANQUES POPULAIRES" . . 286

Local Circumstances favouring Co-operation—"Unions du Credit"—Need of more Popular Credit—Léon d'Andrimont, the Schulze-Delitzsch of Belgium—His Early Difficulties—Eventual Success—Statistics—Instances—The People's Banks of Verviers, Ghent, Liége—The Problem of Credit to Agriculture still unsolved—The

CHAPTER XI.—*continued*.

Reason why—Some Prejudices against the Raiffeisen System—Ultramontane Raiffeisen Banks—M. Mahillon overcomes the Prejudice—Present Prospects of Success.

CHAPTER XII.

CO-OPERATIVE BANKING IN SWITZERLAND . . 305

Distinctive Character of Swiss Money Co-operation—Co-operative Purchase of Cattle in Thurgau and Zurich—Local Substitutes for Popular Credit—Easy Mortgages—Caisses Ouvrières—Co-operative Business Banks—The "Schweizerische Volksbank"—Other Co-operative Banks—Some Lessons to be Learnt from Swiss Co-operative Banking—Pioneer Raiffeisen Banks.

CHAPTER XIII.

CO-OPERATIVE BANKING IN FRANCE . 321

Backward State of Co-operative Banking in France—Ingenious and Costly Experiments in the Past—An Adverse Law—French Etatisme has much to answer for—"La Furia Francese"—The Silos of Algiers—The Start of the Movement—The "Crédit au Travail"—The "Société Mère" and its Offspring—Disastrous Effect of the War of 1870—Italian Example reanimates the Movement—Viganò's Bank at Cannes—The Bank of Mentone—It creates Village Banks and becomes the Centre of a new Movement—The Second Centre: M. Durand's Caisses Rurales—Their Astonishing Increase—The Third Centre: The Syndicats Agricoles—Objections to their Methods—The Bank of Productive Associations—The Crédit Coopératif de Lorraine—M. Rouzès' little Bank at Paris—Hopeful Prospects.

CHAPTER XIV.

CONCLUSION 356

The Sum **of the** Tale told — Economic **and Moral** Results — The Underlying Principle is one—Merits of **the** various Systems —And Dangers besetting them—The Lesson for the United Kingdom—Why it may be held that there is Room for Co-operative Banks among us—Our Needs—Existing Institutions evidencing the Existence of a Want and the Applicableness of the Co-operative Remedy—Our Hindrances—Our Advantages—Unreasonable Objections—A Flaw in our Savings Banks System—People's Banks might correct it—Our Pioneer Banks in England, Wales, and Ireland—A Needful Warning—An Association gone astray—It is absolutely essential that Co-operative Banking should be built up upon Self-help and the quickening of Responsibility—No Gifts or Patronage allowable—Encouraging Progress of the Movement in England and Ireland—Banks to be found in Australia—The Need of India—Relief in Prospect—"The Resources of People's Banks **are** Illimitable."

PREFACE TO THE SECOND EDITION.

So much new matter has been added to the earlier "Record" of People's Banking, that this Second Edition may almost rank as a new book.

In our own country the idea of Co-operative Banking has, as I must gratefully own, met with a far more ready reception than I had any reason to anticipate. The interest betokened has appeared to me to call for fuller and more detailed description of many points affecting the subject than I felt warranted in entering into in the first edition.

I owe thanks for information freely given to so many kind friends that it would be hopeless to attempt to mention all by name. I must, however, single out one, namely, Mr E. W. Brabrook, the Chief Registrar of Friendly Societies, whose ready help in the preparation of Model Rules, alike for PEOPLE'S BANKS and for VILLAGE BANKS, has proved invaluable.

Please God, the good cause having succeeded in enlisting interest, will now speed here as it has sped elsewhere, to the benefit of millions! So far as I am able, I shall always be happy to assist with further explanation in whatever quarter such assistance may be asked.

H. W. W.

June 1896.

PREFACE TO THE FIRST EDITION.

THE subject discussed in the following chapters is new to most English readers. The kind interest with which articles dealing with one portion of it, recently published in the *Economic Review* and the *Agricultural Economist*, have been received, the attention accorded to lectures delivered in various places, and the direct bearing which the matter obviously has upon our present social—that is, at bottom, economic—troubles, encourages me to hope that in some quarters, at any rate, some information upon one of the most signally successful movements of our century may prove not unacceptable.

I desire to record my sincere acknowledgments for information very liberally given, orally and by letter—in some cases at no small sacrifice of time and trouble—to a considerable number of gentlemen connected with the cause of provident action and co-operation, more particularly to the Hon. L. Luzzatti; Herr R. Raiffeisen; M. E. Tisserand, *Conseiller d'Etat et Directeur de l'Agriculture*, in the French Ministry of Agriculture; Dr von Langsdorff, of Dresden, and other heads of Agricultural

Departments of German States; Dr von Jekelfalussy, Chief of the Statistical Office of Hungary; our Chief Registrar of Friendly Societies; Dr von Keussler, of St Petersburgh; Director Cremer, of Neuwied; Professor Concini, of Rome; M. A. Micha, Secretary-General of the Federation of Belgian *Banques Populaires;* M. A. Yersin, Director-General of the *Schweizerische Volksbank;* M. L. Durand, of Lyons; and the Very Reverend Father de Besse.

H. W. W.

February 1893.

PUBLICATIONS BY THE SAME AUTHOR UPON THE SAME AND ALLIED SUBJECTS.

PEOPLE'S BANKS. A Record of Social and Economic Success. 1893. Longmans. 7s. 6d. (*Out of print.*)

AGRICULTURAL BANKS. Their Object and their Work. Agricultural Banks Association, 7 & 8 Palace Chambers, Westminster. 1894. 1s.

VILLAGE BANKS. How to start them—How to work them—What the Rich may do to help them. With Model Rules and Model Account Sheets added. P. S. King & Son. 6d.

A PEOPLE'S BANK MANUAL. Rules and Directions. P. S. King & Son. 6d.

CREDIT CO-OPERATION IN GERMANY. *Economic Review*, October 1892.

PEOPLE'S BANKS FOR ENGLAND. *Economic Review*, October 1893.

OUR VILLAGE BANK. *Westminster Review*, May 1894.

CO-OPERATIVE CREDIT. *Economic Review*, July 1894.

PEOPLE'S BANKS. *New Ireland Review*, August 1894.

THE POOR MAN'S COW. *National Review*, October 1894.

CATHOLIC BANKS. *New Ireland Review*, May 1895.

CO-OPERATION IN AGRICULTURE. *Contemporary Review*, October 1895.

THE CASE FOR AGRICULTURAL BANKS. *Contemporary Review*, April 1896.

THE CO-OPERATIVE BANKING MOVEMENT. *Economic Review*, April 1896.

ESSAIS DE CRÉDIT POPULAIRE EN ANGLETERRE ET EN ECOSSE. *Cinquième Congrès des Banques Populaires Françaises. Actes du Congrès.* Imprimerie Coopérative, Menton. 1894.

LES BANQUES POPULAIRES AU POINT DE VUE COOPÉRATIF. *Sixième Congrès des Banques Populaires Françaises. Actes du Congrès.* Imprimerie Coopérative, Menton. 1895.

LE CRÉDIT AGRICOLE. *Journal des Économistes*, December 1895.

LE CRÉDIT AGRICOLE. *Huitième Congrès des Banques Populaires Françaises. Actes du Congrès.* Imprimerie Coopérative, Menton. 1896. (*Shortly.*)

*Information on the subject dealt with in this book will **be found in** the following publications:—*

SCHULZE-DELITZSCH, H.—"Vorschuss- und Creditvereine als Volksbanken," 1876.
RAIFFEISEN, F. W.—"**Die** Darlehnskassenvereine."
——— "Kurze Anleitung zur Gründung **von** Darlehnskassenvereinen," **1890**.
WUTTIG, N.—"Friedrich Wilhelm Raiffeisen."
BRANDT, O.—"System Raiffeisen."
SCHMID, F.—"**Die** Genossenschaftssysteme," Wien, 1887.
LUZZATTI, L.—"**Rapport du** Président de l'Association **des Banques** Populaires Italiennes," **Rome**, 1889.
——— "La Diffusione del **Credito, Padova**," **1863**.
LEVI, ETTORE.—"Manuale **per le Banche** Popolari," Milano, 1886.
MANGILI, F.—"La Banca **Popolare di Milano**," 1881
CALLIN, ANGELO.—"Guida per **la Fondazione** delle Piccole Banche **Popolari** nelle Città e nelle **Campagne**," Venezia, **1886**.
ANDRIMONT, LÉON D'.—"**Le Crédit Agricole**," **1888**.
MICHA, A.—"Le Réescompte," **1892**.
LAVELEYE, E. DE.—"De l'Organisation du Crédit Agricole."
DURAND, L.—"**Le Crédit Agricole**," 1891.
SAY, J. B. L.—"**Dix Jours dans la Haute Italie**," Paris, 1883.
ROSTAND, E.—"**Une visite à quelques institutions de prévoyance en Italie**," 1891.
VIGANÒ, FRANCESCO.—"Banques Populaires de 1865 à 1875," **1875**.
ROCQUIGNY, LE COMTE DE.—"Les Syndicats Agricoles **et le** Socialisme agraire," Paris, 1893.
——— "LA COOPÉRATION DE PRODUCTION DANS L'AGRICULTURE," Paris, 1896.
COURTOIS, A.—"Banques Populaires," **1890**.
VALLEROUX, HUBERT P.—"Les **Associations** Coopératives en France et à l'Étranger, **Ouvrage Couronné**," 1884.
LECOUTEUX.—"Les Syndicats **et le Crédit** Agricole, in *Le Journal d'Agriculture pratique*," 1890.
BESSE, P. LUDOVIC DE.—"Deux **Rapports**," Paris, 1892.

LIST OF AUTHORITIES.

RAYNERI, CH.—"Le Manuel des Banques Populaires," Guillaumin, Paris, 1895.
CRÜGER, H.—"Die Erwerbs- und Wirthschafts-Genossenschaften," 1892.
CONRAD, JOH.—"Handwörterbuch der Staatswissenschaften," Jena, 1889, &c.
FASSBENDER, Dr M.—"Die Bauernvereine und die Landwirthschaft," Paderborn, 1884.
STÖGER, Dr O. F., in *Schmoller's Jahrbuch*, 1891. Heft III.
"REPORTS BY HER MAJESTY'S REPRESENTATIVES ABROAD ON THE SYSTEMS OF CO-OPERATION IN FOREIGN COUNTRIES," 1886.
"LANDWIRTHSCHAFTLICHE JAHRBÜCHER, 1875 and 1876."—Berlin (containing the Report of the Royal Commission).
MINISTERIO DI AGRICOLTURA, &c.—"Le Società Cooperative, &c., nell' anno, 1889," Roma, 1892.
―――― "Statistica delle Banche Popolari," Roma, 1885.
―――― "Banche Popolari, anno 1893," Roma, 1895.
―――― "Bollettino delle Società per Azioni" (monthly).
"EXPOSITION UNIVERSELLE DE 1889."—Congrès International d'Agriculture. Rapport, Paris, 1889.
"EXPOSITION UNIVERSELLE DE PARIS," 1889.—Rapport présenté par Leone Wollemborg : Les Caisses Rurales Italiennes, 1889.
"EXPOSITION UNIVERSELLE DE PARIS," 1889.—Rapport présenté par M. A. Micha.
"BANQUE POPULAIRE DE LIÉGE."—Rapports (annual).
"FÉDÉRATION DES BANQUES POPULAIRES," Liége, 1887, and subsequent Reports.
ANNUAL REPORTS OF THE CONGRESSES OF BELGIAN *Banques Populaires.*
"DENKSCHRIFT DER SCHWEIZERISCHEN VOLKSBANK," 1869-1889.
"BERICHTE DER SCHWEIZERISCHEN VOLKSBANK," Berne (annual).
"JOURNAL DES ÉCONOMISTES," Paris, vols. for 1886, 1891, and 1895.
"L'ÉCONOMISTE FRANÇAIS," Paris, more especially vols. for 1886 and 1888.
"JAHRESBERICHT ÜBER DIE AUF SELBSTHÜLFE BEGRÜNDETEN DEUTSCHEN ERWERBS- UND WIRTHSCHAFTS-GENOSSENSCHAFTEN," Berlin (annual).
"LANDWIRTHSCHAFTLICHES GENOSSENSCHAFTSBLATT," Neuwied.
"BLÄTTER FÜR GENOSSENSCHAFTSWESEN," Berlin.
"DIE GENOSSENSCHAFT," Wien.
"DEUTSCHE LANDWIRTHSCHAFTLICHE GENOSSENSCHAFTSPRESSE.'
"ARBEITERFREUND," vols. for 1873 and 1881.
"CREDITO E COOPERAZIONE," Roma.

"La Cooperazione Rurale."
"La Cooperazione Popolare."
"L'Union Économique," Paris (more particularly III., 2 and 3).
"Bibliothèque Universelle," Genève, vol. for 1889 (June).
"Reports of the Annual Congresses of French People's Banks," Imprimerie Cooperative, Mentoni.
"Bulletin du Crédit Populaire," Guillaumin, Paris.
"Bulletin Mensuel de l'Union des Caisses Rurales et Ouvrières."
"Verein fur Socialwissenschaft, Schriften," vols. 20, 22, 23, 24, 25, 28, 30, 35, 38.
"Russische Revue," 1874 and 1890, IV.
"Baltische Wochenschrift," Nov. 23, 1891.
"Magyar Statistikai Evkönyv."
"The Economic Review," 1892 and after.
"Report regarding the Possibility of Introducing Land and Agricultural Banks into the Madras Presidency," Government Press, Madras, 1895.

PEOPLE'S BANKS:

A RECORD OF SOCIAL AND ECONOMIC SUCCESS.

CHAPTER I.

INTRODUCTION.

AT a time when every mind appears busy with schemes of "social reform," when every effort, alike of statesmen and of philanthropists, seems bent upon doing something to raise the social status and improve the material condition of the poorer classes, no excuse should be needed for calling attention to an institution which—British, as some of its supporters hold it to be, in its prime origin, but adapted and developed abroad—has in some neighbouring countries proved more helpful than any other in furthering the objects aimed at, but which among ourselves has thus far strangely escaped notice. The problems which at present perplex us are not, we ought to remember, our peculiar monopoly. They call as clamorously for solution elsewhere. In France, in Germany, in Austria, in Italy, in Belgium, as among ourselves, Labour jostles Labour, the rapidly increasing host of those who have to earn their living by toil demand with a voice growing louder and louder the boon of independence and a larger share in the rights and comforts of life. There, as here, the plaintive cry of the desti-

Social Importance of the matter.

Its bearing on the Labour Question.

tute, the suffering, the helpless, homeless, foodless—whom the country has brought forth and the country, it is contended, ought to sustain—may be heard appealing for relief. There, as here, in one shape or another—whether as a matter of possession or as a problem of providing more ample means wherewith to improve what is already possessed—the troublesome Land Question casts its dark shadow across the scene. It cannot, of course, be argued that other nations have been more successful than ourselves in *finally* solving the problem with which we are all grappling. But in respect of one or two points, amid a good deal of profitless experiment and actual blundering, some of them seem at any rate to have come nearer to sound remedial action. They have discovered that it is not necessary to assume, as many among ourselves appear to do, that Capital and Labour, whose recurring strife is responsible for one of our main perplexities, are necessarily antagonistic forces, with different interests, different aims, different aspirations—belligerent parties, between whom peace can be established only from time to time, as a matter of terms. In one instance, at least, they have managed to bridge over the dividing gulf and blend the long-opposing interests into one, by making, in the apt words of Schulze-Delitzsch, the working-man "his own capitalist." And they have shown that other means are available for adjusting differences arising between various factors of national production than encroachments upon production itself; that it is not an inexorable law of Nature that whatever is given to Labour must necessarily be taken from some one else—be it capitalist employer, or be it ratepaying community. Not everywhere is it contended that Labour should be benefited—one might almost use the term "protected"—by a restriction upon output. Emigration, though necessarily tolerated, is looked upon by some of our neighbours rather as an evil to be put up with than

Its bearing on the Land Question.

Capital and Labour are not necessarily antagonistic.

The Workingman "his own Capitalist."

as a desirable remedy. When employment runs short, the **Want of Employment remedied by increase of Production.**
first question asked by them is, whether it is not possible to provide more, by creating new sources of production. Foreign methods may not be our methods—in some instances they distinctly cannot be. It does not seem likely that the resource which various German Governments have found so useful, of stimulating cottage industries to furnish employment for the hands overflowing from the larger workshops, will recommend itself to ourselves, at any rate at present, amid totally different circumstances. There is more to be said for the modern German practice of multiplying small holdings, which has proved most signally successful, and the results of which might well have been taken into account in our own recent attempt to deal with the same matter.* By far the happiest solution yet discovered, and apparently the most adaptable to varying circumstances, is that for which our neighbours are beholden to Schulze-Delitzsch, Raiffeisen, the Hon. L. Luzzatti, M. d'Andrimont, and Dr Leone Wollemborg—who have taught them to establish "People's Banks," and thereby to create large capitals providing abundant employment without cost to any one.

One can scarcely help remarking upon the curious **Two Californias.** coincidence of facts which opened to Europe at exactly the same period, about 1849, two essentially different roads to vast riches. It was while our first emigrants were rushing to the newly discovered gold-fields of California—big with promise, tempting to the eye with the alluring glitter of precious metal—that in a small village in the bleak Westerwald, and in a petty provincial town of that portion of Saxony which Prussia annexed in 1815, the first spade was thrust into a "gold-field" of a very different type, looking

---

* See my article on "Repeopling the Land," in the *Contemporary Review*, May 1895.

at the time bare and barren, but concealing under its unpromising crust a store of wealth, larger and more beneficent in its effects by far than the gold deposits of the State which the American Confederation had then just finally made its own. Which of the two gold-fields has thus far yielded to Society the larger volume of tangible riches, it may be open to question. Which has more enduringly benefited our race—the metal which began by provoking robbery and disorder, and which, along with much good service, forms a standing incentive to greed, envy, and dishonesty; or the "capitalised honesty" which plants virtues where there were vices, makes people thrifty, industrious, sober, honest, and enables them to build for whole classes habitations which no financial crisis can wash away—to such question there can be but one answer.

Success of People's Banks.

What untold riches these People's Banks have within the forty-six years of their existence made available for small folk's needs, what millions they have added to the wealth of the countries in which, as M. Léon Say testifies, they "flourish throughout"; what vast amount of misery, ruin, loss, privations, they have either averted or removed, penetrating, wherever they have once gained a footing, into the smallest hovel, and bringing to its beggared occupant employment and the weapons wherewith to start afresh in the battle of life, it would tax the powers of even experienced economists to tell. Propagating themselves by their own merits, they have overspread Germany, Italy, Austria, Switzerland, Belgium. France is trying to graft them upon her own economic system. Russia has in her own rather primitive way followed the excellent example. Servia and Roumania have adopted them. And now we hear of their spreading from Italy into far Japan—China has got something like them already—while we in Great Britain scarcely yet know of their existence.

INTRODUCTION.

The solution has all the more to recommend it among ourselves, because it is essentially based upon a principle of which this country has long been regarded as the specific home: the principle of self-help. Self-help, it is quite true, has of late gone a little out of fashion. We are taught sometimes to look to other deities to bring us up out of the Egypt of want and distress. Nevertheless, whatever it be reserved for State-help to accomplish, in England self-help is not likely long to want adherents. Unfortunately we have thus far given to this great power only half its practicable application. "It is self-help," phonographed, early in 1890, Mr Gladstone to a delighted body of correspondents across the Atlantic, who thought that they had never heard their co-operative principle so neatly and tersely vindicated —"It is self-help which makes the man; and man-making is the aim which the Almighty has everywhere impressed upon Creation. It is thrift by which self-help for the masses, dependent upon labour, is principally made effective. In them thrift is the symbol and the instrument of independence and liberty, indispensable conditions of permanent good."

A system based upon Self-help

Mr Gladstone on Thrift.

Yes, that is admirably said, and with the truth of Mr Gladstone's words no one will be disposed to quarrel. That is the interpretation which we have thus far put upon "self-help." "Save, lay by, economise, make the most of your pence, alike in provident accumulation and in economic outlay," that is the familiar counsel which for many a year back we have persistently addressed to our poorer brethren. Going further than counsel, we have provided for them facilities beyond what are known in other countries, and, to do them justice, they have readily profited by them. Our Savings Banks, our Provident Societies, our Co-operative Stores, remain unsurpassed in the known world, and secure to us without question the first place among nations in respect of the practice of thrift.

But does not all this, after all, represent only one side of self-help? Could not the same power which enables us to garner the ripe fruit be impressed into service also to assist us in tilling the soil and producing it?

Self-help made Productive as well as Provident.

It seems strange that we should never seriously have turned our thoughts to this problem, which for us, one would think, ought to possess no less practical importance than for any of our neighbours. There are so many bits of waste lying unproductive in our economic system which self-help, if it is within its power, might with advantage be called in to cultivate. There is so much labour which cannot be brought to the point at which our orthodox form of self-help begins—the point of being able to save and lay by. And even where there is employment, there is still so much available labour and ability running unprofitably to waste! There is so much skill and opportunity which for want of means cannot be turned to full account! We are rich, no doubt. But the daily conflicts between Capital and Labour show that with all its abundance Capital is among us not equal to the demands made upon it; that, rapidly as it has grown, Labour has grown very much faster; and that, for want either of will or of power, it is still relatively too small for our national needs—too small, at any rate, at the fructifying points. Then, is there no means of supplying the want, of creating the capital which is wanting, and, where there is admittedly opportunity and working power, of placing also the material to work upon at the command of the willing workman, to the diminution of misery and destitution, and the happy increase of the productive power of the nation?

What relief it may bring.

The answer, given in the affirmative, is to be found in "People's Banks." To state one instance of what they may do—we well understand the all but hopeless difficulty of dealing with the huge mass of helpless misery which daily, articulately or inarticulately, calls upon us to be relieved.

INTRODUCTION.

Though our charities flow very unevenly from different purses, in the aggregate no nation in the world gives more largely, nor more readily. For all that, if Gregory the Great is right, it is to be feared that even the most charitable among us are sorry sinners—even in their very charities. For although they "offer rightly" enough, they most evidently do not "distribute" at all as they should (*si recte offeras, non recte dividas, peccâsti*). Now let us suppose that through this vast, unwieldy mass of distress a line might be carried, separating, not the deserving from the undeserving—that is not our affair—but those in whose hands money might be counted upon to fructify, to give them employment and repay itself out of their toil, from those in a different case; and let us suppose that to each and every one of the former category could as much money be advanced—readily, easily, and at a cheap rate—as they think that they have employment for. By what a substantial proportion would the tax upon our resources, both of purse and of application, be reduced! Not only would the mass of destitution to be dealt with dwindle very materially, but former victims would at once become effective helpers—taxpayers, it may be employers, givers of charitable support instead of claimants to it. Let us further suppose that, even beyond the limits of actual want and non-employment, all those willing workers among us who, like our well-known heroes of self-help, see their opportunity for a great enterprise, who have the ability, but want the means, could go to the same source of supply and there obtain, without the indignity of begging, without having to make a special favour of the loan, what they require—let us assume that the farmer or the allotment-holder could obtain the wherewithal to drain, to manure, to improve his field according to modern principles, the householder the wherewithal to set up and furnish his home cheaply, the small tradesman the means wherewith to stock his shop, the small artisan the funds for carrying out profitable work —whatever the want, whatever the calling might be, suppose that it could be supplied—what a vista of wealth and prosperity beyond the wildest dreams of hope, profitable to the individual, profitable to the community, appears to open itself to one's view! It seems almost like a vision of fairyland.

Well, and can People's Banks accomplish all this?

What People's Banks may do. The answer is to be found in that vast network of flourishing banks spread out over Germany and Italy, numbering by the thousand, turning homeless labourers into cultivating owners, unemployed journeymen into thriving traders, starving peasants into substantial yeomen, stimulating everywhere, in M. Léon Say's words, commerce, industry, and *la petite culture*, which under their beneficent shelter develop "with increasing energy," in those neat, prosperous villages, encircled by smiling gardens, orchards, and heavily bearing fields, which spring up, as if by magic, not in the fertile valley of the Rhine only, but in the barren Westerwald, on the erst neglected plains of Venetia, and in

In Towns. the wild Rhön mountains. It is to be found in the bustling business going on daily in that palace of the *Banca Popolare* which you may see in the *Via San Paolo* in Milan, where a full hundred of clerks are continually at work, besides about 140 unpaid officials, passing tens of thousands of pounds through their hands every day, £80,000,000 in the year, a stream of gold steadily and rapidly increasing in volume. All that work is done with a clockwork regularity and an exactitude in every detail which could not, says M. Say, be surpassed in London or New York. And all has grown up out of genuine "People's" business. Most of the transactions are small—drafts of ten lire (eight shillings) are not at all uncommon. Lira by lira has that magnificent fabric been reared up out of small folk's business—"drop by drop," says its founder M. Luzzatti, "like a stalactite grotto"—till it has grown to be one of the largest banking establishments in all Italy. There are more than seven hundred banks of this order, small and great, in Italy, doing among them a full third of the country's banking. In Germany there are thousands. Or, to ascertain the results in a different aspect, you should, once more in Italy, go out into the country and ask the *muratori* and the *braccianti*, whom you see there building and making roads without a master to control them, where they got the money from which enables them to do the job on their own account, putting the middleman's profits into their own pockets. Or else you should walk into one of those thriving villages in Venetia, in which Dr Wollemborg has set up his *casse rurali*. A few years ago, under the evil influence of hindrances not unknown among ourselves — the accumulation of landed property in few hands, habitual absenteeism, and, moreover, a rigorous exaction of rents such as, happily, we have no conception of—that district was the usurer's favourite hunting-ground, and the poor drudges who cultivated it had not a centesimo to call their own from week's end to week's end. Now the usurer is gone, and the cultivators are doing well, and laying by. Or, again, you should go into the valley of the Rhine, where the Raiffeisen Banks have been longest at work, and observe to what extent homes have been made habitable and comfortable ; how culture has been improved ; how machinery has been purchased, and the best manures and feeding stuffs ; how the vintner has been enabled to sell his produce for cash at double the former rate of return ; how the small peasant can now buy his implements and manures, of the best quality, at the cheapest wholesale prices, and yet—thanks to a large reserve accumulated in his bank, raised up seemingly out of nothing, as if by fairy hands— at six months' credit ; you should see how small industry and trade have been developed, how the usurer, once all-

[margin: Working-men their own Employers.]

[margin: In the Country.]

powerful, has been driven out of the field, and those once poor men have become small capitalists. One is afraid of falling into a strain of rhapsody in describing all these results. "I have seen a new world," broke out, in explicable admiration, the Hungarian deputy, Professor von Dobransky, charged with a mission of inquiry, on seeing this country of newly created plenty, "a world of brotherhood; it is a world of brotherly love and mutual help, where every one is the protector and the assister of his neighbour. An isolated man here finds himself transplanted into the bosom of a community whose resources multiply a hundredfold the productive power of its labour, and crown it with success." This seems high-flown language. But other visitors, dry, sober political economists, like M. Léon Say, M. Rostand, Professor Held, and M. Fournier de Flaix, speak in exactly the same strain. The late Emile de Laveleye expressed himself with less of rapture but not less of emphasis. The wealth which this new instrument has brought forth, as by a touch of Midas, wants to be seen in order to be understood. Looking at it, and reckoning up its benefits, one feels indeed as if on economic ground "a new world had been called into existence to redress the balance of the old." And "all these wonders which I have seen," writes M. Léon Say, "are the wonders of private initiative and decentralisation. It is private initiative, it is the decentralisation of credit which is the dominating cause of all this progress in wealth. It is co-operation which has created it all (*la mutualité a tout créé*)."

And the tale of our "wonders" does not end here. "The moral results," writes M. Rostand, after his second visit to these humble banks of Italy, "are to my mind superior still to the material." To apply Signor Wollemborg's apt illustration, the golden sunshine of thrift and co-operation, wherever it has cast its rays, has "unveiled," and brought to view in plenty, unlooked-for virtues which had long lain hidden like flowers shrouded by the night. The idle man becomes industrious, the spendthrift thrifty, the drunkard reforms his ways and becomes sober, the haunter of taverns forsakes the inn, the illiterate, though a grandfather, learns to read and write. It sounds like a tale from wonderland. Yet it is all sober fact. We find a Prussian judge officially reporting that litigation, especially in respect of claims for debts, has very sensibly diminished in his district—thanks to the establishment of a co-operative bank. We hear a German priest confessing that the new Loan Bank in his parish has done far more to raise the moral tone of his parishioners than all his ministrations. In Italy we have another parish priest—one among many —Dom Rover, the *paroco* of Loreggia, writing only a brief time after the setting up of the co-operative *cassa* in his parish :—

"People go less to taverns now, and work more and better. Since only respectable folk are admitted as members of the Association, we have seen habitual drunkards promise never to set foot again in a tavern—and keep their word. We have seen illiterate folk, of fifty years and more, learn to write, in order that they may be able to sign their application for a loan. Poor people, excluded as being in receipt of parish relief, have vigorously exerted themselves to have their names erased from the paupers' list, and instead of living on alms, we now see them living on their labour—thanks to the small capital lent to them by the Association. Poor fellows, who could previously scarcely support themselves, have been enabled to purchase a cow, out of the milk and cheese of which they repay the debt contracted, keeping the value of the calf as net gain."

Learned professors and Ministers of State, dry economists, parsons, men of business from all countries—all, in fact, who have had an opportunity of judging by the test of their own eyes of the merits of this new Fortunatus's purse, join in the chorus of laudation. One is not surprised to find foreign Governments steadily encouraging institutions whose aim, in the words of one of their founders, Schulze-

Delitzsch, is "Peace"; in the words of another, M. d'Andrimont, "Order and Economy"; while in practice they prove, according to the testimony of M. Léon Say, "the most effective weapon against the development of Socialism."

<small>Appreciation by the Poor.</small>

But to gauge the value of People's Banks at its fullest, one should go among the people whom they have benefited—the small tradesman, the peasant, the cottager, who has by their help purchased, rod by rod, a little holding which he surveys with pride. One should go, as I have done, stick in hand, walking from cottage to cottage, and hear these people describe the contrast between erewhile and now, and listen to them telling of their little troubles and embarrassments, and how the bank stepped in to relieve them. Many such a tale there is which could not fail to warm a philanthropist's heart. If there is one proof more conclusive than any other, as showing the practical utility of these banks, it is the devotion and the gratitude which they evoke from those whom they support and who in turn support them.

<small>Simplicity of the System.</small>

And, so inquired into, the system seems so simple! Every peasant appears able to understand it. He delights in bringing out the books, in showing them to you and explaining what all the entries mean. He can make the whole organisation clear to you.

<small>Its Security.</small>

And, moreover, the business is so safe! "Not a *sou* has been lost," declares M. Rostand, the chairman of one of the largest Savings Banks in France, on behalf of the Italian *casse rurali*. "Our losses have been altogether trifling; in the times of economic crises less than those of other banks," writes to me Professor Concini, on behalf of the *banche popolari*. "Not a *pfennig* has ever been lost, either to creditor or to depositor," so the heads of the great Raiffeisen Union make it their boast, after an experience of forty-seven years, and speaking on behalf of a union now increased to beyond two thousand associations.

INTRODUCTION.

It must seem strange indeed that, with our acknowledged needs, with our large means, and our familiarity with banking, we should never before have seriously directed our attention to an institution which with so slight an effort can produce such marvellous results, which goes on spreading its network continually over new districts, meeting with the same success everywhere, going nowhere but to conquer—we, who otherwise are not slow in our appreciation of money and of opportunities for business. It seems doubly strange that we should so long have neglected this modern development of banking, when we are told that it was our Scotch "cash credit"—which is indeed abroad credited with far more helpful popular work than it has ever had the chance of accomplishing—which first suggested the idea to foreign co-operators. In their earliest days our Co-operative Congresses did indeed nibble a little at the subject. Their members had heard of the "wonders" wrought abroad, and were anxious to reproduce them on British soil. They were not, however, quite clear among themselves as to what they really wanted—whether People's Banks, to help poor folk by loans, or purely co-operative business establishments, to earn banker's profits for their shareholders. And so the inquiry ended in two abortive experiments. Some years ago—in 1886—our Government made these foreign banks a subject of consular inquiry. The Blue Book which has resulted from those labours gives them very becoming credit. But, unfortunately, in its information it is—barring the portion dealing with Italy—full of inaccuracies and errors, such as unhappily occur in not a few of our Blue Books when embodying merely a *relatio relatorum*. I can say nothing better in respect of later official publications issued in London. They are all wanting in accuracy and fulness of information — excepting only the admirable digest just published at Madras, which, of course, has scarcely yet been

Our past indifference to the subject.

studied in England, and which treats only of agricultural banks.

In real truth our knowledge on the subject, as a nation, is still little more than a blank. I hope that I have made out my case so far as to show that there is some ground for endeavouring to fill up that vacant space, and that the People's Banks ought to possess some interest for us. To the fullest extent they carry into practice the admirable maxim on which the Alsatian philanthropist, M. Dollfus, avowedly based the generous and useful work which has helped to make him famous: *Aidez-à-faire*. They do not *give*, but they *help*. They help those to help themselves whom by other means, long experience has proved, we cannot adequately help. If in the following chapters I can but make clear by what services and methods the People's Banks accomplish this, how they have grown up abroad in a variety of form which seems to indicate an almost inexhaustible capacity for adapting themselves to any description of circumstances, how wonderfully they have thriven, and what truly astonishing amount of good they have accomplished, more especially among the poor and neglected—the struggling toiler, alike in town and country, the usurer's victim and the exactor's drudge—my tale ought to be worth the telling.

But I need scarcely add that I hope to do more; that by the account which I shall give of the "wonders" accomplished—the work of enrichment, of education, and of a diffusion of sound principles, alike economic and moral, I hope to induce some good philanthropists to make practical trial in our country of that which has succeeded so magnificently abroad.

"Aidez-à-faire."

CHAPTER II.

THE GENERAL IDEA.

THE bare **idea** of co-operation in matters of money was not by any means new when the two originators **of** the co-operative movement in Germany resolved to create for their country a co-operative speciality. There are traces of it to be met with in **the** history **of most** nations. The Spanish *compañia gallega*, the Portuguese *sociedade familiar*, **the** Italian *monti nummari*, the Russian *watagas*, the South Slavonian *droujinas*—all these institutions show the **principle** of co-operation **for the common** obtainment of money put into practice in **some more or** less elementary way. It cannot occasion wonder that, when the second French Revolution quickened the desire for full emancipation among the toilers of an impetuous nation, the idea thus **far** rudimentarily applied should have been made **to** assume more definite form. It was in those days of emancipation **by** fire and sword that the German chemist Gall—**the same** who invented the method of sweetening **sour wine by** the addition of fruit-sugar during the process **of fermentation**—conceived the idea of "fighting Capital **by a com**bination **of** the many small purses of Labour." *[The general idea is not really new.]*

But it was one thing to grasp the bare idea, and quite another to put that idea into really workable shape. Gall's crude proposal to fight cash with cash—cash which could bide its time, with cash which might, every penny of it, be called for any **day to keep its** owner's body and soul together—erred, **of** course, wide of the mark. What gives *[Difficulties of its application.]*

the capitalist his main advantage over the man with no capital, is not his hard cash, but the *credit* which that cash commands, and which multiplies its producing power five and ten fold. If, therefore, the poor man was to be made "his own capitalist," it must be by assuring to him the help of *credit*—the very last thing which in the ordinary state of affairs is accorded to him, but of which, in Signor Viganò's words, "he stands in far greater need than does the rich." "He has no credit," says Giustino Fortunato, "because he is destitute; and he continues destitute because he has no credit; and so he moves on hopelessly in the same vicious circle, from which there is no way of escape."

<small>Efficacy of Credit.</small>

The question to be answered then came to be: Could by some means or other credit be provided for the poor? Fortunately, Credit is, as Professor Laurent rather happily points out, in words quoted with approval by M. d'Andrimont, satisfied with very little. "Credit," says the professor, "is not the creator, but simply the mover of capitals. It multiplies indefinitely their services; it quickens their movement, as the rail quickens the revolution of wheels; it annihilates the obstacle of time, as steam annihilates the obstacle of space; but it does not create. It uncovers, it awakens, it fructifies; it does not invent. It is a marvellous power, without which the economic movement would not exist; but it is not a panacea. Even with enormous effective values it cannot do everything, and with nothing it will never accomplish anything. *However, with next to nothing, and that is the case of the People's Banks, it will effect wonders.*"

<small>Only small Funds required at starting.</small>

The experience of People's Banks has fully justified this opinion. Schulze-Delitzsch, who has long been looked upon as the main pioneer of modern credit co-operation, began his work with very little. It was but like a grain of sand. But in Signor Viganò's words, it gave co-operation the ποῦ στῶ, from which the world might be lifted out of

THE GENERAL IDEA.

its hinges. It was a paltry beginning, one would have thought, to lead up to the present riches and influence, in the possession of which the Schulze-Delitzsch Banks, according to M. Courtois' rather exaggerated estimate, dispense to trade and industry annually somewhere about £180,000,000 in loans. Raiffeisen borrowed £300, which had to be repaid within a comparatively brief time, to begin his work upon. Commendatore Luzzatti started the giant establishment at Milan, which now commands a paid-up capital and reserve exceeding £500,000, with a puny sum of £28. Signor Leone Wollemborg began his banking operations for his *casse rurali* with literally nothing at all except credit. And yet these co-operative banks among them have created milliards' worth of property, besides becoming themselves substantial institutions with great wealth, in M. G. François' words: "*Une véritable puissance financière, dont l'importance économique n'a pas besoin d'être démontrée.*"

In 1849, however, all this was experience still to come. *Early Co-operation in Spain* In Spain and Portugal, unobserved by English or German *and Portugal.* co-operators, the poor peasants of the *compaña gallega* and the *sociedade familiar* had in their own elementary way solved the problem of co-operative credit up to a certain point. Their shrewd common-sense had taught them that by converting their family, so to speak, into a joint-stock concern, endowed with continuity and common liability, they would be offering very much better security to the money-lender, and thereby enabling themselves to obtain very much more favourable terms. And on this principle they continued through generations to contract their little loans, unconsciously providing a useful stimulus to thrift and economy, and attracting into the family home or holding many a *real* which without such inducement would have gone in finery and dissipation.

But these men had at any rate something to pledge. *The Problem* Schulze-Delitzsch's problem was, in his own words, " to *to be solved.*

procure capitals without a capital of guarantee"—"to find," as M. F. Passy puts it, "means for giving credit to those who have no security to offer in exchange." The question to be solved, in fact, was this: Could labour be pledged for money? Sir Robert Morier, in an excellent paper contributed to our first Co-operative Congress, held in 1869, answers that question in the affirmative. He says: "The skilled artisans of a community are as good a subject for a mortgage as the steam mill which supplies it with flour, or the broad acres which furnish the corn for the mill. All that is wanted is some equally safe means of assigning to the creditors a lien on the former as on the latter." That is the very point. In practice, of course, the problem did not in every case take this extreme shape. For, as in the case of the Iberian peasants, there was often something, at any rate, in the borrower's possession, which might serve as security—a holding, or a house, or some chattels. But these in most instances did not amount to very much; and in the main the problem still remained as Sir Robert had put it, and resolved itself in M. Luzzatti's words into one of finding "moral" guarantees, and devising means for "the capitalisation of honesty," to serve as a pledge or security.

Sir R. Morier's Opinion Labour can be Mortgaged.

"The Capitalisation of Honesty."

The work has been accomplished, as will be seen, by a variety of methods. Still, looking at the banks collectively, one may agree with M. Say, who says that, differing in details, in principle they "all belong to one family." The family has proved a lucky one; for all its members have been singularly successful, though successful in different degrees. And even that difference is not without its value. For it teaches us what an essential element of success in this matter is the frank adoption of the principle of self-help. It clearly shows that the more fully and undilutedly banks have accepted that principle, the better, in the long run, have they thriven. All leaning on foreign supports, whatever ostensible gain it may have brought at the

The Workingman to work out his own salvation.

moment, has in the end **turned** out to be nothing but loss, and it has been proved **beyond the** shadow of a doubt that, **in Schulze's** words, to become "his own capitalist," the working-man must be "the instrument of his own emancipation *(lo strumento stesso della sua redenzione*")*.* "The **only capital (in this** application, of course) which will endure," so says Professor Laurent, with **the approval of Emile** de Laveleye, "is the capital created by the working-**man** himself. It would **be** idle to lend to him or to give him the implements **for** his work. Such gifts, like an inheritance under **the touch of a** spendthrift heir, would be squandered in little time."

We ought to know that this **is** so, though we have given little evidence in the past of our having mastered the fact. **The record** of our benefactions designed to help and raise the working classes is a record, **to a** great extent, of desires and efforts which **do our** philanthropists credit, but to **the same** extent it is also a record of practical **failures. Millions** upon millions **have been** thrown **away,** as uselessly **as if** they had been **cast** into the sea, **in** kindly intended, **but** injudiciously executed attempts **to do** good **to others** according, not to their own, but to our ideas, to give them **ruffles when they** wanted a shirt, and to give **that luxury in a** way calculated rather to make the **receivers** careless, than to make them thrifty. Only a **few** years ago we had proof **of a** fresh instance of this given **us** in the complaint publicly expressed by a nobleman who **had** liberally purchased at his own cost "a large tract" **of** land beyond the sea, on which he had purposed, likewise at his own expense, to settle English emigrants. The **men accepted the free** passage gladly, and, that done, **made** their **way to a more** congenial settling **ground** in the **United States.** Their

<small>Wastefulness of Charities as compared with Self-help.</small>

---

* Not having the German words at hand, I quote from Signor Ettore Levi's *Manuale.*

intending benefactor had thrown his money away. He had pressed upon his beneficiaries what they had not asked for and did not want, and what they considered that they might relinquish without ingratitude. Hundreds of similar instances might probably be quoted, if one cared to ransack the history of our charities.

Throughout history there seems to have been a peculiar bane of failure attaching, like a Pandora's curse, to those provident or charitable enterprises which did not rest absolutely on self-help. Either they did not reach the right people, or they failed in their effect upon those people, making them unthrifty instead of thrifty; or else the method chosen proved unsuitable, or the safeguards were insufficient; or else, lastly, the funds were misapplied by their own guardians and turned to improper purposes.

<small>Instances quoted from France.</small>
France has a long tale to tell of very well meant but injudiciously conceived or else mismanaged enterprises— from that wretched waste of money downward, which in 1848 Thiers branded as "*cette grande folie*," to the present day. The Emperor Napoleon III. tried his hand at such beneficent work. First he created a *Caisse d'Escompte*, endowed with a million of francs, of which he himself provided one-half, which was to advance funds more especially to productive co-operative associations. As it turned out, the rules had been so stringently drawn that no borrower could be found willing to comply with them, and the institution died without having done any good. Then the same Emperor started a *Société du Crédit Agricole*, which was more especially intended to benefit rural borrowers. The institution came to these men in such a questionable shape, it looked to their eyes so unfamiliar and suspicious that, timid as they habitually are, they shrank from claiming what was willingly offered, and the *Société*, not knowing what to do with its idle money, invested a large sum in loans to the Khedive Ismail, which very soon put an end

THE GENERAL IDEA.

to its existence. The Empress Eugénie fared no better with her *Société des Prêts de l'Enfance*. Gambetta experimented with the same ingenuity, but unfortunately also with the same disappointing result. His *Caisse Centrale*, formed with the very best object, soon found itself on the straight road to failure, because it could not attract the one class of customers whom it wanted, and in the end it saved itself only by converting itself from a philanthropic into a business bank.

The truth is, it is not by any means easy to attract poor people of the right sort to the lending counter. With an ingrained sense of very honourable delicacy they shrink from accepting what either is, or else appears to be, a gift. There were non-co-operative philanthropic lending banks in many places in Germany before Schulze-Delitzsch and Raiffeisen entered upon their benevolent career. The late Duke of Saxe-Coburg—the father-in-law of our Queen—more especially, had been careful to found some such in his dominions—at Gotha, at Ohrdruff, at Zelle, at Ruhla, and elsewhere. But nowhere did these capitalist establishments accomplish any real good. In Berlin, Dr Crüger tells us, no man "with any sense of honour in him" would apply to them for a loan. Vagabonds came in plenty, but vagabonds were not to be supplied—though, to the loss of the institution, unfortunately a good many of them were. And when, for want of business, the banks at length closed their doors, though their capital had considerably dwindled by injudicious loans, a large portion of the funds remained unemployed.

Difficulties of inducing the honest poor to borrow.

Such unwillingness on the part of poor people, especially the poor peasantry, to come for loans to persons whom they do not know very familiarly, and by whom they do not know themselves to be known and understood, has been the standing *crux* of the Governments both of France and of Belgium in their endeavours to carry into effect their pet hobby of establishing a form of personal agricultural credit. They tried to do this with the help of the large resources at their disposal respectively in the Bank of France and the State Savings Bank, and through the medium of local committees—*comptoirs d'escompte* and *comptoirs agricoles*—whose members were selected with as great care as was possible, so as to secure persons acceptable to the local *clientèle*. It proved all in vain. The borrowers would not come. "If in a village," so complained the Belgian Minister M. Graux, pouring out his griefs on this subject in the Chamber, "it becomes known that an inhabitant borrows, people at once begin to suspect that his financial position must be shaken. The trader, on the other hand, glories in his credit; the larger is his credit, the higher stands his repute. The peasant will not borrow till his affairs decline, and then he puts off borrowing as long as he possibly can; he will rather pay a high rate of interest to some avaricious notary, who may be trusted to keep his secret, than frankly apply for a loan where interest is low. Such are the ideas of our *campagnards*. In their view a loan brings with it a stigma of discredit." This description is true all the world over. The French Government has had much the same experience in its own country. And in Germany, Herr Cremer, Chairman of the Union of Co-operative Loan Banks of Neuwied, tells me that even the Raiffeisen Associations, which are thoroughly popular and self-administered, have in some of their districts found themselves compelled to put forward one or other of their richer members, so to speak, to "bell-wether" the poor to the lending table. Evidently it is only to lenders of their own place or district, and lenders of their own class, or familiar with its affairs—who may accordingly be fully trusted to understand the position and the objects of the borrower, and to think none the worse of him for his borrowing—that this shy class of customers—as it happens, the only right ones to trust with money—will come.

THE GENERAL IDEA. 23

And if it is only to such that the right borrowers will come, it is only such also who may be trusted to adapt their methods to the case, and be liberal without being careless as regards security. In the most typical cases already quoted from French economic history there has always been either too much or too little caution. To what extent official administration can shipwreck even a good fund, is shown by the fate of the *Legs Rampal*, liberally left by a philanthropist for the benefit of co-operative societies. Unfortunately Rampal entrusted the keeping of the fund to a Committee to be appointed by the Municipal Council of Paris; and that Committee simply strangled the fund with red-tape. Framing its rules with municipal wisdom, it lent to those to whom it ought not to have lent, and did not lend to those to whom it ought, and by this means very effectually frustrated the entire object in view. By this means the *Legs* is being systematically frittered away. In 1887, out of 437,000 francs lent out, 100,000 francs were reported irrecoverable. In 1889, out of forty-nine associations lent to, eighteen were found to be bankrupt, eighteen more in course of liquidation, and three suspiciously in arrear.

<small>Security is not obtainable otherwise than by Self-help.</small>

Even co-operative loan associations, it has become plain, from experience collected, more especially in Italy, must not step outside the district within which they are genuinely local and co-operative, unless they would miss their effect. Co-operative banks, endeavouring to extend their work over a wider district by means of branch offices, where there was not sufficient touch, found themselves making a loss. The branch districts afterwards organised their own independent banks, based on touch and mutual knowledge of one another among members, and the new institutions throve. The losses sustained by co-operative credit associations in Germany in the course of their operations occur almost without exception amongst such as have attempted to work outside their own district or without a recognised district at all.

Self-help has succeeded where Charity has failed.

It is interesting to note the difference in the fate which has befallen, on the one hand, genuine co-operative loan institutions, supported and officered by those for whose benefit they are intended, and, on the other, loan institutions of a different type, be they official or philanthropic, however well conceived and organised.

Instance of Alsace.

One case in point is that of Alsace. The German Government, on taking possession of the newly conquered province, found popular credit unprovided for, and at the same time millions of marks, either savings banks' money or else communal funds, lying idle in its tills. With sound judgment, as it appeared, and great thought, it organised popular Advance Banks (*Vorschusskassen*), by which such available moneys were to be lent out to the peasantry and other small folk on very liberal terms. Every precaution was taken; yet the practical effect proved next to *nil*. A few years ago Herr Raiffeisen planted one of his co-operative Loan Banks on the same ground. Within five years that one multiplied to seventy-three. In 1892, when I visited M. Chèvreton, the Chairman of the Provincial Committee, at Saint Hippolyte, there were 126, all thriving, all doing a large business, alike in granting loans, and in taking savings. Since that time the number has been very largely increased. Never had grain of seed fallen on more fruitful soil than that on which the official variety had barely germinated.

Experience in Italy.

Something very similar has happened in Italy. In 1869 the Italian Government, being anxious, like its neighbours in France and Belgium, to provide small agricultural cultivators with cheap and easy personal credit, by a special law authorised the formation of *banche agricole*, very similar in constitution and practice to the French *comptoirs d'escompte*. In 1882, of the thirty-odd *banche* so established, all but nine had collapsed. Of those nine only two were doing any business to speak of, and that, as it turned out, only owing to special circumstances acting in their favour. One would have thought that in that district surely there could be no demand for credit. Yet, scarcely had Commendatore Luzzatti's *banche popolari* set up their tables on the same seemingly barren soil, but business flowed to them from all sides, and they grew in a few years to most successful establishments.

In Berlin, where the late Emperor William's money, granted in 1865, on Prince Bismarck's urgent recommendation, to endow socialist associations of the Lassalle type, proved a hopeless waste, and where those philanthropic loan banks already referred to had to close their doors for want of business; and in Thuringia, where the banks supported by the various small Crowns accomplished very little—the Credit Associations established by Schulze-Delitzsch have found a most ready and favourable market. *Experience in Germany.*

One very striking and characteristic instance comes to me from the Grand Duchy of Saxe-Weimar. There, in what not long ago was a forlorn district, something like a rural Seven Dials, stands the erst forsaken village of Frankenheim—poor, neglected, it was, with tumbledown houses, all of them heavily mortgaged, badly tilled fields, and an uncouth, barbarous-looking race of inhabitants, rightly or wrongly reputed capable of any misdeeds, and possessing some few famished cattle, nine-tenths of which really belonged to the "Jews." In pity the Grand Duchess had some model dwellings set up, erected at comparatively considerable cost, but to be let at a nominal rent of 30s. a year. The success was not particularly encouraging. Some time after, the Lutheran vicar of the parish resolved on trying the effects of a Loan Bank of the Raiffeisen type. With the help of the money so secured—on these poor people's own collective credit—he built houses, each of which, with the ground upon which it stands, and the *Frankenheim.*

garden surrounding it, cost a little under £60. For these houses the occupiers are required to pay 4½ per cent. interest, plus $\frac{1}{15}$ or $\frac{1}{20}$ of the principal each year, by way of sinking fund, therefore in all, according to circumstances, either £5. 12s. or £6. 12s., in consideration of which the houses become their own after a certain period. All these houses have been readily taken up, the tenants pay their rents regularly, and, thanks to the money brought into the village, the whole face of things has become changed. The dwellings have become decent, the gardens well kept, the fields well tilled, the "Jews" have been paid off, the cattle are well fed, and the human inhabitants are known throughout the country as orderly, well-conducted, industrious, saving and thriving folk.

The Lesson to be drawn.

From all these instances, and more which are on record —no doubt they might be matched in this country—it seems unmistakably evident that institutions like those now contemplated, formed to assist poor people with money which is to be well expended, and honestly repaid, must not, if they are to be of real benefit to the borrower, to promote useful outlay, and thrift, and honesty, come to him like little Providences from outside, with a strange face and a condescending air—Providences whose gifts cost him nothing, and for aught that he is aware of may cost no one else anything, and may be repeated *ad libitum*—but must be his own creation, raised up, as Commendatore Luzzatti, the founder of the *banche popolari*, puts it, "by a heroic levy on his daily wages." *If he is to value the gift, he must be his own benefactor; if he is to deal scrupulously with it, he must be its guardian.* The rich man's dole, coming as from a rich man, is held in comparatively slight estimation, as issuing from a full treasury in which it will not be missed. Hence those ruinous losses, by repeated default, in the French philanthropic funds founded by the State, or the Emperor, or the Empress.

Wherever, on the other hand, the lending institution has presented itself to the borrower as genuinely popular and genuinely co-operative, there has been found to be no more regular and more scrupulous repayer than the small man. Even the French *Crédit Agricole*, which was but moderately "popular," has not lost a penny by its peasant customers, as M. Josseau honourably testifies. The debtor who wrecked the institution was the Khedive. The peasant may be tardy in his payment, so says M. Garreau in *Les Sociétés Coopératives*; but once his sense of responsibility and honour is aroused, he is sure to pay. Similar testimony comes from all quarters. In **Germany** we have Herr Raiffeisen bearing witness, who has never lost a penny; in **Italy** Commendatore Luzzatti; in Portugal Senhor Costa Goodolphim. In Italy, in the *casse rurali*, ministering to the poorest of the poor, not a centesimo has been lost. Emigrants send in their debts from America, and when by chance a man is so hopelessly out of pocket, through things going wrong, that he really cannot repay, his fellows with a creditable sense of class honour make up the amount. It is just the same thing in America. What the "People's Banks" were which flourished in the United States before the Civil War, to revive in later time practically as Building Societies, we do not quite know. There is no precise record left of their operations. Except in New York, where they were made the instrument of reckless speculation, they did well. And evidently they were more of lending societies than are their modern antitypes. For we find the Commissioners appointed by the United States Government to inquire into their practice and success reporting that they have "demonstrated beyond doubt that, with equal prudence and intelligence on the part of the lender, *loans to the industrious and economical poor are as safe as those made to any class whatever of the rich.*"

<small>The Poor Man is the most scrupulous Repayer.</small>

By what methods such "prudence" should be exercised Sir Robert Morier has very accurately pointed out in his paper already referred to. He mentions as the three main conditions of success, the pillars upon which the credit structure must rest, the following:—(1) Maximum of responsibility; (2) minimum of risk; (3) maximum of publicity. Perhaps the elements of successful organisation might be grouped under other headings, but in substance it would come to the same thing. However, beneath these supporting pillars, experience—ample by this time, alike on one side and on the other, confirmatory or refuting—has made it quite plain that, if the fabric is to stand and to show itself equal to the burden placed upon it, there should lie a foundation which makes the structure entirely popular, familiar to those who are to use it, a thing with which they can identify themselves, therefore co-operative, and in the best sense "democratic." "*Avec les banques populaires,*" so says M. d'Andrimont—explaining the fruitful work which he has accomplished in aid of the poorer classes in Belgium —"*le crédit est démocratisé.*" "Capital," he goes on, "which was previously beyond the reach of workers, has been brought close up to their doors." Making this principle his own, M. Léon Say affirms the object of People's Banks to be—"*la démocratisation du crédit.*"

Sir R. Morier's Cardinal Rules.

"Democratised Credit."

That hits a weak point in our economic system. We pride ourselves, on both sides of the political boundary line, upon our "popular" institutions, which make us, as we think, the most "democratic" nation in Europe. Nevertheless in respect of the main supports of the two great divisions of our economic fabric we are distinctly anti-democratic. As the basis of agriculture we have land laws which, for good or for evil, are, from a democratic point of view, a century at least behind those of other countries. And as the basis of commerce we have credit still almost the monopoly of the rich. We do not, accordingly, know that which, thanks

In England Credit is still the Monopoly of the Rich.

to their People's Banks, the Germans and Italians have well learnt, namely, what an **ample and** practically inexhaustible resource of productive power **there** lies hidden in the labour, **the** frugality, the honesty of the nation's workers, as material **for** what Commendatore Luzzatti calls "capitalisation"— just as people who have not seen rivers like the **Danube or** the Rhine, could not possibly estimate from the **little rills** and driblets which go to make them **up**, what **a vast** volume of water may be collected from **those** insignificant sources. It is the object of the **founders of** "People's Banks" to bring those scattered streamlets together, to give them aim and force, and by doing **so** to make the very **atoms** which **compose** them more fruitful, more productive —**by** the sense of responsibility awakened, the principles of business instilled, the knowledge of dealing with money and an appreciation of its productive power diffused. It is **quite** true, as **Dr Johnson** unkindly reminded Goldsmith, that it takes 240 poor men's pence to make one capitalist's sovereign. But once the sovereign is so put together, **it is a** totally different sovereign from that taken out of the rich man's safe. It has behind it 240 wills, 240 pairs of watchful eyes, 240 thinking brains. It has, so to speak, become **an** animate sovereign, with prudence, energy, vigilance, diffused through all its parts. **Every** spring, every wire of the **composite machine takes a** personal interest in **the** collective doings, watching the other parts, guarding against **loss** and waste, correcting the slightest irregularity. And the more completely the distribution **is** carried **out, the** lower the "democratising" organism descends, so as to gather up from the lowest strata all available and useful elements, the more fully, so we see in the practical application of the principle abroad, does it realise its beneficent aim. Not without reason, accordingly, did Commendatore Luzzatti inscribe upon his banner, when he started on what proved to be a triumphal progress of economic success, the **apt** motto: *Aspirare a discendere.*

"Aspirare a discendere."

CHAPTER III.

THE TWO PROBLEMS.

<small>The Task is two-fold.</small>

IT may be well, before entering into a detailed explanation of the several systems of co-operative banking to be reviewed, to consider briefly the general nature of the task to be dealt with. That will help us better to understand, not only the merits of the several systems, but also the differences subsisting between the one and the other.

Obviously the task set is not a simple one. There are more problems than one rolled up in it. I speak of two. It may be urged that there are really more. Employment, surroundings, class, locality, all these things necessarily impress in each case a distinct character upon the work. And there are a variety of ulterior objects which People's Banks are designed to serve, often quite as important as the primary aim. However, for practical purposes it will be found that we can well group all the objects to be kept in view under two great heads.

<small>Its economic Aspect.</small>

In the present consideration I propose to leave out of account all those "ulterior" objects referred to, and to confine myself exclusively to the one economic work which to ourselves in the United Kingdom is likely to present itself as the most important. That work is the provision of cheap credit for those who require it and cannot at present obtain it. We stand in this respect upon rather a different footing from what our neighbours did at the time when they took the task in hand, and to some extent do even now. In Germany and Italy, when Schulze and

THE TWO PROBLEMS. 31

Luzzatti set out upon their work of economic reform, popular credit was wanted, but there was something else wanted even more. Provident institutions were very sparingly developed. Savings Banks were few and far between, and situated mainly in great centres, where they were accessible only to comparatively few. People accordingly required above all things to be taught to *save*. And while being taught to save, they must also be provided with suitable receptacles for their savings, and means for keeping those savings in their *own* districts, available for their *own* use, instead of allowing them to be drained away into large towns. *People's Banks as Savings Banks.*

I am far from denying that in the United Kingdom there is room still for the development and multiplication of provident institutions. The results of which happily our "Collecting Banks" are able to boast afford proof of the substantial gleaning which may be accomplished on ground seemingly well harvested already by provident agencies. The "Collecting Societies" send volunteer officers about to collect, as a labour of love, the pence and twopences which workmen receive, and which, without collectors to carry them into safety, they so often manage to fritter away. The collectors call at the right time, when the money has just come in, snatching up the coppers before they can find their way into the public-house or into the shop where little luxuries are sold. As a rule the societies allow no interest on deposits. They could scarcely afford to do so. They tell depositors plainly that if it is interest which they want, they must take the trouble of carrying their deposits to the Savings Bank themselves instead of having them collected for them. They act merely as a money-box, hoarding up small sums up to a certain limit—I believe it is £5. By such modest work the "Collecting Banks" have managed to gather together in very short time, in the parish of Fulham something like £2,000; in that of St Anne's, *"Collecting Banks."*

Soho, between £300 and £400. Surely here is an institution richly deserving of public favour.

However, generally speaking, there is not in this country the same need of additional depositories for savings which undeniably exists in Italy and Germany.

<small>People's Banks as fixing Savings in their own localities.</small>

Again, it cannot be affirmed that we stand in any very urgent need of additional money reservoirs to collect, and fix in the locality of their production, those local accumulations of money, which in a healthy economy there ought to be, instead of allowing them to be sucked up into the great monetary "wens." M. Luzzatti's able lieutenant, M. Enea Cavalieri, is at times wroth with me for not putting forward this plea with the same emphasis in England, with which it is pressed by himself and his chief in Italy. However, the plea does not apply to us in the same degree. In Germany and Italy, where the whole banking apparatus is less developed, the arteries intended to promote circulation either do not exist, or else are periodically choked; and the consequence is that plethora in one place is apt to become chronic, and to produce as enduring anæmia in another. In our country money circulates freely and readily, and were I to urge M. Luzzatti's and M. Cavalieri's pet point, I should simply prejudice my cause by using a misplaced argument.

There are different grounds upon which it appears to me to be desirable to eliminate from the present consideration those moral and educational merits of co-operative banking which attract many others as well as myself far more than the economic. However, we must grow our tree before we can look for fruit from it. The economic question lies at the root of the whole system, and serves as its foundation. Accordingly, let us be logical, and deal with the purely economic aspect of the matter first.

<small>The first economic Object is cheap Credit.</small>

The work, then, which we have now to keep exclusively in view is the making credit accessible on cheap terms to those to whom the way to credit is at present barred, no matter whether they be **farmers,** or artisans, or anything else. It is all one work, **and to** whomsoever it may be applied, it has some main features in **common.** It can only be effected by a union of forces. And that union of **forces, it** is important that we should understand, must be directed *less at bringing together driblets of means*—to collect such, as into a common treasury, from which afterwards to redistribute them—*than at creating some new security* recognised in the market, which may be relied upon as a magnet to attract **that** cash which is wanted. The pence and shillings **and pounds** which may **be collected to form** a common capital may well be **made to** contribute towards such security. But collect them as carefully as you will, once you have got them together, in nine cases out of ten they are sure **to** prove wholly inadequate **to the** purpose aimed at. **The** provision of money towards which so many well-meaning **but insuffi-** ciently thinking men direct their main effort is really altogether **a** secondary **consideration.** "Money," so said Lord Salisbury not long **ago in one of his** public speeches, "is so plentiful that you can hardly get money for it. **It is** overflowing in the coffers of capitalists and the bankers." Money is always to **be** bought at its price, which price is **security. Again, as** a distinguished nobleman, high in the country's estimation, remarked to me some time ago—" The mere belongings of a number of poor people, to whatever extent you make those people liable, could never of themselves respond to the claims for security which **are** likely to **be** raised." Indeed, without something more to respond to those claims, these people, as collective borrowers, themselves could not in justice be asked to make themselves liable. The whole undertaking would **be** too hopelessly unsafe. If these people are to contribute their pound to a common fund, or if they are to make themselves collectively or severally liable, they must have **a** good trustworthy guarantee that the money which they make themselves

The Question is not one of Money but of Security.

Lord Salisbury on "Money."

C

answerable for will not be lost or jeopardised. They must accordingly address themselves to the question of *credit among themselves* before they begin to think of *credit outside*. If the money is made safe within, it is sure to come in from without. It is not, then, the grouping of *means* together so much as the grouping together of *elements of security*—the creation of sufficient knowledge of one another among the members, of touch with one another, of control of one another, and of responsibility for one another, which constitutes the effective factor of the system. Such elements only union can supply, organised on well-drawn lines, of which experience has established the efficacy.

Scotch Cash Credit.

We find the principle contained in germ in Scotch Cash Credit, which has, as its eulogists rightly boast, "in the space of a hundred and fifty years raised its country from the lowest state of barbarism up to its present proud position," covering it with flourishing farms, and filling its harbours with well freighted vessels. The Lords and Commons Committee of 1826 on Scotch banking explained the cause. "This system," says the report, "has a great effect upon the moral habits of the people, because those who are securities feel an interest in watching over their conduct; and if they find that they are misconducting themselves, they become apprehensive of being brought into risk and loss from having become their sureties; and if they find they are so misconducting themselves, they withdraw the security." It is the linking together of close local and personal knowledge, which can discriminate between good cases and bad, deserving borrowers and undeserving, the joining of interest, of responsibility entered into, with the power of enforcing responsibility in others, which supply backbone to the whole system. There must be touch, power of control, knowledge of members among one another, and a common interest, which carries the security of the pledge given far beyond what a writ or a summons could do

Once these demands are satisfied, it matters little, in the abstract, which of the two roads open to co-operative credit, as M. Leroy-Beaulieu has distinguished them, you take, whether that of "a small capital of guarantee," which under efficient management, we know, may be made to command a considerable multiple of its own amount in credit; or that of the simpler expedient of "collective liability," which makes skilled management dispensable, and accordingly meets the requirements of scattered and rural communities backward in commercial education. The selection of the road must depend on local circumstances. The ground is mapped out with sufficient clearness to make the choice easy. But the first and essential principle for both courses is, that responsibility be made fully effective. *[Two Foundations for Security.]*

So far the problem is the same. It is beyond that point that the two roads diverge.

At first blush one would imagine that agricultural and industrial or urban banking must present dissimilarities which render a common working hopeless, mainly because in the one case lending is likely to be required for long terms, in the other for short. In practice, however, to some extent the very dissimilarity of the needs indicated neutralises the difficulty which it seems to create; and there are many experts who insist that the two practices should in any case be blended, in order that the one may dovetail into, and so strengthen, the other, and each supplement what the other wants. This argument—approved by experience in a multitude of cases—is, however, open to some objection, and is, accordingly, not everywhere accepted. There are many banks which have adopted the combination of twofold work advocated, to undoubted advantage. There are some few which keep the two types of banking carefully distinct, in the same locality, and flourish no less. But in either case, so far as what may be called *large* agricultural banking is concerned, that is, credit banking for *[Agricultural and Industrial Credit.]*

farmers, for peasants, for all but the very humblest class of cultivators, the question of essential difference as between agricultural and industrial credit does not arise. The same methods are found equally serviceable, and even the extension of time, absolutely necessary for agriculture, is found practicable under a system originally framed for very short lending only.

The Point of Divergence. It is on another point that the division of problems really begins. There are, on the one hand, more or less dense populations to be ministered to, or populations with a dense nucleus and outliers sufficiently answering the characteristics of a dense population to admit of being dealt with as such. Such outliers I take to include fairly substantial agriculturists of recognised position. There are, on the other hand, the sparse populations of the ordinary rural parish, and it may be, some small towns or suburbs, embracing too few to give to a bank the same *prima facie* financial strength, and at the same time less qualified, it would seem, for engaging even in elementary banking business. It will be seen that, although, as a rule, greatly wanting in commercial education, those sparse populations provide elements of strength which stand for very much indeed in the solution of the problem of co-operative credit—on distinctive, but very safe lines. Generally speaking, in the former class, there will be, if not actually greater wealth, at any rate more available money—whether it be of a small capital already realised or of regular earnings—facilitating cash transactions, even though on the top of it credit may still be needed. In this class of banks the number of members is likely to be large, if not at the outset, at any rate not long after the bank has got into working order. Indeed it must be. But there is likely to be comparatively little touch between units. The *clientèle* will be a comparatively large, money-earning population, possessed at any rate of some rudimentary notions of business, but shifting and unstable, on the individual member of which it may be difficult to establish a very firm hold. Amid such surroundings needs may be large or small, but they will generally be for short periods and for industrial or domestic uses. There may be material to be purchased for the workshop, or furniture for the house, or else money wanted for wholesale purchase of food stuffs to save expense, or for some little building job, or else cash to enable the borrower to tide over the time till he can dispose of his produce without falling into the hands of sweaters; or, it may be, money, to get him out of the usurer's clutches.

In the other case the population will be fixed, but sparse. The banks will have to be small, sometimes very modest indeed. Most members are likely to prove uninstructed in matters of business. They are pretty sure to be short of money. They may be genuinely poor. They may merely hold their small wealth in an uncoined shape, or labour for wages in kind. They will want their loans generally for a long term, because, if independent, they turn over their money slowly; if wage-earning, their earnings are scanty, and it will take a long time to make up the sum. It does not matter, in this respect, whether they are agricultural cultivators or village traders. For the village trader has to adapt himself to the needs of his customers, who are necessarily tardy payers. But such *clientèle* will have this advantage, that touch between them, knowledge of one another, checking and controlling one another, are really very easy and may be relied upon, and that generally they make a dependable class of persons to deal with.

The specific characteristics of the two classes clearly determine the methods which should be applied to answer their several cases.

In the former class, where you have both numbers and a comparative command of money, moreover presumably a large number of transactions, a rapid turnover of money, Characteristic Requirements in Dense Populations and some familiarity with business, you will be able to rely upon these factors in your organisation. However you limit or fail to limit liability, you will make a prominent feature of your "small capital of guarantee"—a share capital, that is, paid up and serving as a guarantee to those whose credit you ask—and base your system mainly upon it. You will adopt commercial methods of banking, secure skilled management, which you will generally be able to command without difficulty, but which in both cases you will have to remunerate, however you may supplement salaried services by gratuitous supervision. You will rely more directly upon your directors than upon the shareholders, who are too many in number, and too loose in texture as a mass, to be able to control the business effectively, much less to carry it on. Though not ignoring employment of the loan, you will look more to the man than to his promise respecting the use of his money. You could not effectually control the latter. Therefore you will have to make all the more sure that you have a solvent and trustworthy borrower to deal with, and place your reliance in a very great measure upon the sureties who pledge themselves for him. And since you can do that, it becomes a matter of less importance, though still of importance, how you select your members. Mere election does not involve any direct risk. Moreover, you may, for the sake of earning the management expenses which you *must* meet, have to do business on some lines or other with non-members, although that is really a doubtful practice. Still a bank, to do work, must live.

In Sparse.
None of all this would do for a constituency of the second sort. There you cannot rely to any extent upon the petty contributions of money which the few men whom you enlist can bring to your till, even though there be plenty of money's worth at their back. You must base your system more or less upon liability, the value of which

you are in a position to assess with some accuracy, and which you must study to render more effective by a very careful selection of members. Your man must be absolutely trustworthy. Your transactions are likely to be comparatively few. Loans will be demanded for long terms, the turnover will be slight. The margin between incomings and outgoings will be small. You will have to cut down expenses to the utmost, and make gratuitous services the rule, which you can the better do since the call made upon your officers is not likely to be very exacting. You cannot adopt commercial methods, which your clients will not understand, and which would be out of place. But you have all your members well under your eye. You can control every one of them, and make them control one another. You can interest the mass of your members even in the petty affairs of the bank, and so make your machinery more effective by arming it, to repeat my earlier simile, with watching eyes and checking hands at every point. You can effectively check your clients' employment of their loans. You can bring class feeling and local feeling, and moral and social influences to bear. Therefore, if you have to be very careful in the selection of your members, you may also stoop very much lower in the social scale, and admit even very poor persons, so long as you can make tolerably sure that they are honest. Business with outsiders becomes an impossibility. Finally, resting your system mainly on liability, you must apply yourself to strengthening your available capital by carefully raising up a reserve fund, which you can scarcely make too strong.

So stated, the two cases appear—to me, at any rate—fully to explain themselves, and there seems no room for even theoretical antagonism between them. The two methods are not rivals. Each directly supplements the other; and, indeed, each seems incomplete without the other to supplement it. It is satisfactory to think that,

The two kinds of Credit are not antagonistic, but complementary.

after long, needless, and bootless hostility between the advocates of the two, the view to which I am giving expression is coming to be more and more accepted, and on this score peace between traditional rivals seems at length in prospect. In what precise manner the two methods are practically applied in different countries and localities I shall have to explain in subsequent chapters.

CHAPTER IV.

THE TWO ASPECTS OF THE QUESTION.

CO-OPERATIVE banking, like every other kind of **co-opera-** "Mutualism"
tion, has two aspects. You may co-operate merely to help and "Co-oper-
yourself, to **secure, by** combination with others, support ation."
intended **to** procure for you personally **an** advantage,
an equivalent direct return for that which you put into
the common concern. That is what our neighbours in
France, more discriminating in these matters than **ourselves,** call "mutualism" (*mutualité*). **Or else you may
co-operate** to help, yourself indeed, **but at** the **same
time** also to help others, **or** by your support **to place**
them **in** the position **to** help themselves. You **may take**
your choice between these two principles. They are
both legitimate, and both have **been** found **to** produce
useful results. According as you select the one or the other
you will give a different colouring **to** your enterprise. **We**
have specimens of co-operative **work** of either species **in**
this country—co-operative associations which measure their
success by the direct benefit obtained, as **in** a joint-stock
company, and study **above** all things **big** profits; and
co-operative associations which, remaining true to **the aim**
which the **first Rochdale Pioneers** kept in view, **regard**
those **immediate** profits only as a means to an end, **only as**
supplying the **wherewithal to** pursue loftier objects, and
study above all things to provide steady employment,
greater independence, and generally a better position to
the classes whose cause they **have** taken **up.**

The latter principle is, I believe, more likely to recommend itself to generous minds. It seems to take a broader and fuller view of its object, and to aim at higher ends. There is, moreover, by the light of experience, this to be said in its favour, that its success rarely fails to include, like the divine response to Solomon's choice of a blessing, the narrower, more material gain which it seems to spurn, or at any rate not to desire for its own sake. Certainly, also, it is better calculated to generate a feeling of satisfaction, and a propagandist zeal and enthusiasm in its adherents.

Advantages of purely Economic Co-operation.

However, let us not despise the former principle. It is more prosaic; it appears less lofty. But it is the principle which is best understood and recognised in the world. And for economic purposes it has this advantage, that it may be absolutely depended upon. A mere sense of duty may lose its impelling force when that duty begins to grow irksome.

Interest stronger than mere Sense of Duty.

Once you make it a man's distinct interest to do a thing, you may depend upon it that do it he will, if to do it be at all possible. Nor should we take too narrow or too low a view of the results which this principle, worldly and selfish as it may appear, places within reach. Good economy and morality, as Minghetti and Mr Goschen have both shown, lie very close together, and have a great deal of connection with, and influence upon, one another. We have ere now heard it said that the most effective propagators of European civilisation in uncivilised countries are, not our missionaries, but our traders. I do not pretend to affirm that this is entirely correct. But certainly it may be said that under the training of good co-operation, and more particularly co-operative banking, sound economy, business habits, mechanical training to commercial honesty, have been found to act as admirable moral educators at home. When you are dealing with the poor, or the comparatively poor, the mere providing of means for better education, for the acquirement of greater comfort and a better social position—which, once secured, are sure to be valued—is bound to tend in this direction. But there is more educational power in good co-operative banking.

Now let us consider how the two principles may severally affect our problem in hand. There are leaders in the co-operative movement, founders of co-operative banking systems, who look upon co-operation merely as an economic junction of forces, the binding together of so many sticks to a bundle. They are strong in their protestations of the necessity of pure self-help, by which they mean self-help for individual gain, the self-help in which not a group of weak and strong unite to help themselves and help one another, but in which every person studies his own interest. In this aspect co-operation is nothing but combination resorted to for egotistical ends. Under this principle very much is made of individual effort. Every gain secured is to be entirely *earned*. But the effort made is to benefit the particular person. There is to be a strict debtor and creditor account between the association and its member. The gains from self-denial are to be carried rigidly to the personal account of the self-denying one. Whoever is too poor to contribute his quota in money is roughly bidden to remain outside in the cold till he has collected enough to enable him to take up a share. There must be no common fund created, to his proper portion of which each individual has not a distinct and indefeasible right, and from which each individual is not free upon due notice to withdraw his own portion. We often speak of this kind of co-operation as pure joint-stock trading. Perhaps it is no more. But it secures very serviceable results. Generally speaking, the largest and strongest co-operative banks which exist have been raised up upon this egotistical, purely calculating, self-seeking system.

Not many months ago I was speaking to the manager

How this applies to Co-operative Banking.

> "L'esprit de lucre domine tout."

of a bank of this type in the South of France about his own establishment. M. G—— had little to say in its praise, from a co-operative point of view; for as a business establishment it is sound enough. "There is no co-operation in it. It is a bank like other banks. *L'esprit de lucre domine tout.*" There are no gratuitous services, no limitation of dividend, no "loans of honour" to the poor, no study of high aims. Members pay in their money, it may be franc by franc, and for so many francs they purchase such and such advantages, among which they are taught to expect, as gauge of all, a decent dividend. Surely this is a picture without any attractiveness about it. And this particular bank, I may add, is not looked upon by officers of the best of its sister establishments as a peculiarly com-

> It is nevertheless useful.

mendable specimen of its type. "But have you not made credit accessible to small folk, to whom formerly it was inaccessible?" I asked. "Oh, yes, certainly." "Have you not popularised, democratised, decentralised credit? Have you not taught people to bank, to place their money on deposit and draw it out when they need it? Have you not taught many small folk business habits?" "Oh, decidedly, we have." "Do you not lend money to people who even now cannot go to other banks, say, to working men?" "Oh, yes, distinctly we do. Why, there was a cabinet-maker here only to-day who works for a firm. Formerly he was in abject dependence on that firm. Now he comes here whenever he is short of money, to hold over his goods, it may be, or to buy material, or for household purposes. We have many such."

Are not all these distinctly useful services? Is not the country the richer, the happier, the better endowed with producing power for them? Unquestionably banks of this class, which will neither give nor take anything for nothing, which scrutinise their member-customers with a keen, selfish, discerning eye, which think nothing of educating,

THE TWO ASPECTS OF THE QUESTION. 45

of elevating the poor, which apply only the hard, cold principle of purely economic co-operation, have rendered perfectly inestimable **services to** the small trading classes, the agriculturists, the working population of **their countries,** and have strengthened the social fabric of their nations **just** where strength was most needed and tells to best effect.

But now let us turn to the other aspect of the question. There are persons, as everybody knows, **who are not in a** position to take their place in the former kind **of** co-operation, who have not the means to take up **a** share, or at any rate to pay for it **in** cash, to remunerate directors **and** secretaries, and allow a handsome reward to capital. **Are these** people **to be** left altogether without help? It **is they who need it most.** And it is they for whom co-operation was really intended, because only by co-operation **can they** mend their lot. Is it "co-operative" to tell them, **as advocates of** the first principle sometimes do, that they should go to "charity" and live on patronage till they can **manage to** scrape enough together **to** make them "ripe" **for** co-operation? That is equivalent, in a "co-operative" sense, to sending a man to hell in order that he may there qualify for heaven. Your object and your duty is to train him to self-help. And you bid him prepare for it by deliberetely estranging himself from it. Persons in this condition can co-operate like the others. But in the same proportion **as** their **needs** are greater, are **their** objects likely to be larger. **They want** financial assistance badly. **To** obtain such they have a good **deal** that they can give, and must **expect to** give freely—time, labour, attention, application. You cannot procure either money or credit for nothing. **But you must** in fairness allow the equivalent given to be *value*. **It is nonsense** to maintain, as has been done, that such co-**operation** is not self-help. **When** you give what you *can* give to obtain what you cannot, **you are** not receiving "charity," but exchanging **one value for** another. However, all this

Altruistic Co-operation.

It is genuinely Co-operative.

co-operation to obtain, not profit in return for money, but money in return for exertion, implies objects of a different kind, which are necessary for the purpose, and which, apart from being necessary, persons in this position instinctively feel to be desirable. It brings out the social, educating, moral side of the question. To people, such as we are now thinking of, the co-operative association or bank becomes, not merely a shop in which goods or credit may be bought, but an economic hearth and home, a school for all kinds of economic action, for business training, and for higher social virtues, a social as well as an economic money-box. This co-operation, like the other, must be built up upon pure self-help. No serviceable co-operation is possible on other lines. It is exertion which must purchase every gain. To alloy or adulterate self-help would not only be perfectly gratuitous, it would be distinctly prejudicial to the object for the attainment of which co-operation is resorted to. It must necessarily defeat that object. However, I cannot for a moment admit that self-help loses one particle of its economic purity when it is made to embrace a number of men instead of being confined to one. I cannot concede that self-help becomes less self-help when it is impressed in the service of a group of persons, who, being individually weak, and weak in varying degrees, and on various points, combine for the purpose of turning their weakness into strength, and supplementing one man's feebleness by another man's comparative power, each supplying his own quota of what he can give, to benefit by a similar though different contribution from his fellows. That is the self-help by which a community or a nation rises to greatness. So far from being questionable, it appears to me even to be the purest and fullest co-operation.

<small>And based upon Self-help.</small>

<small>Its Effects.</small>
Now, see how co-operation of this kind acts upon the men who engage in it. It knits people very much more closely together; it enlists very much higher senti-

ments than the mere pursuit of gain. It links interest. It binds people together as with the ties of one single family, bringing sentiment, aspirations, the consciousness of common needs into the co-operative enterprise. It sets very much higher motives at work. And it opens a door through which others, not needy themselves, wishing to help rather than to be helped, may legitimately come in, helping, but only by helping people to help themselves. Here is the feature which has particularly endeared this kind of co-operation to so many noble minds, and has generated that peculiar ardent enthusiasm which cold-blooded economists wonder at and cannot understand, but which has helped more than anything else to spread this movement and impel it forward. You can now *help without giving*. You can help while carefully safeguarding yourself against the danger of being made to give—money, that is—while insisting that every assistance rendered in money shall be fully and promptly repaid—help by lending guidance to the unskilled, experience to the inexperienced, time, labour, interest, attention, safeguarded liability, all on a footing of equality. And by doing this you help those whom you wish to benefit infinitely more than by giving them money. This kind of co-operation does not draw a strict dividing line between those who have money wherewith to take up a share and those who have not. It does not, Shylock-like, bring to the business only its commercial ledger and its bond. It does not go into places in which gold chinks freely and discount business is brisk. It goes abroad among the outcast and poor, dropping help into seemingly waste places, and picking up seemingly helpless persons from their misery. It goes into the villages where money is scarce, and the other kind of co-operation difficult. The structures which it raises are not as large or as resplendent with gold as those built up under the more commercial system. But on its own modest lines it does a great deal of good, and good which absolutely no other agency could accomplish. Surely I need not stop to explain why it is that those who work for the principle last described seem generally fired with a peculiar fervent and contagious enthusiasm. They feel, to quote the words of P. de Besse, that they are engaged not in an affair of business (*une affaire*), but in a good work (*une œuvre*); that they are, as F. W. Raiffeisen, the first who applied this principle to regulated practice in respect of banking, has put it, "working for God."

Recriminations between Partisans of the two Types.
The world would not be the world if such aspirations as these had not prompted in the mouths of rivals unkind sneers at high religious professions of "Christian principle," "Christian Socialism," and "Love of one's neighbour," which sentiments they judge to be quite out of place in work which is, after all, mainly economic. Nor is it surprising that the altruists should have retaliated by taxing the other side with "greed," and "egotism," and "deliberate dividend-hunting." These mutual vituperations are all the less called for since it would be difficult to draw a hard and fast line between various systems, to serve at the same time as boundary between the several applications of the two principles described. The territories overlap at more points than one, and there is promise of the principles blending in some neutral region. Indeed, in some places it has already been found possible to bring them from war into union. Where this is not possible, surely there is no need of antagonism. There is room for both principles. There are places in which the one is not called for; there are places in which the other could not act. Accordingly we may well be content to "give to rigid economy the things which pertain to rigid economy, and to altruism the things that pertain to altruism," and allow both systems to grow up and overspread the ground and produce good fruit, side by side.

CHAPTER V.

CREDIT TO AGRICULTURE.

I HAVE spoken thus far of co-operative credit as a help intended for the poor, in the ordinary and most familiar sense of the word—the wage-earner, the toiler, the man of muscle, whose powers must run to waste unless money can provide both material upon which to set them at work and a stock of necessaries wherewith to keep him alive until his labour may bear fruit in a marketable shape. However, poverty in our present sense ought to have a much wider application. Obviously, it ought to be taken as including every one who has a productive use for money or credit, and yet finds himself unprovided with the one and practically cut off from the other. There is one great calling to which this description pre-eminently applies. That calling is agriculture, which, from being a cornucopia yielding almost automatically, not one, but actually those "three" livings of which Lord Beaconsfield spoke something like twenty years ago, has recently, under the stress of adverse circumstances, become changed into a business standing very sorely in need of help, and, if evidence collected in many quarters is not altogether wrong, in need of help more particularly in the shape of money. It may be convenient to consider the position of agriculture as an interest calling for credit, if not exactly *in forma pauperis*, yet at any rate by other means than those which are now available, in the present chapter, although I am quite aware that so placing the subject will expose me to the charge of in some measure

<small>Why Agriculture must be classed as a "Poor" Calling.</small>

anticipating what I have to say with regard to England at the end of the book. Credit to agriculture has so important a bearing upon all the systems which I shall have to discuss, that it will be well to realise beforehand what are its particular needs in respect of credit.

Agriculture has become a "Business" without the Resources of a "Business."

Under pressure of advancing times agriculture has become, from the easy, self-rewarding occupation which it is understood once to have been, a business of money and enterprise like all other callings, an industry like any other industry—having the same tasks set to it, but not the same means at its disposal wherewith to accomplish the task. We should probably be in a better position to consider what are its needs for the future could we bring ourselves more fully to realise this fact. I ventured to insist upon it—upon the hopeless incongruity between an old system and totally altered circumstances, as a condition almost necessarily leading to a crisis—some years ago at one of the half-yearly meetings of the Royal Agricultural Society, and I had the whole meeting with me. We congratulate ourselves upon the amazing growth and development of our commerce, our trade, our industries, our banking. But what resources have we placed at the disposal of those callings, or allowed them to secure for themselves? Had we treated them as we have treated agriculture, it is only too likely that they would find themselves in precisely the same backward and depressed condition in which agriculture now is. However, we have treated them differently. We have fed them with large supplies, alike of money and of education and intelligence. We have replaced slow and sparing hand labour by the rapid and creative labour of the engine and the loom, multiplying harvests while increasing their bulk. We have introduced perfected machinery, we have removed anachronistic shackles and insisted upon full freedom of practice. We have recast all the organisation of the industry, arranged our commerce so as to enable men to take advantage of even the slightest change in the market, of every opportunity which may offer even an infinitesimal gain. All these things mean a larger command of money. They are absolutely impossible without it. But for additional money invested they assure a pretty safe return. And to provide that money we have developed a system of credit which places funds almost without limit at the disposal of the respectable trader or manufacturer—credit, without which, every man of business will readily allow, all this huge world of industry could not subsist for a day. The capital of those of whom it is composed would be utterly inadequate to its purpose. So we have created the "acceptance," which buys at pleasure, just as occasion may demand, for every enterprise which promises a profit. Could we treat agriculture in the same way, is it not at any rate conceivable that, what with production cheapened and facilities afforded for taking advantage of the market, we might make it fare as other industries have fared? All evidence available on the subject seems to support such a conclusion.

"Agriculture," to quote the words of a Minister of Agriculture, spoken in the Belgian Senate, "is changing, and *must* change. Change is for it a condition of existence. It finds itself to-day in conflict with conditions altogether different from those of earlier days, and in such conflict it can have no prospect of success, except by arming itself according to the fashion of the day. We want more artificial fertilisers to-day, and more powerful ones. We want machinery, and many other things that our fathers never dreamt of. These new appliances ensure a higher yield, but they demand, on the other hand, a larger working capital." Those words, spoken at Brussels, and with reference specifically to agriculture in Belgium, apply to the very letter to agriculture elsewhere, not least to agriculture in Great Britain. Indeed they have been, since quoted by me, echoed

Its Need of Money.

in the Report of the Royal Commission on Agriculture.*
I have recently† quoted a case illustrating their truth—I
admit, under exceptional circumstances.

Instances of the Utility of Money: Woolwich.

It is that of a small farm held by a Co-operative Supply
Association which in twenty-seven years has grown up from
the most modest beginnings to a position of great prosperity.
The Society ten years ago decided to purchase for its own
use a freehold farm of 52 acres. (It has since purchased
another of 20 acres.) The farm, which was in a very poor
and neglected condition, would, it is admitted, have speedily
reduced any ordinary tenant, coming to the holding with
the traditional small working capital, to ruin. The Society
came to it with practically as much money as it might

---

* The Royal Commission on Agriculture, in their second Report, recently published, fully recognise the existing call "for increased outlay on improvements necessitated by changes of agriculture," and they propose as a means of meeting it State loans to landlords, for which, they explain, there is "ample precedent." They practically disavow their own recommendation by adding: "We do not contemplate that the demands upon the Exchequer would be of a *serious* character." In that case, it is to be feared, they will furnish no "serious" relief, and do no "serious" good. In all probability State aid, to make up for "the very serious reduction of rents," would be very acceptable to the persons affected; though it is not quite clear why a merchant or manufacturer, when the market goes against him, should be expected to sell out and make room for some one stronger in capital, while the landlord is to be artificially propped up by the general taxpayer, whom he is keeping out of the possession, by honest purchase, of his coveted land. To most people, certainly, economic action unsupported by the State, such as the German *Landschaften*, and the much more democratic and more successful "mutual" *Landwirthschaftliche Creditverein von Sachsen* have shown to be practicable, will appear preferable. The loans here contemplated do not, however, affect our present problem, which is, how to provide money, not for such extended periods as twenty-five, thirty, and forty years, for the permanent improvement of the *property*, but for shorter terms, to make the *business* of farming more profitable.

† *Contemporary Review*, October 1895.

want. It had, moreover, its own market to depend upon, which constitutes, I admit, quite as great an advantage as the possession of an unlimited capital. But just let us look at the increase of production which it brought about with the help of its large capital, leaving the market out of account. It set up new buildings, it trenched the land two feet deep, gave it a bottom dressing, so to speak, of sixty tons of manure per acre, in short, it laid itself out for the highest farming. It sank a good deal of money in the farm, to such an extent that at the present time, what with rates and assumed rent (at the rate of 5 per cent.), it has to write off from £30 to £35 of the gross profits per acre every year as expense. However, it produces magnificent crops—£43 worth an acre of cabbage, £36 of peas, £30 of potatoes, £39 of sprouts, £90 of tomatoes, £90 of marrow, and so on. Its takings from a piggery, mustering from 300 to 350 strong, figure at nearly £500 a year. In 1894 it realised £2,283 from its produce. The original loss has been recovered, in addition to 5 per cent. being steadily drawn on capital invested, and a rate of depreciation allowed which now gives the farm—to state one example—its horses absolutely for nothing. Good "capitalist" farming makes the farm pay in spite of bad times.

Similar cases may be quoted from abroad. In the *Journal d'Agriculture Pratique*, M. Zolla tells the story of a farm at Fresnes in the Loiret, which by an increase of working capital, has been raised from a state of ruin to a condition of fully remunerative prosperity. The farm is one of about 335 acres, and used to be worked on the old-fashioned three-field shift, with a capital of not quite £6. 10s. per acre. The working capital was increased to £16 an acre. The expenses per acre have grown from about £1. 4s. to £3. 1s. per acre. By that means it has proved possible materially to improve the system of husbandry, to manure better, till better, plant 125 acres with sugar beet, and accordingly the profits netted have risen from about 12s. to more than £2 per acre. And in consequence of this change, not only is the tenant better off, but he employs more labour in the bargain, and pays it better.

<small>Dippoltshausen.</small>

A very similar case was recently reported upon at Weende, near Göttingen, by Oekonomierath Beseler, who, by similar methods, has converted his property of Dippoltshausen from a white elephant into a remunerative investment.

<small>Attested by the Report of the Royal Agricultural Commission.</small>

But let us look at things more generally. We have had a Royal Commission sitting to inquire into the griefs of agriculture. If the evidence collected teaches anything, it teaches this, that wherever in agriculture there is ample command of money for working a farm, for manuring, feeding, cultivating, and holding over produce, just as circumstances may dictate, without stint and without limit, the effects of distress are very much mitigated. We might almost, applying the word "worth" in our commercial English sense, say

<small>"Tant vaut l'homme, tant vaut la terre."</small>

with the Berrichons, *tant vaut l'homme, tant vaut la terre.* I may add that men of business who have habitual dealings with farmers, have, in addition, long since discovered that business ability and business habits, a capacity for forecasting and reckoning up results and proceeding accordingly, and for keeping accounts, which M. Leroy-Beaulieu terms "the soul of business," constitute a potent factor making for success, that, in spite of all his technical experience, it is not the old "leather-jacket" farmer, well versed in the rule-of-thumb lore of practices handed down by his ancestors, who best weathers the storm of present troubles, but the cultivator who possesses business knowledge and has the habit of calculating, purchasing, adapting himself to altering times and changing markets, even if for technical learning he be dependent upon others, whose services are always to be bought.

The upshot of all this appears to be that, if we want to

improve agriculture, **we** shall have to place it in the same position in which we have put its sister callings, and, as I have ventured to call it on another occasion, "commercialise" **it** —call in the ledger and the ready reckoner to take their places by the side of plough and grubber, and, last, **not** least, open to it a drawing account proportioned to **its** requirements.

Proceeding farther, and applying this lesson in practice, we shall obviously have to distinguish between two kinds of agriculture. There **is** the *small* man, whom our neighbours think of chiefly **when** they talk specifically of the **need** of agricultural credit. **In** his case the question seems **scarcely to call for** argument. It stands to reason that to cultivate to advantage the land which we are, most of us, at **any rate** professedly willing to place in his possession, he must have the use of money. He must buy his tools, manure, seeds. He must have the wherewithal to live while his small crop is ripening. We know that he can secure a remunerative return for such money. We discover it when we inquire into the results of small cultivation. We show that **we** know it by doubling and trebling the rents charged to the small man in **comparison** with the large. Even though weighted with this additional charge, he finds the acre or two worth keeping and cultivating, making them yield in milk and potatoes, even in corn, what will repay him for his labour and outlay. Thus, in return for an exaction which is not always fair, he helps to teach us a lesson which it is odd that as a nation we seem so firmly resolved *not* to learn. There is scarcely an agent who does not admit that in these trying times small farms and small holdings pay out and out the best. And, in the bargain, small tenants as a rule pay their rents most **promptly, often** in advance. The trouble is, how to convert large holdings into small. Money is wanted to do that. And for employment in agriculture even large landowners have difficulty in raising money, even

[margin: The Small Cultivator's Needs.]

[margin: Profitableness of Small Holdings.]

though it be admitted that the additional outlay would insure a satisfactory return. Thus we are brought back to our first problem of credit to be created—agricultural credit, in this instance, to serve the requirements of landlords, for improving or subdividing their estates, such as experience has shown can by a good system of agricultural credit be easily and cheaply provided. I have recently related* some happy results obtained abroad by wholesale division of large estates into small holdings by the agency of, though without any pecuniary help from, the State. The method adopted represents the greatest advance made in Germany in agricultural economy since the legislation of Stein and Hardenberg. In this case money is furnished to effect the conversion in whatever quantity it may be required, without a tax being laid upon any one, to the material benefit of all concerned. But even after all this has been done, when the roads and drains and buildings have been provided, it is found that the small holders, coming to *good* land, ready laid out for them, with comparatively full purses—since they are required to give proof of their possession of a certain minimum of capital—need additional working funds, if they are to do full justice to their opportunities. In Italy precisely the same discovery has led to relief in a case perhaps even more telling. The Government was long distressed about the unsettled state of the wild forest stretch of Montello in Venetia, which was peopled with disorderly hosts of gipsy squatters. To convert these into an orderly and settled population the Government gave them holdings in that forest, which was public land. The gift proved of no avail. The gipsies soon deserted their holdings, which they had no means of cultivating to advantage, and turned themselves loose once more. Then it occurred to M. Chimirri, who was at the time Minister in charge of Crown

---

* *Contemporary Review*, May 1895.

Lands, to sell off part of the area which had been designed for their settlement, and to employ the purchase money realised as a fund wherefrom to make loans to the gipsies resettled on a portion only of that land. The remedy proved strikingly effective. The gipsies settled down and became decent and orderly folk, and the erewhile wild forest has now become a civilised and progressing district—all owing to the provision of money. There is surely no **need to** argue the point any further with respect to **these** small men. Their want of money is written **large upon** all their economy; and their power to do justice to credit, provided that it be **granted** on fair terms and under proper safeguards, is as amply testified.

However, "agriculture" to our English mind **means a** different thing. It means the calling of the *farmer*, the man who habitually complains of **his want** of money, but yet protests that to **borrow money at 6, or 5, or 4** per cent., while he is netting **scarcely 2 or 1, or even 0, on** what he has invested, cannot **possibly be good** business. Farmers are notoriously bad account-keepers, and it may **be that** that 2 or 1 per cent. includes **some** "living" which ought not to be charged to the farm. **But let** that pass. Possibly our large manufacturers might find their factories as unprofitable "one-per-cent." concerns, were they to endeavour to work them with a capital proportionate to their **establishment in the same ratio in which that of the struggling farmer is to his farm. Take a farm at its very worst—worked out, full of** weeds, understocked, undrained. **I put** it to the most sceptical pessimist, whether on that farm some *one* point could not be discovered **at which** additional outlay would **be, humanly** speaking, certain to earn a profit. If it be but the additional food that could be given to a pig, which can always **be counted** upon to make a return, **there would be 4, or 5, or** 6 per cent., surely, if not more, earned on that **outlay.** And the farmer would be the better for such small

The Case of the Larger Farmer.

Where Money may help.

profit, however embarrassed he might continue otherwise. Probably there would be a good many more opportunities for the profitable investment of money open to him. That swampy, moss-grown pasture would repay draining and liming. That starved, couch-covered field which now bears a thin, withered crop of wheat, which in the accounts must spell a certain loss, would return good value for a dressing of superphosphate or some other manure. It now barely repays the expenses of cultivation. Those expenses would not in themselves be increased by the addition of a good dressing of manure. Reckon up the difference between the bad crop and the good, and see if the surplus value does not pay fair interest on the money outlay and leave a profit, however small! Many crumbs make a loaf. Some excess labour employed at the right time, the purchase or loan of a machine, new drainage, the mere holding over of produce when prices are ruinous and money is wanted—all this, if the requisite money be but available at the proper time and on fair terms, may improve the farmer's position, very little it may be—but when things are bad every little helps. We import annually, as Mr J. Collings complains, £38,000,000 worth of the smaller farm produce—apples, milk, potatoes, vegetables, &c.—from abroad. The chances are that with a larger working capital our native agriculture might raise that and more, and so keep the profit for itself. We cannot compete with the foreigner in cheapness of rent or of labour. But we can produce larger crops per acre. And we can successfully compete in the command of money, which is more plentiful and cheaper here than elsewhere. And the question is, whether with the help of money, meaning businesslike and highly productive farming—say, such as Sir A. Cotton is labouring to bring to perfection in Surrey—we might not on some points beat our competitors in the race. We talk of the ruinous effect of "gambling in wheat." At last year's International Co-operative Congress, Rektor

Abt, of **Winterthur,** in Switzerland, pointed out how, by means very similar to those here advocated, such gambling is kept in bounds, if not altogether prevented. Then there is the question of stock. Keep is plentiful **or** short; **stock is** excessively dear, **or** else **dirt** cheap. **There would be** nothing in these fluctuations if you could take advantage of **them—quite the reverse.** But instead of being the **person** to profit, by reason of your want of money at the **right time,** you become the victim. When keep is plentiful you cannot afford to buy **stock.** When **stock** is cheap you have to sell it. Find **a bank** to draw **upon** which will **lend** you the money at a fair commercial interest, and these troubles may **become to** you sources of direct profit. You may do as does the merchant **or** the stockbroker—you may buy things when **they are cheap and** sell **them** when they are dear. In the great drought of 1893 Agricultural Banks helped not a little to moderate the loss sustained by **the German** peasantry. *How Credit helped in the Drought of 1893.*

I have before now quoted an example which appears to me singularly **deserving of** notice in **this country, as** showing the way in which credit has **been made actually** conducive to profit to farmers **situated very much as are** our **own.** A record of **it** may **be** seen in the official publications of the French Ministry of Agriculture. But I have been **to the** spot. There is **not a** bit of the **Continent** which resembles **our own** agricultural **counties** like **the** country **of the** Nièvre in France. **What** with **its large** properties — there **are some of over** 30,000 **acres—its** tenant holdings, ranging generally from 125 to 1,250 acres, its **leafy forests,** its green hedgerows, its lush pastures, and its wholesale cattle-feeding, **that** Department might **be taken for** a part of **Sussex** or of Surrey. The farmers live by fattening cattle—cattle of a local breed noted for its early maturity **and the** tenderness and delicacy of its flesh, which qualities make **the beasts** highly prized **in the** Paris market. **There is** a well-established method **of work-** *An Example from France.*

M. Giraud in the Nièvre.

ing these farms, which is still adhered to. The grazier purchases his lean stock in February or March, to prepare by a few weeks of stall feeding, then turn out to grass, sell in August, in order to put fresh beasts in their places, and dispose of the second lot in October or November. That is considered very fair business, and on every bullock the farmer is supposed to net about £3, after allowing for the cost of the keep. M. Giraud, when in 1865 he took charge of the local branch of the Bank of France, found that for want of money these farmers were not turning their land to adequate account. The pastures were generally understocked. Perhaps M. Giraud would not have been quite so eager to remedy the defect had he not at the same time discovered that the very same cause which hindered farmers in their calling also seriously inconvenienced the local banks. There was a great "draw" of money in early spring, which emptied the tills. Then in August there succeeded a general scramble, money coming in and going out, causing a great deal of trouble and bringing in very little profit. And in October and November in poured the money realised on the market, in huge unmanageable volume, to embarrass the banks with a plethora all through the slack season. A little ingenuity enabled him to set the matter right, and kill two birds at one blow. The better to push his scheme he became a member of several agricultural societies, and so secured opportunities for explaining his plan at farmers' meetings. To farmers known to his bank he was willing to advance whatever money they might require for the purchase of stock, on their acceptances only, backed in every case by two other good men, for three or four months, with one renewal for the same term allowed as a matter of course, at 1 per cent. above bank rate plus a trifling commission. Farmers not personally known to the Bank of France were required to send in their acceptances through their own local bank, backed by that establishment and by another person besides, and **they would** be served for the same term at a fixed rate **of 6 per cent. That** meant that for the very time for which graziers wanted money, to buy, fatten, and **sell two** lots of beasts, they **would be supplied with it at a** moderate rate of interest, enabling **them to earn an additional profit.** Farmers were not slow to turn **this offer to account.** The new practice spread, and **in a little time** became an undoubted success. When, ten or **eleven years** after, M. Giraud was promoted from his managership to a higher post at Marseilles, he found that in the way indicated he had lent out in all between 130,000,000 and 140,000,000 **francs**, netting the additional 1 per cent. interest on behalf **of his bank,** and putting, **as he** himself estimates, not **less** than **25,000,000** francs—£1,000,000—into farmers' pockets. And **the transaction** proved perfectly **safe.** Only in one **instance did** M. Giraud's bank suffer any loss, and then he admits that it was by his own fault. He had failed to satisfy himself that the borrower's rent had **been** paid. **As it** happened, the borrower was heavily in arrear. And so, very naturally, the landlord swooped **down** by distraint upon the cattle, representing £2,000, seizing them at the **expense of the** bank.

I might couple **with** this example, which **surely is to** the point, similar instances culled from **actual** experience in Germany. In that country it is the potato **distilleries,** providing a mass of fodder—the refuse mash—free **of** cost, or at any rate very cheap, during the winter months, which furnish the groundwork upon which to build up a profitable credit transaction. The distilleries take **care of themselves.** An advance is always readily obtainable **on the** produce, sufficient to keep them going. **But the** refuse fodder would be valueless **to many a** farmer, if he could not buy his lean stock on credit, to fatten and sell for money, and **so to** repay the first outlay out of **the** proceeds of the fattening. **Exactly the** same practice prevails **in** Austria. No doubt

Similar **Cases** occur in Germany and Austria.

something of the same sort may be done here, but at what price? The profitableness of the thing lies in the fact that these have become recognised ordinary transactions, like a manufacturer's purchase and working up of materials, practicable at a commercial rate of interest, without any admixture of a sense of obligation due on the borrower's part —beyond the obligation of repayment. There is nothing of "favour" in the matter; the borrowing is done as a matter of course. The drawer being "good," the bill is taken without the slightest demur.

<small>A Sussex Landlord's Application of the Lesson.</small> In spite of objections which still may be heard, I think that the fact is now little disputed, that the command of more money for working capital distinctly constitutes an urgent need of agriculture in Great Britain. The press has, I think, been unanimous in drawing this conclusion from the evidence given before the Royal Agricultural Commission. And such practices as the following—which does not stand alone—go to show that the conclusion cannot be far wrong. Colonel Clifton Brown, a landowner in the Western Division of Sussex, recognising the fact that farmers want more capital than as a rule they command, advances to his own tenants, if they ask for it, money up to the actual amount of the "valuation," and considers that in so doing he furthers his own interest as well as theirs. The effect of the loan granted at 5 per cent. is not actually traceable in higher rent. But he says this of his system: "In the hard times of the last few years it has enabled me to let all my ground satisfactorily." "The point I want to make out," so he goes on, "is that high valuations cripple the farmer when he enters upon his farm, and he is obliged to borrow the money, and has nothing in hand to work with. That means, as I have said, that farmers *require more working capital* than they possess." Colonel Clifton Brown is in no manner of doubt that what he is doing is right and useful. He assures me that agents

of adjoining estates entirely agree with him, that his system is deserving of **imitation**. It places **the** tenant in a far **better** position than he otherwise would be, and the loan given is worth **the** interest **paid**. **Unfortunately it** is **not** every landlord **who** can afford **to do as Colonel** Clifton Brown does. And if he could, it is more than questionable whether he is the right man to do it. **Colonel Clifton** Brown admits that **upon the** point of security **his system is** weak. "If the law were altered, so that it would give the same power to the landlord to collect the interest on valuation advanced as the landlord **now has for rent,** that would make my plan work well, and would be a great benefit **for farmers.** If I **could collect** rent and **interest of** valuations **on one same footing (a first** claim), it would make security good for valuations advanced by landlords." Yes, but we **are talking of** restricting rather than extending the process of distress. **And why** should the landlord advance both land and money? **It is** unfair to him to ask him to do so, and, moreover, from the tenant's point of view, such **action** is liable to abuse. The **proper body to** advance money **is** a bank, which has **means of** making good its security, such as the landlord **does not** possess. Colonel Clifton Brown fully agrees with me, that if a bank were created capable of **making the tenant's** security effective, and loaning upon it, **the system would be** all that could be desired.

It **may be** objected that there is actually already some sort of agricultural credit. **There is, no doubt.** But what **does it** consist of? What Credit the Farmer has now.

There is, first, the falling in arrears **in payment of** rent, which **makes the** landlord the **lender, and** the lender ostensibly without interest, but which is nevertheless paid for rather dearly, in **the continuance of** the law of distress, in restrictions upon cropping, in covenants and the like, all of which conditions serve as security. At best this credit cannot **be** looked upon as a profitable and beneficial kind of credit. Landlord's Credit.

Dealer's Credit.

There is, secondly, the dealer's credit. If there is any one disposed to dispute the legitimacy of credit in its application to agriculture, let him look at that! You may say that farmers do not want credit, that it is too dear for them. Farmers themselves show that they *do* want it by practising it—in the wrong way and in the dearest possible form. There is no more expensive or improvident credit than dealer's. Reckon up what it costs in interest, in bad quality of goods, in dependence upon your dealer in your purchases, and you will find the cost total up to a considerable figure. Mr Chadwick some time ago stated that, according to his calculation, the same sum of money which a working man spends on one-and-a-half day's support for himself and his family, when buying his goods on credit, will pay for two days' support if the goods be bought for cash in small quantities, and for three days' support if they be bought for cash in large quantities. The difference between the farmer's credit and cash purchases may not be in quite the same proportion, but it will probably be found considerable enough. I do not know if the dependence, the sacrifice of freedom of action, may not be taken to rank as the heaviest item in the account. Some twelve or thirteen years ago, I tried to form a co-operative farmers' supply association in East Sussex, for the common purchase of better and cheaper feeding-stuffs, seeds, machinery, manures, and so on. The proposal was very well received. The need of such a thing was felt, the argument in its favour was accepted as sound. Everybody approved. But nobody showed himself willing to join. Why not? "You will never get these men to join," so said to me a large farmer of the district, who knew his class well—a man himself of ample means. "They are all on their dealer's books and cannot get off." They were tied by the leg. They were not free agents. They must buy their goods at the dealer's prices, of such quality as the dealer chose to give, not as they wanted them, **but as the** dealer was willing to deal them **out**. They paid dearly for their credit. Co-operative Credit Banks, wherever they are established, have done away with this. They have enabled farmers to combine for the common purchase of goods—to which they are now slowly adding combined selling—and the 4 **or** 5 per cent. per annum which they take in interest **is** shown to be **a** cheap set-off for **the** benefit assured.

Again, there **is** banker's credit already available for Banker's farmers—banker's **credit** of a kind. Not the free, ready Credit. credit always obtainable as a matter of course, and always to be depended upon, such as the trader may claim, and does not claim in vain; but an occasional loan on "character" —or rather on the security of property which the farmer is supposed to possess—or on standing crops—credit which is intended rather to help **the borrower out of** a difficulty than to supply him with the **means** for engaging in some profitable enterprise. There is always a smack of favour about this kind of credit, and a suspicion of embarrassment. It seems to cut a notch into the borrower's financial reputation. In any case it is a matter of bargain and negotiation, to be treated for in every particular instance, granted for **a** certain length of time, stated or understood, and **is, accord**ingly, resorted to only in the hour of need—very **often** when credit comes too late to be of any **use**. It **is a** specimen of **what M. Léon Say** has well stigmatised **as** "illegitimate" credit—"consumer's credit," **M**. Leroy-Beaulieu calls it—credit given to meet expenditure already incurred, credit which accordingly cannot yield a profit; as contrasted with "legitimate" or "productive" credit, credit given for **a** purpose of production which may, if judiciously employed, assure a **gain**.

There is the Scotch **Cash** Credit, of course, which **has** Scotch Cash done so much to raise Scotch agriculture. "The far-famed Credit. agriculture of the Lothians," so writes Mr H. D. Macleod,

E

"the manufactures of Glasgow and Paisley, the unrivalled steam ships of the Clyde are its own proper children." "A friend of mine," so Mr Fowler stated some years ago at the Bankers' Institute, "was travelling in one of the northern counties of Scotland, and there was pointed out to him a valley covered with beautiful farms. My friend was an Englishman, and his companion, who was a Scotchman, pointed down the valley and said, 'That has all been done by the banks,' intimating his strong opinion that but for the banking system of Scotland (the cash credit) the development of agriculture would be in its infancy compared to what it is now." Unfortunately, there is now very little of this useful credit left—so far as it applies to agriculture. It seems to have gone out with the nineteen years' leases. It was invented to provide a circulation for bank-notes issuable at that time without limit. It is not worth pushing, from the banker's point of view—as involving risk—after issue has ceased to be profitable business. South of the Tweed it has scarcely developed to recognisable proportions as specifically agricultural credit under its English name of "overdraft." It is to the borrower's interest, of course, to have such a convenience. And that is a telling argument in favour of Co-operative Banks, because they supply the only means by which the borrower can provide it for himself.

Usurer's Credit.

Lastly, there is the usurer's credit—very much of it, more than most people are at all aware of. Evidence of its presence and its ruinous influence comes to light sometimes, like a discovery under the bull's eye glare of a stray prosecution, and then people cry out in horror at the systematic blood-sucking in progress where blood is least plentiful. We notice these exceptional cases. We do not see that steady sapping of our most precarious industry which is ever going on like the gnawing of a rat at the timbers of a house doomed thereby to eventual ruin, and which results meanwhile in the impoverishment of a large number of useful workers to the enrichment of unprofitable drones. Surely on this point a substitute for the borrowing which is sheer suicide is urgently called for.

I come back to the question which I **asked** above :— Why cannot ordinary credit provide for **the** farmer what he needs ?

Why Ordinary Bankers cannot provide what is wanted.

There are very potent reasons, one **of** which the President **of** the Imperial Bank of Germany, Dr Koch, made very clear when speaking upon the subject of credit to agriculture not long ago in the German Parliament.*

Opinion of the President of the German Imperial Bank.

Returns, so he says, **are in** agriculture incomparably slower than in trade and industry. As a rule, it may be **said** that a twelvemonth is required for turning over a sum **invested.** If there should be a failure of crops, or any other misadventure, one year may not suffice. Dr Koch quotes Professor Marchet as laying it **down in** his standard book on " Agricultural Credit" **that** the farmer **is** not in a position to repay his debt till after the close of the "period **of** vegetation," and that at that point of time he can repay it only on the supposition that his new harvest should prove adequate for making good the deficiency of the last. "That **very** uncertain factor, **Nature,**" so Dr Koch observes, "enters into the calculation. It is from this cause as well, and not only because the turnover is in agriculture so much slower **than in other** callings," that the difficulties arise. **The** Imperial Bank of Germany, so Dr Koch went on to explain— an institution corresponding in importance in Germany to what the Bank of England is among ourselves—advances to agriculture in the course of the twelvemonth not less than £12,000,000. Generally speaking, **he** added, the farmer who borrows the money **is** not at all aware of the fact that it is from the Imperial Bank that he procures it, because he

---

* See *Cologne Gazette* of 27th March **1895, No. 269.**

collects it from brokers and dealers who act as intermediaries. But these men would be wholly unable to grant the credit had they not got the Imperial Bank at their back —an institution strong enough and willing to grant such inconveniently long loans.

<small>"L'échéance agricole n'est que nominale."</small> Other bankers who deal in credit to agriculture entirely confirm Dr Koch's statement. "L'échéance agricole," so remarked to me M. Scotti, Director of the People's Bank at Acqui, which does mainly an agricultural business, "n'est que nominale." Losses are infinitesimal. But you can never tell when the money will come back to the bank. So it is at Lodi, at Cremona, at Rovigo, at Augsburg, at Gotha, at Cosel, at Insterburg. At Insterburg I have found that there were agricultural loans outstanding which had been running for more than fifteen, even up to twenty years.

Agricultural credit, then, is a kind of credit which it is not worth the ordinary banker's while to give—in the first place, because it is asked for an inconvenient length of time —a time which may be altogether uncertain, and which will certainly be too long for occasional lending, and too short for permanent investment. The banker and the capitalist lend as a matter of *business*, not as a matter of philanthropy or public duty. Conditions must be made somehow to square with their interests, or they will have none of it. There is no other unwillingness on their part. They are ready to undertake any business which will keep them safe and give them market value for their money. The limited lending already done to agriculture, even to very small agriculture, by some banks in Scotland and in Ireland, and, I believe, by a bank in Cornwall, distinctly prove this. It was undertaken, not because it particularly suited those banks, but because the banks were willing to render a service so far as they judged that they could safely do so. Abroad, great banking institutions like the Bank of France, the National

Savings Bank of Belgium and Italian Savings Banks, show themselves most anxious to find an outlet for their funds into a channel which may turn to the profit of agricultural industry. But the difficulties prove formidable, and accordingly little or nothing can be done by those banking giants by direct means.

There is a second difficulty, to which Dr Koch does not refer, because it **does** not apply specifically to what he was talking about, and does not affect his own bank, a banking institution dealing, not with farmers directly, but with Central Co-operative Banks, which form the intermediate connecting link. The first requisite which a lender is entitled to ask for is *security*. Many well-meaning people in this country and elsewhere, **approaching** the problem of credit **to agriculture** and to the poor, have approached it from the side of "money." They would provide funds, and deal them out to the needy according to their needs, or according to a supposed standard of merit. That is putting the cart before the horse. The first thing to be provided is *security*. Find security, and you will have no need to call for your money; it will come of its own accord. In respect of security for personal credit, however, the farmer, large or small, stands in a totally different position from the merchant or trader. Nobody pretends that he is not "good." He repays, generally speaking, with scrupulous honesty, though he may be provokingly tardy. But just on account of that tardiness, and, moreover, because there is no great money market in which he is known, as is the trader, his signature is not of negotiable value. If you would give it a value, you will therefore first have to create some new machinery, some banking appliance which will make it good current security. Co-operative banks have shown themselves capable of effecting this; and therefore I have ventured to say that in the case of a farmer or cultivator they actually *create* a security—which is true to a fuller extent even than may appear at

<small>Necessity of creating a marketable Personal Security to justify Personal Credit.</small>

first blush; for they do not only make a security negotiable which was not so before; they distinctly establish one where there was none before. That is their peculiar merit. How they accomplish this, how they at the same time create a security, and make lending for what has otherwise been found an inconvenient period possible, I shall have to explain in detail as I try to make clear the various systems of People's Banking. My present object is to insist that credit made easily accessible, cheap, and in every way convenient, may be of very great service to agriculture, and that the ordinary money market, in its present organisation, does not provide a source for such credit—that accordingly some new source has to be created.

CHAPTER VI.

THE "CREDIT ASSOCIATIONS" OF SCHULZE-DELITZSCH.

THE merit of first putting the idea of co-operative credit-banking into practical shape belongs to Germany. Before the two great German apostles of Co-operation, Schulze-Delitzsch and Raiffeisen, began their useful creative work, both about the same time, though quite independently of one another, far apart—one in the East, the other in the West of the Empire—in respect of credit co-operation all was chaos. To the eyes of the world it was Schulze (popularly named, after his birthplace, Schulze-Delitzsch) who first raised order out of confusion, and infused system into the rude mass of half-formed notions. As a matter of fact, Raiffeisen was, in his quiet, unobtrusive way, the first in the field by a very short space of time. It really matters very little, though of course the *furor teutonicus* has seized upon this point eagerly as a pretext for a pitched battle, over which minds have grown curiously heated. Some people will have it that Credit Associations were not Schulze's original creation at all, but that he picked up the idea from an obscure German jeweller, one Biski, who died an officer in the Federal army of the United States. If he did, it matters not a jot. The idea of co-operation for credit was, as has already been shown, "in the air" when Schulze's mind was first attracted to the problem. Gall had suggested something of the sort in 1830. About the year 1845 one Liedke had organised co-operative savings

<small>The Germans the first Organisers' of Co-operative Credit.</small>

<small>Schulze-Delitzsch.</small>

banks in Germany, with a view to lending pecuniary assistance, in a very cumbrous way, to co-operative supply associations. About the same time that Schulze took up his apostleship, in 1851, a Moravian named Staudinger, without any knowledge of the work going on in Prussia, established something rather similar to Schulze's "Credit Associations" in his own native town of Klagenfurt. All this can detract nothing from Schulze's merit—even supposing him to have been cognisant of it. It was one thing to have a vague shapeless idea floating in one's mind; it was quite a different thing to give to that idea definite form, to make it workable, and to set it actually at work in thousands of establishments throughout the country. That is what Schulze did; and he did it with the skill and rapid success of a born organiser, to the incalculable benefit of his country. To neutral observers a matter of far greater interest than these hot disputes about rival claims to priority is the fact, that up to the present day the two systems of co-operative credit formulated severally by Schulze and Raiffeisen have remained the two specific types of such credit, the parents of two distinct families of associations, and the models, upon one or other of which all similar institutions have been shaped. Of the two, thus far, Schulze's system has been the most freely copied all over the Continent, and has attained the largest economic results. Its success has been marvellous. Nevertheless, I shall have some fault to find with it. As a matter of course, it is the child of the circumstances which brought it forth, and it bears their impress plainly upon its form.

His first Beginnings.

To Schulze, as to his fellow-labourer Raiffeisen, the idea of co-operation was first suggested by the miseries brought upon many of his neighbours by that trying dearth and famine which swept across Germany during the years immediately preceding the last Revolution. He was then living in his little native town of Delitzsch, filling a judicial post corresponding, roughly speaking, to that of a County Court judge in England. By this means he was brought into contact with many small folk, and led to understand and appreciate their sufferings. Schulze had visited England, and knew something of our provident societies and our early beginnings of co-operation. Accordingly, it occurred to him to apply for the mitigation of their sufferings the same means which had already proved effective here. In conjunction with his friend Dr Bernhardi, of Eilenburg, he set on foot, first of all, a sort of provident fund. Next, the two philanthropists organised an institution which has since become exceedingly popular in Germany, a co-operative association for the joint purchase of raw material. German co-operators sometimes express astonishment at our not having adopted the same convenient form of co-operation in this country. The reason probably is that our trade is generally carried on on a larger scale, and that our wholesale dealers have better accommodated themselves to the wants of their clients. Moreover, none of our traders would wish his rivals to know how much raw material he himself purchases. But to the joiners of Delitzsch and the shoemakers of Eilenburg the new institution came as a veritable godsend. They took it up readily, their example was followed elsewhere, and to the present day, among a considerable number of associations for the purchase of raw material, co-operative shoemakers' societies continue numerous and flourishing in Germany, more especially in Saxony, Brunswick, and the adjoining districts of Prussia.

From the co-operative purchase of raw material to other co-operative supply, and from that to the co-operative supply of money, was in each case but a step. Schulze took both, one by one, and the year 1850 saw his first "Credit Association" established. That association was not in the fullest sense co-operative, and hence its early

The first "Credit Association," 1850.

weakness. It was a capitalist institution, philanthropic and condescending, supplied with funds by members who did not themselves expect to become borrowers. Evidently Schulze was cautiously feeling his way. But he made his bank co-operative at any rate to the extent of insisting that no one should obtain a loan who did not himself become a member of the bank, and so pledge himself to regular payments (*ergo*, to savings) up to a certain figure, and, moreover, that the loans granted should be treated, not as a matter of charity or favour, but as a matter of business. There was a notable advance in this upon old methods. The German apostle of co-operation did not long halt at this half-way station. While he was away meeting one of those numerous vexatious prosecutions with which his Government unpleasantly seasoned his career, his friend Dr Bernhardi worked out at Eilenburg a more fully co-operative scheme, upon which he modelled his own local bank. The experiment proved a decided success. As many as 396 members joined, paying in in the very first year 2,242 thalers (£336) in deposits, and so enabling the association, with the help of 3,703 thalers (£555) of borrowed money and its own small capital, to lend out in the twelvemonth 8,801 thalers (£1,320), and to realise a net profit of 142½ thalers (£21. 7s. 6d.), which was considered exceedingly encouraging. Schulze, returning to Delitzsch in 1852, at once recognised the superiority of his friend's system, and forthwith grafted its principle upon his own less perfect institution, with the result of increasing the number of members from the 30, to which it had fallen, to 150, and raising sufficient funds to enable him to lend out something like 5,000 thalers (£750) in the first year after the change.

Thus was the first stone laid of a fabric which was destined to become a great co-operative stronghold, the first seed planted of a crop which was to overspread the entire Continent. In substance the Schulze-Delitzsch

CREDIT ASSOCIATIONS.

associations are the same still; in the main the original type has been adhered to. It was a bright light which Schulze had set a-burning, and he was not the man to hide it under a bushel. He may be described as a born economic missionary. His striking personality, his convincing eloquence, his invincible faith in his own cause, and his truly contagious enthusiasm made him an almost ideal propagandist. He "stumped" the country with a will, making clear with a remarkable lucidity of exposition to audience after audience the principles of his system, the benefits of its application, the incalculable gain which it must bring alike to individuals and to the community. Thousands flocked to hear him; thousands became converted to his idea. I personally well remember the wonderful effect of his propaganda; for during the time when he gained his most signal triumphs I happened to be in Germany, and in one of his own best working districts. His economic gospel took the country by storm. Everywhere new "Credit Associations" sprang up — followed in many cases by supply associations — and everywhere they accomplished astonishingly good work. When in 1883 the great German champion of co-operation was called home there are said to have been no less than 4,000 associations of various sorts established in Germany, organised on his rules, comprising something like 1,200,000 members, disposing of capital of their own to the amount of more than £10,000,000, and doing business at the rate — so Herr Schmid, of Vienna, calculates — of at least £100,000,000 a year. That is without including a large number of associations formed avowedly on Schulze-Delitzsch lines in adjoining countries. Without doubt Schulze had carried his idea to triumph.

Schulze's path was not at first altogether strewn with roses. He had to fight his way to success by his own efforts. Those were the days when in Germany there was still a common talk of the "limited understanding of

His Difficulties.

subjects." The "first," and really the only, "duty of citizens" was declared to be, "to obey." Governments must do all the thinking, as well as all the governing, and the State alone was reputed competent to render help. When therefore this "Democrat"—as he happened to be, and a Liberal was at that time almost a social outcast—presumed not only to think out his own scheme for benefiting his fellow-men, but topped this offence with the arch-heresy of suggesting that men could actually help themselves without the interference of the State, the Manteuffels and Bismarcks felt their prerogative invaded, and resolved to make the audacious innovator suffer for his presumption. He was an obnoxious person to them to begin with; for not only did he openly avow himself a Liberal, but, in addition to this, he was a leader of the party aiming at German Unity—to belong to which was at that time reckoned next door to high treason. The Government began by worrying the poor man out of his judgeship. When they could not refuse him sick-leave as a judge, they granted it coupled with the condition that he must not, while on furlough, visit his native town. When, knowing this condition to be illegal, he nevertheless proceeded to Delitzsch, where he was received like a hero returning from victory, they promptly announced that a month's allowance would be stopped out of his salary. Indignant at such arbitrary treatment, Schulze threw up his judgeship in disgust, and resolved to devote himself from thenceforth entirely to his philanthropic work.

Government Persecutions.

But he had not yet done with "paternal" Ministers. Every conceivable hindrance was laid in his way. When in 1859 he convened his first Co-operative Congress—the most harmless Congress, one would think, which a man could convene—under the dictation of the Government in Berlin even fair-minded King John of Saxony dared not open his dominions to the supposed traitor, who was accordingly compelled to summon his adherents to that one available refuge, as it **then** was, for persecuted Germans, the Thuringian duchies. When it was seen that in spite of all this official harassing and badgering, prosecutions in **courts of** law, and tabooing in the press, Schulze still kept gaining ground with the people—who were not by **such** means to be dragooned out of benefits apparent to all and appealing to all—Herr von Bismarck, the unsparing anti-Socialist of later days, raised up a Socialist Jannes **to** withstand him, in the person of Lassalle. This man was systematically petted and caressed, favoured even to the length of the acceptance of his idea of Socialist workshops. At the instance of Herr von Bismarck, who personally introduced the forerunners of Bebel and Liebknecht to King William, some experimental *ateliers*, endowed with money **from** the King's privy purse, **were set up** at Berlin, and **carried on for** a brief time—of course with the result of **losing** His Majesty every farthing ventured. In 1865 the Prussian Diet appointed a Committee to draw up a law on co-operation. By explicit direction of Herr von Bismarck the one person in the House who knew anything about co-operation was deliberately excluded. And so this harassing and baiting went on. To the end of his career was Schulze, who enriched his country by more milliards than **Prince** Bismarck conquered for it in 1871—to say nothing of instilling the principles of thrift—mercilessly harassed on his course. And to this day the odium of political partisanship **of** which Sir E. Malet speaks in his Blue Book— evidently under a false impression, because he applies the charge to the wrong party—as **still** attaching to the co-operative movement, is clearly attributable to that long-continued official boycotting.

Of course all this childish persecution entirely missed its aim. Every **weal which** Prince Bismarck's sharp whip raised on the popular favourite's skin secured the latter fresh hosts of admirers and converts. There is absolutely nothing to be said in justification of the official badgering. To make it the less excusable it was directed altogether against the wrong point—not the point at which, unfortunately, the system eventually proved to be vulnerable, but that at which it was absolutely blameless.

<small>Schulze's Problem stated by himself.</small>

Schulze himself has stated the problem which, when forming his first People's Bank, he set himself to solve, to be—how to obtain the use of borrowed capital without a "capital of guarantee." Taking this view of his case, it is not surprising that he should have made it his first aim to create the "capital of guarantee" which he found wanting. That really is the pivot upon which his whole system turns. Sir R. Morier, writing as a warm admirer of Schulze,

<small>Unlimited Liability.</small>

describes *unlimited liability* as the "keystone of his whole system," its indispensable support, "just as the principle 'all for one and one for all' is the soul and breath of all co-operation." He goes on say that "*with* unlimited liability" the fulfilment of these two conditions—the selection of trustworthy officers, and the acceptance of sound rules, both being known to the public—will "suffice to attract the local capital to the market." In respect of the latter point Schulze-Delitzsch himself seems to have taken rather a different and a more timid view, for he designedly resorted to more powerful means of attraction. And although in his day he insisted quite as strongly as ever Sir Robert could afterwards do upon the absolute necessity of unlimited liability ; and although his chosen champion and pupil, Dr Crüger, writes that "without the unlimited liability of members it would be almost impossible to do anything, and no money could be obtained," in these present days unlimited liability has come to be looked upon as a practice which even Schulze-Delitzsch banks could very well dispense

<small>It is not indispensable.</small>

with. In Belgium, in Italy, in France, credit associations more or less of the Schulze-Delitzsch type have done very well without **unlimited** liability. And in Germany they are learning to cast it aside with equally good results. It is now indeed generally accepted as a maxim that, although for a bank in its earliest stages unlimited liability is unquestionably a substantial help, **as** securing a larger **credit,** nevertheless a bank which has once been fairly put upon its legs may very well dispense with it, and a bank **which by success** has become strong is without **doubt better** without it.*

There will be something **more to say on the subject of** unlimited liability in the next chapter, **in connection with a** system in which unlimited liability **is** undoubtedly indispensable, but in which also it has been successfully disarmed of its terrors. Outside Germany the constant insistence by advocates **of** the Schulze-Delitzsch system upon unlimited liability has proved really the most serious hindrance to the spread of co-operative credit associations. In Germany, at the time when Schulze began his **work,** no other form **of** joint liability can **be said to have** been known. Even we, the original inventors **of** " limited liability," had not **yet** passed our " Limited Liability Act." And even after it was passed, our neighbours did not show themselves particularly eager to appropriate its benefits **to** themselves. And evidently, even in spite of some serious mishaps, in Germany people have become so much accustomed to this form of guarantee, **that in the teeth of all its dangers, which Dr**

---

* Dr Crüger and his fellow-champions **of** the Schulze-Delitzsch system profess to look **upon the question of limited or unlimited liability as immaterial. For** ourselves (as for the Italians, according to the testimony **of Commendatore** Luzzatti) it **is** decidedly material. Signor Ettore Levi will have it **in** his later days Schulze himself strongly **inclined to acceptance** of liability only limited. This **is,** according to **the** testimony of Herr Siegl, a mistake. According to Herr Siegl, Schulze **was with difficulty persuaded by his friends in** his last days to **agree to the sanction of limited liability.**

Schneider, one of the foremost of writers on the Schulze-Delitzsch side, has compared to those of a "two-edged sword,"* they still prefer it to any other, as assuring advantages not otherwise to be secured. Of 4,401 credit associations furnishing returns for the year ending 31st May 1892, as many as 4,169 are shown to have been based on unlimited liability. And that was after a law had been passed in 1889 which specifically authorises, and, in fact, rather invites, unlimited liability associations to limit their liability. Even though at that very time a new class of credit associations had sprung up, basing their action upon limited liability, from 1890 to 1891, the number of limited liability credit associations had risen only from 41 to 146, and on 31st May 1895, out of a total of 6,295 credit associations registered (leaving out of account 122 unregistered) as many as 5,932 adhered to unlimited liability. That may be taken as indicating with sufficient clearness that, generally speaking, German co-operators are not afraid of the unlimited form of liability. And provided that proper safeguards are adopted, under their own circumstances there is certainly something to be said for adherence to an institution which long practice has made familiar, and which increases the credit purchasing power of capital very considerably, while adding an incitement to vigilance where vigilance is particularly needed. No, Schulze selected unlimited liability, not because he considered it absolutely indispensable, but because he found it the familiar and accepted German tradition; and, no doubt, it also promised him the most rapid success.

The real "Keystone of the System." The real "keystone of the system" is the compulsion brought to bear upon members to *save*, regularly and

---

* Dass die auf unbeschränkter Solidarhaft beruhende Genossenschaft in ungeschickten Händen eine sehr gefährliche Waffe sei, die in den minder bemittelten Volksklassen viel Unheil anrichten könne.— *Blätter für Genossenschaftswesen*, 1886, p. 81, *ss.*

steadily, and by their savings to raise up a "capital of guarantee," a capital sufficient to command benefits which are offered, not wholly as an end in themselves, but no less as an inducement to members to practice the great economic virtue of thrift. Hence, Schulze-Delitzsch's associations have been popularly called "Compulsory Savings Banks" (*Zwangs-sparkassen*). For moral results Schulze looked no higher than thrift. He himself and his followers have often openly sneered at the "religious" objects kept in view by "Christian Socialists"—such as our Judge Hughes and E. Vansittart Neale. But thrift they are thoroughly willing to stimulate. "Compulsory Savings Banks."

The Schulze-Delitzsch banks, then, may be not incorrectly described as, in their founder's original intention, savings banks first and credit banks afterwards. The want of credit urging people to apply for membership was to be used as a means for turning them into habitual savers, as the first condition for enabling them to satisfy that want. At the outset, then, at any rate, and for a considerable time afterwards, the *lender's* interest was placed before the *borrower's*.

Schulze's scheme, in his own original conception, may be briefly summarised thus. Every member joining is expected to take up one share. He is not allowed to take more, partly because, his unlimited liability being pledged, no more is held to be wanted to provide security; partly, also, to prevent the capture of the association by a few greedy capitalists for their own selfish profit. Schulze's System described.

The value of the shares Schulze advisedly fixed high. The original figure was, I believe, £30. Of course, it is provided that that sum need not be paid down at once; rather is it assumed that it will be made up by instalments, which may be very small. This principle necessarily commits the newly-joining member to a long course of saving, which is just what Schulze desired to bring about. With the help of the capital in course of formation, of savings Large Shares.

F

deposits invited in addition to the accumulating instalments, of other deposits, and of the credit which the small capital and the unlimited liability of a large number of members among them are sure to command, the banks ought to be—and in fact are—in a position to raise all the money which may be required from them in loans. They have now even arrived at raising more, in fact quite enough sometimes seriously to embarrass them.

Interest was at first high.

The loaning is to be done freely, but not necessarily very cheaply. The borrower came from a market dominated by usury. And as he was willing to pay, both Schulze and M. d'Andrimont maintain (as quoted by M. Ettore Levi)—against M. Luzzatti and Raiffeisen, who plead for kinder consideration — that there is no wrong done in taking from him fairly high interest. The usual charge at the outset varied from 12 to 14 per cent.; not very long ago it stood generally at 8—though ostensibly at only 6, the additional 2 being tacked on under the guise of a "commission" of $\frac{1}{2}$ per cent., reckoned for three months. A flooded market has more recently reduced it.

Security rather than Specification of Object insisted upon.

The banks practically ask no questions as to the object of the loan, or the person of the borrower, except that no money is now (since 1889) lent outside the association (it is the new law which makes this condition imperative)—however willing the latter may be to accept deposits or loans from outsiders. What the associations look to in the matter is *security*. And they allow practically any form of security—mortgages, pledges, sureties, bills—although, wisely, at headquarters mortgages are viewed with decided disfavour, as constituting an inconvenient, and even dangerous, pledge. However, generally speaking, provided that the security is acceptable, the banks are willing to grant credit to any amount which appears safe, in the shape either of current accounts or of specific loans, the latter being generally secured by an acceptance or promissory note.

The loans may be large **or small**. But they must be short for *short* terms. Schulze **has laid it down** as a cardinal rule that a banker cannot **lend** out money for a longer term than that for which he himself has received it. Any banker's clerk could tell the learned gentlemen at Berlin, who still write in defence of that doctrine, that it is practically nonsense. What the banker **has to do is, not to** collect money in distinct pieces of coin and dispose of such pieces for **just as** long **as he is allowed the use of each**, but to take care that in his lending he does not exceed the term for which in some way **or** other, **not** making the transaction unprofitable, he can make reasonably sure of obtaining **money himself, no** matter whether that be by the **steady automatic** inflow of deposits **or** by specific loan. However, the principle has a neat and "taking" ring, which makes it still a **favourite** in theoretical discussion, though practical credit bankers have long abandoned it. According to the strict principles of the system, then, three months constitutes the ordinary period of a loan, with one renewal, for another three months, permitted, but not favoured. A member, accordingly, can, on this supposition, always obtain money for **a short** term, provided that he has security to offer which **is** acceptable to the Committee. That body, upon whom the main burden of administration falls, invariably **consists of three**. It is elected by the members **at their annual** general meeting, and in **consideration of the services** rendered, is paid a regular salary, with a commission added, the latter being regulated by the amount of business done. **To** check the Committee, and to audit their accounts, a Council of Control or Audit is added, being likewise elected every year at the annual meeting, and generally consisting of nine members. This Council meets, of course, much less frequently. It has the decision on the granting or refusing of loans constitutionally reserved for its judgment. But for practical reasons that provision remains, as

Short Lending.

a rule, a dead letter. There is more business than the Council could effectively control. Schulze was a great believer in the principle which says that "the labourer is worthy of his hire." Good work, he maintained, was to be secured only by payment. Accordingly he was an opponent of gratuitous services. Even the members of the Council are under his rules entitled to remuneration, according to their attendances. That regulation still holds good in nearly all the banks.

<small>Large Districts.</small>

One important feature in the system is, that the banks are allowed a very large, and almost unwieldy, area to work in. The bank sets up its counter in a convenient centre, and invites all who live within an accessible distance to come and join it. It is contended that, to secure a sound foundation and to work satisfactorily, the bank should have as *large* and as *mixed* a constituency as is at all procurable, consisting of members of all callings, whose blending is calculated at all times to equalise supply and demand of money, security and risk. The large area, of course, means a considerable number of members, and correspondingly substantial business. And with such support the Schulze-Delitzsch associations have grown comparatively large, and represent, generally speaking, far more substantial numbers and capitals than do their rivals. And this, it is pleaded, not only provides greater financial strength, but, moreover, saves management expenses.

<small>The Success of the System.</small>

Whatever be the theoretical merits or demerits of the system, it certainly has secured a very large measure alike of support and of success. In Germany alone, according to the last return published, the number of credit associations which had accepted the Schulze-Delitzsch principles numbered in 1894 something like 2,700. But only 953 of these had actually become members of the Central Union. Indeed, it is not strictly speaking quite correct to call even all those 953 "Schulze-Delitzsch banks," inasmuch as one

or two consider themselves of an independent type. The difference is almost one of name only. And one or two more have actually converted themselves into joint-stock companies. There has been a slight diminution in the number during the past few years, which does not necessarily mean a loss of strength. The same thing has happened in Italy. I am not in a position to state the precise amount of transactions done by all these banks. But it will give some idea of the magnitude of the collective operations if I quote the following figures referring to 1,047 credit associations that have furnished returns, all of them being of the Schulze-Delitzsch type, though not all incorporated in the Union. The 1,047 associations, then, lent out among them 1,550,012,619 marks (£77,500,630), that is, on an average, 1,480,432 marks (£74,021) per association. That, of course, includes renewals. Probably the approximate amount of *bona fide* new borrowing was somewhere about £50,000,000.*
The total number of members was 509,723. Therefore on an average every member had had 3,040 marks (£152) placed at his disposal. The collective property (capital and reserve funds) of the 1,047 associations is returned at 155,680,698 marks (£7,784,035), the money borrowed or received on deposit at 457,734,531 marks (£22,886,726). Of this large sum, which compares very favourably with the total of the association's own funds, only 13,541,531 marks (£677,076) had been borrowed from large banks. As much as 380,917,418 marks (£19,045,871) had been collected in deposits and savings, 57,252,243 marks (£2,862,612) stood to the banks' debit on current accounts, and 6,023,124 marks (£301,156) was due from the bank on acceptances. Thus, in all, these associations disposed of a working fund of 613,415,229 marks (£30,670,761), which is

---

* The annual return gives the figure of renewals at £16,746,678 only, which would raise the new lending to £60,763,952; but that leaves both mortgages and current accounts out of consideration.

surely a very considerable sum. The clear profit netted is returned at 9,487,700 marks (£474,385). The roll of members, it may be added, was made up of all varieties of classes, 31.5 per cent. being, roughly speaking, persons engaged in agriculture, and 26 per cent. artisans working for their own account.*

<small>Extended beyond Germany.</small>

It should be borne in mind that the business of these 1,047 banks making returns, represents, roughly speaking, only one-half, perhaps less, of what Schulze-Delitzsch credit associations are actually doing in Germany alone. Moreover, the same system has spread far beyond the German border. Herr Schmid, of Vienna, in 1886 calculated the entire number of Schulze-Delitzsch banks then existing at 4,500, with 1,500,000 members; and attributed to them collectively an annual business of £450,000,000—a huge sum. Surely this is a most satisfactory measure of success, and it tells of an almost incalculable amount of good done by the supply of cash for productive purposes. And as for dividend—the result by which many among ourselves, it is to be feared, will be inclined to gauge the success of the undertaking — though some "Credit Associations" have done badly, others have declared 10, 12, 14, up to 20, and even 30 per cent. On an average they have, in a year which was not particularly favourable for business, netted 5.19 per cent. on their working capital, after allowing £3,913 for charities, and £48,359 for losses, the latter averaging only about 1s. 11d. per member. Looking at this all together, it cannot be pronounced an unsatisfactory result, even though there be a diminution upon some preceding years.†

---

* For more complete statistics, see the note at the end of this chapter.

† The figures for some preceding years were considerably more favourable. Commercial depression has affected co-operative like other banks. In 1891, for instance, 1,072 associations returned a share capital of £5,853,993, that is, £11. 6s. per member. The entire transactions amounted together to £138,745,134; the credit granted to £82,078,709; the sums raised by loan to £12,691,313.

And in the main the business done has been done smoothly and in a business-like way. The losses, as has been shown, although severe in some particular instances, are not heavy, taking the whole volume of business. The lending has been done on every variety of security; to some extent—small, but still too large, viz., £592,043 on the year, and £2,478,395 in all—on mortgages; £4,722,953 has been lent on simple note of hand. The main lending has been done on acceptances or promissory notes, on discounts, and, in the last place, on current accounts. The last-named form of credit, copied from the Scotch "cash credit," and resembling what we in England know as "overdraft," is rightly much favoured by the leaders of the movement, as being convenient alike to bank and borrower, and a form of transaction training to business habits. The leaders of the movement continue also to urge upon their followers the advisability of extending the use of cheques, which is at present still very little practised in Germany. Generally speaking, the acceptance or promissory note is the instrument favoured for loans, notwithstanding that there is among some classes in Germany a very pronounced feeling against this form of bond, because it is very often put to improper use, and the German law is exceptionally severe upon drawers making default. The loans granted by the 1,047 Schulze-Delitzsch referred to on acceptances or bills of exchange figured in the past year in all at £29,342,628, of which sum £14,442,745 stands for new business, and £14,899,884 for renewals. The sums employed in discounting bills figure at £15,819,418; and the current accounts (overdrafts) at £27,023,583. The credit associations are much appreciated as savings banks. Most of the banks are open every day. Their credit in the open market is excellent. Altogether, the Schulze-Delitzsch credit associations have in respect of magnitude of business, of extension of their system, and of work done, an exceedingly good record to show.

Smallness of Losses.

Securities taken.

Success assured in some measure by Departures from Theoretical Rules.

But that record has not been secured, it ought to be explained, without some rather remarkable departures in practice from the rules laid down in theory. That is, I take it, no blame to the system, even though Schulze be originally responsible for some of the precepts which practical men have put aside, but which his teaching successors still cling to, no matter how conclusively experience may have shown them to be unsuited or however much circumstances may have changed. Schulze's *system* was self-help —self-help undiluted, unalloyed, individualist* almost to excess, purely *economic* self-help—giving to every man in proportion to what he had expended in effort. Oddly enough, while insisting with great emphasis upon the strictly *individualist* character of his co-operation, Schulze made himself (unintentionally) guilty of a curious piece of inconsistency in adopting unlimited liability, which as a matter of course gave the system a *collectivist* character, with an application which many of his followers have seen reason to deplore. That, as I have shown, could not be helped. Schulze knew what circumstances he had to deal with, but he could not tell in precisely what manner his methods would act, whether they would prove too drastic or too little effective. He operated on untried ground, at a period when money was scarce; saving undeveloped, and the individual feeble. Naturally—or, at any rate, excusably —he argued that he could not do too much to attract both numbers of members, to act in union, and capital. He must have capital; he must have good administrators; he must have a lively sense of self-interest awakened. These things are to be got, if you will offer them a proper reward.

---

* Compare Dr Häntschke's "Individualismus und Kollektivismus in der neuen genossenschaftlichen Bewegung" in "Zeitschrift der Centralstelle für Arbeiter-Wohlfahrtseinrichtungen," 1895, Nos. 14, 17. Dr Häntschke is one of the Secretaries of the Union of Schulze Co-operative Associations.

Hence those high rates of interest allowed, the salaries and commissions permitted for services, and the non-limitation of dividends, which has spelt up to 20 per cent. in a good many cases, and in some even to 50 and 60 per cent. However, times have changed. And, moreover, some of the expedients used have proved too powerful. They were ingeniously conceived, like the cogged wheels for "grip," and the curved rails for "swing," without which our early railway engineers imagined that they could not possibly get their prospective train to run forward. Experience has shown that the train moves very much more easily and swiftly without cogs and curves.

Schulze bankers—I mean the practical men—have made analogous discoveries with respect to ingenious contrivances in their own business. Moreover, money, which in Schulze's time was scarce as rubies, has meanwhile become plentiful, and is now almost a drug in the market. In all the great Schulze-Delitzsch banks which I have lately visited, I have heard the same complaint. There is too much money. The difficulty is not, to provide capital, but to find investments. Practical men have of course accommodated themselves to the altered "environment," even though theorists continue pedantically consistent in their preachings. The result is a startling discrepancy between theory and practice. After reading about the imperative necessity of large districts, of unlimited liability and of good payment for capital and for services, and about the utter unpardonableness of long credit, it makes one rub one's eyes to find districts confined within well marked-out limits—unlimited liability gradually being thrown overboard by the largest and strongest of Schulze-Delitzsch banks, councillor's fees declined, and credit given, not for the orthodox three months only, but, if the borrower have at all a good character to show, practically—by renewals—for thirty months, almost as a matter of course, and in exceptional instances even for

On what Points Deviations have taken place.

fifteen and twenty years. Only by such deflections from the course marked out has the system managed to do as well as it has done. It stands absolutely to reason. Things which at one time were a help have now become a hindrance. The unwieldy districts which Schulze believed to be necessary, to provide numerical strength, have proved to mean, quite necessarily, a loss of touch and knowledge among men in a concern in which touch and knowledge are essential, but none too strong to begin with. There is no breach with the "system" in the abandonment of an inconvenient detail. In the same way those monstrously large shares, which are bound to keep out any really poor man, have been found a direct hindrance when money is plentiful. Schulze knew very well what he was about when he recommended them; but his methods have proved too effective, and circumstances have changed. Banks now complain of having too large a share capital, which makes them pay dividend rates instead of deposit interest for their money. They are accordingly everywhere trying to reduce it. They cannot reduce shares; but they are cancelling them whenever an opportunity offers—in one or two banks, I am sorry to say, by gradually weeding out women members—and they insist that only part of the share shall be paid up, a comparatively small portion, which in Augsburg is limited to £5 on the £50 share, in Cassel to £15 on the £37. 10s. share. That, again, is no sacrifice of principle. In the same manner those tremendous dividends, which certainly did attract capital, but capital which now shows itself to be capital of the least desirable sort— capital bringing no business and swallowing profits—have proved in the long run detrimental rather than helpful to the object in view. There is no class of persons more detested by Schulze-Delitzsch bank managers than the "dividend-hunters," who do no business, but seek to get out of the bank all the profit that they can. Dividends have wisely

<small>Shares are practically made smaller.</small>

been reduced, in the most legitimate way, by lowering those exorbitant rates of interest on loans which Commendatore Luzzatti has denounced as "usurious," and which made the bank smell very malodorously in the nostrils of well-meaning men. In the majority of banks now money is obtainable at from 5 to 5½ per cent., and dividend has, *on an average*, sunk to the same level. The banks are answering their purpose all the better, and are doing perfectly well. Even in respect of paying the "labourer worthy of his hire," Schulze's studied consistency has proved excessive. Directors, of course, have to be salaried. But the practice is gaining ground of members of the Council refusing their fees and being content to serve a good cause for nothing. Overflowing coffers must certainly in any case have proved fatal to that pedantic limitation of time to three months. The practice has been found indefensible on other grounds, as being inconsistent with the object of the bank ; and, generally speaking, a man of good character may make sure of being allowed to retain his loan for thirty months—repaying by instalments—and if he can make out a good case, even for very much longer. At Augsburg, Major Weinmann, one of the directors of the bank, was good enough to go through some of the borrowers' accounts with me. In them every particular affecting the case is set forth. When a man appears not to be making good use of his money, that money is called in as fast as is possible, consistently with the terms of the loan. But if he is judged to be doing well with it, time is readily accorded. As a case in point, there was a poor pointsman on the books who owed money since about ten years. It was altogether contrary to the rules ; but the man was evidently doing his best—slowly repaying what he could—and the bank heard that he was an honest man, and gradually bettering his position. Then why should it defeat the very object for which it had been started by pressing him ?

Dividends Reduced.

Terms for Loans extended.

The real fact is that all these matters of practice must necessarily be left to practice to determine, and therefore should have been settled by practical men. The writers who tenaciously hold to old precepts, and vindicate details as if they were essentials, have with the best intentions really done no service to their cause.

<small>Agricultural Credit.</small>

It is entirely owing to the distorted description which those theorists have given of their own system that the impression has got abroad that the Schulze-Delitzsch banks are powerless to render assistance to agriculture. No impression could be worse founded. What the Schulze-Delitzsch collectively have done in the way of agricultural lending we do not know. But we know enough to be able

<small>Its large Amount.</small>

to judge that they have in the matter of *amount* done more than any other system. We have some partial statistics. We know that in 1885, 545 such banks, having among them 270,808 members, 72,994 of whom were purely agriculturists, lent out to these latter no less than £6,982,996, about one-fifth of their aggregate lending; and that in 1894, again, 546 such banks, having among them 261,521 members, 82,513 pure agriculturists, lent out to these £8,853,751.

It will be well to devote a page or two to the subject of this agricultural credit.

<small>The Advantages of Schulze-Delitzsch Banks.</small>

The difficulties in the way of such credit, and the favouring factors to be set against them, have already been indicated.* The former consist mainly in the length of time for which loans are ordinarily required, the uncertainty of the date of repayment, and the absence of a recognisable marketable security. The latter are to be found in pretty absolute fixity of abode, in the ease with which information is obtainable about borrowers, and in a general predisposition to honesty. The great crux of the question is the

---

* Chapter V.

finding of money for just the right period. Now, to provide this, the Schulze-Delitzsch banks are in a peculiarly favourable position. **In the first place, they** are all, or nearly all, **well-established—for** there is no propaganda now in progress —well-known in the market, therefore commanding a good credit, and very strong in capital. Accordingly deposits and savings may be counted on pouring in, so to speak, automatically, and really the difficulty which, **as I** shall **show**, puzzles co-operative bankers in some other countries not a little, may be said not to exist for the Germans. In **the next** place, the Schulze-Delitzsch banks are, **after** all, mainly industrial banks. It **may** be **said** to be a moot point among co-operators whether agricultural credit should be dispensed in union with industrial or by itself. **In** Italy **we shall come across** some co-operative banks, almost purely agricultural, working **side** by **side with** industrial banks in **the same** locality. The followers of Schulze-Delitzsch are thorough believers in blending of as great **a** variety of types of business as is possible, in order that one may dovetail into and supplement the other. The broader **the** basis, the safer the superstructure. This principle applies with special force to the relations between agricultural and industrial credit, since it is found that agriculture borrows most when times are bad, and when industry and trade, having less use for money, restrict their borrowing. From a banking point of **view, the old verselet holds true—**

These Banks are mainly Industrial.

<blockquote>
Rustica gens
Optima flens,
Pessima ridens.
</blockquote>

In **the** Schulze-Delitzsch banks, generally speaking, the majority of members, and even in a greater degree the majority **of** borrowers, are industrial men, who contribute a volume **of** business generally rapid, and so large that it will well carry along with it a certain proportion of slow agricultural work. We have seen **that in the 545** banks agricultural members numbered one-fourth, but borrowed only one-fifth. At the present time the average proportion among banks doing agricultural business appears to be respectively as one-third and one-fourth. We have therefore, so to speak, a tolerably solid wall to lean upon, sufficiently well secured by industrial "binders" to admit of filling up with agricultural "rubble."

More fully to explain the system in operation, I cannot do better than quote some specific instances.

The Credit Association of Augsburg.

There is, then, first, the great "Agricultural Credit Association" of Augsburg, the premier bank of the whole connection. It is really not a Schulze-Delitzsch bank at all, as one of its directors was careful to point out to me, though it has for practical reasons attached itself to the Union. But the differences in the two systems are so absolutely trifling as practically not to come into account. The bank was really created for the benefit of agriculture, and was originally endowed in part, and of course more than correspondingly controlled and directed, by the State. That State interference the director, Herr Hederer, soon saw, must be got rid of at all costs. It was so, and with it the State endowment, and the bank is all the stronger for the loss. True to Schulze-Delitzsch rules, the bank adopted unlimited liability, and, to raise ample money, it issued large shares of £50 a piece, of which members were allowed to take several. Since 1889 not only has this plurality of holdings been rigidly eliminated from the system—except in the case of older members, who are allowed to retain two as the maximum number—but, moreover, in the case of new members, the bank declines to allow more than one-tenth, that is, £5, to be paid up. That small proportion may be paid up by instalments of as little as 2s. a month. The bank has now about 11,500 members, who have among them subscribed about £200,000, of which about £100,000 is paid up. The reserve fund accumulated represents £25,000 more. The bank is administered, like ordinary Schulze-Delitzsch banks, by three directors, forming the Committee, and a Council of Control of nine, which nominally decides upon the loans to be granted, all materials for decision being got ready for it by the directors and the staff. The admirable and complete way in which all information required for reference is kept, always handy, well arranged in boxes, books, and card catalogues, is particularly deserving of notice and commendation. The bank grants every year about £1,000,000 in loans. All such loans are under the Act of 1889 restricted to members only, and accordingly not a few members go "in" and "out" just as necessity may prompt them to join or to resign. Of all that lending only about £200,000, that is, about one-fifth, is done to agriculturists, scattered over the whole of Upper Bavaria. There are about 7,000 of these, and in the course of a year the bank may issue 6,000 or 7,000 agricultural loans, amounting on an average to £30 each, though some of them mount up to £1,500 and more. The smallest do not exceed 50s. Much industrial lending is done by means of current accounts, that is, cash credits or overdrafts. For agricultural purposes that method is found inconvenient, because transactions are too few. Therefore borrowers, as a rule, raise money on acceptances or promissory notes, on which generally both the date and the name of the payee are left blank, in order that both the expense of a fresh stamp on renewal and the trouble of obtaining new endorsements may be avoided. Such loans are held on from three months to three months, the longest term allowed for borrowing without repayment of any kind being eighteen months. Provided that part-repayments are made, the loan is often allowed to go on for a long time, five years and more, according to circumstances. The interest charged is generally speaking about 5 per cent., but commissions raise it practically to $6\frac{2}{3}$ per cent., all of it payable in advance. The losses sustained have in the twenty-five years of the existence of the bank proved so trifling as practically not to come into account. Alike for its own convenience and for that of members living at a distance, the bank has stationed agents all over its province, wherever there appeared to be an opening and wherever a suitable man could be found. It is the special office of one of the directors to appoint these. There are in all something like 250 agents, generally merchants or tradesmen in a good position in their particular locality, remunerated at the rate of ⅛ per cent. on business done through them. None of these agents have a definite district assigned to them. Any member is free to apply to any one of them for a loan. But should he go far afield to make his application, when he has an agent near, of course inquiry is instituted into the presumable cause of such conduct. There appears to be considerable scope for the exercise of energy in such agencies, for Major Weinmann told me of one agent who had in little time increased his takings for commission from *nil* to something like £40 or £50 per annum. The agent is given no power whatever. He simply forwards applications, makes inquiries, advises the Central Bank, and pays out moneys at his principal's direction. It is the authorities at Augsburg who decide on the applications made. The better to be able to form a judgment, they secure the assistance of a "man of confidence" in each district, who is unpaid, and whose name and person it has proved practicable to keep altogether secret. By such means the bank manages to serve a very large district effectively and with safety. And its services appear to be appreciated, for its position keeps improving.

Insterburg.   To take another bank, very differently conditioned—there is that of Insterburg, in Eastern Prussia, reputed one of the best banks in the Schulze-Delitzsch Union. This bank, founded in 1860, has a smaller area in which to carry on its business, and its members' roll does not exceed 3,800, 1,700 being persons engaged in agriculture, and cultivating from 2.5 to about 2,500 acres each. A share capital of £64,000, which is considered more than ample for its requirements, enables the bank to dispose of about £200,000 annually in loans, at a rate of interest varying from 4½ to 6 per cent., according to the "goodness" of the borrower, of which amount about £126,000 goes to agriculture in amounts varying from as little as 5s. up to £1,500, but averaging generally £17. 10s. The lending is always done on acceptances or promissory notes, drawn for three months at a time, but renewed on very easy terms—that is, in consideration of very trifling repayments—so that there are loans outstanding which have run for fifteen and even twenty years. For the purpose of providing information as to the qualification of borrowers, the bank—which confines its operations to the area of something like a petty sessional district — has "men of confidence" stationed in various localities, all of them being members of the bank, unpaid, and all of them considered persons who may be relied upon to give trustworthy information, not only in consideration of their known character, which determines their selection, but also because their unlimited liability pledged to the bank makes it their interest to do so. I have found the same engagement of liability relied upon as sufficient in France, in the Indre-et-Loire, where the Agricultural Syndicate of the Department lends on much the same principle, less developed.

The Credit Association of Gotha is another bank often held up as an example in respect of its agricultural lending. This is a bank which has, by a long and successful practice, made good its hold upon almost the entire little Duchy of Gotha. It is particularly popular as a savings bank, and twice a week, on market days, its office is more than crowded with depositors. The general centralisation of local business life in the little capital of course helps the bank very materially to obtain information with respect to borrowing members. To inform itself more fully, it has fifty-three local committees, consisting of from three to five persons each, understood to be men of independent position, and therefore likely to be unbiassed, appointed in various localities. These committees subject all applications made for loans in their district to a careful investigation, and advise the bank, each member by himself, writing down their answers to the questions put on printed forms, and forwarding these, folded like voting papers, to the central office, which holds itself in no way bound by the opinions expressed, but decides absolutely at its own discretion. The questions asked of agents are put mainly with a view to ascertaining whether the applicant is a trustworthy person and doing a good business, not what he is actually worth. In a stable and steady population like that of the Duchy of Gotha, it is not difficult by this means to avoid bad business. The local committee men receive a very small commission on business negotiated, which very often goes in a harmless little common jollification at the end of the year. It does not amount to very much. By such means the bank manages to cater financially, very effectively, for the 2,000 or so of its members (out of a total of 3,000) settled in villages. They are not necessarily all agriculturists; many are tradesmen or artisans. The loans, though granted in each instance for three months only, are readily renewed up to thirty, provided that one-tenth is paid off at each renewal. Strong in its command of money, the bank renders very useful service in lending, not only to individuals, but also to agricultural supply associations, co-operative dairies, societies letting out threshing machines, cattle-breeding and sheep-raising associations, and similar bodies practising co-operation in the service of agriculture, as well as to village councils and other local bodies.

To quote a third instance—there is the little village bank A small Bank of Walldorf near Meiningen, a very much smaller institution, Walldorf. but of the same type, which has a capital of only £1,400, and about 240 members, in a village peopled by about 1,500 inhabitants. It has its regulation three officers, one of whom is the schoolmaster, who receives an annual salary of £15. His two colleagues between them receive only £11. In so small a place of course neither "men of confidence" nor local committees are required. The Council of Control and the Committee know pretty well all that it is requisite to know about applicants for loans. They manage to lend out annually about £3,000 or £4,000, not counting cash credits, of which, when I was in the place, there were nine outstanding, amounting in all to £1,240. The maximum loan allowable to one person is £300. I ought to mention that in this bank, as a departure from ordinary Schulze-Delitzsch practice, all money is lent simply on note-of-hand, no promissory notes being issued. There are practically no losses, and the management expenses total up to about £50 a year, including salaries. The little bank, which has been growing since 1869, has, I may add, successfully managed to oust a usurer from the village who was a curse to the district. What pleased me particularly in this bank was the close touch and active interest maintained among members, not a usual feature in Schulze-Delitzsch Banks, but to be accounted for, of course, in this case by the smallness of the district and the absence of other objects of interest. I have noticed exactly the same thing in some of the smaller agricultural banks of the Luzzatti type, more notably in that of Spigno. The utility of the bank, its educational value, and its security as a business institution as a matter of course increase as such community of interest becomes more marked and realised.

I must quote just one bank more, because it appears to Cosel. me particularly interesting by reason of its locality and peculiar circumstances. The bank of Cosel, in Silesia, is situated in a district almost entirely agricultural, and still rather primitive in its institutions. The population to a large extent consists of Poles, some of whom are so illiterate that the bank managers have found themselves constrained to dispense in many cases with those written applications and receipts which the Schulze-Delitzsch authorities at Berlin hold to be absolutely indispensable. Very much of the work has to be done by verbal instruction, such as pointing out to the sureties that it is to their own interest to watch over the men for whom they go bail, and prevent the bank from suffering loss. In spite of all this the losses sustained are so trifling that within the last fifteen years, on a business amounting to £6,400,000, not more than £1,500 has had to be sacrificed. The bank was originally started as an industrial bank. Agriculturists, however, soon found out its value, and came crowding in in such numbers that at the present time they represent about 67 per cent. of the total of members, that is, about 850 out of not quite 1,300. There are agriculturists of every description, some of them substantial yeomen, owning six hundred acres and more, others small illiterate peasants. The bank has a capital of about £10,000, with about £6,000 accumulated as reserve fund, and generally about £20,000 or £23,000 of savings in its keeping. It has generally about £50,000 outstanding in loans. Most of this is lent for comparatively long terms. It is interesting to note that, on an average, loans contracted to make good a deficiency in the crops, or due to some other accidental misadventure, are repaid in about two years; loans contracted for the purchase of live stock in three; and loans contracted for acquiring land or putting up buildings, or else for carrying out agricultural improvements, in from six to eight years. The bank never presses borrowers unduly, but is of course careful to make sure that the money will come back to it. For purposes of inquiry it maintains its own representatives in different localities, but it appears to rely really more upon the self-interest of sureties, whom it does not accept without adequate inquiry. To serve a quasi-detached district, some distance from Cosel, which includes about thirty villages, the bank maintains a distinct branch establishment in the Moravian settlement of Gnadenfeld, which forms the centre of that district. There is an accredited agent at Gnadenfeld—a local tradesman, who receives a commission of 10 per cent. on all interest collected. He has no voice in the granting of loans, but merely transmits applications and information. The practice has proved perfectly satisfactory. There are now about 300 members enrolled in this branch establishment, all of them being of course members also of the parent association, and having the option of doing business, as they may prefer, with the one or with the other. In all there are 155 parishes in which the bank does business, lending out annually about £170,000 or £200,000. To be able to do this it borrows at times considerable sums from other banks, which it finds that it can do without difficulty.

These five instances, taken from different districts, in widely different parts of Germany, and representing typical cases, demonstrate, I should say, with sufficient clearness, that banks of the Schulze-Delitzsch type are, when well officered, and managed with common-sense, perfectly capable of meeting the requirements of agricultural credit, so far as they are strong in capital or credit, or else in a steady receipt of deposits.

So far so well. But in spite of all that has been said, in spite of all these magnificent services and the phenomenal success recorded, it may still be questioned whether the Schulze-Delitzsch associations to the *fullest* degree realise the ideal of co-operative banking. To begin with, a system in which failures and liquidations occur so frequently, that even one of its chosen eulogists not many

<small>Defects in the Schulze-Delitzsch Organisation.</small>

years ago could not help admitting "9½ per cent.,"* and from which numbers of associations have seceded and still secede, in order to convert themselves into joint-stock companies, cannot from either a business or a co-operative point of view be judged *absolutely* perfect—let alone that it is altogether contrary to our idea of co-operation, that the humblest classes, the working men proper, should be excluded and bidden to wait outside until they have accumulated sufficient funds to qualify themselves for membership involving the taking up of big shares. There are working men, no doubt, in the Schulze-Delitzsch associations; but only a very small proportion. From the last official statistics, we learn that on an average only .9 per cent. of the members of Schulze-Delitzsch banks were "servants and commissionaires"; .7 per cent. "shopmen and shopwomen"; 2.3 per cent. "railway employees," and the like (not "hands"); 5.6 per cent. "factory hands, miners, and journeymen"; and 26 per cent. "artisans working for their own account," that is, the best-to-do of their class. That is in all only 35.5 per cent. not really of working men and women. The bulk of the members is nearly everywhere made up of small tradesmen, small landowners, and men of similar independent or quasi-independent position, men of the classes, in fact, from which our Loan Societies ordinarily recruit their ranks. *Our* idea of co-operation is, that it should above all things benefit the working classes.

If Herr Siegl—who writes with a great deal of specific knowledge—is right, Schulze, having originally learnt co-operation in England, at the outset desired, like ourselves, to bring working men within the sphere of his beneficent action; and "in the early years of the movement he

---

* Dr F. Schneider, writing in 1885, in the *Arbeiterfreund*, admitted 184 failures among 1,910 banks, and pleaded that that was a *small* percentage, "*only* 9½ per cent."

occasionally succeeded in doing so" (*was ihm anfangs auch mehrmals gelang*). It is to be regretted that he himself and his followers did not persevere in this course. However, working man co-operation is absolutely incompatible with very large shares.

The frequency of failures and liquidations has, it ought in justice to be added, very substantially decreased, as Dr Crüger rightly points out in *Jahrbücher für Nationalökonomie und Statistik*,* since the law of 1889, shaped to some extent upon our Industrial and Provident Societies Act, has made a biennial audit imperative. The first effect of that measure was, we are told, temporarily to *increase* the number of liquidations, because the shaky associations were at once found out. But, that first shower of collapses over, there has been an appreciable diminution, and no doubt the remaining associations are all the more healthy. The effect suggests this question: why did not the Central Board of the Schulze-Delitzsch Union, which now recognises the merit of the innovation, but which will not hear of further modifications, and which had quite as much to say for the unimprovable excellency of its system *before* 1889 as it has after, resort of its own accord to so useful a practice as that of periodical audit? The pedantic sticklers for the system absolutely as instituted by Schulze give their case away by such inconsistent argument. The average proportion of failures has no doubt steadily decreased, but there have nevertheless been some very awkward liquidations and suspensions. The very last return issued records five failures and thirty-one liquidations. And, moreover, there has been that ugly crash at Weimar, which is particularly instructive from our point of view, since it reveals with great clearness the crucial point upon which the Schulze-Delitzsch organisation is weak. The Bank of Weimar a few years

Failures and Liquidations.

Salutary effect of a Compulsory Audit.

---

* Dritte Folge, Zehnter Band, Fünftes Heft. Jena, Fischer, 1895.

ago made a loss of £175,000, leaving it with an actual deficit of £123,000, which, it is satisfactory to be able to add, is now gradually being worked off, and so, thanks to the forbearance of its creditors, the bank is recovering its solvency. But how was that disastrous collapse brought about? Why, the members of the Council of Supervision, the men of all others to whom the shareholders looked for the safeguarding of their interests—who ought to have made it their supreme aim to keep the bank safe—had themselves borrowed sums amounting to £20,000 and £30,000 apiece, which they were unable to repay; three of them had borrowed £75,000 among them. £20,000 and £30,000 borrowed from a *People's* Bank! Does not that in itself show that the institution had been wholly turned aside from its proper purpose? How come People's Banks to allow such colossal lending? This Weimar case is of course a peculiarly glaring instance, but it is by no means the only one of its kind.

Conversions into Joint-Stock Banks. And then there are those conversions into joint-stock companies. I must speak of them at once, because both collapses and conversions arise to some extent from an identical cause. There is no denying the fact of frequent conversions. We find Dr Schneider bewailing it in the official organ of the Union, the *Blätter für Genossenschaftswesen*. In the kingdom of Saxony alone, according to an official return prepared by the Ministry of Justice, out of 115 "Credit Associations" existing on the 1st October 1889, by the 31st January 1891 no fewer than twelve had converted themselves into joint-stock lending banks pure and simple. In July last year, when I went to visit the great People's Bank of Leipzig—hitherto, next to the Bank of Augsburg, the premier bank of the Schulze-Delitzsch Union: a bank having about 6,000 members, and a share capital of £150,000, and doing business annually to the amount of £7,250,000—I found that bank converted **into a** joint-stock company, and *congratulating* itself upon the change. **It** still adhered to the Schulze-Delitzsch " Union," **of** which it could scarcely be described as a *bona fide* member, rather **on** personal than **on** logical grounds. In its new shape it found itself much less cramped in its action ; management had become more convenient. But, then, the main object of the bank **had been** sacrificed. **Loans** are still **made to** small people. But what guarantee is there that that practice will be continued? The direct interest and responsibility of borrowers in behalf of its prosperity, the union of interests between lenders and borrowers, **are** certainly gone. Already, I found **the** preference was being given to large business, and *higher* **rates were** *being charged in proportion as the transactions* **grew smaller.** Italian banks, upon Commendatore Luzzatti's injunction, even when they grow capitalist—as unfortunately some of the older sort do grow—still, at any rate, remain **so far** faithful **to** their original principle as to give **the** preference systematically to small business.

What is the reason of this twofold deterioration—the decline in safety and the abandonment of the democratic, popularising, co-operative principle ? The exclusion of the poor classes has, no doubt, a great deal to do with **it.** It eliminates the element which as a matter of course makes for a popular character. Those tremendous shares of £30, £40, and £50—they average now between £15 and £25— **are** bound to keep **out the** class **which** I have in **view.** How are working **men with prudence** to pledge themselves **to saving up so** large **a sum out of** their small earnings ? The **idea is** preposterous. But **the main cause** is that Schulze, when adopting co-operation as a form, did **not at** the same time adopt with anything like **sufficient** fulness what **we now everywhere recognise** as the co-operative principle—to **wit, consideration, above** all things, **for** the *consumer.* Our stores are not intended **to** provide a profit

_{The Causes of Deterioration: Exclusion of the Working Classes by large Shares.}

_{Excessive Consideration originally for the Lender.}

for those who do not buy of them, who only hold shares. They are to provide goods cheap and good for those who *do* buy. Analogously, co-operative banks should not exist to provide a large profit for the shareholder, but aim, so far as is practicable, at cheap credit for the *borrower*. However, Schulze at the outset reversed the order of things. The consequence is that, so far as his followers have in this matter adhered literally to his teaching, his banks have become mere ordinary trading banks, in the words of my friend at Nice, "*des banques comme les autres*," what the late Professor Held has called "simple trading banks (*einfache Handelsbanken*)."* They have studied above all things business and large dividends. They have acted as our co-operative stores would act if they were to lay themselves out for "corners" in any produce in which they deal, in order to be able to declare a large dividend. Obviously, business, studied for its own sake, is in a co-operative institution nothing but a snare; and "big dividends" are to the same institution what M. Elie Reclus has rightly called them in a report (on this very subject) presented to one of our early Co-operative Congresses, "a greater danger than heavy losses"—manifestly so, because they estrange the institution from its proper purpose. The danger of business-hunting has in the Schulze-Delitzsch banks been rendered greater by the allowance of a commission to directors on "business." All other systems of People's and Agricultural Banks make it a paramount rule that no risky or speculative business shall on any account be engaged in. Under the stimulus of the commission promised, some Schulze-Delitzsch directors have directly *sought* it, for the sake of pelf, lending money on the most questionable security. In Heilsberg they lent money on a river-mill which was bodily washed away by the stream. In Cannstadt they lent money on a

Ineffective Provision against Unsafe Business.

---

* *Arbeiterfreund*, 1873.

theatre which they eventually had to seize by foreclosure—a most inconvenient pledge to **become** possessed of. Moreover, there is in **these matters such a** thing as depreciation of security, more particularly **when that security consists of** real property. When **things came to a crisis, the real** danger of the **unlimited** liability adopted **in this** system became at once apparent. Members were suddenly called upon to make good **serious** deficiencies. The very sad experiences gone through, even by retired **members, who** had considered themselves perfectly safe—not a few being absolutely ruined—makes painfully **clear the danger of** unlimited liability adopted **on** such lines. **Unlimited** liability no doubt is extremely **useful,** and may be entirely harmless, when the **management of affairs is** committed *to the same persons* who **have to bear the burden of** liability. **But** in the case under consideration the burden does **not lie with** the same weight upon the managers who direct the enterprise, speculative or otherwise, **and the** general number of members ; because the former are to a considerable extent indemnified by their commission, which serves practically as an insurance. Under improper guidance, unlimited liability has in **very truth** shown itself the "two-edged knife" as **which Dr Schneider** has himself described it, spreading ruin among shareholders **as in the case of the** City of Glasgow Bank. The head **of the Agricultural Department of one of the German** kingdoms **writes to me (privately) on the subject to** the following effect :— *[margin: This makes Unlimited Liability a Source of Serious Danger.]*

"The credit associations **(of the** Schulze-Delitzsch type) aim at high dividends by the largest **possible** extension **of their** business, as regards both territory and operations. This has in many instances led to speculation for the sake of gain (the acceptance of unsafe mortgages in consideration of a higher interest, the dealing in speculative shares, or else the investment of the reserve in such effects, the discounting of bills without sufficient knowledge of such business), more especially where officers are remunerated by *tantième* (*i.e.* commission). These **are,** briefly summarised, **the causes why the** 'credit associations,' which had been much in vogue up to the company-promoting years, 1871 to 1873, have in this kingdom found themselves compelled to call up very considerable payments from their members, in order to enable them to continue their existence, or else to go into liquidation. . . . The very painful experiences in respect of credit associations, by which many an agriculturist, required, after years had gone by, to meet unexpected calls, has lost all his property, made people at first so shy that for a long time they could not be convinced that the Raiffeisen Loan Banks, in striking contrast to these associations, afford *almost absolute security*, since they are administered on totally different principles (no dividend, no speculation, salary only to the cashier, small districts, confined only to one parish or to one or two adjoining ones)."

Once you introduce the element of individual gain-seeking and make its pursuit allowable in a co-operative institution, as a matter of course you plane the way for transformation into a joint-stock company, which is the legitimate body for such an enterprise. Indeed, you may be said actually to start your association as in principle a joint-stock company, even though you call it co-operative. And you also open the door at once to such abuses as those revealed in the case of the Bank of Weimar.

Committal of Business in the main to three Salaried Officers.

All the dangers already indicated are immeasurably aggravated by a feature in the constitution to which writers on the Schulze-Delitzsch side have thus far failed to pay proper attention. Their associations are deliberately made large, alike in numbers, and in respect of the area which they cover. There is, therefore, from the very outset, an inherent danger of looseness of organisation, and want of touch in them. In small banks, like that of Walldorf, and in the Spar- und Gewerbebank of Leipzig, I have found far more touch, interest in common affairs, and generally a more co-operative spirit prevailing. However, those cases, unfortunately, constitute the exception rather than the rule. Instead of endeavouring to neutralise the danger existing, by somehow tightening the inter-connection among members, and providing additional means of control, Schulze has deliberately added to it by concentrating practically all administrative power in the hands of the three salaried officers, the very men who are entitled to draw the commission, and therefore are least exposed to the penalty involved in liability. Wherever I have inquired—and I have been to see some of the best banks—I have had the admission made to me that the supervision committed to the "Council" is almost purely nominal, inasmuch as the business is far too voluminous to make it possible for its members to exercise any effective control. Hence comes that frequent incurrence of risks which Dr Schneider and Dr Crüger attribute simply to happy-go-lucky easiness, to *Vertrauensdusel*—infatuated confidence—which lends money on insufficient security: the "careless giving of credit, loose control and indifference, and unparalleled fatuity of confidence," bewailed by Dr Schenck, the chairman of the Union. In the Italian and Belgian People's Banks the governing body is a *committee of unsalaried members, which appoints and checks the administrative officers*, being itself checked by the Council, for which the work is accordingly rendered manageable. The difference in organisation is one of extreme importance. And its results are seen in this, that, although in Italy and Belgium there have, no doubt, been suspensions and liquidations, those collapses have shown themselves neither as numerous nor as disastrous as those occurring in Germany. Dr Crüger in his article already quoted, practically confirms the view which I here take by stating that within the last fifteen or twenty years failures and liquidations of Schulze-Delitzsch banking associations have, as a rule, been due to "large credits granted to members of the Committee or the Council, or of both, without taking adequate security in return, therefore to a shameless abuse of the trust reposed in them by members of the association." The defect, surely, is capable of rectification. And leaders who have accepted the

German law of 1889 as an improvement, ought not to be above adopting other improvements so clearly indicated by experience. "*Rien ne naît à l'état parfait,*" so writes in the *Economiste Francais* M. Maurice Block, a careful student of these things; "*il faut donc perfectionner aussi les principes sur lesquels l'organisation des associations de Schulze-Delitzsch repose.*"

<small>In spite of all, the Schulze-Delitzsch System has done inestimable good.</small>

Very true. However, I am anxious not to be thought unduly severe upon the oldest, in one sense the most sturdy, and still the largest of organisations, of Co-operative Credit. That organisation has blemishes, but its foundation is good. After what I have said, I should not like it to be thought that the Schulze-Delitzsch associations are generally unsound. Quite the reverse. Practice is wiser than theory. The striking figures which I have quoted sufficiently prove that practical men have been able to bend imperfect rules into a shape making them serviceable. Besides, all men are not rogues. If the Council of Weimar, and the Committee-men of some other Credit Associations, have abused their opportunities and their discretion, the vast majority of officers of the Schulze-Delitzsch banks have shown themselves not only unquestionably honest, but also very capable men. It would be most unfair, on the score of one or two weak but remediable points, to disparage the system, which has done more for Germany and Austria—and indirectly, as stimulating to imitation, in other countries—for the poorer classes generally than it would be easy to express in words.

However, it must on the face of things be apparent to every one who can judge of the circumstances, that whatever surprising good the associations spoken of may have done in Germany and kindred Austria among Germans, their system is not suited to the habits of other countries, and, more particularly, entirely unsuited to our own. Dr Crüger, in fact, glories in its being specifically "German."

Italy has found itself compelled to modify it considerably before accepting it in practice; Belgium has had to modify it, France has had to modify it. We are in exactly the same position. It deserves, moreover, to be noticed that even in Germany the system of Schulze-Delitzsch has ceased to spread. Other systems are multiplying their banks at a rate which is truly astonishing. We hear of no new "Credit Associations" formed. The number of associations, of members, of business remains pretty much the same from year to year. There is much writing in the press, much talking on the platform. But that writing and talking is mainly defensive, and directed against other systems; it does not represent the same pushing oratory and argument which in Schulze's own days fired the public to action, and made banks start up like legions under the stamp of Pompey's foot. There must be some reason for this; there ought to be something like a warning in it. Rome did not worship "the god Terminus" until after it had passed the zenith of its greatness. Evidently some new stimulus, or else some remedial modification, is wanted. One cannot help regretting to see a power so large and so well tried in practice as the Schulze-Delitzsch organisation, which is still undoubtedly the centre of co-operative action in Germany and the largest union of co-operative credit institutions in the world —although some other systems number more banks—condemned to the mere maintenance of its ground. Of course, it has accomplished much of the work which it set out to do. It has covered much ground, on which now provision is made for democratised credit—credit which is dispensed freely, and on the whole cheaply, to the benefit of millions among the humbler classes. But such a giant as this ought still to be going forth conquering and to conquer. There are still kingdoms to be won. Even now, the Schulze-Delitzsch Union is performing one of the most useful services that Germany stands in need of in presenting a bold front to

State Socialism, advocated and pushed in high quarters, and in insisting on the sufficiency of self-help. It sent out the promptest and the clearest note of protest against that utterly reprehensible proposal, put forward, and unfortunately carried, by the most State-Socialist of all governments of Europe, the Government of Berlin, in favour of the endowment of a Central Bank, to give credit to agriculture under State supervision, with State funds, the amount of which within a twelvemonth has had to be quadrupled. But while feeling grateful for all that it has done and is still doing, one would wish to see it taking M. Block's advice and perfecting its machinery even still more—it may be, by studying what its own imitators have done elsewhere—in submission to the demands of modern times, and turning itself once more, phœnix-like, into a propagandist force, advancing, as everything which exists has advanced since 1850, becoming more democratic in its government, more popular, more of the poor man's friend. There is surely room still for very much work even within the lines of its own programme.*

---

* The following figures will give some idea of the lines on which the work of the Schulze-Delitzsch banks is carried on, and of the magnitude of their operations. There were, on 31st May 1895, 953 credit associations belonging to the veritable Schulze-Delitzsch Union, which is divided into 32 sub-unions, and comprises, in addition, 454 supply associations, 14 building societies, and 53 miscellaneous societies—1,474 in all. Some of these associations, that is to say, 10 credit associations and 1 supply association, had registered themselves as joint-stock companies, and 5 credit associations as companies *en commandite*, that is, having a small number of persons liable without limitation of their responsibility, and a large number limited up to a fixed amount. The admirably compiled Annual Statistical Report, prepared by Dr Schenck, chairman of the Schulze-Delitzsch Union, does not say how many of the 1,047 credit societies sending in returns belong to the Schulze-Delitzsch Union proper. They may, however, all be assumed to be organised on Schulze-Delitzsch principles. There are now about 2,700 credit associations of this type in Germany. The 1,047 associations furnishing returns muster among them 509,723 members, that is, on an average, 487 members per association. That figure remains pretty steady. The number of members per association varies from under 50 (in 14 associations) to more than 6,000 (in 2 associations), 11,436 being **the maximum** number, with a long interval between it and the next. About half the number of associations have members' rolls ranging from 100 to 400. Of 479,353 members of associations, of whom a special census has been taken, **45,888 are** shown to be women, nearly one-half of them women without an occupation; but **there were** 1,264 female servants, and 1,022 women of the artisan class. The total of 479,353 members is shown to **have been** made up as follows:—31.5 per cent. (as compared with 31.3 in the foregoing year) were independent agriculturists, market gardeners, &c. (142,432 men and 8,662 women); 3 per cent. (against 3.1) salaried persons employed in agriculture, market gardening, &c. (12,974 men, 1,166 women); 3.1 per cent. (no change) were manufacturers, owners of mines, and builders (14,608 men, 406 women); 26 per cent. (26.3) independent artisans (120,174 men, 4,636 women); 5.6 per cent. (5.5) factory hands, miners, journeymen (25,700 men, 1,022 women); 8.7 per cent. (8.6) independent tradesmen and dealers (38,786 men, 2,983 women); .7 per cent. (no change) shopmen and shopwomen (3,289 men, 188 women); 4.8 per cent. (no change) jobmasters, barge-owners, and public-house keepers (20,494 **men,** 1,640 women); 2.3 per cent. (2.2) postmen, railway employees, waiters, **and** persons employed **on** barges and boats (11,014 men, 134 women); .9 per cent. (no change) commissionaires and servants (2,958 men, 1,264 women); 6 **per cent.** (6.1) medical men, pharmaceutical chemists, teachers, artists, authors, and municipal or parish officers (27,707 men, 1,194 women); and 7.4 per cent. (7.2) persons without occupation (12,899 men, 22,593 women). It will be seen that the working classes are very sparingly represented. A special census shows that in 974 associations there were 151,094 members **of** the farming **class.** In 546 **of these** there were, among **261,521 members in** all, **82,513 of** the **farming class.** These had among them raised £6,982,495 **in loans. The total** paid-up share capital of the **1,047** associations **is returned as** £6,025,623; the accumulated reserve as £1,758,912, making up a collective capital of £7,784,035, which is £7,435 per association (£1,680 being reserve), £11. 16s. per member. In addition to this working capital, the associations raised £22,886,726 **by loan,** £21,860 per association, £44. 18s. per member This **gave the** 1,047 associations an entire working capital of £30,670,761. **Of** every £100 working capital raised, £19. 12s. stood for paid-up share capital, **£5. 14s.** for reserve, and

£74. 14s. for borrowed money. The 1,047 associations lent out in all £77,500,631, made up as follows :—On bills of exchange issued directly to the association, £29,342,628 ; on bills of exchange brought to be discounted, £15,814,418 ; altogether on bills, £45,157,046 ; on current accounts, £4,722,953 ; on notes of hand, £27,023,583 ; on mortgages (new lending), £592,043. This makes £7,435 per association, and more in all by £850 than in the preceding year, and shows an indebtedness per debtor of £152. In addition to the £27,023,583 of cash credits or "active" current accounts, there was a total of "passive" current accounts (balances in hand on drawing accounts) of £26,709,603, which shows that in practice the one class nearly balances the other. These moneys represented the balances of 51,529 drawing accounts. About £950,000 more had been lent out in the year against acceptances as compared with the preceding year. The losses recorded amount in all to only £48,359, which is about 1s. 11d. per member. The management expenses figure as £323,504, which is at the rate of about 20 per cent. of the gross profits. The transactions resulted in a total net profit of £474,350, of which sum £122,293 was carried to the reserve fund, £15,371 forward to next year's account, £3,914 was employed for charitable and educational purposes, and £330,634 was paid out in dividend at the average rate of 5.19 per cent. on the capital employed. The returns record 31 liquidations and 5 failures. One of the failures is due to embezzlements to the amount of no less than £15,000. The return shows a smaller amount of business than some of the earlier years, which is owing to slack times, and also probably to a diminution in the number of banks in this particular Union, which may be only apparent, since, as Dr Crüger has verbally explained to me, for some years associations appeared in the lists which were really dead. There is, however, a rather notable increase of business and in the number of members as compared with 1893, and the proportion of losses keeps decreasing.

CHAPTER VII.

THE RAIFFEISEN "LOAN BANKS."

No two people, setting out for substantially the same goal, could have started from two more directly opposite points than did Schulze-Delitzsch and Raiffeisen. <small>The Origin of Raiffeisen 'Loan Banks."</small>

It is rather a curious tale the story of the origin and the gradual growth of Raiffeisen's co-operative organisation from its tiny beginning, as a veritable grain of mustard seed, planted on the barren soil of the neglected Westerwald, to its present commanding position, in which, to adhere to the simile, it resembles an "exceeding great tree," spreading out its branches over all Germany, and Austria, and Italy, and Hungary, affording shelter to innumerable living beings rejoicing in its shade, with offshoots already penetrating into France, Servia, and Russia. It is of banks of this type that the economists quoted, MM. von Dobransky, Emile de Lavaleye, Rabbeno, and Léon Say—to mention no more—write in so rapturous a strain about "wonders" and "marvels." The whole thing may be said to be the result of a bodily infirmity, which brought hardship to one man, but inestimable benefit to more nations than one.

Born in 1818 at Hamm, in Westphalia, F. W. Raiffeisen found himself in his youth destined for a military career. Before, however, he could obtain his commission, he was compelled by a constitutional ailment, which impaired his eyesight, to retire. An opening was found for him in the Civil Service, and the year 1845 saw him installed as <small>Their Founder.</small>

Burgomaster (under the French law still prevailing in Rhineland) at Weyersbusch, in the bleak forest district of the Westerwald. In due course he was promoted to the Burgomastership of Flammersfeld, likewise in the Westerwald, with a union of twenty-five parishes under him to administer. It was in this position that Raiffeisen had the crushing troubles of the poor peasant cultivators brought vividly before his eyes in the famine years of 1846 and 1847. His was one of the districts which the scourge of those years visited the most severely.* It was a poor country to begin with, with barren soil, scanty means of communication, bleak surroundings, indifferent markets. Nature had proved a very stepmother to this inhospitable bit of territory upon which the half-starved population—ill-clad, ill-housed, ill-fed, ill-brought up—by hard labour eked out barely enough to keep body and soul together with the support of the scanty produce of their little patches of rye, of buckwheat, or potatoes, and the milk and flesh of some half-famished cattle, for the most part hopelessly pledged to the " Jews."

The "Jews." That reference indicates a peculiarly sore point in the rural economy of Western and Southern Germany. In this country we have no idea of the pest of remorseless usury which has fastened like a vampire upon the rural population of those parts. Even the gombeen-man cannot compare with the hardened blood-suckers of those parts of Germany. The poor peasantry have long lain helpless in their grasp, suffering in mute despair the process of gradual exinanition. My inquiries into the system of small holdings in those regions have brought me into personal contact

---

* Sir E. Malet is entirely wrong in placing Raiffeisen's first labours "in Silesia," as he does in his Blue-Book Report. Probably our Ambassador had heard of the great distress prevailing among the handloom weavers in that province, and was so led into his mistake. Raiffeisen had no connection whatever with Silesia.

with many of the most representative inhabitants—heads of agricultural departments, judges, parsons, peasants—and from one and all—here, there, and everywhere—have I heard the self-same, ever-repeated bitter complaint, that the villages are being sucked dry by the "Jews." Usury laws, police regulations, warnings, and monitions have all been tried as remedies, and tried in vain. There are not a few Christians, by the way, among those "Jews," though originally the evil was no doubt specifically Hebraic—not altogether owing to a predilection of those who made a practice of it. They were practically *driven* into it. Germans do pretty well even now in the way of anti-Semitism. But that is nothing to the outlawry everywhere practised against the obnoxious race before 1848, when in scarcely any town were they allowed even to trade, except by sheltering themselves behind some friendly Christian, who could be brought to lend them the use of his name. The consequence was, that all the humbler Jews flocked into the villages, where, being practically debarred from taking up other callings, they fell back with all the peculiar aptitude and ingenuity of their kindred upon the small trade—the trade in cattle, goods, corn, money, whatever it might be—of which in many places they secured an absolute monopoly. Of the iniquitous practices to which that monopoly soon gave rise this is not the place to speak at length. Whole volumes have been written on the subject in Germany, after careful inquiry, by men with practical experience, quoting chapter and verse, and painting all the hideous horrors of the system in ghastly detail. The "Draconic" laws with regard to bills, and the peculiar regulations applying to foreclosure, the personal liability of the debtor for any balance of debt remaining uncovered by a forced sale, and lastly, the convenient practice of lending out live stock, as *Einstellvieh*, to remain the creditor's, though fed at the cost of the debtor, materially and terribly

Their Usurious Practices.

facilitate the crafty practice. Plenty of cases are cited in which the poor peasant has been compelled to take the usurer's lean and dry cow at a high price, in order to feed it up and return it, in exchange for a fresh lean one, when brought into condition and in calf. It is a current saying, that once you are beguiled into trading with one of these Christian or Mosaic "Jews," you are infallibly lost, as surely as is a fly caught in a spider's web. You are made to buy from him, to sell to him—all at his own prices. One of the greatest mischiefs practised is that connected with the sale of real estate, which is habitually done by public auction, on condition of the purchaser's agreeing to pay the purchase money by a number of instalments. In one aspect that is an admirable practice for both parties— being small, cultivating folk. To the vendor it raises the price; the purchaser it enables practically to pay for his purchase out of its own proceeds. Only it has this drawback— the vendor may want his money. And as, under the old state of things, in nine cases out of ten he sold his *Verkaufsprotocolle* (his bonds for payment of future instalments) to a "Jew," in the event of every payment not being met to the day, the purchaser found himself at the Jew's mercy. Thousands of families, I am assured, have been ruined in this way.

<small>Excessive Distress calls forth a Remedy.</small>

Under this oppressive system, in 1846 and 1847 the "Jews" were "making hay." Among the poor peasantry the distress was great. And the peasants' distress was the "Jews'" opportunity. Every little wattle cottage and tumble-down house was mortgaged; most of the peasants' cattle belonged to the "Jews"; there was little employment on the roads or in the forests—the sole available means for netting a few additional shillings; the poor land yielded but a bare pittance; and famine and ruin stared the poor inhabitants in the face. There was no one to turn to for help but the "Jews." The whole district accordingly was converted into a usurers' hell.

THE RAIFFEISEN "LOAN BANKS." 119

Naturally, Raiffeisen's heart was touched at the sight of so much misery. And when, in 1848, he was removed to a rather larger, but equally distressed district, in the same Westerwald, he promptly resolved to take up the cudgels for the poor oppressed peasants, and declare relentless war against the plague of usury. He set to work at once. His first raising of funds was by no means the easy process which Sir E. Malet's account in the Blue Book seems to suggest. But some small funds he managed to scrape together, and with their help he forthwith established a co-operative bakery. Co-operative bakeries have since become a popular and familiar institution in every country, and as a rule they pay. This one at Flammersfeld proved on its small scale a signal success, for it enabled the peasantry to purchase their bread at just half the current price. The next step taken was the formation of a co-operative cattle-purchase association. That, likewise, has become a familiar feature abroad. In half the Swiss Canton of Thurgau little cattle is purchased, at any rate by small folk, by other means. This move attacked the "Jews" in one of their strongest outworks, and reduced their mastery at a vital point. But still they held their bonds and mortgages for money debts. Raiffeisen now put his scaling ladder to the very citadel. With a balance of the £300 which, in all, he had succeeded in raising with a good deal of trouble, in 1849 he set up his first "Loan Bank" (*Darlehnscasse*), and offered the peasantry, who would subscribe to his rules, to supply them with money for their needs. *A Co-operative Bakery. Co-operative Purchase of Stock. The First "Loan Bank."*

In the retrospect it seems a small undertaking. To Raiffeisen's neighbours it appeared hopeless. "Where was the money to come from?" "From there," answered Raiffeisen, pointing upward to the skies. It was in that very year, possibly in that very month, that on the banks of the Seine Proudhon with a noisy flourish of trumpets *A Small Beginning.*

opened his own far more pretentious "People's Bank," which was, as he thought, to regenerate France. One can scarcely help remarking upon the striking contrast between that splendid enterprise, flush of funds, big with promise, hopefully watched by thousands of expectant Frenchmen —and yet doomed to end in nothing but smoke in less than two brief months; and, on the other hand, the modest little bank, scarcely daring to show its face, with barely a few hundred pounds of borrowed capital, unheard of outside its own small parish, and yet destined to grow up a flourishing institution, distributing millions through its thousands of channels, and establishing plenty everywhere where it set foot—proceeding victoriously on its triumphal progress long after its early rival had been forgotten, except as a curiosity in the reading of political economists. That little bank, to which no one has ever contributed a penny in share capital, which has lived by lending money as cheaply as it possibly could, and finding means for borrowing still more cheaply, a few years ago resolved upon dividing its reserve (having forsaken its founder's co-operative principles), and discovered that that fund, the product of tiny surpluses arising from petty transactions among its members, had grown to more than £2,000.

Triumph of the Movement.

The Flammersfeld Loan Bank did its work well. The "Jews" found themselves compelled to relax their grasp, and the peasants were given a new lease of life. Like Schulze-Delitzsch, Raiffeisen had carried his idea to practical triumph, which it only remained for him to follow up. As an advocate of his cause he was as unlike his rival as could be. Modest, unassuming, content to do his work in his own limited sphere, he attempted no advertising and no noisy propaganda. If his work was good and useful, he trusted that it would prove its own best advocate. The result has amply justified his confidence. His system at first sped very slowly. It was five years (1854) before a second bank was formed—and of that bank Raiffeisen was again the founder, on his removal, once more as Burgomaster, to the district of Heddesdorf, close to Neuwied. Not till 1862 was a third established, not till 1868 a fourth. Really not until 1874 did the Loan Banks become at all widely known, and not till 1880 did they begin to multiply perceptibly. From that time forward, however, they spread with astonishing rapidity. By 1885 their number had, in Germany alone, grown to 245, by 1888 to 423, by 1891 to 885. The very material service which they rendered to agriculture in that terrible year of drought, 1893, added a further stimulus to their multiplication. In that period of trial it was shown that they could do more to give assistance, by self-help, than the State with its well-filled purse. They enabled cultivators, by co-operation, to remove their live stock, for which they lacked keep, to districts in which it would still fetch a decent price. They laid up stocks of feeding stuffs, which, being bought in good time, could be sold cheaply to members, and help them to tide over the period of distress. And when the drought was over, they supplied cash wherewith to re-stock farms and folds on easy terms. By New Year 1896 their number had increased to 2,000, by 1st May to 2,169, not counting even more kindred associations independently organised. Wherever they went, as Laveleye says, they succeeded, and made themselves general favourites. Governments now encourage them, provincial Diets ask for them, priests and ministers pronounce their benisons upon them, the peasantry love them. When in 1888 it was announced that Raiffeisen had breathed his last, half Germany mourned over her benefactor by the name by which he is still fondly remembered, that of "Father Raiffeisen." At the present time, not a day passes without notices coming in of the establishment of one, two—as many as five. Dr Schenck in the last issues of his admirable and very impartial Annual

Report candidly owns that the largest increase recorded in the returns belongs to them. Both their spread and their reputation seem deserved, especially since, after forty-six years' experience, they can make it their boast that by them *neither member nor creditor has ever lost a penny*.

<small>Never a Penny lost.</small>

It is rather difficult to compare Raiffeisen's banks with those of Schulze-Delitzsch. Both have grown up amid essentially different surroundings, in different spheres of action, with different tasks. Schulze worked in a town, among townsmen, and mainly for the benefit of townsmen, not of the poorest class. His banks could not benefit the very poor. Raiffeisen's specific object was to benefit those very poor people left out in the cold, and to benefit them in the most effective way. So he came to the conclusion that he must exact nothing from members joining, and that he must make long credit the rule. Calling upon a poor man, who deliberately joined in order to borrow, to pay down money, would to his mind have amounted to sheer mockery. His very reasonable principle was this: to make a loan at all serviceable to a poor or embarrassed man, time must be given the borrower sufficient to allow it to repay itself; to tax other resources for repayment would be, not to help, but to cripple the borrower. He might want the money for buying manure, or seed, or feeding stuffs. In that case he could scarcely be expected to repay it before a twelvemonth. He might want it to improve his herd of live stock, or to build a barn, or sink a well, or else drain a field. In such cases he must be given credit for two years, for five, or ten, or even more.

<small>Raiffeisen's Aim.</small>

In brief outline, the system upon which the Raiffeisen practice is based is this. Raiffeisen begins by confining each association to one particular district—a parish by preference, but if one parish be too small (he does not favour districts with less than 400 inhabitants), and if the matter can be conveniently arranged, a union of two or

<small>His System.</small>

three. Within these narrow limits members are elected, **Election of Members.** on application, with **great care and** discrimination, by those who have already joined. The object **is** not to secure a large roll of members, but rigidly to exclude every one who is not really eligible. That done, the association is organised **Democratic Government.** on entirely democratic lines. No difference of any sort is recognised between poor and rich, except that the rich, bearing the brunt of the liability, are by accepted understanding allowed also to take the leading part in the administration.* **Both on** the Committee—in every case consisting of five, and charged with all the executive work— and **on the** Council of Supervision—consisting, according to the size of the district, of from six to nine members, and entrusted with checking and supervising the Committee, overhauling all that it has done at least once a month—it it is understood that the richer members (without a sprinkling **of whom** Raiffeisen would have no association formed) should be in a majority. **Neither** members of the Com- **No Salaries.** mittee nor members of the Council of Supervision **are** allowed to draw **a** farthing of remuneration, **be it** in the shape of salary or of commission. Every chink and **crevice** is deliberately closed against the intrusion of a **spirit of** cupidity or greed, so as to make caution and security **of** necessity the guiding principles of action. One man only is paid, namely, the cashier; **and** he has **no say whatever**

---

* **This shows how very far** Mr Yerburgh, not having studied the question **of** which he **has** set up as **a** master, has strayed from that "Raiffeisen scheme" which at public meetings he tells people that his "Agricultural Banks Association" has "adopted" on the ground of its satisfactory results, obtained abroad, in prescribing in Rule VI., that there may be "Honorary Members," who shall "not have any of the liabilities of Ordinary Members," but "be eligible for election on the Committee." Whatever Mr Yerburgh pretends as to his "scheme," so long as he adheres to that preposterous rule, he is, in respect of cooperative banking, at the very opposite pole from Raiffeisen, his scheme is an absolute negation of Raiffeisenism.

in the employment and distribution of the money, being merely an executive agent. To make quite sure of everything being kept safe and square, the Central Office employ a body of auditors continually travelling from association to association, examining books, inspecting accounts, and overhauling the whole business of every association, at least once every two years. Furthermore all "banking," in the ordinary sense of the term, is strictly forbidden. The associations are *loan* associations, and the sole instrument which they employ is credit. Banking profits are very acceptable in their way, but they must mean risk. And risk is the one thing which the Raiffeisen associations set themselves to avoid. There are no acceptances, no pledges. "*Ce qui me plaît dans les banques populaires agraires, c'est qu'elles font du crédit personnel—le crédit tout court, sans phrase,*" so says M. Léon Say. And they supply that personal credit only by borrowing, and borrowing on the credit of the association. As the rules were originally framed, no member was asked to pay down anything on joining, either for shares or in entrance fees. The Legislature, by its law of 1889, overruled this regulation, and ordered that there must be shares. The Raiffeisen associations met this dictation by making their own shares as small as possible, generally 10 or 12 marks, at most 15 marks, payable by instalments. Raiffeisen advisedly would have no dividend, because there is to be no direct profit. Once more the Legislature overruled him. However, the members of the "Loan Banks" have voted all their dividend away, once for all, to two different reserve funds, keeping back only sixpence a head, which goes in subscription for the official publication of the associations, in which the balance sheet of every bank has to be published. All through, it is one of the essential features of the organisation, individuals are to derive no benefit except the privilege of borrowing, and every farthing which is left

Strict Audit.

No "Banking."

Personal Credit.

Small Shares.

No Dividend.

over out of transactions is rigorously claimed for the two reserve funds instituted. One of these is an ordinary reserve fund out of which to meet occasional deficiencies. The other, called "Stiftungsfond," * to which without fail two-thirds of the annual profits must go, is an entirely peculiar feature. It belongs wholly to the bank, and must not be shared out on any account or pretence. This second reserve fund really is the backbone of the whole system. Little by little only it keeps increasing, but with "mony littles making a muckle," it is bound to grow up in course of time to an impregnable rock of financial solvency. Its first object is to meet deficiencies or losses for which only with hardship could individual members be made responsible. Its next, of course, is to supply the place of borrowed capital, and so make borrowing cheaper to members. Lastly, should it outgrow the measure of such employment, it may, at the discretion of the society, be applied to some public work of common utility benefiting the district. Not even in the event of the association being dissolved is any sharing-out permitted, lest a rich association be tempted to dissolve for the sake of the spoils. In the case of a dissolution it is provided that the money must be handed over to some public institution to be kept on trust until required for the endowment of a new association formed in the same district, and under the same rules. Or,

_{The Indivisible Reserve.}

---

* This name was adopted in 1889 under the new Act, which made the designation of *Vereinsvermögen* (property of the Society) no longer suitable, inasmuch as such "property" must be disposed of in some way by vote every ten years. That would have been a deathblow to Raiffeisenism. Therefore the Act had to be circumvented somehow. We are much in the same precarious position, since our Friendly Societies Act does not allow us to create a permanent fund not divisible on the dissolution of the Society. The German Parliament has just passed a short Act reinstating the "Property of the Society" in its old rights. We must hope that our own Parliament will some day help a good cause in a similar way, by granting similar powers.

that failing within a reasonable time, the reserve may be employed for some useful local public work. Thus the whole fabric is built up on the lines of pure co-operation, of safety, caution and stability. This same principle is applied also to the practice of lending. **Loan** association though the association is, for safety's sake, it deliberately makes borrowing, not easy, but difficult. Indeed, the whole machinery is so framed as to *check* borrowing rather than encourage it. Money is, indeed, to be found for every one who needs it; but in every instance he must first make out his case, and prove alike that he is trustworthy and that his enterprise is economically justified. There is nothing which the associations more determinedly set their face against than mere improvident borrowing, stopping up one hole by making another. If an applicant make out his case, be he ever so poor, the money will be placed at his disposal. Without such proof, be he ever so rich, the money is sure to be refused. And once the money is granted, to the specific object for which it was asked must it be conscientiously applied. Once every three months the Council of Supervision meet for the special object of reviewing the position of debtors and their sureties, and considering the employment given to the loan money. Should a surety be found to have seriously deteriorated in solvency or in trustworthiness, a better surety is at once called for in the interest of the association. And should that demand not be complied with, or should the debtor be found to have misapplied the money, under a special clause the loan is at once called in, at four weeks' notice. This may seem harsh dealing. But it is absolutely necessary for the security of the association. And in practice it has not been found to work at all harshly. Those who apply it are the debtor's own neighbours, who are sure not to have recourse to this *ultima ratio* except in cases of positive necessity. As a matter of fact, it has scarcely been resorted

Safeguards adopted.

to at all—which just shows its value as a birch-rod on the mantelpiece. In another respect the banks are—wisely—equally inexorable. Alike interest and principal, they insist, must be paid to the very day. The principal is, for all loans running any length of time, made repayable by equal instalments; and on any point rather will the association give way than on that of prompt and punctual repayment. Not only does this arrangement materially facilitate the carrying on of the business, but it is far more valuable still as training the borrowing folk to habits of punctuality. Our country folk—so says M. Garreau, a man of some experience, in agreement with many other writers —are capital repayers, but without training they have absolutely no idea of the lapse of time. The service, then, which these associations render by instilling into them both business habits and the sense of a duty to meet engagements promptly, is very considerable.

In the matter of method, lending is advisedly made as simple and as easily intelligible a process as possible. All that, as a rule, is asked for is a note of hand, unbacked, or else backed by one, or more generally two sureties, according to the circumstances of the case. That, of course, precludes all raising of money by passing on acceptances. Every farthing that is wanted, so far as it is not supplied by the savings or other deposits paid into the banks, has to be raised by borrowing. At the outset that may appear rather a cumbrous proceeding. But what with a high reputation secured by exemplary business habits, and the substantial guarantee of unlimited liability of all members, the banks have long since gained for themselves a position commanding such very easy credit, that they have no difficulty whatever in borrowing all that they want, be it from public banks, be it from private individuals, at the cheapest market rates. Confidence in their security is so well established that (as

Simplicity of the Method.

How the Loan Banks are trusted.

128 PEOPLE'S BANKS.

appears on official evidence from a report published in 1875) in Rhineland Law Courts actually allow trust moneys to be paid in to them on deposit; and in those two critical epochs of crucial testing of German credit, the years of the two great wars, 1866 and 1870—when deposits were withdrawn wholesale from other banks and when even diplomatists like Sir R. Morier found it difficult (so he himself reports) to supply themselves with money—deposits were actually *pressed* upon the Raiffeisen Banks, for safe keeping, though it should be without any interest at all.* In truth, the savings banks deposits alone go a long way. Some banks have, at the outset, to do as good as altogether without them. But in not a few of the older established they supply actually all the local demand and even more.

Federation of the Banks.

The multiplication of Loan Banks has as a matter of course led from co-operation between individuals to co-operation between associations. Every large district has its own Union, with a Representative Council meeting to

The Central Council.

discuss the common affairs of the district. And at the apex of the whole fabric stands the *Generalanwaltschaft*, with its Representative Council, and the Annual General Meeting, to check and direct its action. Since 1877, more-

The Central Bank.

over, the union of associations possess their own Central Bank, in which the affairs and interests of the whole system are, so to speak, focussed, and which has proved a very appreciable convenience and source of common strength, and, moreover, a most useful intermediary between local banks and the general market, as the president of the Imperial Bank of Germany, Dr Koch, has recently testified in the German Parliament.† The Central Bank is really a joint-stock company, based on *limited* liability

---

* Dr Schneider says that the same thing happened in the case of the Schulze-Delitzsch Banks.

† *Kölnische Zeitung*, 27th March 1895, No. 269.

THE RAIFFEISEN "LOAN BANKS." 129

only. It derives its strength from the local associations, the vast majority of which—at the present time 2,094 out of 2,169—are shareholders in it. Every local bank is allowed, and invited, to become a shareholder, but none is obliged to do so. It is entitled to the services of the Central Bank whether it holds shares or not. The collective share capital of the Central Bank now stands at 5,000,000 marks (£250,000), distributed in 5,000 shares of 1,000 marks each. The small balance not taken up by societies is held by individuals. The bank is intended as an institution only for the benefit of the Raiffeisen associations. It does absolutely no business beyond that of the Union. It is intended to serve as common cash box, equalising excess and want, and facilitating common business. Since the dividend payable on capital is limited to 3½ per cent.—all surplus being carried to the reserve fund—and since the business has become large, the bank can lend out to local associations at very reasonable rates, all the more so since the Imperial Bank has, in consideration of its financial strength and soundness, put it on the "most favoured bank" footing, and agreed to discount its acceptances at 2 per cent. The Neuwied Bank is the *only* co-operative bank now admitted to such preferential terms. It lends out to local societies at the rate of 3¾ per cent., and allows them on deposits 3¼ per cent. up to the sum of £500, and 3⅛ per cent. beyond. Its business is so simple—I have seen it all done on the spot—that 1 per 1,000 of the turnover suffices for all expenses. The turnover has grown very considerably. In 1877 (four months only) it was £9,000. By 1880 it had risen to £56,000, by 1890 to £500,000, and by 1894 to £1,400,000. It was then decided to create provincial branch banks acting as *succursales* to the Central Bank. There are now ten such, severally established at Königsberg, Danzig, Berlin, Erfurt, Breslau, Cassel, Wiesbaden,

Its Services.

I

Strassburg, Nuremberg, and Wachenheim in the Palatinate. None of these branch banks did a considerable business in 1895. But the aggregate turnover rose at once in that year to £3,000,000. In the first four months of the present year it amounted to 33,260,500 marks (£1,663,025). That does not by any means represent the total amount of lending and borrowing done between bank and bank in the Raiffeisen connection. Very much business—about £10,000,000 in the year—is done between local banks without the interposition of the central institution. General Anwalt Cremer estimates that, thanks to such co-operative banking, the current rate of interest generally has been reduced by about 1 per cent., and credit has been cheapened to that extent. The Central Bank with its branches has become a veritable Little Providence to the local institutions, enabling new banks to establish themselves and grow up with a credit granted to them, which places them in a position to do without other borrowed money, and to dispense even with local savings, while weak and not calculated to attract such. The Central Bank has already a strong reserve fund standing at present at something like £12,000.

Co-operative Supply.

The possession of a Central Bank has enabled the Central Office to multiply its services in a very acceptable manner to the local associations and their members. Among other things, it has helped it to establish during the past few years a system of co-operative supply, mainly for agricultural purposes — implements, feeding stuffs, manures, seeds, and also coals—which was very much needed. Like the focussing of business in a central bank, this new feature of Loan Bank co-operation has been pretty widely copied by other co-operative and *quasi*-co-operative institutions, and by this means agricultural co-operative supply has of late years spread very rapidly all over Germany, so as to have outstripped anything that we have in our country. The Central Bank is not by its rules permitted to carry on such business **itself.** Accordingly it has proved necessary to form another Central Institution, a Trading Firm, which among other things also does the association printing. This firm buys the manures, and other commodities, for which the Bank first collects the orders from **the local associations,** and delivers them for cash to **the Bank. The Bank delivers** for cash **to the associations. Whatever lending is done, accordingly, is done only by the local associations to their** members, not as a giving **of** credit **for goods,** but **as an** independent loan transaction. **In** this **way the** Raiffeisen Firm has become the means of supplying already **as much** as £80,000 or **£90,000** worth of goods in the twelvemonth; **and the figure keeps steadily** growing.* Considering of how **recent origin is this** business, that certainly appears no unsatisfactory **result.** And, really, it represents only a part of the co-operative supply done for the associations. For the local associations have long **since learnt to carry on not a little co-operative** trading **on their own account in their own** localities, forming supply associations by **the side of the** banks, which employ bank **money raised** by credit, but keep their operations and liabilities strictly separate. **As I shall** show, there **are** local associations which in **this way do as** much as **£2,000** worth of supply business in the **year, and,** indeed, this **business is now** increasing very rapidly. **Like** the Bank, the Trading Firm is a *limited* liability **concern,** acting under self-denying rules which preclude any **dividend,** applying the profits to the defrayal of establishment charges, travelling **expenses, or any other** outlay **required for the common service.** Whatever is left over **beyond that is** carried scrupulously to the **general reserve.**

The uses of the **system do not end here.** A co-operative **Insurance Department is** in course **of formation—to**

Further Developments: Insurance, Dairies, Vinegrowers' Associations.

---

* During the first two months of the present year the Trading Firm did a business of £46,007.

insure, among other things, cattle against disease. There are co-operative dairy associations in connection with the system, a co-operative hop-growers' association, and, lastly, a most useful speciality, co-operative vine-growers' associations. These last-named societies are organised on two different methods, as dealing either wholesale, or else retail, and in either form they have proved an inestimable boon to the vine-growers in the valleys of the Rhine, the Moselle, the Ahr, and in Transylvania, actually doubling cultivators' receipts. In olden time every peasant used to press his own grapes and prepare the juice ready for the market, being almost absolutely dependent for the sale upon dealers, who knew how to turn the transaction to good account. Now, as I have myself seen it done in the Ahr valley, all the grapes gathered go at once to the common press, where they are immediately tested for sugar, and credited to each grower according to a scale previously agreed upon. By means of the credit open to it, the association is enabled to pay cash down, reserving a small balance to be distributed *pro rata* at the end of the year. The pound of grapes which formerly sold at from 18 to 20 pfennigs (2¼d. to 2½d.) now sells at from 30 to 48 pfennigs (3¾d. to 6d.); the pound which fetched 12 pfennigs (1½d.) now goes for 25 pfennigs (3⅛d.), and so on in proportion. The public find this innovation advantageous, because it enables them to buy their wine pure, and also to buy it very cheap. One-shilling-a-litre Ahr-wine from a co-operative cellar is very drinkable liquor; two-shilling wine is as good of its kind as you can buy anywhere.*

---

* I am glad to be able to state that there is a fair prospect of these co-operative methods being copied alike in Italy and in some parts of France, where there is ample room for their application. What I have written on the subject in the *Journal de l'Agriculture* and the *Démocratie Rurale* has attracted the attention of some active associations whose leaders profess themselves anxious to put the matter to the test.

THE RAIFFEISEN "LOAN BANKS." 133

For the formation of co-operative dairies the "Loan Banks" are found to be most valuable institutions. They have no difficulty in raising the money required, which they advance to the dairy associations at easy rates, stipulating for gradual repayment. Keeping back 1 pfennig ($\frac{1}{8}$d.) on every two pounds of milk delivered enables the association as a rule to pay off such debt in about ten years.

Even this does not exhaust the utility of the "Loan Banks." Of late they have begun to practice co-operative selling of agricultural produce as well as co-operative purchase of farming requisites. The problem is not an easy one. But some little successes have already been secured. At the provincial headquarters at Cassel last year I found the chairman of the district, Herr Rexerodt, a landed proprietor, who has given himself up to this work as a matter of Christian duty, seated in his office like a broker in his shop, with samples of seeds, grain, and other produce ranged all round. Some common sales of corn have also been effected, securing the seller in one case a gain of 30s. per ton, in another a profit of £5 per truck, an excess return not to be sneezed at in bad times. No doubt the organisation, which is still in its infancy, will be perfected and yield even better results.

Co-operative Sale of Produce.

With so great utility, in such variety, to point to as a recommendation, and a degree of success which in its financial application may be summed up in "millions of money lent, mostly to poor people, and not a farthing ever lost," it is not surprising that, once the Raiffeisen Banks became really known, they made way exceedingly fast, and that now they are meeting with ready imitation all over the Continent. To trustworthy persons their establishment has made want of money for productive purposes absolutely a thing of the past. Every one can obtain whatever he wants at about 5 per cent. interest, and he can obtain it for practically any length of time. M. Courtois

Benefits of the Loan Bank System.

has ascertained that of the tens of thousands of loans granted—of neither the number nor the amount of which there is a complete return extant—only about 15 per cent. are granted for one year or less, 43 per cent. for from one to five years, 34 per cent. for from five to ten years, and 8 per cent. for longer. So long as the borrower continues regular in his payments, and applies the loan to the object for which the money has been granted, he may be sure that this will go on. If a member has money that he does not know what to do with, there is the savings bank open or the deposits department. If any one finds himself helplessly in his creditors' power, his property mortgaged, and his credit gone, so long as there is any margin of solvency left, the bank with its inexhaustible resources is ready to step in, take over his estate, and see that it goes for its proper value, handing him over the balance for a fresh start. This has been done in hundreds of cases. And in all this large and complicated business, in about a thousand associations, during forty-three years, there have been only ten cases of embezzlement or misappropriation, which were in every case met out of the reserve or by the sureties. I have no more recent figures; but cases of loss continue few.*

---

* In 1893, 610 Raiffeisen Associations had among them 17,720,871 marks (£886,043) outstanding in loans, in addition to 3,068,334 marks (£153,411) advanced in cash credits, therefore £1,039,454 in all, at the rate of about £1,706 each. They held only 473,758 marks (£23,688) in share capital, but in addition 1,176,389 marks (£58,814) in two reserve funds, and 24,620,600 marks (£1,231,040) in savings deposits. The total of management expenses was returned as 240,905 marks (£12,045), not £19. 13s. apiece. As much as 6,830,114 marks (£341,505) had been lent out in the course of the year, in addition to 4,380,452 marks (£219,022) in cash credits, £560,527 in all (nearly £919 per association). Savings had been taken in the course of the year to the amount of 10,542,561 marks (£527,128), and loans had been repaid to the amount of 5,030,473 (£251,523). This shows the business to be

THE RAIFFEISEN "LOAN BANKS." 135

It may be well to stop at this point to examine the causes of such signal success. The Causes of Success.

Above all things, there is the common, the joint and several liability—call it "unlimited" if you like—without which a sound Raiffeisen Bank is inconceivable. The liability is not really "unlimited," as I shall show. It is to the interest of the society itself that it should be *rigidly* safeguarded—far beyond what can be done by the very obvious and desirable expedient of limiting the lending powers of the governing body, in the case of collective lending as of individual loans—and that no risk of any kind should be incurred. But so far as the "one-for-all and all-for-one" is adopted, the adoption of that principle must be *absolute*, and absolute with *full equality* as between members, assigning equal rights and equal liabilities to all. That is the very pillar of the system, the pivot upon which the whole organisation must necessarily turn. The avowed object for which you co-operate is, by means of collective

Common Liability.

---

sound, and serves as a conclusive refutation of M. de Malarce's gross misstatement, avowedly made on hearsay evidence, that repayments are backward. Profits amounted on the balance to only 70,502 marks (£3,525). In 1893 there were a little more than twice the number of banks in existence of those which had furnished the returns here summarised. At the present time there are nearly four times that number. The turnover of the Central Bank, now that the provincial branch banks have been constituted, amounted in the first eleven weeks of the current year to 18,629,620 marks (£931,480), the turnover of the Trading Firm to 1,414,777 marks (£70,739). Of 2,107 associations existing on 15th March, 2,026 had joined the Central Bank. In the year 1894 the entire turnover of the Central Bank amounted to about 28,000,000 marks (£1,400,000). The paid-up capital stood at 1,300,000 marks (£65,000); the reserve fund, including an addition of 29,913 marks made out of the profits of the year, at 196,356 marks (£9,818). The expenses did not reach 28,000 marks (£1,400). The profit realised was 81,000 marks (£4,050). The co-operative supply done for members in respect of manure, feeding stuffs, seeds, implements, and coals, amounted to 1,426,188 marks (£71,309).

effort, by, so to speak, the creation of a "faggot-liability," to obtain for yourselves the credit which in an isolated condition you do not, or every one of you does not, command. That means that *within* the association you must provide an efficient substitute for that pledge credit which M. Say condemns, and which your members have it not in their power to purchase; and *outside* the association create security ample for your borrowing, and such as will make inquiry by the outside lender in every specific case superfluous. The ostensible financial "goodness" which you collectively pledge to the outer world may be that of one man only in the whole association. That is his contribution to the common stock, perfectly legitimate if it is safeguarded. But please observe that in this application "credit" and "liability" do not at all mean the same thing as "money." We do not ask any man to give a single penny, be it to a fellow-member, be it to the association collectively. Quite the reverse. We particularly beg him *not* to give. We tell him that, not in his own interest only, but far more in the interest of the association, it is essential that he should carefully *abstain* from giving. He is to support—to help others to help themselves. The employer, who has his employee financially well in his power, may unhesitatingly assure him credit by lending him the use of his name. The banker who holds, not perhaps directly negotiable, but ultimately adequate, security from his client, may well grant that client an overdraft, or accredit him with another institution. In the same way in the Raiffeisen associations we try to create—and have indeed succeeded in creating—a security which acts as an efficient substitute for a pledge, and secures those who lend their credit by making it their fellow-members' direct interest, not only to be honest themselves, but also to see that others are honest. That is Raiffeisen's great triumph; the creation of such security, where previously there was none, is his peculiar

THE RAIFFEISEN "LOAN BANKS."   137

merit as an organiser of co-operative credit. The lively sense of responsibility **required, for one's** self and others, is absolutely not to be assured without the enlistment of liability, not only direct, but going a good deal beyond the value of a share or a good many shares, be they small or be they large. There is nothing to sharpen the **wits** of people concerned, to make them watchful, critical, observant, inexorable, like effectual liability. You have the principle **in germ—and** in germ only—in Scotch cash credit.

Let me quote upon this point the Report of the Lords and Commons Committee **of 1826** on Scotch Banking. "Any person," so says the Report, "who applies to the **bank for a** cash credit is called upon to produce two or more competent securities, who are jointly bound, and after **a** full inquiry into **the** character of the applicant, the nature of his business, and the sufficiency of his securities he is allowed to open a credit." "This system," so the Report goes on, "has a great effect upon the moral habits of the **people,** because those who are securities **feel an** interest in watching over their conduct; and if they find that they are misconducting themselves, they become apprehensive of being brought into risk and loss from having become their securities; **and** if they find they are so misconducting themselves, they withdraw the security." Here are two important elements of security indicated—establishment by inquiry of the borrower's trustworthiness, and control of his action of employment. There were at the time spoken of about 11,000 cash credits outstanding collectively for about six millions of money. **In addition to the 11,000 borrowers,** there **were,** as the evidence points out, between **30,000 and** 40,000 persons liable for the loans, acting as checks and controllers; 30,000 or 40,000 pairs of eyes, directly interested in **the** case, watching the borrowers on behalf of the bank; 30,000 or 40,000 **tongues to remind them** of their

[margin note: Scotch Cash Credit contains the Principle in Germ.]

duty, and warn them if they threatened to go wrong. That explains the whole satisfactory working of the system. Here are the two main pillars of co-operative credit recognised—*joint liability* and *individual checking*. The sureties become an intermediate body between capital and want, helping the latter, but also effectually safeguarding the former.

Now this is co-operative banking applied in a very halting and middle class sort of way, among people who possess property and also some commercial education. Our object is to dive deeper — in the words of Commendatore Luzzatti, " *aspiriamo a discendere* "—so we must proceed upon very much broader and more popular lines. We must multiply our sureties and quicken the vigilance and control by responsibility carried still further.

The Germ Developed.

The fundamental idea of co-operative credit banking has already been explained. It is, that a number of men, poor alone, or poor and rich, join together to pledge their credit in common, in order thereby to obtain the temporary command of money which individually they cannot secure, with a view to disposing of that money among themselves, likewise for temporary employment, and for profitable purposes. The practicableness of the scheme hinges upon the feasibility of ensuring repayment from members, and thereby creating a good foundation for credit by securing—*absolutely* securing—those who pledge what they possess, practically " up to the hilt," for the benefit of others. That is done by selecting your members, by watching the borrower, by watching the loan, and reserving to yourself effective power for calling it in, and by subordinating everything that is done to the one consideration of safety. Now see how unlimited liability directly serves to supply all this.

Common Liability secures careful Selection of Members.

Without unlimited liability, to begin with, you can never make sure that your bank will be sufficiently careful in the selection of its members. Such selection, limiting your membership to persons absolutely trustworthy, is the first condition of **your success**. With only his 5s. or £1 share at **stake no person in town or** village would **care to** say "No" to the application for **admission of any but an** openly disreputable neighbour. Why should **he** disoblige him? However, we **know** from experience **that** co-operative banks have had to be broken **up simply because one or two black sheep had found** their way into **the fold.** Make people understand **that** in electing the new member they practically make themselves liable for any **default** which he may make, and all considerations of etiquette and mere neighbourly courtesy are **sure to vanish.** The breeches-pocket knows **of no** etiquette. **Hence,** in a great measure — though not **solely** — that marvellous morally **educating power which it is** generally admitted that Raiffeisen banks **exercise upon their members.** This it is which has helped to make the **Loan Banks** such admirable moral reformers, instilling principles which **previously were** not altogether common. People soon find out the value **of** a cheap lending institution, when they see their neighbours regularly employing it. Once they are made to understand that membership is altogether dependent upon their **good** character and good conduct, **and its** continuance upon **their** perseverance in such **virtues,** it is astonishing how fast **the drunkard forsakes his sottish ways, the** spendthrift **his extravagance, how** fast **the idle becomes industrious,** the quarrelsome man peaceful, **and** the reckless careful.

Next, without unlimited liability, you would not, at any rate to the same extent, secure the admirable management which is admitted to distinguish these little village **institu-tions.** M. Alphonse Courtois recognises **this** as one **of the** chief causes of their **success:** "*Elles sont d'ailleurs re-marquablement administrées; cette division très* **nette des** *attributions* **entre** *pour beaucoup, présumons nous,* **dans le** *succès de ces unions.*"

_{It secures Good Administration.}

It is not only that the unlimited liability of members prompts those members to be careful to select none but the most competent officers. We know that that is necessary. "*Il ne suffit pas d'avoir une bonne machine*," remarks M. Léon Say, addressing himself to this very point; "*il faut aussi avoir un bon mécanicien.*" At the outset, at any rate, the success of the banks has, as Emile de Laveleye, one of their warmest admirers, has pointed out, invariably been the work of some individual zealous workers who have taken up the cause for the sake of the good to be effected—*des hommes dévoués*. The attractive idea—the *idea morale*, as Commendatore Luzzatti calls it—may suffice to secure such. But the unlimited liability of officers at the same time leads them to be extremely critical in their disposal of bank moneys—very strict in their demand of prompt repayment, which is one of the most essential conditions of success, economic and educational. Not only their own money is at stake and may be lost; any risk incurred would jeopardise other people's money as well, the money of those whom they particularly desire to benefit. If this consideration touches more particularly wealthy people who may be in the bank, and who may be answerable in a higher degree for its liabilities than others, such wealthy people will of course be represented on the governing body. And since it is they who supply at the outset the apparent backbone of solvency, and their presence in the bank is on that account sure to be desirable, they have the power practically of insisting upon anything which they may consider necessary in the interest of safety. They may, therefore, adequately secure themselves.

It secures Efficient Watching of the Loan.

Without unlimited liability, furthermore, there could not possibly be all that watchfulness and control which really make up the system of Raiffeisenism and which keep it safe, that "admirable" principle, as the Duke of Argyll calls it, " of strict payments and watching the loan." You keep your members generally under control. More especially do you control your borrowers, and take care to ascertain that they remain honest, thrifty, careful, deserving of credit. You watch specifically the employment of the loan, its application to its proper purpose, failing which you call it in unmercifully—otherwise there can be no success. You insist upon prompt payments. You build up your whole fabric upon a system of mutual checking, the borrowers being checked by the committee, the committee by the council, the council by the mass of members, all without offence or invidiousness, all in the interest and for the protection of the very people checked. "*Ecartez la solidarité,*" so says Father de Besse, "*et personne ne voudra même dans une association, ni corriger son prochain, ni se laisser corriger.*" "*Semo in cento che se femo la spia un con l'altro onde x imposibile che nessun fazza un bruta parte.*" So explained a member of the first Raiffeisen bank formed in Italy, that of Loreggia, of which I speak at greater length elsewhere, in his uncouth Venetian patois. It means: "We are a hundred persons who watch one another like spies; it is not possible that any one of us should fail in his duty." And all this, as observed, without offensiveness. Quite the reverse. All that zealous, lively, warm, and loving interest in their local association, which every observer remarks upon as a distinctive, striking feature among members of the Raiffeisen Loan Banks, is plainly traceable to the principle of unlimited liability, which makes every one feel that he and his fellows have become "members one of another." Under this system an association becomes what Ettore Levi says that every genuine co-operative association should be—*una famiglia onesta e laboriosa*—an honest and industrious family, with a community of aims, of interests, and of sympathies. Every one knows that there is no hostility in this mutual observation. In no system of associations have I witnessed the same manifest feeling of "belonging together," and at the same time the same lively interest in the affairs of the association as in this. In the Schulze-Delitzsch associations and the Luzzatti banks 100 members will attend a general meeting out of 1,000 or of 15,000. I know of a bank in which 11 men could with difficulty be whipped up out of 11,500. In the Raiffeisen Associations you may be sure that the members will be represented to a man, so far as that is at all possible, and that every member will bring his ears and wits with him. Often may you see members about the office when there is an important committee meeting. It is to their interest that they should know what is going on. And they *will* know it. Publicity in respect of everything except savings, and democratic government, the full equality of all who are in the association, are absolutely essential for success. However, that close touch, that insistence upon full equality where equality appears at first sight sometimes difficult, that strong feeling of social and moral, as well as financial, solidarity—all these things are impossible without common liability. When the poor man knows that he may have to pay for his submissiveness, his shyness and his awe of social superiors soon wear off.

<small>Small Districts Conducive to Safety.</small>   Another very important element of success, that is, of the safety which has in this case been combined with unlimited liability, is the smallness of the district assigned to every bank. The followers of Schulze-Delitzsch will not understand this, because in their own system—which is essentially different in its entire construction—success means a large "business." In the Raiffeisen system, where there are no salaries, no expenses to speak of, and where "business" consists merely in simple borrowing and lending, whether the sum be 1s. or £1,000, the object to be aimed at is not "business," but absolute safety. Profits

scarcely come into account. In any but a small district there could not possibly be that knowledge, and vigilance, and checking of one another, upon which stress has already repeatedly been laid as constituting a *sine qua non* of success. "It is the smallness of the districts," writes, officially, Herr Gau, of the Agricultural Department of Saxe-Weimar, "which makes the Raiffeisen associations so generally trusted." Creditors know that in such districts strict control and supervision are likely to be efficient. The Raiffeisen system is, in truth, essentially one designed for small, self-contained rural districts. Raiffeisen dubbed his associations specifically "agricultural." He never contemplated the application of his system to towns. He kept in his ideas to the modest country parish. Signor Contini has tried to apply the system among an urban population in Milan, but thus far without success. Even should success be obtained, it will only be like the success of keeping a tropical plant alive in some exceptionally sheltered spot out of its own climate. I know of one or two Raiffeisen banks only which flourish in larger districts than those which Raiffeisen himself contemplated. One of these is at Dahlen in the Kingdom of Saxony. It is really abnormally large. But its success is entirely due to the peculiar organising capacity of its chairman. The other is in Trebus in Prussian Lusatia. The district of this bank—which its founder, Herr Becker, formed after about two years of careful preparation—covers about 22 square miles. It is decidedly successful. But the district is peculiarly constituted. There are, so to speak, five little hamlets, each of which contributes a committee-man. Certainly good touch appears to be maintained. And General Anwalt Cremer himself admitted to me when I spoke to him of that very successful bank—which, when I was there in 1894, had an annual turnover, after not three years' existence, of £5,000 among a constituency of about 120 members, taking up a share of 5s. each, and had accumulated about £50 in its two reserve funds*—that something more might probably be done in the way of grouping small parishes or villages. But under ordinary circumstances a parish is the ideal area, because within such a district watching can certainly be made easy, and every one is in reach of the bank, and moreover every one knows one another. The creation of such a bank, it ought to be remembered, is not purely a question of numbers. In the new agricultural settlements of the eastern provinces of Prussia, where truly admirable work is being done in cutting up more or less bankrupt large estates into small holdings—by which means entire new villages are being raised up—although the use of more money is unquestionably appreciated, Raiffeisen banks can be formed only very sparingly and slowly, because the settlers, gathered together from all parts of the Empire, do not yet sufficiently know one another. This explanation was given to me by President von Wittenburg, who is a zealous admirer of the system, and has himself, as *landrath* in Silesia, formed two Raiffeisen banks by means of advances of public money made from the savings bank of his district—so safe is the business considered to be—at the ordinary rate of 4 per cent., which advances he found repaid much faster than he either anticipated or desired. In the great majority of cases it is just the smallness of the district which ensures success, not merely by making the vigilance required possible, but also by giving to every association an entirely local character, and bringing thoroughly home to members their personal interest in it.

---

* This bank limits its loans to one member to £50; it pays 3½ per cent. on deposits, and charges 5 per cent. on loans; it also grants current accounts, and has established a co-operative cattle insurance society, which at that time 60 of its members had joined, insuring among them about 200 head of cattle up to three-quarters of their value. There was an appreciable saving on premiums.

THE RAIFFEISEN "LOAN BANKS."

This really cannot be understood at a distance. To realise it you must go among the people, and see and talk to them, watch the pride with which they contemplate their successful institution, the zeal with which they make themselves acquainted with all its transactions. They can show you the books and explain everything to you. They are not a bit afraid of what on paper appears espionage among themselves; rather do they accept it willingly as an effective bulwark of safety. They have their savings bank and put into it, because it is *their own*. They watch at all points to make sure that the association may suffer no hurt. They discuss all that goes on in connection with it. It has linked them together with a new bond of union which firmly establishes peace and kind feeling. The seemingly rapturous language of M. von Dobransky is not a bit too strong for the case. I have never been more interested in my life than when going into one or other of these villages, in which there is a co-operative loan bank, and judging from the evidence presented what that bank has done for its members. Here is one, to me particularly interesting, case—that of the village of Mülheim on the Rhine, not very far from Coblentz. The peasant of the Lower Rhine is as a rule—whatever the "peasant girls with deep blue eyes" may have been in Byron's days—not a particularly genial and attractive specimen of humanity. But it is surprising what a metamorphosis the advent of this humanising instrument has brought about. The best among the population of Mülheim, some two hundred and fifty persons, have joined the bank. Though the soil around is rich and well watered, the place is said to have been some time ago rather neglected, and not a little pestered with "Jews." The latter have quite disappeared.

They quicken Interest.

That is another advantage of small districts. "*L'usure ne peut être combattue que de près,*" rightly urges M. Léon Say. In Germany it has baffled even Bismarckian methods

They facilitate the Suppression of Usury.

K

of eradication, which do not usually err on the side of gingerliness. What the Prince's "blood and iron" could not accomplish, co-operative gold and the silken bond of union have brought about with ease. Whole battalions of these greedy gentry have been put to the rout, and driven discomfited from the field.

Instance of Mülheim.

To come back to my instance of the Loan Bank at Mülheim—the old wattle and post-and-pane houses, with their rickety timbering and ramshackle roofs, have disappeared, and given place to neat, substantial stone buildings. There is an unmistakable look of plenty, of order, of neighbourliness observable everywhere. Of course, according to the teaching of our own agricultural authorities, these people are farming on an entirely wrong system. But there are no signs of agricultural depression about their properties. The gardens are tidily kept, the fields and orchards look throughout *bien soignés*, and everything appears prosperous and flourishing, so that, after all, perhaps facts are more correct than theories. Land fetches about £1 the German rod, which sums up to £288 an acre. On such soil of course good husbandry tells; and co-operation has perceptibly stimulated it. You see drainage, new implements—even a steam threshing machine has been provided by co-operation, one of those expensive implements, which our English journalists—writing down *la petite culture* as Goethe's "German" portrayed a camel which he had never seen—periodically assure us that the small peasant could never manage to purchase out of his small purse. Here is one purchased by him—and purchased without money, to begin with, and without cost in the end. He has let it out, to members at 8s. 6d. per hour, to non-members at 9s. 6d., and that has paid for the machine. He does a good deal in the way of co-operative supply, agricultural and otherwise. By the side of his co-operative credit association he has set up a co-operative supply association, which does from £1,800 to £2,000 worth of business in the twelvemonth, for all of which it borrows the requisite money from the bank. Himself and his neighbours pay in about £2,000 in savings every year. There is at Mülheim a considerable revenue from cherries. This is one of the three German districts which supply us pretty liberally with cherries in three successive periods. From this village alone in good years we now receive some £3,000 to £4,000 worth of cherries. In July 1891 cherry-growing members of the association paid into their bank 23,945 marks of cherry money on deposit, after deducting what they required for current expenses. Moreover the association does a considerable business in *Verkaufsprotocolle*— bonds pledging purchasers of small real estate to certain payments by instalments. All the dangers arising from that once very formidable process have been overcome with the assistance of the Loan Bank. It buys them at a moderate discount, and all goes on peaceably, and merrily, as if there never had been any "Jews." This little bank has annually about £2,200 worth of these bonds coming into its possession, and holds generally something over £6,000 worth in its hands. All in all, it has an annual turnover of about £35,000, leaving a net profit of about £250, every farthing of which goes to the reserve. By this means, though the bank serves all its customers very cheaply, since 1880, when the association was formed, a reserve has accumulated of about £1,500, enabling the bank to allow to its customers six months' credit on co-operative purchases without adding a penny to the wholesale price. The bank employs a cashier, who acts also as secretary, at the small salary of £37. 10s. a year. He has got all the bookkeeping at his fingers' ends, and knows all, financially, about every one with whom he has to do.

The gratuitousness of services is another distinct factor of the success attained, and an additional safeguard to the *Advantages of Gratuitous Services.*

common liability pledged. The idea of the association is, that members should give that which they have got in order thereby to purchase that which they have not. They have *not* got money, which under ordinary circumstances purchases credit; so they give vigilance, labour, effort, time. In giving it it is only reasonable and consistent that they should labour without demanding remuneration. But there is further justification. What is, under circumstances like those here contemplated, freely given, among neighbours, is most likely to be honestly given. Schulze objects that "the labourer is worthy of his hire." True. But, then, his hire may be worth something to him. He is dependent for it upon the votes of his fellow-members. Those fellow-members may be applicants for loans. Their applications may be improper. Is every officer likely to stand firm when the member who can give him his salary or take it away puts to him the brutal Bismarckian "do ut des"? "Officers of co-operative credit banks," says Commendatore Luzzatti, "should have a conscience free from all personal pre-occupations and from pressure of any sort." They should know "neither father nor mother," and consider business coming before them purely on its own merits.

Benefits of Disallowing Profits and of the inalienable Reserve Fund.

There is another important feature making for success, closely allied to the last, and that is the disallowance of all profits, all individual pickings out of the bank, which is not intended as a profit-bearing institution; and, necessarily allied to that, there is the creation of an inalienable reserve fund belonging absolutely to the bank and not divisible under any circumstances. That fund is a monstrosity to purely economic and commercial co-operators like those of the Schulze-Delitzsch school. An "anomaly" it may well be called, but an anomaly which, as Felice Mangili has said, is justified by its circumstances and results. There is no magnet, nothing to bind members to their association, like money **laid up**, in which every one entitled is naturally anxious to retain his interest. There is no danger of breaking up an association or diverting it from its object when there is a good "Stiftungsfonds." And everything that tends **to** keep members **together,** to **make** it their interest to strive **to** continue worthy of membership, that stimulates their interest, everything **also which** tends to attract others to **the** association, and **accordingly incites** them to make themselves morally eligible, amounts **to a** direct gain. **Beyond this, the** direct benefit arising from the inalienable reserve fund in fortifying credit, in providing funds for useful enterprises, in cheapening credit, and making it more convenient for members, is considerable.

Lastly, there is the simplicity of business. Raiffeisen rules most positively interdict "banking," **or** business, or risk, **or** speculation **of any kind.** Their "business" is simply to **lend and to borrow.** If **a** loan should go **wrong,** under such circumstances you **know exactly what you can** in the worst case be made **liable for.** That **£1 or £10** *absolutely* limits your loss. **There can** be nothing ulterior. And joined to this simplicity **of** business is the simplicity of business arrangements, bookkeeping, organisation, and so on. **Everything is** simple, everything **is** intelligible. M. Durand says after careful investigation :—"*Avec les garanties présentées par l'organisation des Darlehnskassen, la solidarité n'a aucun danger et **ne saurait effrayer** les grands propriétaires.*" *Simplicity of Business insures Safety.*

By such means, simple in themselves, **but** telling, Raiffeisen has made it **his task to raise** up his system **of** educating **and** lending **banks. It cannot** be doubted that he has succeeded. His **work** has been subjected to many **a** test. Unfortunately, like **every** good work, it has had opposition and obloquy to contend against, which **have,** however, led only **to** its **more** brilliant vindication. In 1874 **the** late Emperor William **appointed a** Royal Commission to inquire into its work, presided over by the late Professor Nasse, and having Dr Siemens for a member. The Report, published in 1875, proved so favourable that the banks have from that time forward counted the Imperial Family among their warmest patrons, including the Empress Frederick, who has more than once given proof of her interest. The late Emperor William testified his approbation by a gift of £1,500 from his privy purse, to which his grandson has recently added another £1,000. Among the evidence collected by the Commission mentioned occur the statement already referred to of the Rhenish parson, who confessed that the Raiffeisen bank in his parish had done far more to raise the moral tone among his parishioners than all his ministrations, and the deposition of the presiding judge of the Court of Neuwied, which shows how materially litigation has diminished in his district, owing to the conveniences afforded, and the good principles instilled, by the local Raiffeisen Loan Bank. Those good effects have been sustained. In 1886 the Diet of Lower Austria sent two experts to inquire into the system, who expressed themselves so entirely satisfied of its merits, that that Diet, and other Diets of the Austrian Empire following in its footsteps, at once resolved to encourage the formation of Raiffeisen associations in their several provinces, and backed that resolution with grants of money. In Saxony, in Baden, in Hesse, in most provinces of Prussia, Governments are giving proof of their desire to have these banks multiplied.

And by economists and philanthropists who have seen them they are warmly eulogised and recommended as justifying the verselet (in German it is one) with which a writer on the subject recently headed his pamphlet: "The setting up of Raiffeisen associations means the pulling down of workhouses." M. Rostand commends as their distinguishing traits: "extreme simplicity and cheapness, non-allowance of any dividend, limitation of the district to a parish or a hamlet, the strict prohibition to touch the reserve, the support of the clergy, the common liability replacing the helplessness of agricultural units, the prevailing spirit of devotion and sense of social duty." Mr F. A. Nicholson, in the preface to his Report, sums up the teaching of the inquiry into various systems of co-operative credit for agriculture which he has carried on under orders of the Madras Government in these words: "Find Raiffeisen!" "I have examined many systems," so writes M. Durand, who has himself become a zealous and most successful apostle of co-operative credit in France; "I have not found one which reconciles so fully the demands exacted by Credit: security of operations and the social and moral requirements of rural populations. I do not hesitate emphatically to pronounce the *Darlehnskassen* of Raiffeisen the finest creation, alike from a moral and an economic point of view, which has ever been invented for agricultural credit." To the mind of M. Rostand they conclusively settle the question whether the small agriculturist requires credit at all. It has been denied. It has been affirmed that if he had it he would abuse it. Here, says M. Rostand, is the answer.

It is undoubtedly a great work which Raiffeisen has achieved—in one aspect, greater even than that accomplished by Schulze, although, developing more slowly, it has not yet proved the means of raising quite so much money—greater, because it begins upon less, compasses more in a moral point of view, and rests upon a safer and more popular foundation. To the system of Herr Raiffeisen as to that of the **banche popolari** may justly be applied M. Rostand's felicitously-worded phrase: "*C'est l'heureuse union de l'esprit d'affaires avec les sentimens d'une véritable, d'une pratique philanthropic.*"

CHAPTER VIII.

OFFSHOOTS AND CONGENERS.

Spread of Co-operative Banking.

ONCE co-operative banking had, under Schulze's and Raiffeisen's skilful guidance, shown itself a decided success, the idea was of course readily taken up in many quarters. Every wind, so to speak, caught up seeds dropping from the fruitful and richly bearing tree, to waft them across the Continent, and indeed beyond Europe, scattering them here and there as the soil seemed favourable. On some land they struck root rapidly, and grew up luscious plants. Elsewhere, under a less clement sky, their growth proved more sparing. In one or two places the pushing sprouts found indigenous kindred produce to mingle with, and so helped to bring forth new types and to afford fresh proof of the astonishing adaptability of the newly discovered system.

Offshoots in Germany.

In such a way, first among all countries, was GERMANY overspread with offshoot associations, thriving, and tillering, and intertwining, and multiplying to a very forest. A very provoking feature about all this German money co-operation, however, is, that *more teutonico* it has become split up into a bewildering multitude of sections, all of them independent in organisation, and all most orthodoxly jealous of one another. Could they but bring themselves to sink their differences, to co-operate loyally among themselves as members of the same family, instead of deliberately hindering co-operation by venomous opposition, they would represent a truly colossal force, capable of conferring untold blessings upon the struggling **classes**. The 7,000 or 8,000 associations now existing—in **spite of all** their internal bickerings and hostilities, which are bound to cripple their action—keep in circulation, fructifying **in** people's employment, and bearing ample fruit, **a** sum of money for which £120,000,000 can scarcely be an excessive estimate. What might the result be if the soldiers of this Colchian army were loyally **to** join hands among themselves! **However in** Germany that seems too good a thing to hope for on this side of the millennium.

The Schulze-Delitzsch system has in Germany itself sent forth very few independent shoots. There are, as has been shown, some credit associations organised outside the recognised union. Of such are the ninety or so associations established in Posen and West Prussia, for the use of the Polish population, of which the Rev. P. Wawrzyniak is **chairman**. These banks are exceedingly good, and they dispense a great deal of agricultural credit. They are specifically Polish, and owe **not a** little of their success **to** the assiduous labours of the Roman Catholic priests who, in societies formed **altogether of** Roman Catholics, have, of course, free scope allowed them for their well-directed energy and parental solicitude, strikingly falsifying the impression often owned to among English co-operators that Rome is unfavourable to co-operation. The banks maintain a useful and well-managed central bank at **Posen**. Of such associations also is the Bank of Augsburg, already referred to; and there are others—for instance, the credit associations of Würtemberg. In all these detached growths of Schulze-Delitzschism the deviations from the parent system are so slight, and affect the general principle so little, that they cannot seriously come into account. <small>Of the Schulze-Delitzsch Type.</small>

The system of Raiffeisen has been far more productive of both genuine and spurious offspring. Some **of** its offshoots are legitimate children enough, thoroughly of a piece <small>Of the Raiffeisen Type.</small>

with their parent in organisation and principle, and independent only because they choose to be so. Such are the Raiffeisen banks of Silesia, organised originally inside the Raiffeisen Union, by Herr von Huene, popularly known as "the Silesian Bismarck," strong-willed like his prototype, but, unlike him, a staunch Ultramontane. To some extent, of course, his peculiar denominational leaning is reflected in his associations. There are different reasons for the independent organisation of the majority of Raiffeisen banks in Bavaria and Würtemberg. Their secession has been prompted purely by that peculiar German speciality of political feeling which passes by the name of "particularism." Patriotic Bavarians or Würtembergers could not bring themselves to remain long in a union of which the headquarters is in Prussia. Accordingly Würtemberg has organised its own unions, alike of Schulze-Delitzsch and of Raiffeisen banks, and Bavaria has organised even two unions of the latter type, both unnecessarily independent. The Würtemberg Federation has formed its own central bank, which a few years ago got into difficulties through bad management.

"Particularist" Secessions.

By far the most important secession from the Raiffeisen army has been that of the banks directed by Herr Haas, the prefect or administrator of a political district in Hesse. His dissenting union of banks has already grown to more than 1,500, many of them strong and flourishing; and it is growing still. I do not like to criticise these banks with any degree of severity, because they form an integral portion of a very much larger union of agricultural co-operative associations or "syndicates," which are doing a great deal of good to German agriculture, and are pushing ahead in their practical application of co-operation to husbandry, far more than any other body of associations. They are remarkable for an inspiriting amount of "go." They buy, they sell, they unite their members for work, they form co-

The Haas Associations.

operative dairies, vintries, and strike **out** new paths with a degree of energy and practical sense which do them all credit. The banks following the **lead of Herr** Haas are likewise distinguished by some peculiar features, which may be argued to tell in their favour—even, it may be, in comparison with the Neuwied banks—such as admirable book-keeping and an aptitude for accommodating themselves to altering circumstances, in respect of cash credits and of facilities afforded for the collection of savings.

Their leaders, to be fully fair, do not own themselves to be seceders. Two of them, at any rate, Kreisrath Haas himself, and his countryman and fellow-labourer Dr von **Langsdorff, have in** their days been Raiffeisen's recognised **lieutenants;** and in the teeth of their master's own state**ment, to the** effect that they do not show themselves animated by the same "spirit" as himself, profess themselves now his "true" followers, and call the Neuwied section the apostates, notwithstanding their boast of apostolic succession. It **is** very possible that some of the defects which the Haasists allege as justifying their **own** defection may have shown themselves in practice in the Neuwied Union. Evidently personal considerations—personal dislikes—play a considerable part in the feud. But it is very likely that the Neuwied organisation became too strongly centralised, therefore wanting in elasticity and local autonomy, and that Neuwied at times did pose a little too much like Rome in the Church. We know that Germans are constitutionally pedants. These defects are, however, rapidly being remedied. The creation of great district banks necessarily carries decentralisation in its train; and the autonomy of provincial unions—which has, subject to acceptation of the main rules, always been recognised—is being more fully developed. The main objection **on** the part of the Haasists appears to be, that the Neuwied rules present themselves to them as inconveniently severe. Propaganda, they thought, was not being sufficiently pushed. The stern Sarastro kept his temple gates too relentlessly closed against unregenerate Taminos. Co-operative banking would spread far more rapidly, and help would be brought far more largely to the suffering multitude, if principle were made to bow to temporary expediency, and the conditions were relaxed. Rather cleverly, from a strategic point of view, Herr Haas allied himself with Raiffeisen's great foe and persecutor, Schulze, to arrange with him some middle course which should be Raiffeisen while also being Schulze, and so disarm Schulzist criticisms. In deference to Schulze, he sacrificed two of the main pillars of the Raiffeisen system, to which Schulze more particularly objected—the refusal to issue shares, or else the reduction of the value of such shares to a minimum, and the accumulation of an indivisible reserve fund. Such evisceration obviously corresponds very much to the taking of the part of the Prince out of the play of "Hamlet." The admission of the poor without a tax, the appropriation of all profits, to the exclusion of dividend, to a common fund, are what make Raiffeisenism what it is. However, Herr Haas did not evidently mean to apply his Schulzoid rules as they were laid down. If he recommended shares of £25, he was content to collect only 50s. upon each. Indeed, he left his banks to do pretty well as they chose, provided that they would affiliate themselves to him, which has resulted in his gathering together under his banner a large army, doing a considerable amount of good, no doubt, whilst things go smoothly, but heterogeneous as regards principle and organisation, and wanting generally in the backbone, wanting certainly in the morally educating, the economically disciplining element, which constitutes one of the most essential and attractive features in the true Raiffeisen system—uniting members simply for the purpose of enabling them to obtain money, as a matter of temporary, personal convenience, and uniting them under

Their Peculiar Features.

a latitude with regard to rules, which makes the union a veritable *omnium gatherum* of good, indifferent, and very bad. I will give an instance. At Bürgel, close to Offen- A Bad Bank. bach, so to speak under the very nose of Herr Haas himself, I found in a populous parish an association of this Federation, composed of only about forty members, who keep themselves scrupulously select. Their shares are for 50s., all paid up. Until recently they levied an entrance fee of 25s., but that they have lately reduced to 15s. They constitute a most solvent bank, with a capital of £1,200, and excellent credit. But they will not do what Raiffeisen banks were intended to do. They will not take in the poor. There are about 700 savings deposit accounts, contributed, of course, mainly by persons left outside. Savings, in fact, pour in at the rate of £40 or £45 a week. On such the bank allows $3\frac{1}{2}$ per cent.—only to pay its members 10 per cent. on their shares. Such a rate of interest is totally opposed to the Haas rules. But even within a few miles of his own headquarters Herr Haas is powerless to prevent the abuse. Here is a usury shop, known to be a usury shop, set up under the style and title of the "True Raiffeisenism!" I was warned before going that I should find the bank a bad one. But, then, why is it kept in the union? The Neuwied Union would turn it out. There are more like it. I will not say many. But obviously being in the Haas Union affords no sort of guarantee for the character of a particular bank. Generally speaking, the system is Raiffeisenism un-Raiffeisenised—the educating, elevating, altruistically helping element extracted, and merely the economic and commercial accommodation left, which has, generally speaking, thriven thus far—though there have been more liquidations and collapses than in the Neuwied system—but which offers no guarantee that it will thrive in trying times. It is not—it is not intended to be—a thing to generate enthusiasm. It is calculating, gain-seeking co-operation, like Schulze's, only less consistent. Its growth is in no small measure due to the countenance which it has very openly received from the followers of Schulze. It must have been mortifying in the extreme to those gentlemen to find that, when the State-Socialist Government of Prussia, at the instance of one of Herr Haas' colleagues, Herr von Mendel Steinfels, set up at Berlin a Central Bank, subsidised by the State, and intended to prop up agricultural banks by artificial means, the Neuwied Union, like the Schulze Union, promptly and frankly declared that it would have nothing to do with that mischievous introduction of State help, since a sound cooperative union must be strong enough to support itself—whereas the Haas Union at once jumped at the proposal, and readily seized the hand held out to it with money—which has already proved insufficient for its purpose, as State grants invariably do, and is now to be quadrupled! With every wish to do justice to Herr Haas' scheme, with every recognition of his good work on other co-operative ground, I cannot bring myself to look upon his banking system as altogether perfect; I cannot think that it is "co-operative" to dissociate education, discipline, opening the door to the very poor, from pure economics. And no one can yet say with what degree of success these banks will weather trying times.

The "Peasants' Associations." Next to the Haas Associations the "Peasants' Associations" (*Bauernvereine*) may well claim a place in this record, inasmuch as they have all written co-operative credit, to be given to small agriculture, conspicuously upon their rather comprehensive programme. The absolute necessity of popular credit as one of the main wants of agriculture is indeed now so well understood and so generally appreciated in Germany that it appears as if no propagandist society of any sort or any tint or shade of opinion—social, political, or denominational—could be formed without at any rate *promising* financial services. That accounts, among other things, for the creation of that Conservative Junkers' Association, formed and officered by Herr von Broich, which is to "primrose" the agricultural population with the help of easy credit, not unsubsidised from above, but as yet only promised. **For the** actual business of these **associations is** next to *nil*. **The "Peasants'** Associations" have likewise a political, and, even more, a religious flavour about them. " Mother Church," if not clearly set forth upon **their** banner, is known **to be** invisibly present in their councils, and to have a hand in directing their work. And benevolent large landowners, who are not likely to require much assistance themselves — more particularly such **as** are faithful to Rome—take a leading part in the proceedings. The first Peasants' Association was the creation of the late Herr von Schorlemer Alst, a staunch leader of the Ultramontane party in Parliament. From Westphalia the institution has spread into Upper and Lower Rhineland, Baden, Hesse, Nassau, the Eichsfeld country, East and West Prussia, and Silesia, and nearly everywhere the associations have attained strength. That is attributable to the fact that, in addition to propagating "sound" religious and political views, **they** also practise **very** wholesome co-operation, and **give the** peasants very much assistance in respect of **things** needed —instruction, legal advice, opportunities for inquiry and **discussion, as** well **as cheaper and** better manures, seeds, **feeding stuffs, and the** means for **co-operating in** agricultural production. Their "co-operative law" is very much appreciated. The Peasants' Associations constitute themselves, so **to** speak, the guardians of the peasants, and take their part to such an extent against sharp-witted and **over**reaching dealers and usurers, that the **mere** mention of the name " Bauernverein" is often quite sufficient to cause the **greedy** aggressor to beat **a hasty** retreat. Upon a question **of** law arising, any member has the right to take gratuit-

Marginalia: Political Banks. "Co-operative Law."

ously the opinion of the association lawyer, paid and retained by the association. Should he advise proceedings and the member lose his case, the association undertakes to pay the major part of the costs. The largest of these associations at present is that of Kempen, which employs agricultural chemists to analyse and advise, sends dairy instructors about, teaches peasants bookkeeping, does a large business in agricultural goods, and maintains for the benefit of its 41,000 members no less than 138 agricultural banks in a district already fairly well-stocked with such establishments from Neuwied. All over Germany the Peasants' Associations practise, for agricultural credit, the Raiffeisen system pure and unadulterated, as the one best approved by experience. The associations of Hesse and Nassau have indeed wholly handed over the management of this part of their business to the authorities at Neuwied. Oddly enough, the Peasants' Associations—there are at present ten—maintain no sort of touch or union among themselves, which accounts in a large measure for the provoking absence of statistics as to their aggregate work, which must be considerable. When attending a meeting of the Rhenish associations last year, I ventured to suggest inter-association co-operation, at any rate to the extent of collection of statistics, and I believe that my suggestion will be acted upon. As it is, the credit given by the Peasants' Associations is not included, even by way of estimate, in any of the statistics published.

Belgian "Peasants' Associations." An institution so useful for propagandist purposes was sure to be copied outside the borders of its own native home. Under the leadership of Professor Francotte and Abbé Mellaerts, Belgium, which is, co-operatively speaking, either darkly Ultramontane or else glaringly Socialist, has readily grafted it upon its social system; and some of the earlier French syndicates seem, in principle, with their *membres fondateurs* and *membres effectifs*, and their patronage and oligarchic **government, to** have been, so to speak, "made in Germany," or at any rate inspired from there.

AUSTRIA **and** HUNGARY have **not** shown themselves slow to learn the useful lesson taught by their neighbour, Germany. Indeed, on the Danube co-operation **for** credit **has become the** most popular form of co-operation known; for **in** 1893 Austria possessed, out **of** 2,825 co-operative associations in all, no fewer than 2,118 credit associations. In 1889 the number of credit associations was in Austria actually greater **in proportion** to territory **than that** registered in Germany, namely, 1,312 **as** compared with 2,200. But the German associations are larger, and also do a more voluminous business. Statistics find their way into print very tardily in the Empire on the Danube. The last trustworthy figures published are those relating to the year 1891, which **are** given in the *Statistisches Jahrbuch* of 1893. For 1891, 1,599 associations had sent in returns, showing a collective roll of 635,206 members, and **an** aggregate lending in the year of 290,898,000 florins (£23,271,840), nearly a third being lent on mortgages (which should not be), more than half on acceptances. Their collective property amounted to 32,180,000 florins **in** paid-up shares, **and** 15,472,000 florins in reserve funds, all in all 47,652,000 florins (£3,812,160). They held among them 289,037,000 **florins** (£23,122,960) in savings deposits, and 11,783,000 florins (£942,640) in loan money.
<small>Austria and Hungary.</small>

There are some peculiar features **about** co-operative banking in Austria and Hungary which make it an interesting study **for the inquirer.** Above all things there is that almost Babylonian medley of races—Teuton, Latin, several varieties of Slav, and even Turanian. In such a realm manifestly an institution **may** be said **to be put** searchingly upon its trial for adaptability. Co-operative credit has been taken up by all these races—least readily, oddly enough, by the Italians—and **everywhere it has**
<small>Co-operative Banking among various Races.</small>

Slav Associations.

been found to answer, with varying degrees of success. The Slavs, we know, are almost born co-operators. Some of the earliest forms of co-operative organisation are to be met with among their families. At the present time the specifically Slav provinces of Austria—Bohemia, Moravia, and Galicia—decidedly take the lead in co-operation, maintaining the largest number of associations. Of the 1,599 societies referred to above, there were 439 in Bohemia, 347 in Moravia, 248 in Galicia, moreover 15 in Carniola, and 34 in Bukowina—1,083 in all, claiming 509,490 out of the 635,206 members, holding 20,529,000 florins in share capital, 12,635,000 florins in reserve funds, and lending out annually 230,173,000 florins. (I have not included Silesia among the Slav provinces, although a large portion of its population is Slav.) It is true, the associations enumerated were not all Slav. Among the 439 of Bohemia there were 170 or 180 German. But evidently Slavism stands for much in the co-operative organisation of Austria, though, unfortunately, its associations are not generally speaking as good in quality as they are plentiful in number. In Austria generally, as Mr Maude points out in his Blue Book Report of 1886, administration of co-operative societies is a little lax. Among leaders of the movement this is frequently made a subject of complaint. Nevertheless the record of the Slav societies cannot be called a bad one. There were in 1895 no less than 728 specifically Czech credit associations collectively in Bohemia, Moravia, and Silesia, of which 486 numbered 292,132 members, held 8,375,692 florins in share capital, 11,929,588 florins in reserve funds, and 201,069,753 florins in savings deposits. The amount of collective lending is not stated in the *Genossenschaft*, from which I take these figures. But as in 1891, 420 banks had lent out among them 111,754,425 florins, and as the 486 banks referred to had raised by deposits and loans 205,205,341 florins, in addition to their own property of 20,285,280 florins, it is evident that their business must have been considerable. Dr Wrabetz, in his comments, remarks on the rapid growth of the business of these Czech associations, and expresses regret at the want of equal union and common action among the German banks. The Slav societies study union as an essential part of co-operation. Whereas of the 180 German credit associations in existence in Bohemia in 1895 only 31 had joined the common union, nearly all the Slav—Czech, Polish, and Slovenian—had affiliated themselves to their several central bodies. Among the German associations there is generally a want of union and of common action, which tends to weakness and bad practice. Of 2,428 co-operative banking associations known to have existed in Austria alone in 1894, and doing a business of probably somewhere about £30,000,000 in loans, only 120 had joined the recognised German Union. The German Union has for some time been, in the bargain, weak at headquarters and feebly led. Under the remarkably able leadership of its present chairman, Dr Wrabetz, who is more particularly valued as a man of practical business knowledge, it is rapidly consolidating its strength. Of course Slavs decline to have any dealings with Germans and Magyars, just as Germans and Magyars decline to deal with Slavs. And so there are divisions running through the entire organisation, and business is made needlessly difficult.

Another peculiar feature in Austrian and Hungarian credit co-operation, on which Dr Wrabetz rightly insists, is this, that the co-operative banks organised under the two-headed eagle recruit their members to a far larger extent than their sister establishments in Germany from the agricultural classes. Even in the Schulze-Delitzsch banks of Austria agricultural membership preponderates. The credit associations of Podersam, Eger, Radonitz, Langenlois, Tachau, Kaaden, two in Krems, and most of

Prevalence of Agricultural Members.

the Polish, Czech, and Slovenian associations are made up mainly of agriculturists.

Communal Loan Banks.
To some extent Austrian credit associations have found themselves forestalled by a far less perfect, specifically local, lending institution, the *Gemeindedarlehnskasse* (parish loan fund), the presence of which has more or less influenced their own development. The *Gemeindedarlehnskassen* are very numerous. Galicia alone has 2,521. They dispose of tolerably considerable funds, which were handed over to the parishes out of the compensation paid in exchange for peasant rights attaching to manor lands when feudal services and dual ownership were abolished. It very soon occurred to the inmates of the parishes so endowed—as it has occurred to the inhabitants of parishes in France receiving State compensation for failure of crops after the drought of 1893—that the funds placed at their disposal might with advantage be employed in occasional advances to the parishioners. A good deal of lending is done in this way. But it is not generally good lending. Borrowers claim the money as a matter of right, and have learnt to look upon the money borrowed as belonging to themselves, for which reason they often show themselves remiss in repayment. However, these *Darlehnskassen* have unquestionably given a stimulus to the formation of other more or less co-operative banks—in many cases, it is true, only very imperfectly co-operative—which are rather numerous in Austria.

Visitors to Carlsbad may see one such, rather a typical one, at Pirkenhammer. It has existed something like ten years, and has a paid-up share capital of 8,705 florins—243 shares distributed among 182 members—in addition to a reserve fund of 1,083 florins. The main reason given to me to explain why this bank had not adopted the Schulze-Delitzsch rules was, that members like having *more* shares than one. Besides, they do not appear to relish a very strict régime, more especially since all services are rendered gratuitously. Theirs is a very easy kind of lending. Pirkenhammer lives on Carlsbad, and in the season nets good earnings. So the lending practically resolves itself into an anticipation, during the slack winter months, of the earnings expected to be made in the brisker times—not a very provident kind of borrowing. Members can always borrow up to the amount of their shares, and should the bank require more money than it has, the provincial treasury at Prague is ready to assist it with funds. The annual business in lending amounts to about 43,000 florins.

The Austrian co-operative banks adopting the Schulze- Delitzsch system now probably number more than the 2,428 given by Dr Wrabetz in his last returns as the number for 1894. Generally speaking, the German credit associations of this type are strong in capital. Accordingly we must not be surprised to find limited liability more largely prevailing than in Germany. Of the 2,428 referred to above as many as 986 limit the liability of their members to the amount of their shares only, or, more generally, to a multiple of that figure. Of 117 associations sending in returns for the year 1894, 43—doing something less than a corresponding amount of business—were limited liability associations. These 117 associations had in 1894 a paid-up share capital (including reserve fund) of 7,235,743 florins, on the strength of which they had been able to borrow 40,324,255 florins. Of course the societies adopting limited liability are apparently strongest in capital of their own, which means, that they have been able to borrow least. Thus, among the limited liability associations in Styria, the proportion of share to borrowed capital is as 1 to 2.3. In Lower Austria and Moravia, where liability is unlimited, it is as 1 to 5.4 and 5.5. Not taking into account renewals, the 117 banks, it is shown, had lent out in the year 54,682,267 florins, which means, according to

German Credit Associations.

Dr Wrabetz's explanation, that, including renewals, they had probably lent out 80,000,000 or 85,000,000 florins—£6,400,000 to £6,800,000. That is not bad business. The losses appear to have been trifling. Of course the number includes bad and indifferent banks as well as good—the best presumably being members of the Union. Like their sister banks in Germany, of the same system, the Austrian associations are much encumbered with funds, which they do not quite know how to employ. It may be a useful hint to our own co-operative supply associations, similarly embarrassed, to quote Dr Wrabetz's opinion to the effect that this embarrassment is owing to the fact that co-operative production, which could provide ample and very legitimate employment for such funds, is insufficiently developed.

As a type of a good Austrian Schulze-Delitzsch bank, I will quote one which I have the authority of Dr Wrabetz himself for considering one of the very best of his Union. The Credit Association of Kaaden in Bohemia was founded in 1870 by sixty members. It now numbers more than 1,000. Among these there are 754 engaged in agriculture, from allotment holders up to owners of fairly considerable properties. The bank has a share capital of 159,924 florins (£12,800), and in 1894 lent out 871,979 florins (£69,800), not counting cash credits. Within twenty-five years its annual turnover has risen from £8,552 to £233,064. It has done a business of £3,635,908 (including £1,360,000 lent out on acceptances), and has lost in all not more than £128. Its business management is simple. It has tried the *castelletto*, which assigns to every member an available credit open without question, but has abandoned it as complicated, and now judges each application on its merits. In the place of Schulze's three, it has four members on the Committee, and, moreover, as many as twenty-four on the Council of Control. That of course ensures better supervision and inquiry. Its management expenses are very small—3,647 florins on 2,913,342 florins of turnover. Add to this 2,615 florins for rates and taxes, and you have a little over 2 per 1,000 as representing all establishment charges. The bank serves large and small without any distinction, granting a cash credit to a large landowner for more than £2,000, and advancing petty sums to small folk. It holds about £55,416 in savings deposits, for which it allows 4 per cent., charging 5 per cent. on purely personal and 4¾ per cent. on secured credit. Its large Council of Control, recruited from all parts of its area, enables it to serve an extended district (which nevertheless covers only half the ground of what is usual in Austria) without appointing local committees, or agents, or "men of confidence." Notwithstanding the comparatively small margin allowed between interest charged and interest given, this bank has on an average of the last ten years paid dividend at the rate of a trifle over 6 per cent. It has had credits offered to it by several large banks, but has been so well supplied with funds of its own as not to require them. There can be no doubt that this bank has rendered admirable service.

Very near it, at Schlackenwerth, is a credit association which shows the Schulze-Delitzsch system in a less attractive light. It is organised nominally on the identical principle, but with very much less of a co-operative spirit to apply the common regulations. It deliberately keeps down the number of its members, so as to secure a large profit. The Bank of Eger, again, not very far off, studies profit (10 per cent. dividend) by keeping down its share capital and borrowing very largely, much beyond what Dr Wrabetz considered safe. These instances of abuse of course do not stand altogether by themselves. Dr Wrabetz points out their danger with great persistency. He is urgent in recommending all round a limitation of dividend, the simplification of accounts, and an advance in respect of management in sympathy with advancing times.

Schlackenwerth.

Eger.

Credit Associations in Galicia. Speaking of abuses, a word or two may be due to the credit associations established in the province of Galicia. As has been already observed, credit associations are unquestionably strong in Galicia. But they are not credit associations of the most perfect type. Galicia is the chosen home of a peculiar race of Jews strongly given to profit-seeking. These men of course find their way into the banks, to such an extent that 50 per cent. of the members are said to be Jews, whereas there are only about 11 per cent. of Jews among the general population. Of 248 associations existing in 1891 (265 in 1892), the majority are said to have been officered and administered by Jews. Between 1890 and 1892 no fewer than sixty-three such associations were started specifically by Jews, to be managed by Jewish committees. It is of course fully as legitimate for Jews to join credit associations as for Christians, and for dealers of one kind as for dealers of another. And the partiality shown for co-operative credit associations by the sharp-witted Jews of Galicia goes a long way to establish the economic merit of the institution. However, there are two sides to the question, two uses to which credit associations may be put. And the high rates of interest prevailing among these Galician associations appear to suggest that among their members there are more than the average number who have found out the specifically weak point of the Schulze-Delitzsch system, and know how to turn it to account for their own advantage. The Galician credit associations are said not to stand in the best of odours with the general public, and to be considered as profit-mongering rather than co-operative. As a rule they occupy large districts, districts comprising from 80 to 120 parishes. The number of their members is stated (at New Year 1893) as 169,663, including 90,786 (54.6 per cent.) small agricultural freeholders. Their aggregate share capital is given as 5,373,039 florins, their reserve funds as 1,323,746 florins, their savings deposits as 15,592,948 florins, their loans raised as 4,529,405 florins, placing at their disposal a working fund of about £2,045,000. With the help of such resources the banks had in 1892 lent out collectively £2,040,504 only, but at such rates as to leave them a net profit of £38,936.

On the eastern bank of the Leitha, the Schulze-Delitzsch associations are as fully in the ascendant in comparison with Raiffeisen banks as in Austria. However, Dr von Jekelfalussy, the President of the Statistical Department of Hungary, refuses to recognise them as fully co-operative. Dr Wrabetz finds fault with them for departing to a serious extent from orthodox Schulze-Delitzsch rules, which probably means that, as in Galicia, they have become rather profit-earning institutions, for the benefit of the few, than co-operative, in the service of the many. The Statistical Year Book of Hungary for the year 1894 shows that in 1892, 658 credit associations were in existence, whereof 610 were in Hungary proper and 48 in Croatia and Slovenia. There is no information given as to membership or business. For 1891 there are, however, returns extant for 645 associations. These banks held among them 34,223,000 florins (£2,737,840) in share capital, 2,163,000 florins (£173,040) in reserves, accordingly 36,386,000 florins (£2,910,880) as collective working capital, and had at the close of the year 66,563,000 florins (£5,325,040) outstanding in credits. All these items show a very substantial increase upon the business of 1882. The credits have something like doubled. But the figures afford no clue whatever to the character of the business.

Schulze-Delitzsch Banks in Hungary.

Under the head of Austro-Hungary some special reference may perhaps appear due to a small group of associations of a peculiar type, in which membership is restricted to officers in the army and navy and civil servants, on active service or retired. There were, in 1887, 77 such, with a total capital

Army and Navy Loan Associations.

of 7,028,218 florins, and a reserve of 399,103 florins. The number of associations has decreased. There were in 1893 only 48 in Austria and 22 in Hungary—70 in all. But the share capital had grown to 9,753,285 florins, and the reserve funds to 656,848 florins. The amount outstanding in advances is given as 11,915,579 florins. As much as 997,402 florins had been taken in savings deposits, and 770,290 florins had been borrowed (including 640,334 florins from the Life Insurance Departments of the same associations at 4½ per cent. interest). These societies numbered in all 32,120 members.

Raiffeisen Banks. The Raiffeisen associations are far more sparingly developed in both halves of the monarchy. But they are multiplying rapidly, and have become very popular. They are individually very much smaller than the Schulze-Delitzsch institutions, so much so that Herr Siegl calculates one Schulze-Delitzsch association to be equal in number of members and financial strength to no less than thirty or forty Raiffeisen associations. The latter owe their remarkable recent increase and growing popularity in Austria, and to a lesser degree in Hungary, more specifically to an inquiry, which was set on foot as late as 1886. Since that date there has been a pitched battle going on in the Hapsburgh empire between the two systems. Very hard things have been publicly affirmed against the Schulze-Delitzsch system. It has been alleged that it has failed to satisfy the demands which it professes to meet. The administration of the associations, it has been stated, is not what it ought to be ; it has been said that there have been speculation, losses, excessive interest, disappointment, and disgust. In Lower Austria, the metropolitan province, a sharp attack made in the Diet resulted in a vote of funds granted, to

An Official Inquiry. enable two expert officers to proceed to the Rhine and examine on the spot the practical merits of the Raiffeisen system. They came back delighted with what they had seen. Their report was wholly favourable. And since that **The Result.** day the Raiffeisen associations are the official and popular favourites. Other provincial **Diets have followed** in the **footsteps** of the Lower **Austrian. The Austrian Chamber** of Deputies has taken favourable note of these associations, accepting Professor **Marchet's declaration** made in 1889, to the effect that **they** form "the only means known calculated to satisfy **personal credit** in a manner which could be approved." **Herr Schmid, one of** the auditors of the Austro-Hungarian **Bank, having** inquired carefully **into the** matter, added **his** testimony: that the Raiffeisen banks "are better calculated than any other form of association, in a **crisis such as** the peasantry, alike of Germany and of **Austria, have** never before been subjected **to,** to afford **efficient** assistance, **not only by actual money help,** but also **by** counsel, and instruction." With such recommendations **the** Raiffeisen banks **have pushed** their way rapidly to the front, spreading over **Lower and Upper** Austria, the Tyrol, **Styria, Carinthia,** Vorarlberg, Salzburg, Hungary, Transylvania, and other provinces, and ingratiating themselves wherever they went by good work. The provincial governments **were anxious to** encourage **and,** if possible, **to help** them. The question was, how to do it **in a legitimate way.** By votes of the various Diets, a grant of **250 florins** (about £19) **is made** to each association newly **formed, to** defray its first **expenses**—purchase of office furniture, a safe, books, and so on. And in addition to this, a loan of 2,000 florins (about £160) is placed at the disposal of every association so formed, at the rate of 3 per cent., for not longer than two years, to provide it with the first working **funds.** That moderate **advance appears to have** been found adequate, for the associations are everywhere showing signs **of** active life, multiplying and growing in strength. It **is a very** limited amount of help, but it **suffices** to set the **wheels** turning which, once in motion, provide **their own** further propelling impetus. The experiment is interesting, and its results have often been found satisfactory. In all these institutions, from the Raiffeisen and Schulze-Delitzsch firstling banks downward, it has always been the first step which involved the most serious difficulty. Here is a help which ought to be within reach of associations in most places, and which is scarcely open to serious economic objection, provided that repayment is rigorously insisted upon. On the other hand, no doubt, there is a rather serious drawback to this practice, of which we, of all people, whose rich men are so far more anxious to help with money than with work, will do well to take note. The subsidy is really not necessary. Banks can very well do without it. It may help, it may further and develop. But it is also liable to suggest abuse. Under this coddling system not a few *soi-disant* Raiffeisen banks are said to have grown up which are really only political agencies, or else started at the instance of a district administrator to secure him promotion or a decoration. In any case, the employment of such a forcing influence as has been spoken of ought to be applied only with great care and discrimination—better, I should say, not at all.

An Austrian Raiffeisen Bank.

Having given a sketch of the practice of a particular Schulze-Delitzsch bank, I may do well to quote in the same way an instance of well-conducted Raiffeisen banking, as a specimen of what is to be met with in Austria. The Raiffeisen Bank of Brunnersdorf, in Bohemia, close to Kaaden, was formed by Herr Hafenrichter in 1888, with the help of a subvention of 250 florins (£19) voted by the Estates of Bohemia, which grant is nominally repayable, but in fact is not claimed back. The population of Brunnersdorf consists almost exclusively of small peasant proprietors. There were at the outset only twenty-one members to join; there are now 110. The bank has, like most other Austrian associations of its type, issued shares of 10 florins

(16s.), and levies in addition an entrance-fee of one florin. By this means the little bank has gathered together a small share capital of 2,071 florins (£165), which it has strengthened by a reserve fund of 332 florins (£26), the result of five years' painstaking work. But it has attracted 41,233 florins (£3,296) of savings deposits, and has thus been enabled to lend out (in 1894, including renewals) 52,641 florins (£4,208) for varying terms, the longest of which is four years. As in our own country, there seems to be some difficulty in Bohemia about keeping the reserve fund untouched and inalienable on the dissolution of the society. But it is provided that in the event of dissolution the fund shall go to the parish. There have thus far been no losses. And there can be no doubt that, in its humble way, this bank is doing very useful service.

The Slavs appear to take less kindly to the system. In Galicia, where there is a good deal of supply co-operation, there were as late as 1892 only five Raiffeisen banks, all of them due to the propagandist initiative of Professor Stefezyk, of Czernichów, numbering among them 646 members, and having an aggregate share capital of only 614 florins (about £50), in addition to about £60 reserve fund. They had, however, taken no less than £3,228 in savings deposits, and lent out £3,168 in loans averaging 96 florins each, and had made no losses. <small>Slav Raiffeisen Banks.</small>

On the eastern bank of the Leitha, the stronghold of genuine Raiffeisenism is in Transylvania, where there are already about fifty Raiffeisen banks in all, formed and well maintained by the Saxon settlers in the country. These banks are to all intents and purposes genuine Raiffeisen banks, like those of the Rhine. Forty-seven of them, having among them 2,820 members, had at New Year 1894, 762,485 florins (£61,000) outstanding in loans, and 470,906 florins (£37,672) accumulated in savings deposits. By the side of this co-operative credit, a good deal of common supply is <small>Transylvania.</small>

done, and there are four vintners' associations, doubling the proceeds of their members by co-operation, just like their prototypes on the Rhine and Ahr. There are 301 members in these vintners' associations, which sell annually about 20,000 florins' (£1,600) worth of wine.

Hybrid Banks in the County of Pesth. Whatever good the agricultural credit banks of the county of Pesth, established within the last ten years by Count Alexander Karolyi and his helpmate, Dr Bernát, may be doing within their own sphere, it is not altogether accurate to speak of them as "Raiffeisen Banks." On the showing of their own officers, their system represents something of a "cross" between the Raiffeisen and the Schulze systems, which means, that they depend to a somewhat larger extent, than do the Raiffeisen banks proper, upon share-capital, as contrasted with liability only. In a theoretical aspect they may be said to resemble the associations formed in Germany by Herr Haas—with this difference, that the majority of them have, up to the present time, limited the liability of members. Evidently the large landowners, who were mainly instrumental in creating these banks, were afraid of unlimited liability, applied to themselves—just as our big men, zealous for the formation of "Agricultural Banks" in this country, are manifestly afraid of it. Our would-be "Raiffeisenists" invented the anti-Raiffeisen rule about honorary membership as a safeguard to themselves and to others of their class—entitling big folk to come into the bank as patrons, with much social influence, and to direct the management, without making themselves liable, except to pay a subscription, the amount of which may be regulated, and the value of which may be dispensed, according to the varying merit—from a subjective point of view, which may be political—of the members. The Hungarian apostles of this useful but, to my mind, only half-bred Raiffeisenism, started their Central Bank, originally endowed by themselves, and kept under their own control, to supply the local banks with funds. This is the "supporting central institution" of which Dr von Jekelfalussy speaks (as quoted by me in my first edition, p. 47), as enabling "Raiffeisen Banks" to subsist without unlimited liability. The Central Bank has a share-capital of 500,000 florins (£40,000), issued in 100 florin shares, of which at the end of 1894, only about 300 (£2,400) were held by societies. The larger portion by far remained in the hands of individuals, the original promoters. The objection to this half-and-half system is, that it does not produce quite the same results as genuine Raiffeisenism. It does not make members of local banks rely to the same extent upon their own powers and their own efforts; it "gives," instead of stimulating self-help; it does not act as an educator; it does not make its votaries "an honest and industrious family." Our pseudo-Raiffeisenists in England ought to take warning by this. M. György, who attended the International Co-operative Congress in London, states in his Report that, notwithstanding the limitation of dividend payable on Central Bank shares to 4 per cent., laid down in the rules, there is "a disposition observable" to transforming these "Raiffeisen Banks" into "ordinary trading banks"— just as has happened among deteriorated Schulze-Delitzsch Associations. Accordingly, I am not sorry to learn from Dr Bernát, the Secretary of the Federation, that a spirit of more genuine Raiffeisenism is likewise making itself observable, that under its influence unlimited liability is spreading, and that the genuine Raiffeisen banks formed on this system "are working till now quite well." Under the circumstances one is entitled to hope that the more co-operative principle, which scorns "support," and trusts solely to "self-help," will extend and become before long the predominant feature. The number of agricultural credit banks of the type just described, all situated in the county of Pesth, stood at the close of 1895 at 317, having 63,220 members, with

Objection to their System.

125,856 shares issued, to the collective value of 3,332,937 florins (£266,635), of which money, however, only 1,338,928 florins (£107,113) was paid up. To this must be added, to arrive at the total amount of working funds, 90,786 florins (£7,263) reserve funds, and 1,293,396 florins (£103,471) deposits. All these figures show a remarkable advance upon those given for 1894. The number of members (and shares) has almost exactly doubled. The year's transactions balance at 7,918,106 florins (£633,448), allowing for a profit of 116,364 florins (£9,309). The loans outstanding, on bills of exchange and otherwise, figure at 7,633,069 florins (£610,647).

Co-operative Banking in Sweden, Norway, and Denmark. In the three Northern Kingdoms whose shores are washed by the cold waters of the Baltic and the North Sea, co-operative credit has thus far thriven but poorly. There have been beginnings and strugglings; and here and there a bank, raised up when, under the influence of the Schulze-Delitzsch triumphs in Germany, the co-operative fit was on the nation, has lived down to the present day. But, generally speaking, amid the sparse populations of SWEDEN, NORWAY, and DENMARK, little fruit of such sort has been brought to perfection. In countries in which in other respects co-operation has become a power, on soil which has brought forth such picturesque co-operative specialities as the Swedish *bergslags* and forges, and, again, such excellently organised associations as the Danish building societies and co-operative dairies, one would have looked for better things. But the working population—of Sweden, at any rate, so Herr C. Krook contends—with their natural contentedness and their ample wages, are too comfortably off to stand in serious need of funds. There is Mr L. O. Smith's *Aktiebolaget Arbetaringens Bank*, of course, and there are in Sweden some thirty People's Banks, in Denmark much fewer, and in Norway scarcely any beyond the *Kristiania Folksbank*, all doing more banking than loaning.

OFFSHOOTS AND CONGENERS. 177

However, all these kingdoms have something to show which in some manner or other congenial to local ways takes the place of People's Banks. Some means of popular credit, it appears, there must be. Denmark, in addition to a few Credit Unions of the Belgian type, possesses some fairly useful "Aid Associations" and *Monts de Piété*. Norway has Savings Banks, which lend out money pretty largely, chiefly amongst small folk—as would appear from the fact that only 18 per cent. of the loans granted exceed £28 each. And in Sweden, banks provide the poor with what they want by means of the *Kassakreditiv*, an institution of local origin which has become very popular, alike with public and with private banks, for loans of small amount. Not many years ago the accounts opened in this manner amounted in public banks to £1,112,000, in private to £5,600,000.

In the NETHERLANDS co-operative credit has fared little better, owing to entirely different causes. As in the days of Louis XIV., it appears, the Low Countries are still the El Dorado of *marchands de boutique*, the traders, who will allow no one to interfere with their monopoly. Co-operation there is as unpopular as is Judaism in Vienna, and almost as fiercely persecuted. "The opposition of Colonial dealers and other retail tradesmen against co-operative associations," so writes Dr Elias in the *Blätter für Genossenschaftswesen*, "has reached such a pitch that it has become next to impossible for a member of a co-operative association to have himself elected into a Town Council, into the Assembly of Provincial Estates, or into the Second Chamber." Fortunately for co-operation, there is a First Chamber to hold its protecting hand over the poor outlaws, and a Crown to afford them some little sanctuary. The admirably organised societies *Eigen Hulp* and *Nederlandsche Cooperatieve Bond* are now fighting the battle of the co-operative cause with so much success, that without being over-sanguine we may probably look for some early

Co-operative Banking in the Netherlands.

M

development in the direction of co-operative banking, for which there is unquestionably room, more especially in the country districts. At the present time there are one or two very useful little working-men's credit associations, something after the style of our "Slate Clubs," collecting 10d. a month from every member, till the sum reaches 75 florins (£6. 5s.). After that the money is distributed. These associations do some lending to members out of their own funds and funds obtained from deposits (which are taken from 2d. upwards), on which 4 per cent. is allowed to members and $3\frac{1}{2}$ per cent. to non-members; and some of them are Raiffeisenites so far as to insist that the object of the loan shall be stated beforehand, and rigidly adhered to, on pain of forfeiture of the loan. Repayment is exacted by instalments, and interest is charged at the rate of 1 per cent. per ten weeks, that is, $5\frac{1}{5}$ per cent. per annum. A rather commendable feature is this, that on earlier repayment than what is stipulated for (just as among our best Loan Societies) a rebate is allowed, varying from $\frac{1}{3}$ to $\frac{1}{2}$ per cent.*

Co-operative Banking in Russia.

It is very interesting to watch the gropings of RUSSIA —in one aspect one of the oldest homes of co-operation in Europe—after an efficient and popular system of cooperative credit, to supply that working capital which is nowhere more urgently needed. There have been many tentative beginnings, such as, in the country of the *artèles*,† one would have thought, must have led to some satisfactory result. But the country is as yet still too much in Government uniform for anything to succeed in which self-

---

* While these sheets are passing through the press I learn that two Raiffeisen Banks, the first in their country, have quite recently been opened in the Netherlands, one at Bergum, the other at Oenkerk.

† These have recently, very late in the day, attracted some notice in this country. What has been published in English is thus far of very little value, and very belated. The *artèles* are not really co-operative associations in our sense.

help forms an essential factor. Some of the early experiments, indeed, were **not** without promise. "*La Russie marche bien*," wrote M. **Brelay, a** little more than a decade ago, in the *Economiste Français*. And in 1883 Russia could boast that **she had** exactly 1,000 co-operative associations, with 207,259 members and £1,216,960 share capital, and lending out in the year £3,819,920. Since that **time, however,** things have gone backwards. The **number of associations** has dwindled from 1,000 to below **800.*** In truth, even the 1,000 had more **of** show about them than **of** reality. It is Government harassing—the hard-and-fast **rules forced upon** associations from above, **interference, supervision, and** restriction—which **is** killing co-operation. **How** possibly can credit co-operation succeed while the Government categorically forbids associations **to expel** members? How is **it to** keep **so much as** solvent while members, being indeed limited in their borrowing to "productive" purposes only, are allowed to evade that wholesome provision by first improvidently disposing of their "productive" possessions, in order then to have an excuse for claiming association money for their re-acquisition? That seems a device specially contrived to facilitate improvident borrowing. Thirsty moujiks know well enough how **to** adapt **their practice to** so accommodating **a** rule. They sell their **seed-corn, their**

---

* **The latest returns published quote** 764 as **the** figure **of** credit associations **now existing in Russia.** Of that number, 638, scattered **over 280** "districts," **are shown to comprise** collectively 211,400 members. Co-operative banking appears to have pushed its way into Siberia, and even into Central Asia. **There are said to be** 21 credit associations in the department of Tobolsk alone. Of the credit associations mentioned 455 are reported **to** be rural banks, 175 urban, and 32 associations composed of employees of distinct industrial establishments. The collective lending done **in** the past year is returned as 28,000,000 roubles (more than £3,000,000), which is an advance upon the figures of previous **years.**

horse or their cow, and, having orthodoxly got through the sale money in vodka, they have a splendid pretext for falling back upon the funds provided by philanthropic capitalists. Since the law prohibits the taking from them of their horse, their cow, cart, sleigh, harness, implements, farm buildings, seed-corn up to twenty-five *pouds*, clothes, and food and fuel sufficient for one month's use, in satisfaction of any debt, in this little manœuvre they are perfectly safe. The whole thing has been turned into a farce and a caricature of self-help.

Co-operation made a fairly good start in Russia among the German settlers under the Empress Catherine. Since then the Crown has tried its hand at the problem. Great nobles like Count Araktschejeff have done the same; and M. de Louguinine, a zealous and genuinely philanthropic disciple of Schulze-Delitzsch, some time back devoted himself with fervent earnestness to the charitable work. He may be regarded as the "father" of modern Russian credit co-operation, such as it is. Other good men have bestirred themselves—M. Khitrowo, M. Jakowlew, M. Van der Vliet, M. Stokolowski, Dr von Keussler, and more besides. Yet with all this the movement has made but little way except among the Germans in the Baltic provinces. This is an exception which fully proves what everybody who has looked into the matter insists upon, outside Russia and in it—namely, that it is Government interference which fatally checks the movement. Give it but a little liberty, as in the Baltic provinces, and at once it thrives according to circumstances. There were in 1892 in the Baltic coast-land sixty-nine associations, not including some Raiffeisen associations newly formed. Dr von Keussler, in the *Baltische Wochenschrift*, owns to an opinion that the latter are far better qualified than the Schulze-Delitzsch societies to prosper in his own country. The Schulze-Delitzsch associations, he objects, are not at all suited to local circumstances. Outside the **Baltic provinces**, in spite of very zealous encouragement given by the *landschaften*, by nobles, and by Government authorities, credit co-operation can be said to be only vegetating in a languid way, losing more ground than it gains.* Of the 1,438 associations formed in all, less than 800 survive. Of these, some years ago, 699 sent in returns for the year 1890, showing a members' roll of 200,950, a collective share capital of 6,160,391 roubles, and a reserve of 1,274,426 roubles. A larger number of associations (728) reported a total business (money spent and money received) of 79,062,058 roubles; and 722 reported loans issued to the amount of 16,067,929 roubles. For a country like **Russia** that is nothing. And yet it cannot be said that the instinct of the people is opposed to co-operation. Education, no doubt, is deficient, and that is a hindrance. Poverty is great. But in other applications of the principle, Russians show themselves born co-operators. Not a work is undertaken but the men form themselves into a co-operative *artèle*, and that institution works, on the whole, very well. The one fatal obstacle in the way of success of co-operative credit is Government interference, kindly intended, no doubt, but of its very essence so inimical to co-operation that where it is the other cannot thrive.

If Russia is backward in co-operation, its neighbour and whilom protégé **Servia** has in the brief time of its independence set a brilliant example to other nations by organising co-operation, and more particularly co-operative banking, with a degree of assiduity and success which certainly deserve commendation. Servia needed co-operative credit, for usurers were fleecing its peasantry—that is to say, the great bulk of the nation—to the tune of 400, 500,

Co-operative Banking in Servia.

---

* The "Peasants' Banks" of Russia and Poland are not credit institutions in our sense. They are mortgage banks, facilitating the purchase of land.

and even 1,000 per cent. of interest, to such an extent that the Skuptchina felt itself called upon to interfere, and, to prevent all Servia from being swallowed up by the greedy money-dealers, to pass a law wholly anomalous in principle, which vests *all* property in land nominally in the State. Mortgaging and selling are accordingly made impossible without the consent of the authorities. This extraordinary law, for a wonder, is held to have worked well, and to have accomplished its end—thanks, I should say, to the concurrent creation of convenient institutions for providing credit on more reasonable terms. Servia is a country with only about 2,000,000 inhabitants, 99 per cent. of whom are engaged in agriculture, the majority—that is, about 79 per cent.—being occupiers of holdings of from 5 to 25 acres (of land not nearly in the same state of cultivation as ours), 15 per cent. of holdings of from 25 to 50 acres, and only 5 per cent. owning larger properties. With such a population, almost exclusively agricultural, Servia finds business not only for a National (Issue) Bank and three ordinary commercial banks, but in addition for no less than sixty-three (urban) People's Banks, and, moreover, already for sixteen agricultural banks. Probably there are by this time more. All these institutions are of recent growth; for co-operation never entered into Servia till about two decades ago. And some of them are not over-sound. Co-operative banking is, it may be added, practically the one form of co-operation thus far developed in the kingdom. There have been some supply associations, which, being badly organised, have collapsed. There is some little co-operative production —tailoring and shoemaking and the like—but it does not amount to much. Trade is in Servia all on a small scale, and it is actually decreasing. There are no large factories; all is petty trade, very much in want of money; and it was for its relief that co-operative banking was first introduced. The first Servian People's Bank was formed at Belgrade in

1881. In point of organisation it resembles, like its sister establishments subsequently established, the French and Italian type of banks rather than the German. The Servian law allows no unlimited liability, accordingly liability had to be limited from the outset to the actual amount of the share. An entrance fee is exacted, and the share is made payable by instalments of 50 centimes a month. There is no limit to the number of shares which a member may hold, and as business is profitable, and there is no limit set to the rate of dividend—which frequently rises to 10 per cent., and at present stands, for the Belgrade Bank, pretty steadily at 15 per cent.—such freedom of purchase has led to a sad abuse. Investments are scarce in Servia, and no investment is reckoned so safe as a share in the Belgrade People's Bank. Accordingly rich members have bought up shares to the number of 200, 300, and even 1,000 each, practically converting the concern into a joint-stock business. The Managing Committee is in this bank, as in the others, large, comprising fifteen members in the place of Schulze's three. On the other hand, the Council of Supervision consists of only seven. And five members of the Committee are continually told off to act as a "Committee of Discount," which has to decide what bills are to be discounted. The Servian law is very liberal in respect of acceptances, which are given as a matter of course by professional as well as commercial men. Accordingly acceptances constitute the favourite form under which loans are negotiated. Interest is high in Servia. Accordingly from 7 to 9 per cent. is charged on loans. The People's Bank of Belgrade has a paid-up capital of 1,205,000 francs, with 205,000 francs reserve (£56,400 in all). Its holding in savings deposits (on which from 4 to 5 per cent. is allowed) a year ago amounted to 2,800,000 francs, and it had 2,200,000 francs outstanding in loans. The other sixty-two banks are very similar in organisation and practice;

but there is in every case some little peculiar feature of practice to distinguish one from the other. Some lend to members only, others also to non-members. Among them the sixty-three banks* hold 10,184,400 francs in paid-up capital, and 958,680 francs in reserve funds. The number of their members is 43,120.

Not to speak of other quasi-co-operative institutions designed to facilitate common holding of land and common labour of various kinds—zadrouga, moba, pozaimitsa, spreg, and batchié—to provide agricultural populations with loan money, Servia possesses one agricultural "bank" and fifteen "caisses." The difference between the two orders is this, that the former is based upon limited liability, and is more of a business bank; the latter is based on unlimited liability, and very much restricted in its business. To bring themselves under unlimited liability, which the Servian law disallows, the *caisses* have had to bind themselves under a special law of "contract." The oldest of these institutions, the "bank" of Smédérévo, was formed by M. Michel Avramovitch, who is really the leader and the soul of the movement, in August 1893. Nominally it has 10,000 shares of 100 francs each. In truth, only 2,500 of those shares have been issued and paid up. And it deserves to be noticed that the principal shareholders are not the persons for whose direct benefit the bank is really designed, but public authorities. The "department" holds 1,000 shares; each of the seven "arrondissements" of the department holds some shares; the 118 "communes" of the district come next; and actually only 600 shares are

---

* The banks are distributed among different departments as follows:—Belgrade has 7; Nich, 5; Valievo, 5; Vrania, 3; Kragouevats, 8; Kraina, 1; Krouchevats, 3; Morava, 4; Pirot, 2; Podrinie, 3; the Danube, 7; Pojarevats, 6; Roudnik, 3; Timok, 1; Toplitsa, 1; Oujitse, 2; and Tserna Réka, 2.

allotted to *bonâ fide* members—peasants, tradesmen, &c. The bank does practically every kind of business, lending on acceptances or notes of hand, and also making small loans of "honour" to very poor people. The peasantry will not pledge their produce. They consider that *infra dig.* The bank has a Managing Committee of ten members, every one of whom must be a resident in Smédérévo, so as to be handy for attendance. Moreover, there is a Council of Control of five, three being likewise residents in the town, two named by the country members from among themselves; and, moreover, there are representatives of the several arrondissements, four to each arrondissement, to watch the business on behalf of their particular constituents. The bank is not allowed to lend to one single member beyond five times his holding in shares. The lending is done dearly, at 7 or 8 per cent. On the other hand, the bank allows 5 or 6 per cent. on savings, the higher rate on the smallest savings, in order to stimulate thrift. It maintains school savings banks in every large school, issuing halfpenny (five centimes) savings cards, which are handed in as deposits as soon as the twenty squares, standing collectively for a franc, are filled up. On the 30th of June last the bank held no less than 113,662.70 francs in savings, 2,340 francs being contributed by school children. The bank has become a parent of smaller banks (*caisses*), which it supports throughout its department by opening to them credit at 7 per cent., the ordinary bank rate. All these *caisses* are village banks of the Raiffeisen type—without entrance fee, without shares, with gratuitous services, small districts, and an accumulating reserve fund. The oldest of them was founded at Vranovo in March 1894. It has only sixty-two members. Vranovo is a village with a population of 1,560, of whom the majority belong to the smaller class of peasantry. Having a credit opened to it by the Smédérévo Bank of 8,000 francs, and taken 345 francs in savings, this little *caisse* lent out within seven and a half months (15th May to 31st December) 8,150 francs in thirty loans, at what will appear to us an exorbitant rate of interest—namely, 9 per cent. However, since it borrowed the money at 7, the margin cannot be pronounced excessive. The second *caisse* was founded in Azagna in April 1894. It has 226 members, and had within a year taken 5,309.75 francs in savings, including 265.80 francs from school children.

There can be no doubt that these banks are in their humble way doing economic good, though the bulk of the good to be done is of course still to come. As regards their educational results I cannot resist the temptation to translate from M. Avramovitch's Report the following record:—

"Peasants who used to spend their days in the public-house, playing cards and boozing, have thrown off that habit. In the village of Rattarée, before a bank was there called into being, the publican paid 480 francs rent for his café, and did well. This year scarcely could he be brought to pay the parish, which owns the café, as much as 210 francs. And even on that lower rent he has made a loss. One day, making the round of our village banks, I went into the tavern of the village in which I happened to stop, and there the publican at once began complaining to me about the distress in which he had been landed, since scarcely any one now comes to his inn, either to drink or to play cards. And indeed, whereas at other times I have in this inn seen plenty of beer, wine, absinthe, and other liquor about, this time I found none. In the village of Mihailovatz there used to be two inns; but one has had to close its doors at New Year. On one occasion a member of a village bank has been seen playing cards and losing four francs. He was brought before the Committee and summarily expelled. Other members, who were suspected of indulging in play, took warning, and are now rarely to be seen in the public-house. Throughout Servia the municipal elections serve as an occasion for fighting and quarrelling. Wherever village banks have been established, the elections now pass off in perfect peace and good feeling. The Annual Report of the Managing Committee of the Village Bank of Azagna says on this point: 'Our association has drawn us together and made us friends of one another, as should be the case amongst honest and well-conditioned folk. It has taught us to respect one another and to help one another, to enable each to live better and to work better. In little time it has made us learn many useful things which our schools have failed to teach us.' Our schoolmasters and priests (*popes*), who were formerly political agitators, have become agitators for the cause of co-operation. In one year only Servia has seen fifteen village banks start up in three Departments. There would be more if the ordinary banking establishments would open their credit to our *caisses*. They have now promised to introduce provisions providing for this into their rules at their next annual meetings. No doubt the parishes as well will find means of employing their large capitals now invested in various stocks and effects for the benefit of agriculture by the interposition of our village banks."

Servia's neighbour, ROUMANIA, has likewise already begun to organise some village banks about which I have no data.* *In Roumania.*

In the IBERIAN peninsula, to which we owe some of the earliest examples of combination for purposes of credit, such as the *compañia gallega* and the *sociedade familiar*, self-help has, in its modern application, thus far made very little headway indeed. In PORTUGAL, where, according to Senhor Goodolphim, interest runs high—for accommodation loans for poor people up to 100 and 200 per cent.—and where usury is rampant (Lisbon alone boasts sixty-five pawnshops), a formal resolution in favour of cheap credit has been put on record by the Agricultural Congress held in 1888, calling upon the Government to place funds for lending out at the rate of $3\frac{1}{2}$ per cent. at the disposal of *In Spain and Portugal.*

---

* The Ottoman Empire has an "Agricultural Bank," which is to lend out such money as it can to small cultivators at the rate of 6 per cent. per annum, and for terms varying from three months to ten years. The cultivators themselves contribute towards the funds of this bank, but not by any means in a co-operative way, but rather by way of a tax, until the total reaches 200,000,000 francs, which point is still a long way off. I do not know whether the Co-operative Association of Sarona (Jaffa), formed under the German Co-operative Law, and registered at the German Consulate, engages in banking.

cultivators. This request will probably be acceded to when there is found to be sufficient public money available. In SPAIN, where Señor Diaz de Rabago informs us that amid a general lassitude there is so little demand for money that even usurers cannot obtain more than 10 or 20 per cent. for loans, things have not yet matured so far. The *Monti de Piedad* cannot find borrowers enough to take their ready cash off their hands, and, incredible as it may appear, for a good spell of time there was a treasure of 189,697,026 reals (£1,900,000) available in the country for popular credit (£84,000 being in cash), of which from the Crown downward nobody had the slightest inkling. On the 15th of August 1849, the Minister of Finance, having chanced to read in a history book an account of the wealth of the ancient *Positos* which must have made his mouth water, caused an inquiry to be addressed to the provincial authorities asking if there were any such institutions still in existence. There was no answer returned. In 1850 the inquiry was repeated. After a good deal of searching and rummaging, at length in 1863 it was discovered that there were still 3,418 *positos* surviving, possessing among them the treasure already mentioned. The institution is so peculiar that I do not like passing it by without a brief notice, albeit it is not based on either self-help or co-operation, but really represents what to some economists is the *beau ideal* of a public aid institution, a fund belonging to no one, and devoted wholly to lending among the poor. The Portuguese have in times past possessed similar loan-funds, going by the name of *celleiros communs*. But these have long disappeared from the face of the earth. For its *positos* Spain is beholden to King Philip II., who somewhere about 1555 or 1556 set the example of founding them all over the country. They were originally really granaries, over which were set public officers having orders to distribute corn from them in time

The Spanish Positos.

of famine to the poor **at their discretion**, on condition, of course, **of** its being returned. **Spain** was rich then, and pious, and hundreds of people followed the king's example. The Cardinal **de** Belluga alone founded thirty-two *positos* in Murcia. Cardinal Cisneros founded two very large ones, severally **in** Alcala and in Torrelaguna. In 1558 there were some twelve thousand in existence. In 1584 the king ordered an inquiry into their wealth and administration. The value of the corn stored is said to have been something prodigious. But the administration **was** anything but perfect. When famine came, the Governors, with a sound commercial instinct, lent away what grain was available *to themselves*, selling it afterwards to the **poor at** high prices. This was **soon** put a stop to, and the *positos* **went** on flourishing till, **what** with the ravages of wars and revolutions and the growing needs of the Crown, serious inroads were made upon them, materially reducing **both** their number and their wealth. When Napoleon I. overran the land, the small balance remaining was prudently hid away for safety —and then was forgotten, to be unearthed once more in 1863. By a law passed in 1887 the administration has been completely reformed. The treasure has all been converted into money, which the *gobernador civil* of each province is at liberty to lend out at the rate of ½ per cent. per month at his own discretion—but also more or less **on his own** responsibility, which he takes care to safeguard by demanding sureties or other security from the borrower. According to Señor de Rabago's testimony, the *positos* are now doing fairly good work, though it is not certain whether they will be allowed to do so for very long. **For not a** few economic reformers appear **to have cast** a covetous eye upon their treasure with a view to other employment. The *Monti de Piedad* do a great deal of lending, though only a comparatively small portion of it to poor people, for whom their service was intended. In 1890, out of £2,320,000 money available, they advanced on pledges only £320,000, seeking a market for the other £2,000,000 among the better-to-do classes. In the rural districts the joint-stock *Banco Agricolo de Segovia* has begun a promising business of popular lending, for long terms (seven years), at reasonable rates, and in very small amounts, down to £2. The borrowing is made particularly easy by a rule adopted, which indeed demands that the principal shall be repaid by annual instalments, but allows two years of grace during which only interest is collected. In such small loans, never exceeding £40, the Bank has in eight years lent out, to the poor cultivators of the *métayer* and *enfiteuta* class, £586,700, and has, according to the testimony of its managing director, Don C. Lecea y Garcia, never lost a farthing.

Modern Co-operative Banking.

There are, as Don Joaquin Diaz de Rábago informs me, some more agricultural banks of the same type in Spain, and there are some tiny beginnings of ostensibly co-operative credit, which generally take the shape of money clubs or friendly societies, or else carry on mere joint-stock business under a name speciously suggesting co-operation, for the benefit of a few shareholders who admit subscribers or "adherents" to borrowing benefits, without allowing them a voice in the management. Of such institutions is the *Banco Agrícola y Urbano de Valencia*, formed only in 1893, about the business of which there are no data extant. To quote some further instances, the following societies—*La Protección mútua*, of Madrid (composed of civil servants); *El Crédito Obrero*, of Valencia; *La Previsora*, of Onteniente; *La Labrador*, of Alcalá del Rio; *La Constancia*, of Bujalance; *La Cassa de Ahorros y Préstamos del Cuerpo de Telégrafos*, and several others, in addition to a small number of *montepios* (which appear to be a speciality of the province of Valencia), are all of them money clubs rather than co-operative banks, inasmuch as they collect monthly or weekly subscriptions, which they employ in making loans. **The** Civil Service Society of Madrid appears to be doing well. **It collects 5 pesetas (4s.) a** month from each member. **In 1889** its capital stood at 68,075 pesetas (£2,322), plus **a reserve fund of 3,394 pesetas (£136).** It had a turnover of 179,000 pesetas (£7,160), **and netted a** profit of 7,652 pesetas (**£306**). Its management expenses did not exceed **20 pesetas (16s.) in** the twelvemonth. Quite recently **a** society has been formed, under the name of *La Unión Obrera Balear*, for the purpose of diffusing information respecting associations designed **to** benefit working men, and of forming such in the Balearic Islands. Among **such** societies are: savings **banks, co-operative workshops and** supply societies, classes for instruction, **societies for** procuring in **common medical** assistance and **medicines,** funds to insure working men against labour **accidents,** orphan **asylums, and, lastly, genuine** credit associations **or co-operative banks. But** thus far all these things appear **to have advanced no further** than a well-intended programme.

Asia has its rudimentary beginnings of co-operative credit, very imperfect, providing a happy hunting-ground for the dividend-hunter, **but** nevertheless satisfactory as affording proof, not of the existence of want—of that unfortunately **there can be** no doubt—but of the appropriateness of the co-**operative** remedy, and of a predisposition among the **natives to adopt it,** even in **the** "Sleepy Presidency." **The "nidhis," of which Mr** F. A. Nicholson gives a full **account in his admirably compiled Blue-Book** on "Land and **Agricultural** Banks," are **a sort of money club not a little in use** in the presidency of Madras. **They very much** resemble the United States "building **societies," and started** up first about the "fifties" **as** a modern development of **an** older indigenous **institution, the** Kûttan Chit. There are now, **according** to the Registrar's return, 135 such "nidhis" **in existence.** But there have been many more. **For, some years** ago, when

India: The "Nidhis."

the promotion fever was high, the societies started up like mushrooms—one may almost say by the hundred—only to perish as rapidly. The "nidhis" collect money from their members by monthly subscriptions, and, to have more funds to deal with, they take deposits. The moneys so accumulated they lend out, most generally putting the loan up to auction, and letting it go to the highest bidder. That makes the "nidhis" a rather remunerative investment, paying as a rule $7\frac{1}{2}$ per cent. in interest. For the directors there are further benefits, because these gentlemen vote themselves and the secretary—who appears to be the great swallower of all—very substantial salaries. And since the control exercised is anything but perfect, and proceedings under the Companies Act are not altogether simple, there appears to be ample scope for further abstractions without any danger to the abstractors. Malversations are accordingly said to be frequent. The most grasping of these "nidhis," or sham "nidhis," are popularly known as "lubbucks," which means "gulpers" or "devourers," and seems to be the Indian equivalent for "Shylock." There are other grounds on which people's bankers may well object to having the "nidhis" classed as "People's Banks." They do not, as a rule, lend for productive purposes, but to provide a dowry for a marriage, or a fund wherewith to purchase jewellery, or defray the expense of some domestic ceremony. The loaning appears to be generally done for long terms, as much as eighty-four months being not unusual—on the understanding that repayments shall take place by regular instalments. The interest is described as high, ranging from $6\frac{1}{4}$ to $18\frac{1}{2}$ per cent., with $37\frac{1}{2}$ per cent. in reserve as "penal interest," in case of default, which is probably not infrequent. The 135 "nidhis" now existing have among them a nominal capital of 2,33,81,933 rupees, on which one-third is paid up. No statistics are given as to the lending done. It is intimated that very much more could be lent out than there is, if only sufficient money could be provided. No doubt the "nidhis" would provide a useful foundation upon which to rear up some more perfect fabric. The difficulty appears to be, that lenders and borrowers in them form distinct classes.

I do not like concluding my stroll through the Diaspora of Credit Co-operation without just mentioning the co-operative banking of which General Tcheng-ki-Tong some years ago told a Paris audience as having been practised time out of mind in his native country of China, and more particularly in the specifically agricultural districts, such as his own native province, Fo-kien. He does not explain their work in detail, but he calls them *banques mutuelles*, and he assures us that they have yielded exceedingly satisfactory results, without the drawback of any misadventure. They agree in this with Raiffeisen banks that they are allotted severally only small districts. General Tcheng-ki-Tong is careful to explain that his countrymen positively will have none but such. They will not be fellow-members with persons whom they do not know personally, and of whose doings they are not accurately informed. Once they are satisfied on this head, they willingly incur any amount of liability, the one for the other. No small peasant, the General goes on to say, who wants to carry out some structural or agricultural improvement is ever at a loss for money. In his own little district his neighbours know him, and if he is considered trustworthy, they do not hesitate to let him have what he wants. Under all circumstances, supposing him to have been elected, he is entitled to borrow twice the amount of his own share. Money seems plentiful, because all the local savings find their way into the bank. The peasants are, according to the General's description, generally prudent and shrewd, and, understanding the value of agricultural improvements, they are not loath to let others have what they themselves

China.

are sure to want some day. A Chinese proverb has it that "The land is the great debtor of the nation," absorbing all its surplus money. And in practice it is found a safe debtor, who repays the money lent to him with ample interest. Much of that proverbial productiveness for which the popular districts of China have become famous, and that never-resting industry of its people—which there, as everywhere, requires the stimulus of a reward to keep it moving—the Empire of the Rising Sun is shown to owe to the simple but useful contrivance of co-operative credit established among its toilsome peasantry, and providing them with the material on which to expend their ready labour. In a humble and unostentatious way these banks are said to have done, each in its own sphere, an immense amount of good.

Japan.

In the past year Japan has made some progress towards following in the footsteps of China. For in its island realm Heizo Ittō, a disciple of Signor Luzzatti, has constituted himself the apostle of co-operative banking among his own countrymen with, it is said, every prospect of success. And so the girdle of co-operative credit seems to have been slung pretty well round the globe; for in America likewise such credit is understood to have already tentatively planted its foot, by way of first seizure of the territory, with every intention, as it appears, to stay.

CHAPTER IX.

THE "*BANCHE POPOLARI*" OF ITALY.

FROM an English point of view, no form of co-operative credit established abroad is likely to command a greater amount of interest than that which has found a congenial home in Italy. That country, when M. Luzzatti began his excellent work, stood in sore need of popular credit. Usury was rampant, and no less exacting than when in 1430 the Seignory of Florence had found itself compelled to call in the aid of the Jews, to check by their intervention the extortionate rapacity of Christian money-lenders — and, again, when, a little later in the same century, three Franciscan friars, in pity for the suffering poor, gave to the world the valuable institution of the Monti di Pietà, which to us are known only in their deteriorated form. In the nineteenth century, according to Commendatore Luzzatti, it behoved Democracy to render to the poor the service which in days of greater youth and union the Church had discharged, and to draw its sword for "War with Usury" (*guerra all' usura*).

Why Italian Co-operative Banking should specially Interest us.

Moreover, the country was commercially undeveloped. Protracted divisions and oppression had kept it poor in the main sources of national production. The country which had taught all nations banking possessed little commerce; the country in which the Georgics were written owned an agriculture little advanced upon that which Virgil had described. Many attempts had been made to provide help. As Spain had her *positos*, so Italy had her *monti frumentari*,

Past Attempts to create Popular Credit.

her *monti nummari*, and *monti dei paschi*.* Governments had sought to furnish assistance in their own paternal way, and even while Commendatore Luzzatti was taking up his economic apostleship, ministers like MM. Torelli and Grimaldi might be heard strenuously urging banks and public corporations to make their funds available for the rescue of the needy. The measures taken had the effect of bringing relief in the shape of reasonable credit to some *large* proprietors. But to the poor their result was *nil.* All this Government and capitalist meddling and peddling evidently was powerless to ensure real and lasting improvement.

The Italian Savings Banks.

Better success had attended the useful reconnoitring work which two different classes of banks had tentatively ventured upon in the field of popular credit, pointing the way—dimly and vaguely, it might be, but still, generally speaking, correctly—for more thoroughgoing reform. The Italian Joint-Stock Banks have detected very much sooner than any of their sister-institutions elsewhere the immense value of what may, by analogy, be termed "third-class traffic"—the banking business of those millions of comparatively poor people, who make up by their numbers what they lack in individual wealth. By a variety of little experimental expedients they had studied to attract such

---

* All these institutions did good work, but work purely charitable. In 1878 there were still 1,465 *monti frumentari* (or *pecunari*) in existence, dispensing among them 14,781,998 lire in loans. They were practically abolished, compelled either to convert themselves into institutions of a different type, or else to close their doors, by a law passed in 1887. At the present time there is, so far as I am aware, only one Monte dei Paschi left, that of Siena, an important institution which, under remodelled management, is doing admirable work no less as a mortgage and general credit bank than as a savings bank. It is one of the largest and best-managed financial institutions in Italy, and would merit full description here, if it could at all be classed as a "People's Bank."

humble customers to their counters. The Savings Banks did even better. The **Italian Savings Banks** rank among absolutely the best of the world. Evidently they have a thrifty people to deal with, pouring in their millions of lire with a readiness which in a poor country is surprising, and which sometimes appears to become almost embarrassing. In addition to 4,686 Post Office Savings Banks, scattered all over the country and enjoying certain peculiar privileges —such as the power of collecting small savings down to the amount of 5 centesimi (a halfpenny)—there were on 31st December 1894 no fewer than 395 other savings banks in Italy, holding among them deposits amounting to 1,306,919,314 lire (£52,276,772).* Surely that is a satisfactory record, more particularly when it comes to be borne in mind that, in addition, there were 410,436,517 lire (£16,417,460) deposited with the Post Office Savings Banks, 206,825,358 lire (£8,273,014) with the People's Banks, and 75,015,166 lire (£3,000,606) with other credit institutions, making a grand total of 1,999,196,355 lire (£79,967,854). For a population of about 31,000,000, in the middle of a prolonged period of commercial and industrial depression, that is not bad. And it is satisfactory to know that all through the years of distress and crisis, while great commercial establishments crumbled to pieces, and taxes were imposed on the top of taxes, the flow of savings deposits steadily kept increasing. In 1883 the average deposit per inhabitant stood at 39.75 lire, in 1887 at 58.13 lire; by 1894 it was found to have risen to 64.68 lire. Of the 1,306,919,314 lire held by the ordinary savings banks, only 294,914,740 lire was laid out in mortgages. For the remainder a use must be found in small loans, under powers which practically leave the directors *carte blanche* in respect of their

---

* There has been a considerable increase in these figures ever since 1883.

investments. Still, with all these aids, the great national want remained unsatisfied, even though banks and savings banks had often more money than they knew what to do with. Means and end did not fully agree—the machine was evidently not adapted to its work.

Luigi Luzzatti, the Creator of Italian Co-operative Banking.

Luigi Luzzatti, with the shrewdness of a born man of business, discovered what was needed. His has been a career peculiarly fruitful of good work, benefiting the poorer classes. Long before his public services in Parliament secured him the reward of political office all but the very highest, the position attained by him in his country was such that, as his friend E. de Laveleye testifies in his " Letters from Italy," high and low treated him with a degree of respect reserved only for the most valued and distinguished citizens. The reason of this was, that everybody knew him to be giving up his life to the service of his neighbours. Altering only the one word "*regno*," he might well apply to himself the noble words spoken by the first King of United Italy: "*Le classe lavoratrice sono quelle chi me stanno più a core. Il loro miglioramento è il programma del mio regno.*" Substitute "*vita*" for "*regno*,' and you have a precise description of the "great idea" governing M. Luzzatti's life. There has not been a work of social reform undertaken in Italy during the past thirty years of which he has not been either the author, or else at any rate one of the most prominent supporters. And now, though he does not fill an office in the Cabinet, and therefore is—as his friends like to think—all the more free to pursue and further his own good social work, untrammelled by the ties of party —what with his captivating presence, his fascinating and convincing eloquence, his peculiar knowledge, and his transparent honesty, he continues, without doubt, the foremost leader of thought in Italy on social questions, the person whose counsel is most sought, and the man possessing the greatest power of influencing his countrymen, the man upon whom the politicians of Parliament, the scholars of the Universities, and the large masses all look as upon their best teacher.

He began his work of economic reform in 1863, when still quite a young man, and proclaimed to the world his ideas upon "The Diffusion of Credit," in a little book which at once fixed attention upon its author. He had learnt credit co-operation in the school of Schulze-Delitzsch, and to this day to his admiring eyes Schulze-Delitzsch remains "*il sommo maestro della cooperazione*." But he also perceived very clearly that a mere mechanical copying of Schulze-Delitzsch's system must inevitably lead to disappointment. To answer in Italy, the machinery applied must be not only simple and business-like, but also of a distinctly local type. Improving with a happy skill upon Schulze's work, M. Luzzatti produced that of which he might well say with justifiable pride—"We have not copied an institution, but produced a new type, and, impressing upon it the stamp of Italian originality, we have created the *Banche Popolari*." Experience has amply justified his independent action. *[margin: Originally a Follower of Schulze-Delitzsch.]*

Italy wanted People's Banks fully as much as ever Germany had wanted them. But the circumstances of the country, its habits of thought and of action—everything, in fact, which was likely to tell in their creation and work—were different from what corresponded to them in Germany. Accordingly, to be at all useful, the principle must be put into a new garb.

The first stumbling-block to be cleared out of the way, so M. Luzzatti clearly realised, was that obnoxious principle of unlimited liability. In Italy, whatever Francesco Viganò might say to the contrary, that would never answer. "Our people would never have joined an association which threatened them with such grave danger," frankly avows Ettore Levi. Giustino Fortunato goes so far as to say that in the southern provinces of the kingdom the adoption *[margin: His Departures from Schulze's System. He limits Liability.]*

of unlimited liability must have made co-operative credit "absolutely impossible." Sir J. Lumley, in his Blue-Book Report, wholly confirms this opinion. "Unlimited liability," he says, "would have deterred persons of means and education; and at the same time the character and habits of the people themselves would have disinclined them from entering any association involving so great a risk." Signor Luzzatti himself, condemning unlimited liability, pronounces it "an economic tradition of Germany, descended from the propertied classes to the poor."

There are, I am bound to admit, even at the present day, some among M. Luzzatti's followers who consider that his *banche popolari* would be all the better for the adoption of unlimited liability; that unlimited liability would awaken more interest and sense of responsibility, and arouse more of what is known as "co-operative spirit." But such men are to be met with only in places in which the omission of safeguards against excessive capitalism and selfishness, such as M. Luzzatti now strongly recommends, has led the older and richer People's Banks into abuses, the existence of which, unfortunately, there is no denying, but which may very well be guarded against by much less drastic expedients. And the number of persons advocating non-limitation of liability in the *banche popolari* is only small. It was reserved for Dr Wollemborg to show how unlimited liability might after all be made palatable to the Italians. But that was to be under totally different circumstances.

He reduces Shares and the Time allowed for Payment. Another decidedly objectionable feature in the German system M. Luzzatti held to be those forbiddingly formidable shares, which Schulze had deliberately adopted, in order to compel his members to commit themselves to a long course of saving, but which place the acquirement of full membership for poor persons at so remote a distance that to any one ungifted with German patience the task must appear well-nigh hopeless. M. Luzzatti had greater faith in human nature. He considered that people might be led into a steady course of saving by means very much less coercive. Accordingly, he entirely reversed Schulze's method on the point of shares, and instead of issuing *large* shares, to be paid up in a very *long* time, he laid it down once for all that shares must be paid up *within ten months at longest*, so as to give the bank, in the place of an indefinite and unascertainable liability "in the bush," its "bird in the hand"—a definite, if small, capital, absolutely at its own disposal. Paying up within ten months necessarily means comparatively small shares. In the place of Schulze's £15 or £25, with a minimum assigned by Dr Schenck of £5, we find in Italy, in 1893, shares exceeding 100 lire (£4) in only two instances. The major portion of shares (in 505 out of 701 banks sending in returns) vary from 25 to 50 lire (£1 to £2). There are 139 instances of smaller shares (17 of 5 lire or 4s.), and only 60 of larger, whereof 45 fall to the round figure of 100 lire (£4). That places the member's minimum holding rather low. But his liability being limited, there is no reason why he should not, if so inclined, invest in more shares than one, as one after the other becomes paid up, up to the extreme figure which the Italian law, like our own Industrial and Provident Societies Act, allows—namely, £200. The result has fully justified M. Luzzatti's trustful judgment. The figures already quoted for savings deposits demonstrate that Italians have learnt to lay by without having a policeman, so to speak, standing behind them, to prod them into thrift. And what I shall still have to relate will show that with their smaller limited-liability shares Italian People's Banks have proved pre-eminently workable, and have indeed amassed fully as large a working capital in proportion to their requirements as the Schulze-Delitzsch banks, namely, capital standing as one to three in comparison with what they have to borrow.

Once more, in the **matter of** raising money—purchasing cash in the market in order to resell it to his customers—M. Luzzatti decided to take an independent course. To his banks, beginning work with less pledgeable security than the German, the question of raising **excess money** may be said to assume an aspect of even more pressing importance. Time was when the most correct and advantageous method for raising money was, in the case of banks, held to be by the issue of notes. The Italian People's Banks have had an opportunity of testing this. Up to the year 1874 they enjoyed the privilege of issue. In 1872, being then only eighty in number, they had £1,022,000 in circulation, for the most part in fifty centesimi notes. The privilege was withdrawn in 1874, and the People's Banks have suffered no loss by the change. In the best of cases the issue of notes could go only a short way towards providing money.

His Banks are in the first instance Deposit Banks.

Schulze's banks were in the main *borrowing* banks, obtaining what money they required in excess of their own capital by loan. M. Luzzatti had a different conception of a bank. He desired to keep the business business-like, and to make his banks *independent*. Borrowing, he argued, must needs mean dependence upon other institutions of credit. And dependence must mean weakness. The task set to the banks was, in the first place, to localise savings, largely to attract local deposits; and in **the second,** to bridge over **a gulf, to secure access** to the capitalist market to unrecognised solvency—so to speak, to "monetize" hitherto uncoined credit power, by bringing it upon the capitalist market in a recognisable form, and with a recognised *locus standi*. In

The "Acceptance."

that market acceptances constitute the general medium of exchange. Being really the most convenient instrument for negotiating loans—inasmuch as they provide an indisputable record, which of itself insures power for summarily enforcing repayment—while at the same time they supply ready means for raising more money by passing them on—they have, in very truth, become the bankers' currency. For a credit institution standing well in the market, they possess a further recommendation, namely this, that they may be turned into a direct source of profit. A sound bank is always in a position to pass on paper bearing its endorsement at a reduced rate of interest, pocketing the difference. The larger its discount business, accordingly, the more considerable will be its gain. Now, bills of exchange are perfectly understood in Italy, the original home of banks. And the Italian law, so far from being "Draconic," like the German, and therefore adverse, is distinctly favourable to acceptances. It even provides means for easy collection of their value by post, at a mere postage charge, by ordinary letter-carriers, alike in town and in country. Signor Ettore Levi, now Vice-President of the "Bank of Italy," suggests an additional reason for the choice made by his brother-in-law. A bill of exchange, he says, stands as a rule for a productive transaction at its inception; an ordinary loan for a transaction already completed, upon which there is a deficiency. A tailor buying cloth to make clothes of, gives the manufacturer a bill, to mature when he has realised his profit. The man in difficulties, who cannot meet a bill previously drawn, comes to the bank for a loan. The reasoning does not appear altogether conclusive. But whatever its force, for the various reasons stated, M. Luzzatti elected to base his banking *mainly* on acceptances. His banks have in addition adopted other methods, as I shall show. But in the main, whatever be the form selected—even in the case of cash credits, which have grown greatly in public favour—it is the *bill* which forms the basis of the lending.

Once more, M. Luzzatti's choice has approved itself in practice. It has enabled his banks, as I shall show, to take advantage of circumstances unquestionably favouring them, but which could not possibly have been turned to account by other means. It has led them generally into a path of business which has proved manifestly convenient and safe, and at the same time it has educated members of his banks very effectively in habits of business.

Thus far, accordingly, M. Luzzatti may be said to have proceeded judiciously.

How Honesty is "Capitalised."

However, the main factor of success still remained to be supplied. 'If the banks wanted to coin working capital by receiving savings and deposits and passing on bills, they must first of all secure sufficient confidence with the public, and credit with the larger banks. With their limited means, how were they to accomplish this? M. Luzzatti had his answer ready, but it staggered his countrymen by its " Utopian " boldness—the banks were to " pledge their honour," to " capitalise their honesty." The great source of their credit was to be their " high reputation for honesty and solvency (*la grande riputazione di onestà e di solidità*)."

It is made Members' Interest to be Honest and Watchful.

Put into ordinary economic language, of course, M Luzzatti's rather high-flown phrase does not mean that by the touch of some thaumaturgic power the members of the *banche popolari* were miraculously to be turned into saints or angels, but merely, that it was to be made their direct interest to be honest and punctual, and to see that their fellow-members were the same. They were to be put, not upon their " honour "—that is a most misleading phrase—but upon their " responsibility." The main supports upon which the author of the scheme designed to rely in his " capitalisation of honesty " were to be the very simple ones of careful discrimination in the selection of members, such as would constitute the mere election a pledge of the member's trustworthiness; and, moreover, full publicity—a regular, frequent, and frank publication of balance-sheets, capital accounts, &c., relating to each bank. " The best and safest guarantee of prosperity," **Signor** Luzzatti himself **says,** " is the moral worth of the member. The very life of co-operation is bound up with the moral worth of members, and the more it **is** assured by strict guarantees, the more readily will money flow into our banks." He would **not** shrink from expelling unworthy **members.** And hence *la grande riputazione di* **onestà** *e di solidità,* which to-day places the *banche popolari* abreast **of the** best banking institutions.

Fully democratic self-government "*of* the members, *by* the members, *for* **the** members," he judged **to** be indispensable. The interest **of** the entire community of members was to be written large, as a paramount consideration, upon all **the bank's** transactions. Responsibility must accordingly **be made acute,** effective, and general. The Committee **must** represent **the** members collectively, as a British Government represents the nation, not as a foreign Government affects to **represent** it while really representing the **Crown.** Hence **the** substitution of a larger, elected, **and** unsalaried **committee,** appointing and controlling **the** officers, in the place **of the** small and purely administrative committee of three which Schulze had instituted **once** for all. Again experience **has shown M.** Luzzatti **to** have judged rightly. And, indeed, it has taught him that he must carry his co-operative principle **very** much further than, under the influence **of** " practical men " (in Germany), urging excessive consideration for capital **and** administrative capacity, **he** insisted upon at the outset.

Administration is wholly Democratic.

On the free and full publication **of all** details affecting the **position of a bank the** " father " of Italian Co-operative Credit **lays no less stress,** holding it **the** more imperative, the **younger is the bank in question, and** the greater accordingly **is its need** for making **good its** position. Its balance-sheet is to **serve as its** brief **of** trustworthiness.

Publication of Accounts.

Let us stop for **a** moment briefly **to consider some of** the direct results of the system adopted.

PEOPLE'S BANKS.

The Result: Admirable Management.

Nobody who has seen the Italian *banche popolari* has failed to remark upon the admirable management under which the banks have generally speaking found themselves from the beginning—the business-like practices and the astonishing resource of those who were placed at their head. A mere glance at their work must show that, as M. Léon Say puts it, these banks are "as skilfully organised as if the best actuaries of London and New York had given their help." Balance-sheets, the smooth flow of business, the remarkable order prevailing throughout, all go to prove this.

We have had occasion to notice precisely the same thing in connection with the Raiffeisen Banks of Germany: it is all order, regularity, exactitude, down to the minutest detail. Obviously this good management springs in both cases from the self-same underlying cause, the moral discipline, the responsibility awakened, the direct economic interest aroused among the body of selected members. From an actuarial point of view, however, this Italian business, with its technical banking and a perfectly astounding multitude and variety of operations, is a different thing altogether from the elementary simplicity of Raiffeisen work, which, in its own sphere, is one of its chief recommendations, but which seems scarcely suited to the Italian *banche*.

Large Inflow of Savings Deposits.

Let us proceed a step further. As an encourager of thrift there could not be a more effective agency than the *banche popolari*. For M. Luzzatti insists that every *banca* should be at the same time a savings bank; and in this capacity the *banche* have become one of the most favourite species of savings banks known—not because, as Mr Hodgson Pratt suggests in his lecture delivered in 1887, they allow a higher rate of interest ($\frac{1}{2}$ per cent. more) than the public savings banks. The official returns published show the rate of interest to vary considerably in individual banks, descending as low as $2\frac{1}{2}$ per cent. (which is *below* public

THE "BANCHE POPOLARI" OF ITALY. 207

savings bank rate), and rising in some instances as high as 7 per cent., and in one quite exceptional instance, at Scafati, even to 10 per cent. The reason why the *banca popolare* is the general favourite seems to be, that it is the local people's own. In 1894 the *banche popolari* had among them 206,825,358 lire (£8,273,014) of savings money in their tills. The *Banca Popolare* of Milan alone in 1890 held 35,500,000 lire. The little *banca* of Lonigo, which from being a *succursale* of Vicenza in 1877 set up as an independent little establishment, with a capital of 150,000 lire (£6,000), held in 1890 1,522,728 lire of savings banks deposits, in addition to 1,213,706 lire of other deposits (practically also savings) and 366,677 lire balances on current accounts. "*Voilà plus de* 3,000,000 *lire d'épargne constituée goutte à goutte*," remarks M. Rostand. And he goes on to explain: "The local Post Office Savings Bank has few customers; as happens everywhere where the initiative is strong, these intelligent workers prefer independent private action to the action of the State, and understand the advantage which they derive from carrying their money to a place from which it will return to them as a fertilising dew in the shape of loans or the discounting of bills." "But for that institution," Sir J. S. Lumley quotes M. Luzzatti as saying, while applying his observation to the *banche popolari* generally, "the whole of the savings of Lombardy would be concentrated at Milan, and the blessings of commercial and agricultural credit would be unknown, not merely in small places, but even in large towns such as Bergamo, Brescia, Cremona, Pavia, Lodi, &c., where the savings deposited in Savings Banks amount to millions of francs." The *banche* are antagonistic to monetary "wens," they localise and decentralise.

In the third place, let us consider the effect of this system upon the general public, which is indeed a prerequisite to the result last dwelt upon. Applying the co-operative principle — which means avoidance of risk, *Safety of the Transactions.*

thinking of the depositors rather than of themselves as profit-mongering institutions—the banks have taken their place among the *safest* depositories for money known in Italy. Their losses are infinitesimal. Official statistics show that in the year 1893, with their small capital of 114,722,132 lire, People's Banks in Italy had attracted 372,164,388 lire of deposits, whereas ordinary banks, commanding a capital more than twice as large, viz., 260,465,920 lire, had been able to attract only 349,093,984 lire, actually a smaller sum, in the deposit market. There is nothing to account for this striking difference except the *grande riputazione di onestà e di solidità* possessed by the People's Banks, and the very much larger confidence accordingly reposed in them by the public. How fully such confidence is justified by facts will appear from the diagrams accompanying this chapter, which show, on the ground of official statistics, the fluctuations in the holdings of capital, of deposits, and in the business transactions generally, severally in joint-stock and co-operative banks during twenty-two years.* The deviations in the lines standing for the business of co-operative banks are very slight. The lines move pretty steadily upwards. The lines indicating the business of ordinary banks show a considerable amount of zigzagging, expressive of sudden expansions followed by as sudden contractions. The superiority of co-operative banks under this head, as pre-eminently *safe* institutions—even in Italy, where there are not a few indifferent banks—ought to be a recommendation not least worthy of consideration in England.

Two Favouring Forces.

Being organised on the lines set forth, the People's Banks found themselves in a position to take advantage of

---

* See pp. 210, 211, and 213. The diagrams show severally the Total Transactions, the Share Capital and Reserve, and the Deposits held, in the case of Ordinary and of Co-operative Banks. These drawings ought to speak for themselves.

THE "BANCHE POPOLARI" OF ITALY.

two helping forces which kind Fortune had placed conveniently at their command. There were, in the first place, vast stores of money lying ready to their hand in the keeping of joint-stock banks and savings banks, whose custodians were not only willing, but even eager, to let them have them, if they could at all satisfy them of their trustworthiness. The managers of those institutions readily detected in the new organisation an agent who might be turned into an exceedingly serviceable ally. He could open to them a wide additional field of business, all the trouble of cultivating which would fall to his share, while most of the profit would come to them. They resolved to trust him. In M. Luzzatti's words, they actually "vied with one another" in their efforts to take the new People's Banks under their "maternal guardianship." "In doing so," M. Luzzatti frankly insists, in his Annual Address of 1889, "they have only consulted their own interest." But all the same, he gratefully acknowledges the most opportune assistance received.

Bankers befriend the People's Banks to Invest their Money.

The *Banco di Napoli* offered to discount bills at 1 per cent. under the ordinary bank rate. The *Banco di Sicilia* was ready to find four-fifths of the capital required for starting even a considerable number of *banche popolari* within its own district. Under the law as it stood that proved impracticable. But the good will from which the offer proceeded remained available for other methods. On the face of it, if the popular banks wanted to exist any length of time, they must be honest. And M. Luzzatti and his friends had too much at stake in their reputation to play recklessly with their new instrument of credit. Very little of the money thus made available, it ought to be pointed out, could have been conveniently drawn upon by other means except discount. Long loans for fixed periods would not have suited the lenders, and loans always liable to be called in would not have suited the borrowers.

TOTAL BUSINESS OF VARIOUS TYPES OF BANKS, 1871-93.

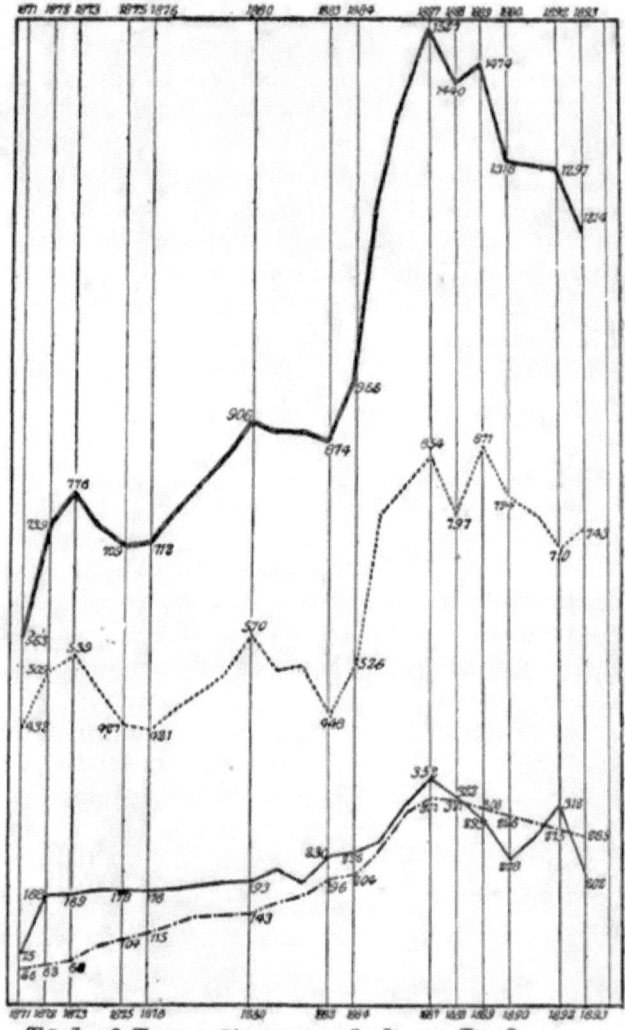

SHARE CAPITAL AND RESERVE HELD SEVERALLY BY ORDINARY AND BY CO-OPERATIVE BANKS, 1871-93.

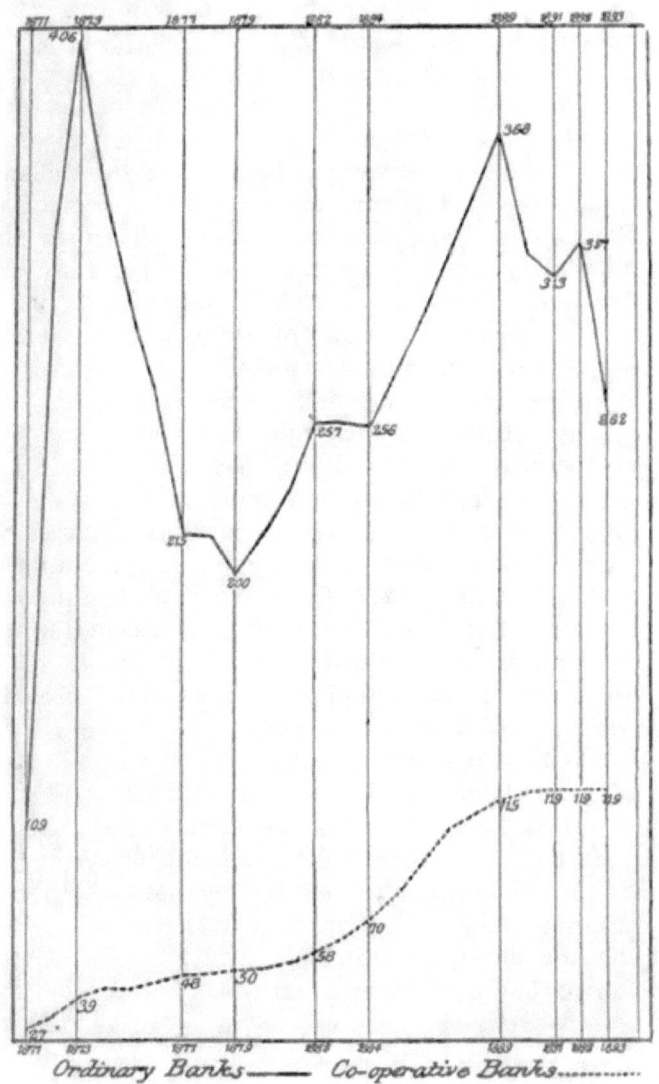

Ordinary Banks ——— Co-operative Banks ············

PEOPLE'S BANKS.

The Friendly Societies support them. There was another helping force which at their birth stood the new *banche* in good stead. "We have issued," so says M. Luzzatti in one of his addresses, "from the maternal womb of the friendly societies (*delle viscere materne de quei sodalizi di reciproco aiuto*)." Friendly societies were well developed in Italy. The point is of importance to ourselves, because it marks a resemblance of direct bearing upon the subject between us English and the Italians. And if we are ever to have an organised system of People's Banks, it will probably have to be built up on the same foundation, and may very well issue, as in Italy, from the " maternal womb " of the friendly societies.

The friendly societies of Italy at once detected the social and economic value of M. Luzzatti's idea, and took it up readily. Such societies were, as a matter of course, wholly debarred by their rules from themselves practising co-operative banking. But if they could not convert themselves into loan banks, they could at any rate supply the *banche* with members and secure to them support by making their system understood among those for whom it was mainly intended. From the first they stood by the *banche*. The two institutions have become sworn allies. And the *banche* have had many an opportunity of repaying the favour of early support by substantial pecuniary services rendered when they had become strong.

With such simple means as those indicated have Commendatore Luzzatti and his lieutenants, MM. Pedroni, Mangili, Levi, Manfredi, Cavalieri, Concini, &c., in comparatively brief time built up a fabric which in the words of M. Durand may well be regarded as "the envy of Europe"—a fabric which, as a financial power, ranks side by side with the Rothschilds; which does a full third of its own country's banking; and which through its thousands of channels dispenses annually a stream of millions, trickling down to the very spots on which help is most needed,

DEPOSITS HELD IN SAVINGS AND ON LONG-TERM BONDS
SEVERALLY BY ORDINARY CREDIT INSTITUTIONS
AND BY CO-OPERATIVE BANKS, 1871-93.

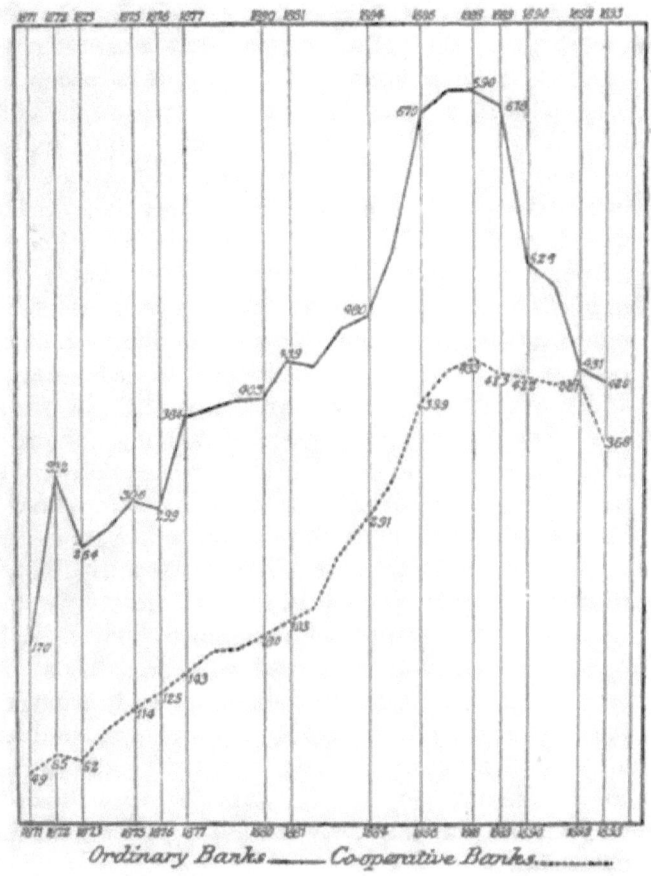

[The three Tables shown on pages **210, 211,** and **213 are reduced** facsimiles taken from larger diagrams **prepared by the Statistical** Office of Italy, for the use of which I **have to** thank **the Hon. Com**mendatore Bodio, President of that Office.]

and bringing forth prosperity in trade and agriculture, planting comfort in myriads of homes, and feeding, by the enlarged market which it supplies, the commerce and industries of Italy.

History of the Movement. Its Beginning. However favourable circumstances might in the course of practice turn out to be, in 1863 and 1864, when M. Luzzatti entered upon his crusade against usury, he found himself face to face with a task of no little difficulty. He had his "plan of campaign" ready. But his army for fighting it had still to be created. He cannot have been in a better position for beginning operations in Italy than would at the present day be an apostle of his economic gospel in England. There were only very few who believed in his "chimera." The very friends who consented to join him were sceptical, and contributed their small subscriptions rather "to oblige their friend," or "as one engages in a doubtful charity," than with any faith in the scheme. Like Schulze in Germany, he felt himself hampered by a socialist Lassalle, one Boldrini, perpetually crossing his path and acting the Shimei by him. However, Boldrini had no Bismarck to back him up, and so his opposition came to a speedy collapse. A more serious hindrance was to be found in the backward state of the Italian law, which recognised no societies with unlimited capital, such as co-operative associations must needs be. Until 1883 the *banche* were compelled to sail—innocently enough—under false colours, styling themselves joint-stock companies, and altering the figure of their "limited" capital from year to year, in order to comply with the law. That helps to explain the comparatively slow progress made up to the date named.

The Pioneer Bank of Milan. In spite of all these hindrances, M. Luzzatti—after a little co-operative experiment made in connection with a friendly society at Lodi in 1864—late in 1865 decided upon starting his first People's Bank in Milan. And on the 25th of May 1866 he opened the doors of his modest little establishment in a small hired room. It was a puny little affair. The bank had but £28 for its capital—oddly enough, precisely the same sum with which our Rochdale Pioneers entered upon an economic reform destined to revolutionise commerce. "*Moi, je souscrivis* 100 *lire, j'étais le millionnaire de la bande.*" Of course they could employ no paid clerks or officers. All work must be gratuitous. But there was a good will at the back of the enterprise. "Half my heart," long after said M. Luzzatti himself, "is wrapt up in the People's Bank of Milan."

The bank began its petty business amidst sneers similar to those which greeted the early labours of our co-operators of Toad Lane, in the humblest of ways. There seemed to be a long uphill fight in prospect. However, in its very first year fortune stepped in to befriend the bantling institution in quite an unexpected way. It had not been in existence many days when a monetary crisis, throwing all business into confusion, furnished to its founders an opportunity for showing their ready resource, and enabled them, by turning that chance to account, to raise their bank at once into public favour and reputation. The late Felice Mangili, who was Secretary of the Bank, relates the incident in his *Mémoire*, published in 1881. Barely had the Bank of Milan opened the doors of its modest office, when Italy was plunged into war. In the then state of affairs war necessarily meant a financial crisis, and the Italian Government, by way of aggravating such, had anticipated the opening of hostilities by enacting forced currency for the notes issued by the National Bank. There was general consternation. The *disagio* went up to 10 per cent. The Savings Bank of Milan alone lost about 800,000 lire before it rightly knew where it was. The public were in a state of ferment, and serious disturbances were apprehended. The *Banca Popolare* promptly came to the rescue, offering to issue *buoni di*

<small>Resource shown in a National Crisis.</small>

cassa—bonds, or bills, that is, not notes—for small amounts, five, three, two lire, against security. The public jumped at the opportune suggestion. The Giunta Municipale readily approved it, and the printing press was at once set to work with admirable effect. A serious crisis had been averted — and the reputation of the *Banca Popolare* was made. Within a year the number of its members rose from 400 to 1,153; its capital grew to 217,000 lire, its reserve to 7,902 lire; at the end of the twelvemonth it had discounted 687,606 lire worth of acceptances, had received 341,251 lire of deposits, the total of its transactions stood at 10,957,086, its profits at 16,030 lire. It was enabled to pay its members a dividend of 5 lire per share, that is, 10 per cent. The ship was fairly launched, and sailing along with a favouring breeze.

<small>Early Troubles. They are overcome.</small>

In its subsequent career the bank has had more than one severe crisis to weather. However, the good fairy which befriended it at its birth stood by it all through. In no experience do the merits of co-operative banks show themselves more brilliantly than in their capacity to live through crises. Every crisis that has visited Italy has left far less impression upon the People's Banks than upon their non-co-operative rivals. Recently, it has taken about six years for the general monetary crisis, which affected ordinary banks at once, in 1887, to penetrate into the citadel of co-operative banking; and when it did reach it, it led only to a diminution of business, not to any disastrous collapses. During the last serious commercial disturbance the *Banca Cooperativa Operaia* of Milan actually went on increasing its roll of members from 4,268 to 4,929, its share capital from 58,547 to 63,856 lire, its available funds from 2,927,350 to 3,192,800 lire. The *Banca Popolare* weathered the storms which troubled it triumphantly. In the first fifteen years of its existence, up to 1880 (inclusive), its losses amounted in all to only 191,636 lire (£7,664), of which 68,567 lire was owing to frauds committed by employés, and 3,606 lire sacrificed in support unwisely given to a co-operative printing establishment. And since that date the bank's losses have remained as trifling. The greatest danger which the bank ever had to face arose, not from a crisis, nor from outside pressure, but from its own midst. In the years from 1871 to 1873, when the promotion fever was raging throughout the world, and in Italy took the shape of what Signor Mangili calls *bancomania*, the shareholders grew greedy, and clamoured for the conversion of their bank into a joint-stock concern, in order that they might through it engage in speculation. The Committee offered a stout resistance, and just managed to carry their point. Their constituents grumbled, but have lived to thank their leaders for their firmness.

The face of things is changed, indeed, since those early days of struggles without and dissensions within. The Milan Bank has become one of the marvels of Italy. It is lodged in a palace. It employs, in addition to 130 or 140 unpaid officers, nearly 100 clerks. The number of its members stood at New Year at 17,860. Its paid-up capital amounted at the same date to 8,598,300 lire, consisting of 171,966 shares, with a reserve fund of 4,299,150 lire at the back, to raise the sum total to 12,897,450 lire (£515,896). In addition to 74,704,454 lire of ordinary deposits, the bank held 30,998,416 lire in savings. It had lent out in the course of the year 96,442,916 lire (£3,857,716) on acceptances, dealing out in this way not less than 196,101 loans — 88,938, to the amount of 11,967,652 lire, of 200 lire or less; 66,157, to the amount of 21,674,343 lire, of sums ranging from 201 to 500 lire; 31,184, to the amount of 22,540,689 lire, of from 501 to 1,000 lire; only 56 loans, to the collective amount of 5,800,000 lire, were for more than 50,000 lire. The average figure per loan stood at 491.80 lire. In addition the bank lent out 69,145,000 lire (£2,765,800) in

Signal Triumph.

other ways. Its business with the 320 other *banche popolari* and various correspondents amounted to 110,653,966 lire. On a total turnover of 1,492,206,739 lire (£59,688,269) it had realised a net profit of 1,219,478 lire, which enabled it, after the deduction of 121,900 lire for the usual profit-sharing and charities, to pay dividend at the rate of 6.40 lire on the 50-lire share. Its management expenses figured at 285,374 lire (not including rates and taxes). The figures for earlier years show considerably better. In 1889 the business with the People's Banks stood at more than twice the figures quoted. Ever since 1890 there has been that cloud of commercial depression pressing upon all business, which, of course, tells even more than on smaller banks on large institutions situated in great commercial centres like this monster Bank of Milan, the organisation and "installation" of which constitute one of the sights of the banking world. "*Toute cette organisation*," remarks M. Rostand, struck with admiration, "*est remarquable comme ordre, ingéniosité, perfectionnement technique.*"

<small>Effects upon Commerce and General Prosperity.</small>

What millions of money dispensed to those who could not by other means have obtained any does the thirty years' work of that bank represent! And really that is the smallest portion of the service which it has rendered. "By its influence on legislation," says M. Rostand, "and by the model which it has supplied, the *Banca Popolare di Milano* has laid in Italy the foundation of co-operative credit." Of those hundreds of banks which dot the Italian territory from the Alps to the Mediterranean, says M. Léon Say, the People's Bank of Milan is either the mother or the nurse. "*La Banque Populaire magistrale de Milan et les grandes caisses d'épargne de Milan et de Bologne dominent, de la hauteur de leurs dizaines ou centaines de millions, tout le peuple de ces petites banques avec leures petites caisses d'épargne qui se meuvent dans leurs orbits et puisent les épargnes partout pour vivifier partout l'agriculture et les petites industries.*"

THE "BANCHE POPOLARI" OF ITALY.

Summing up the history of the bank, Signor Mangili ascribes its success to the gratuitous rendering of services by the officers, the non-limitation of its capital, the smallness of the payments exacted, the restriction of each member to one vote, the refusal of confidence to any member who has shown himself undeserving of it, the preference given to credit services over profit, and the exclusion of any hazardous operation.* {*The Causes of Success.*}

I do not wish to quote the *Banca Popolare* of Milan as altogether a model bank, although in point of strength and wealth it has proved the most successful. There is, as M. Luzzatti himself has urged, actual *danger* in success. In the opinion of some sound co-operators, the *Banca Popolare* of Milan has, with its increasing prosperity, become *too capitalist*. However, Signor Mangili's formula supplies a good epitome of the principles which ought to govern the organisation of a bank set up on the lines already sketched. The main principle, of course, is the application of *co-operation*, to the exclusion of *exploitation*. It will be necessary to devote a few pages to the discussion of the machinery by which this principle may be carried into practice.

Above all things, you must provide machinery for dealing out the bank's money—investing it—with as near an approach to absolute safety as is at all possible. People's Banks deal in *personal* credit—a dangerous commodity even among selected members. And they must open their doors wide. Like Raiffeisen, M. Luzzatti would wish to see wealth fairly well represented in his banks. Unlike Raiffeisen, he would not—or would not at any rate at the outset—have really needy persons admitted into them. Accord- {*Representation of various Classes in People's Banks.*}

---

* La gratuità delle cariche, il capitale illimitato, le quote di tenue imposto pagabili anche con versamenti a piccole rate, l'unicità del voto, il frazionamento delle operazioni, l'elargizione del fido a chi fra i soci si ne mostri veramente meritevole, il credito anteposto agli utili, l'esclusione d'ogni operazione aleatoria.

ingly, it is often made a reproach to the *banche popolari* that they are not sufficiently "popular." Their constituencies very closely resemble those of the Schulze-Delitzsch banks in Germany. Working men are few. And very accountably so. Obviously, the demand of a share, say of 50 lire, to be paid up in ten months, is rather a heavy tax upon a wage-earner, more especially since there is an entrance fee levied in the bargain, which in some cases—for instance, in that of the *Banca Popolare* of Milan——stands for as much as 25 lire. M. Luzzatti lays great stress upon the collection of an entrance fee, unreturnable in case of retirement, because it helps to strengthen the reserve fund, and tends to keep members, unwilling to sacrifice what they have once paid, in the bank. Add to this that in prosperous banks the share rises in issue value in proportion with the growing reserve, by 25, 50, and 100 per cent., and no one can be surprised at finding the "poor" element rather scantily represented. In the last statistics published we have, on an average of 639 banks, 6.56 per cent. of the members classified as substantial landed proprietors, 24.12 per cent. as smaller cultivators, 4.66 per cent. as rural day labourers, 4.77 per cent. as large manufacturers and merchants, 25.25 per cent. as small tradesmen and manufacturers, 8.11 per cent. as factory men, 18.86 per cent. as civil servants, clerks, teachers, &c., and 7.67 per cent. persons as without an occupation. These proportions vary very little from year to year. How M. Rostand comes to class the members generally as about 11.5 per cent. "rich" and 88.5 per cent. "poor" (496 "rich" and 3,814 "poor") I fail to understand. It appears to me that according to the official figures we have 19 per cent. "rich," 68.23 per cent. in a fairly comfortable condition, and only 12.77 per cent. really "poor." As between bank and bank, of course, the proportions vary. In the large People's Bank of Bologna, for instance, you have, out of 4,971 members, 1,842 small tradesmen, 917 small freeholders, 818 clerks and civil servants, 441 teachers, medical men, chemists, &c., and only 301 day labourers. On the other hand, in small banks like the *Banchina* of Bologne and the *Banca Operaia* of Milan, you have the working-class element preponderating. **But such** banks are few. One very satisfactory feature observable in the figures is the rather striking increase in the number of "small agriculturists" who have become members of People's Banks. Such small cultivators figured in 1876 at only 16.80 per cent. of the sum total of members; by 1893 their proportion had **risen to** 24.12 per cent. The proportion of rural day labourers has likewise steadily increased, though only from 3.20 to 4.66 per cent. On the other hand, the number of small traders, &c., had (proportionately) **decreased** from 32.15 to 25.25 per cent., and that of persons **without a** calling from 13.15 to 7.6 per cent. On the whole, accordingly, there has been something of an advance in the direction of greater "popularisation" of the banks, though not, perhaps, at a sufficient rate of progression.

The picture presented shows even more of a middle-class hue when you come to give a turn to the kaleidoscope, so as to bring into view the proportionate *holdings* of the several interests represented. The 6.56 per cent. **of sub**stantial landowners held 17.95 per cent. of the shares, **the** 24.12 per cent. of small cultivators only 14.69 per cent., the 4.66 per cent. of rural labourers 1.80 per **cent., the 4.77** per **cent. of** large merchants and manufacturers 14.90 **per** cent., the 25.25 per cent. of small tradesmen 20.86 per cent., the 8.11 per cent. of factory labourers 4.05 per cent., the 18.86 per **cent.** of the professional classes 15.34 per cent., and the 7.67 per cent. **of persons** of no occupation 10.95 per **cent.** There is, of course, nothing exceptionable in this; it is perfectly natural, and indeed proper, that the better-to-do should have the largest holdings. The figures will, however, deserve consideration when we come to con-

Distribution of Holdings.

sider the question of a limitation of dividend. Group a bank as you will, once you adopt the principle of *shares*, you cannot avoid receiving into it two distinct classes, whose interests *may* become antagonistic; and in the interest of the weaker, if you want to keep the bank co-operative, you will have to interfere to maintain the balance even.

However little the constituencies of the Italian *banche popolari* may fail to satisfy Professor Rabbeno, M. Durand, and others anxious to see relief brought to economically the very lowest stratum, to "*les plus pauvres et les plus déshérités*," from a banking point of view manifestly they present a constituency of very questionable value to deal with, more particularly when you come to consider that the average roll of members in a bank stands at 612. Under such circumstances success is attainable only by the adoption of very safe methods for dealing out and checking credit.

<small>Smallness of Losses an Evidence of Good Management.</small>
The figures appearing in official statistics for the bad and doubtful debts made every year by the People's Banks most conclusively prove that the machinery actually adopted has on the whole answered its purpose. For 1880 the proportion of such debts is given as .28 per cent. on the lending, for 1881 as .33 per cent., for 1882 as .27 per cent., for 1886 as .22 per cent., and so on. Only in 1893—the last year for which I have full figures—a concurrence of adverse circumstances raised it to the quite abnormal height of 1.55 per cent. Barring that one exceptional instance, bankers will agree with me that the proportions quoted are very small. They are very much smaller than what can be quoted for Italian joint-stock banks. If you stop to pick out the best-managed People's Banks of Italy, in which the methods practised are to be seen to greatest advantage, you will find the losses smaller still. In the *Banca Popolare* of Bologna, for instance, in 1894, losses amounted to only 11 centesimi on every 1,000 lire lent out, say 1d. on £40.

The body upon whom the direction of credit operations devolves is the *Comitato di sconto*, a volunteer committee elected at the annual meeting, and consisting variously of from fifteen to forty members, taking their duty in turn, whose special office it is to consider and approve, or else reject, applications for loans or advances, and requests for credit to be opened in the shape of current accounts. There is no more important body of officers forming part of M. Luzzatti's co-operative organisation than this *Comitato di sconto*, upon whose *fiat* it depends whether the credit of the bank shall be pledged or not. M. Luzzatti accordingly will have them amenable to no influence whatever which might in the least degree draw them aside from the narrow path of impartiality and caution. His own wish is, that by a self-denying ordinance they should forego their own right of borrowing. That, however, he has not been able to carry. But he would write over their door words which he slightly misquotes from the Gospel: "I know neither father or mother; only he who follows the truth follows me"—which means, that neither consideration for a vote nor for profit, for friendship or for consanguinity—nothing whatever but strict regard for the interests of the association shall determine their judgment. The *Comitato* prepare themselves for their active work of recommending or disallowing loans, by drawing up, independently of any actual application, a table, kept always in readiness, as their constant guide, but always strictly secret, which shows what amount each member of the association is, in the opinion of the *Comitato*, "good for." This table is called the *castelletto*. It is carefully revised from time to time, and, should the estimate fixed in it for any particular member decline while a loan is out to him, or to any one else for whom he acts as surety—or, again, should securities pledged for a loan depreciate by 10 per cent. or more—the debtor is at once called upon to make good the difference, in the

Organisation of the Banks. The Comitato di Sconto.

The Castelletto.

one case by a new surety, in the other by additional security. On this *castelletto* people may combine to borrow. For instance, if A is considered good for £40, B for £30, and C for £60, on the strength of their joint signatures, any one of them is entitled to a loan of £130—provided that no other paper is out signed or backed by A, B, or C. Supposing that the *Comitato* are correct in their appraisement, the *banca* in this way makes sure of keeping its lending within safe limits; and experience seems to indicate that the valuation is generally trustworthy. Credit given in the shape of a current account is withdrawn, if it shows no business. For that is held to indicate that the credit is asked, not for trade or productive purposes, but merely for accommodation.

A "Mobilised Portfolio." Upon the manner in which the *Comitato di sconto* discharges its duties, it must entirely depend, not only, whether the bank keeps solvent, so to speak, in the abstract, having value for its money; but also whether it keeps actually solvent and prepared for business at any time that such may offer, in the sense of having money available. It does so by means of a "well-mobilised portfolio" of acceptances, which makes the bills which it holds practically worth money, as being readily discountable. Experts, accordingly, agree in laying the very greatest stress upon the maintenance of such a "portfolio," and to the careful study of such writers on the subject attribute the success of the best *banche popolari*. In the crisis of 1880 the People's Bank of Poggibonsi found itself hardly beset. Upon the strength of its little capital of 90,000 lire (£3,600) it had taken 503,000 lire worth of deposits (£20,120), and discounted 550,000 lire worth of bills (£22,000). Under the circumstances its ruin would have been inevitable, if it had not held its funds in bills which could be readily realised. The miraculous development of his principal bank, the *Banca Popolare* of Milan, Commendatore Luzzatti himself

THE "BANCHE POPOLARI" OF ITALY.

ascribes mainly to its consistent practice of meeting all calls made upon it, even when it had a right to "notice," with the cash payments which its "ever-mobilised portfolio" made always practicable.

Some banks have, in addition to the *Comitato di sconto*, a separate *Comitato dei rischi*, which has been found extremely useful. The *Comitato dei rischi* keeps account of all the transactions done with individual members and with non-member sureties. Every loan, every endorsement, is chronicled in its books, as well as any other fact which may have a bearing upon the qualification of members as borrowers. If they are punctual in repayment, if they give trouble—all these things are noted in the books of the *Comitato*, which for reference are invaluable.

The Comitato dei Rischi.

Although bills of exchange form the favourite medium for loans, they do not constitute the only one. Some lending is done on note of hand. One bank, at any rate, that of Bergamo, lends on pledges, *sans dessaisissement*—pledges which remain in the borrower's use, as they might here under a bill of sale, only without the ignominy of any public record of the act. Mortgages are generally forbidden. But the banks lend on "warrants" and on invoices, on labour bills and on a variety of similar instruments, common among trading and manufacturing folk, but not generally negotiable except as an act of special consideration and at a high discount. To be able to borrow on such at ordinary rates of interest constitutes a material convenience to the public. For instance, a tradesman having money owing to him from a customer, need but obtain the latter's acknowledgment of the correctness of the debt—provided that the debtor is "good," or can make himself so by security—to have the account discounted. Under this arrangement builders carrying out contracts can receive the money wherewith to pay their workmen while the work is in progress; a printer working for a publisher who

Variety of the Banks' Operations.

P

demands long credit can obtain his money; that poor lady milliner, come down in the world, of whom we read some time ago in a London paper, who, with a heavy bill due to her, had not money enough to provide for her hungry family at Christmas time anything but bread and water, might have had her good Christmas dinner. It is very common for poor people to buy sewing machines with money borrowed from a People's Bank, which practice of course they find exceedingly useful; it secures to them all the conveniences of the "hire-purchase system," without exacting its extortionate price. It is doubtful if by any method the *banche* have rendered to the humble trading classes and small folk generally more material and more welcome service than by this convenient, popularised lending. The practice has proved useful beyond that; for it has to a considerable extent altered the custom of trade by its example, and made cash payments the rule in the place of credit. Again, banks advance money on rents falling due, or indeed on any prospective claim sufficiently assured and acknowledged. The People's Bank of Bergamo has advanced money on cocoons, secured by the undertaking that the spun silk shall not leave the spinner's house till the debt has been repaid. To the small silk-growers this has proved a substantial benefit.

Short-Term Lending.

All these loans are granted only for short periods. The money is to be kept continually in hand and "rolling." Besides, the leaders of the movement do not wish to accustom their protégés to a practice of long borrowing; and, moreover, Signor Ettore Levi goes so far as to argue that there is less risk in short loans than in long. The ordinary term is three months, and very rarely indeed is a renewal granted beyond another three. Not a few banks charge an additional fee upon renewal, which Signor Levi considers justified. The only exception in respect of time is made in the case of agricultural loans, for which as many as ten renewals are permitted, not to say anything at present about the issue of long-term bonds, of which I shall have to speak under a special head.

As the *banche* prefer short terms, so they also give the preference to small amounts—partly because such are supposed to involve less risk, as more largely distributing the engagements incurred, but also because the very *raison d'être* of the bank is, to furnish credit to *small* folk and for *small* wants, and they strive to remain true to their democratic object.

<small>Small Loans Preferred.</small>

For their supply of funds, in addition to the re-discount (at a profit) of their bills taken, the banks rely upon ordinary deposits, and, not least, upon savings deposits. Attention has already been called to their remarkable utility as collectors of the latter. As receivers of ordinary deposits they appear to have become no less popular. "We have not had to run after the deposits, the deposits have come running after us," on one occasion remarked Signor Luzzatti. However, deposits are always withdrawable by notice, at the option of the depositor.

<small>The Supply of Funds.</small>

Now, what banks mainly value is, to have money lent them for a fixed and tolerably long period. To accomplish this, M. Luzzatti introduced his *buoni fruttiferi a scadenza fissa*, bonds which, like our Exchequer Bills, run for fixed terms and bear interest, which, I find, varies in Italy as much as from $1\frac{1}{2}$ to 10 per cent.* These long-term bonds have not managed to secure a very large market. In 1893 there were bonds only to the value of 48,334,708 lire (£1,933,388) in circulation. That is a material help, no doubt, but it is only about one-tenth of what the *banche* generally speaking must keep at their disposal. Evidently, to issue long-term bonds, corresponding to our

<small>Long-Term Bonds.</small>

---

* In one case only, in Calabria; generally speaking, there is little beyond 7 per cent.

Exchequer Bonds, in any amount, a stronger body is needed than a People's Bank. It is all the more satisfactory that the People's Banks' custom of prompt repayments and their high character have made them so much trusted that large withdrawals of deposits are scarcely known.

The *Comitato di sconto*, which has to sit in judgment upon every claim for an advance made, is not the only representative administrative body appointed in the *banche popolari*. Indeed, their whole organisation is representative and elective. There is the *Consiglio*, or Council, which acts as a General Committee, regularly elected at the annual meeting, in most cases for two years, one-half retiring each twelvemonth. This body, wielding—next to the general meeting —supreme authority, varies in number from about seven, in the smaller banks, to 130 or 140 in the large Bank of Milan, every member of it being unpaid, and, for the security of the members in general, elected with care. M. Luzzatti insists more and more urgently, as time goes on—in opposition to his master Schulze-Delitzsch — upon purely *gratuitous* services. In the larger banks, of course, there must be a paid staff, and, in accordance with a resolution formally adopted at one of the great Congresses of People's Banks, these are paid not only by salary but also by commission on profits—not on "business." That is one of the Italian declarations in favour of profit-sharing. This is found to act as a useful stimulus to good work. Some banks make such payment dependent upon the dividend attaining a certain minimum figure. Signor Levi recommends as a rule that the profits should be appropriated as follows: 70 per cent. to dividend, 20 per cent. to reserve, 10 per cent. to the employés. A provident pension and sick insurance system, according to the rules laid down by Alfred de Courcy, has long since become a regular institution with all these banks. Of the higher officers, the Italian *banche* pay three—the president, the cashier, and the chief book-keeper

The Consiglio.

All Services Gratuitous.

—in about the following proportions: the president, 1,500 lire; the **cashier**, 1,300, the *capo contabile*, 1,100 lire.

From its own number the *Consiglio* elects from three to five *sindaci*, upon whom devolves the daily supervision of affairs. As a rule, they take the duty in turns, each for a week at a time, and after so much sacrifice of time and labour are allowed to retire at the close of a year.

The Sindaci.

Distinct from all these is a board of honorary officers which is altogether peculiar to the Italian *banche*, namely, the three *probiviri*, to whom an appeal may be carried on any point whatever arising in the administration of the *banche*, and whose judgment—to be pronounced only *in banco*—is final. A candidate refused admission, a member refused credit, a member sentenced to expulsion—whatever the question may be, an appeal lies to them, and their jurisdiction has in practice been found a rock of strength in maintaining harmony and keeping things in a satisfactory groove.

The Probiviri.

I have incidentally spoken of the Reserve Fund, which, of course, these banks accumulate out of profit, allotting annually from 15 to 25 per cent. to its formation. The weaker banks are in capital, the more importance, as a matter of course, do they attach to a reserve fund; and thus we see every good bank in Italy building up as strong a reserve as it can—so strong that, in the case of the *Banca Popolare* of Bologna, it actually exceeds the paid-up share capital, standing at 1,292,077 lire as against 1,260,540 lire. I have also already referred to the practice adopted of issuing shares at a higher value, in proportion as the reserve fund increases, so as to make the incoming member pay for the share which he, so to speak, acquires in the accumulated reserve, though, of course, that share cannot be claimed or drawn out by any one. This is another distinct departure from the German system, and is to be accounted for by the fact that in Italy the shares really are

The Reserve Fund.

shares, whereas in Germany they represent merely *parts sociales*. The premium on shares is in Italy everywhere actuarially ascertained from year to year. It varies considerably. In many cases there is none at all. In others it amounts to but a few centesimi. At Parma, it now stands at 12 lire on the 50 lire share; at Milan, in the *Banca Cooperativa Milanese*, at 25 lire on 50; at Tortona, at 44 lire on 50; at Bologna, in the *Banca Popolare di Credito*, at as much as 58.60 on 60 lire. In a joint-stock company, of course, such an arrangement must be held perfectly legitimate. But it may be questioned if it is altogether commendable in a co-operative association. It may lead to such betrayal of the co-operative principle as has become notorious in the cases of the Paris *lunettiers* and the Roman *tipografi*. It has already led to abuses. The shares of some of the older Italian People's Banks are openly quoted and dealt in in the market, like ordinary stock. That should not be. We have had the same thing happening in respect of our own co-operative workshops—for instance, at Hebden Bridge. But our societies have very promptly put a stop to it. Generally speaking, it is true, thus far, no particular hardship has been felt to arise from the Italian practice.

Merits and Defects of the System.

Thus judiciously constructed, "fitly joined together" in all its parts, the fabric of Italian People's Banks has shown itself admirably adapted for the discharge of a surprising variety of functions, of which all have not yet been told. One or two of their best works remain still to be described. Cramped and hampered by the advice of "practical men," to whose judgment M. Luzzatti held himself bound to defer, they began as essentially "business" banks, bidding for support by dividends and salaries, and deliberately excluding *i miseri*, as "unripe" for credit, and likely to abuse it. All these "practical" principles imported from across the Alps have been cast aside long since. "We have suffered, not from scarcity, but from a superabundance of funds," says Commendatore Luzzatti over and over again. "We have succeeded too well." The banks have paid 6, 8, 10, 14, 15, 20 per cent. of dividend. "Yes, but stop that," now urges M. Luzzatti, year after year. "Limit dividends; throw away every inducement to greed! Critics justly urge" (as does M. Léon Say) "that our '*crédit populaire n'est pas bon marché et de plus, il est inégal.*' M. François, in the *Journal des Economistes*, points out that it ranges from 4½ to 10 per cent. The Government statistics show the same thing. Eight per cent." (the very figure which M. Luzzatti somewhere declares excessive) "occurs frequently as the accepted rate. Leave that alone now; cheapen your service, study, not dividend, but cheap loans; and remember the 'womb' from which you have sprung, the womb of the working-men's friendly societies: lend to those societies and to their members, work in co-operation with them, and having attained prosperity, do your best to help the poor!" This exhortation has not remained without result. Existing banks it is not very easy to induce to revise their terms. But new banks are formed with more popular and more generous rules. And all banks that have worked themselves up to any position of wealth now give according to their power for philanthropic purposes and render help to the needy.

Under such impelling influence has sprung up what M. Rostand commends as "that original and noble piece of machinery of Italian co-operation (*cet original et noble rouage de la coopération italienne*)," the *prestito sull' onore*— the "loan of honour." Besides voting money for charitable purposes, some of these banks—seventy in 1893—every year devote a certain proportion of their funds to a special service, granting loans to the poor who have nothing to pledge as security except their "honour," their promise to repay—"a very doubtful security," English bankers will

The "Loan of Honour."

say. But experience has shown that losses under this head are rare and perfectly trifling. In the case of the *Banca Popolare* of Milan, in twelve years they did not amount to 10 per cent. In 1890 the *Banca Popolare di Credito* of Padua reported only 2,000 lire of losses out of 100,000 lire; only 43 "doubtful" loans out of 2,000 contracted. The *Banca Popolare* of Bologna in the same year set down only 2,000 out of 100,000 lire lent as "doubtful." In 1889, out of 9,250 lire lent out in 93 loans, it had lost 313 lire. It stands to reason, says Senhor Costa Goodolphim, arguing on such loans, that the debtors will make their best effort to repay, because they may want to borrow again. In the year 1893 the seventy banks referred to among them granted in all 8,149 "loans of honour," to the amount of 621,471 lire (£24,858). The amount is exceptionally small, because the Bank of Bologna for some reason or other suspended its service of such loans during that year. (During the year 1895 it lent out 17,630 lire under this head.) The number (8,512) and amount (621,426 lire) of loans repaid during the year pretty exactly balance both these figures. The large Bank of Lodi alone granted in that year 54,468 lire in such loans; the Operatives' Bank at Turin 35,676 lire; and the People's Bank of Nocera Inferiore (not a very strong bank) even 210,950 lire.

Of course, the banks do not give their money to every vagabond who may claim it. They have special committees appointed to inquire into cases. Thus the *Banca Popolare* of Bologna nominates a distinct committee of five to deal with the matter. Some other banks—as, for instance, those of Cremona and Bergamo—entrust the distribution of the money voted to some allied friendly society. The *Banca Popolare* of Milan makes a point of having always some representatives of local friendly societies on its "loans of honour" committee. Most of the loans granted are small. But I have come across grants to one man of 500 lire

THE "BANCHE POPOLARI" OF ITALY. 233

(£20), and even more. The *Banca Popolare* of Milan and the *Banca Popolare* of Bologna never grant more than 200 lire to one applicant. The *Banca Cooperativa Operaia* of Milan (founded only in 1884, with a subscribed capital of 134,800 lire) had in 1890 granted 1,455 such loans, 655 being under 50 lire each, 595 between 50 and 100 lire, and 25 upwards of that amount.

The "loan of honour" is always made repayable by instalments—as a rule, in ten months, though in some cases the time of repayment is spread out over sixty weeks or even longer. Some banks charge a moderate interest, others lend gratuitously. From the *banche popolari* the useful institution of *prestiti sull' onore* has spread over the whole network of provident institutions in Italy. The *istituti di mutuo soccorso* have taken it up, and most friendly trade societies—stonemasons', barbers', sign painters', and so on—practise it as a regular part of their work. Thus, thanks to the creative initiative of the *banche popolari*, a stream of gold has been set flowing, far less costly and far more beneficial than our well-sponsored charitable enterprises, watering the desert of distress with fertilising little currents which "return not void."

Even that is not all that the *banche* can do in the way of philanthropic work. When times of trouble arise, and the benevolent subscribe their thousands to help the houseless and starving, no machinery has been found so effective for beneficently distributing the money collected as the People's Banks. They are in a better position to discriminate between deserving and undeserving cases than Government officers or committees specially appointed. They know the country and the people. They can take care that the money given is properly expended. And, lastly, applying their own system of distribution, they are able to make the money go four or five times as far. Thus, in 1879, when the Po overflowed its banks, spreading ruin

Banche Popolari as Agencies for Distributing Relief.

all round, no relief machinery was found to do better service than the popular banks, which, being handed over 100,000 lire each from the relief funds, managed to multiply that sum to about 400,000 lire in the course of distribution, with the help of their credit—it is true, only *lending* the larger sum, but lending it so as to make it repayable by easy instalments spread over five years. And 4 lire so lent was to the poor flooded worth a good deal more than 1 lira given. In 1882, under similar circumstances, the *Banca Cooperativa Popolare di Padova* did even better service. Upon the guarantee of the province it advanced to the sufferers out of its own funds, with due discrimination, in all 295,417 lire, at 2 per cent. interest, demanding repayment by annual instalments spread over as much as ten years.

The Little Bank of Montelupo.

As an instance of what a People's Bank may do, on the very humblest lines on which its work is possible, I quote the record of the little bank of Montelupo, in the Florentine districts, one of the very earliest which was started, as an outcome from purely local initiative. The place is a sort of rural Whitechapel, with a poor population earning a bare livelihood mainly as *stovighi*, that is, makers of the cheapest kind of lucifer matches. Of these poor folk 375 started a *banca* with 10-lire shares, to be paid up in ten months. Accordingly they began with but £15 among them, and never got beyond £150 of share capital, even at the end of the year. Notwithstanding this, with the help of their *riputazione*, in the very first year they managed to attract £1,120 of deposits, and to lend out £1,240 in loans, netting a profit of more than £120, which nearly repaid the shares.

Credit to Agriculture.

Like the Schulze-Delitzsch associations in Germany, the *banche popolari* of Italy have often had the reproach levelled at them that they fail to provide for the needs of agriculture. The charge is as unjust in one case as it is in the other. It is not even quite fair to say that they leave *small* agriculture unprovided for, although, roughly speaking, that statement comes very much nearer the truth. I have already referred to the rather striking increase in the number of small-cultivator members in these banks. These men would not have joined if they did not find that they got some good out of the bank, beyond securing a convenient receptacle for their savings. There can be no doubt that a Luzzatti bank, established in an agricultural district, and having a certain amount of general business to rely upon, can, and in all cases that I know of, does, dispense its helpful loans to small agricultural folk as to others, so far as short-term lending is acceptable to them. Some *banche popolari* also make a point of lending a certain sum annually, after the example of the wealthier savings banks, at an unremunerative interest, really as a charity, to small agricultural folk. But, generally speaking, it is quite true that this system is not adapted to very small agricultural business. It was devised for comparatively dense populations, and it stands to reason that you cannot have an omnibus to carry a load of people along the well-paved streets of a town, which shall also serve as a light buggy-cart, to jolt the isolated peasant over his rough mountain tracks. Wherever the *banche popolare* attempt to serve a secluded rural district, they either become weak and incapable of standing the test of trying times, as has recently been witnessed in Piedmont, or else they really change their character, and become, under humane guidance, very similar to Raiffeisen banks—with this important drawback, that they have not the Raiffeisen clauses written in their rules, and therefore have no fully adequate safeguard against abuse. The two institutions obviously have different spheres marked out for them. M. Luzzatti has himself practically admitted this in his preface to the last official Report, and in his speech delivered at the Congress of Bologna, in both of which he, with sound judgment, pleaded for an *alliance* between *banche* and *casse*, the *banca* to form the trunk and the *casse* the branches, radiating from and supported by the central institution, as is actually already the case in the French Riviera.

Nevertheless, the Italian *banche popolari* without question do a great deal of lending in support of agriculture.

Various Methods tried.
Credit to agriculture has, in truth, long been the peculiar pet child of Italian legislators and economists. It has all along been felt to be so much needed. And at the same time it has proved so difficult! I have already stated that, as the outcome of an agitation immediately succeeding the

The Law of 1869.
establishment of political union, the Italian Government in 1869 passed a special law which authorised a number of banks to issue notes for specified amounts—30, 50, and 100 lire—on the security of certain cash balances held. The notes issued serve as legal tender in their provinces, and pass current, indeed, much beyond. One would have thought that this must be a highly profitable business for the banks. However the country has never taken to the system. The brief term to which lending under this law is restricted—three months—was of course against any large practice. In addition, the difficulty already referred to, of having to be prepared to cash whatever paper was issued, the moment at which it might be presented, prompted the issuing banks themselves to keep their issue within bounds. There are now only two credit institutions issuing under the law, namely, the excellent Savings Bank of Bologna, and the equally well-managed *Monte dei Paschi* of Siena, and their joint issue has dwindled to about £64,000 in all.

Cartelle Agrarie.
Approaching the same task from a more independent, but perhaps a more practical, standpoint, M. Luzzatti endeavoured to adapt our practice of Exchequer Bills and Treasury Bonds to the Italian market. He introduced the

THE "BANCHE POPOLARI" OF ITALY. 237

buoni di tesoro d'agricoltura or *cartelle agrarie*, which under the shape of bills or bonds secure credit for long periods. Before issuing such, he prudently made sure of the willingness of the large banks to discount them. It is interesting to note that in thus adapting themselves to the demands of agricultural credit, the *banche popolari* have introduced into their *regolamento* a rule evidently borrowed from the Raiffeisen banks, requiring borrowers to state the object of their loan beforehand and to adhere to it on pain of forfeiture.* The business actually done has not realised the hopes entertained. In 1881 the *banche* had 12,224,450 lire of agricultural paper outstanding. By 1889 the circulation had contracted to 6,390,210 lire, which is actually less than was recorded in 1876, the first year in which statistics were collected. But the money was apparently all taken up in small amounts. There were 1,425,750 lire outstanding in 30-lire bonds (24 shillings), 760 lire in 40-lire bonds, 1,592,650 lire in 50-lire bonds, 3,188,800 lire in 100-lire bonds, 182,000 lire in 200-lire bonds, and only 250 lire in a bond for that maximum figure. I do not believe from what I hear that the practice has at all extended since these figures were collected. So far as I can gather, the *cartelle* have been taken up in the main by friends of the movement, just as the first shares in the Milan Bank were—as a means of lending support to a good cause. There is no *bonâ fide* business done in them in the market. It wants, as has been already said, a stronger body than co-operative banks to make Exchequer Bills pass current.

In 1887, when the law of 1869 had incontestably proved a failure, the Italian Government decided experimentally to adopt M. Luzzatti's plan, fortifying it by the imposition of

The Law of 1887.

---

* Regolamento Provvisorio per l'emissione dei Buoni agrari prese le Banche Popolari del Primo Gruppo italiano (Rule 4 in Ettore Levi's Manuale, p. 548.)

238   PEOPLE'S BANKS.

<small>Cartelle a scadenza fissa.</small>

Government authority. The Act of that year gives power to credit institutions to issue bonds running for a fixed period (*cartelle a scadenza fissa*), for the length of which no limit is laid down. In practice, I believe, that two years is about the longest term permitted. The loans issued under this law may be secured either by mortgage, or else by a "privilege" equivalent to that given under our law of distress. To ensure this, lenders must have their claim registered. This is done free of charge. But it means a great deal of trouble and delay and entanglement in red tape. The Savings Bank of Bologna, which probably does the largest business of this sort among non-government institutions, had last October about 1,700,000 lire (£68,000) of such *cartelle* in circulation. That is not very much. Generally speaking, the second experiment is admitted to have resulted in failure like the first, and bankers, still retaining their sympathetic fondness for agricultural credit, are expectant as to a new and more perfect law which is said to be on the stocks, and which is to apply some more suitable method to the task.

<small>M. Sani's Method.</small>

To Signor Sani, the Chairman of the *Banca Popolare* of Bologna—one of the largest and certainly the most enterprising and original of Italian People's Banks—the method prescribed by the law of 1887 appeared from the outset so little contrived to serve its purpose, that he preferred to make the ordinary practice of lending, on acceptance or by cash credit, available for agricultural uses. Being exceptionally strong in capital and deposits, his bank is in a particularly good position to do this. Long terms cannot occasion any serious inconvenience to it. The agricultural population of the district consists mainly of freeholders. However, mortgages would be inconvenient as a security. So the bank secures itself by sureties or deposited effects —mainly by sureties—lending on acceptance for the term of six months—after which a renewal may be granted—or by cash credit for the term of a twelvemonth, on the expiration of which the credit may likewise be renewed. In either case the interest stands at 5 per **cent. This** method has proved not only acceptable to the agricultural population, **but** also very safe. It is easily applicable, even without the **precaution of** local committees such as are usual in Germany, because the large Council of the **bank includes** men from all districts, persons who **know** sufficient about the agricultural population to be able to ascertain and advise what borrowers deserve to be trusted. **In any** case there have been no losses.

M. Sani's method, being simple **and practical, is** the *How it is applied.* **method which,** roughly speaking, all agricultural banks dealing at all in agricultural credit have elected to put into practice—**Lodi, and** Brescia, and Bergamo, and Cremona, **and Rovigo, and that whole cluster of** *banche popolari* which **the late** Postmaster-General of Italy, M. Maggiorino Ferraris, **has helped to** raise up in his native country of Piedmont, established mainly **for** the service of agriculture. The cash required is provided **either** by the steady inflow of deposits, the command of a strong reserve fund, or **the** issue of long-term bonds, which, after all, secure **to strong** banks such substantial sums as 680,036 lire to **that of** Lodi, 581,119 lire to that of **Brescia, and 213,922 lire to** that of Rovigo. Those were the figures in 1894. Or else banks of this kind adopt the precaution of keeping a comparatively large proportion of their funds invested in readily marketable securities of steady value, so as to be prepared for sudden calls. These securities are made to answer the same purpose as the "mobilised portfolio." In Italy, where Government **Consols pay nearly 5 per cent.** interest, and Post Office **Savings Banks** accordingly make a profit, this is an easier process than it would be in the United Kingdom. In any case **the** banks show that they can provide the money. To ascertain the borrowing value **of their** clients they employ pretty much the same methods as the German banks. They have *succursales*, or local committees, or else local men to whom they can apply for information. In many cases the task is facilitated by a combination, very usual in the country, of tax-gathering with banking, which provides useful information, brings people to the "shop," secures a small profit, and materially reduces the otherwise heavy taxes levied upon the bank itself. On the other hand, the work is more difficult than in Germany, because among the agricultural population the proportion of *tenants* is very large, and tenants have rent to pay, in default of which, as in England, they may be distrained upon, under a law which is as severe as our own. That is one reason why it is absolutely indispensable that the credit granted should be *personal*. "*Esso è tanto piu importante in una provincia come la nostra nella quella prevale il latifondio e l'affitanza impresaria l'impone come una necessita.*" So writes to me M. Tullio Minelli, Chairman of the Co-operative Bank of Rovigo, which in 1894 lent out, out of 7,900,000 lire in all, about 4,740,000 lire (£189,600) to farmers. "Tenant-farming imposes personal credit as a necessity." In the district of Rovigo, the landlord is generally applied to for information about his tenant, and in many cases he readily goes bail for him. In the Lodigiano, where there are mainly *large* farmers, farming 600 to 800 acres and more, who may require substantial sums, and who consider themselves every bit the landlords' equals, such practice is out of the question. However, really, the landlord's testimony being unavailable, the tenant borrowers are all the more careful to satisfy the bank with regard to the danger of a distress. In any case the losses are infinitesimal.

Credit in connection with Agricultural Syndicates.

The rapid spread in Italy of the institution of agricultural syndicates—which we may consider as simply agricultural co-operative associations with technical instruction added to their programme—has suggested to M. Luzzatti a new method of organising agricultural credit, specifically with a view to facilitating common purchase of goods. The method has been actually put into practice, but not long enough to make it possible to report results. It is in principle the same which has for some time back been practised with good effect in the Raiffeisen associations of Germany. The members of the agricultural syndicate, so far as they wish to avail themselves of credit, join, or else form, a co-operative bank, which upon any demand for credit of course satisfies itself with regard to their trustworthiness, and, if desired, opens to them a cash credit secured by sureties or otherwise. That credit, or part of it, the member assigns to the agricultural syndicate, which thereupon opens him a corresponding credit for the purchase of the articles in which it deals. He may make use of such credit, or he may not. If he does not, he will have nothing to pay. The practice effectually helps farmers over the difficulties which I have found to stand in the way of agricultural co-operative supply in this country—viz., a want of ready cash. The farmer buys practically on credit, like our own poor or thriftless farmers; but having made sure of a credit with the bank, he at the same time obtains all the benefits of cash payment and co-operative purchase in respect of price and quality, being charged only a moderate interest upon the money actually drawn. The method is simple, but it has its distinct advantages.

I abstain from entering in any detail into the semi-charitable or philanthropic lending practised by some co-operative banks, because that is not business but alms-giving.

Quite enough has surely been said to show with what liberal hand the *banche popolari*, lending out in 1893 close upon £40,000,000, deal out their money, be it in showers or be it in driblets, to the small artisan or to the substantial farmer—readily, smoothly, safely, with remarkable adaptability to varying circumstances.

What a stream of almost exhaustless beneficence does this system of People's Banks seem to turn loose upon a thirsting world! And how wasteful do our own profuse, but carelessly distributed, gifts appear by the side of these self-repaying loans! It may be said that we have the money, and need not look to economy. But our carelessness leaves such a wide margin of distress which goes without benefit. And the greatest benefit of all, the lesson which teaches people how to help themselves, how to make the help received from others go farthest, the lesson of thrift and business-like habits, in our free-handed but easy-going giving—which is the product rather of instinct than of reflection—we generally miss altogether.

Spread and Growth of Banche Popolari.

As might be expected, once the "Utopianism" of M. Luzzatti's scheme had been disproved by facts, once the People's Banks had shown themselves truly beneficent associations, hindrances disappeared, and the banks multiplied pretty rapidly. Up to 1883, indeed, the adverse law stood in the way. Their number increased by 9, 2, 7, 5, 10 in the year. Nevertheless, in 1882 it already stood at 206, with an aggregate capital and reserve of 57,822,000 lire (£2,312,880), that is, about £11,200 per bank, and a members' roll of 114,072 (821 per bank); and their collective lending amounted to annually 156,042,366 lire (£6,241,696). By 1889 the banks had increased to 714 (as against 159 non-co-operative credit institutions), with 114,979,542 lire (£4,599,180) capital and reserve, and lending out annually 285,936,946 lire (£11,437,476). Their annual transactions had risen from 206,899,142 to 425,339,827 lire. In 1893 there were 730 banks (of this system only, without counting the *casse rurali*), of which 662 sending in returns under this head showed a collective members' roll of 405,341, the classification of whom has already been given.* The average number of members per bank, which varies a little from year to year, stood then at 612. The collective paid-up capital of 697 banks amounted to 89,949,527 lire, to which must be added 28,278,349 lire reserve funds, bringing up the total of capital of their own to 118,228,000 lire, or £4,729,120. This capital had attracted in all 357,723,000 lire (£14,308,920) of borrowed money (£8,729,480 savings deposits, £3,646,040 deposits on current accounts [cash balances], and £1,933,400 in long-term bonds), and had enabled the banks to lend out on acceptances, current accounts, ordinary advances, and otherwise 992,448,400 lire (£39,697,936). The loans were for the most part of medium amount, 20.97 per cent. in number, 19.37 per cent. in value. ranging from 201 to 500 lire; 10.18 per cent. in number, 21.14 in value, from 501 to 1,000 lire; 4.30 per cent. in number, and 29.00 in amount, from 1,001 to 5,000 lire. Accordingly, close upon 70 per cent. of the money was lent in sums ranging from £8 to £200. Only .53 per cent. in number, 13.45 per cent. in value, go beyond 5,000 lire; and 67.02 in number, 17.04 in value, fall short of 200 lire. The rates of interest charged vary from 1½ to 16 per cent. But the last-named extraordinary figure, which M. Luzzatti condemns as " Asiatic," occurs in the case of one bank only, a small one, peculiarly situated, in Sardinia. However, the rate of interest is generally higher than in Germany, ranging from 6 to 8 per cent., which M. Luzzatti justifies by the high value of money prevailing in the poorer country. Against this it ought in fairness to be pointed out that some of the strongest and largest banks pay dividends of 10, 12, and 14 per cent., which are from our point of view not at all " co-operative." The bad or doubtful debts made upon the 992,448,400 lire of lending are, as already stated, returned at 15,390,164 lire, 1.55 per cent., a figure more than five

---

* See page 219.

times larger than what occurs in ordinary years.* The actual losses made good are given as 1,334,360 lire (£53,375). They are confined to 199 banks, presumably badly managed ones, of which there are more than there should be. There were 74 banks declaring a loss, instead of a profit, of 438,157 lire in all. Of that number, 18 banks are in Campania, where co-operative banking is very so-so, 9 in Apulia, where it is not much better, 6 in Basilicata, 7 in the Marches, and 6 in Piedmont, where there is a good deal of speculative spirit, and there are, as will be shown, a number of banks excessively weak in capital. The net profits realised by 694 banks (including the 74 losing ones) is returned at 6,799,855 lire (£271,994), which, upon a sum of 89,949,527 lire (representing the paid-up capital of 697 banks) would be equivalent to a return of more than 7½ per cent. Of that sum, however, only 4,827.854 lire has been distributed in dividend,† 1,156,755 lire being carried to reserve, 379,738 lire being distributed among the employés with 211,356 lire in addition carried to their provident funds, while 107,529 lire was devoted to charities.

I ought to add that the year 1893 was in every respect an exceptionally unfortunate one. The figures for preceding years show *very* much better in every respect.

---

* This exceptionally heavy figure is owing to bad banking in weak provinces. Basilicata shows 19.07 per cent., as against .47 in 1886, .01 in 1882, &c. ; Apulia shows 4.83 per cent. ; Sicilia, 3.28 per cent. ; Sardinia, 2.22. Emilia has 1.20 per cent., as against .20 in 1886, its ordinary rate. Lombardy .33, which is only a slight excess upon its average figure ; Venetia, in the same way, .27 per cent. It is the bad banks which have been found out by the crisis, and spoil the average for the good.

† The Statistical Report gives 6.36 per cent. as the average return of dividend declared in 1893 by 493 banks furnishing returns, or 4.97 per cent. on capital plus reserve. That is a considerable diminution on the results of the "eighties," when 9.49, 9.48, 9.44, and respectively 7.30, 7.31, and 7.23 per cent. were common.

THE "BANCHE POPOLARI" OF ITALY. 245

The 730 banks were very unequally distributed over pretty well all the kingdom. Ostensibly Campania, which has a large number of small and not always very good banks, takes the lead, boasting, in 1893, 127, which by the end of 1894 had increased to 132. However, the real force of co-operative banking lay then, as it lies now, and always has lain, in Lombardy, Venetia, Emilia, the Marches, and Piedmont. Of the "business" done during 1893 by 649 People's Banks, totalling up to 12,476,186,567 lire (£499,047,462), the average figure per inhabitant of the province is: for Lombardy, 1,439.68 lire; for Emilia, 643.78 lire; for Venetia, 471.24 lire; for Campania, 228.63 lire; for Latium, 89.97 lire; and for Sardinia only 3.53 lire. The average figure per inhabitant of the kingdom is 406.06 lire. Emilia, Lombardy, and Venetia, as M. Luzzatti himself testifies, show both the best banks and the greatest banking strength. Fifty-nine of the sixty banks existing in Lombardy, having 74,163 members, held in share and reserve capital 39,811,120 lire, and in deposits 163,046,660 lire, which is more than twice what the non-co-operative banks of the same province can boast; whereas Campania, with 58,963 members, held only 17,670,321 lire of capital, and 66,410,230 lire in deposits. The figures for Venetia are less striking than those for Lombardy, but still favourable to the co-operative banks. The co-operative banks there held 10,497,384 lire in share capital, and 54,554,036 lire in deposits, against 8,103,783 and 35,014,426 lire respectively held by ordinary banks. The proportion is most telling in Emilia, where co-operative banks held 10,372,695 lire in capital and 52,613,048 lire in deposits, as compared with only 55,918, and 917,487 lire respectively held by other banks. Assuredly these figures show what a power co-operative banking has grown to be in M. Luzzatti's country.

The year 1893 was, as observed, an exceptionally bad

The Crisis has affected Co-operative Banks less than Ordinary Banks. one. It was then that the commercial crisis really began to find out the co-operative banks which had stood, so to speak, like a rock, while the non-co-operative institutions tumbled to pieces, and crash followed crash. As a matter of course, a decline of business tells upon industrial banks, no matter whether they be co-operative or otherwise. In 1887, 608 co-operative banks held a "portfolio" of acceptances discounted of 285,000,000 lire, and deposits of 427,617,000 lire, on a paid-up capital of only 104,109,000 lire. By 1893 the paid-up capital had risen to 118,228,000 lire, but the "portfolio" had shrunk to 214,490,000 lire, and the deposits to 357,723,000 lire. . Among non-co-operative banks the decline was very much more marked. Their share capital went down from 324,605,000 lire in 1887 to 261,873,000 lire in 1893, their deposits shrank from 688,045,000 lire to 419,423,000 lire, and the discount business had gone down from 353,000,000 to 186,000,000.

From 1893 to 1894 the number of People's Banks in Italy diminished by ten. There are now only 720, allowing one People's Bank to every 42,089 inhabitants as compared with one to 165,439 in 1881. There have been several collapses, owing to bad management. Thus the important (industrial) Bank of Brescia, which had speculated in sulphur, had to close its doors. The Bank of Alessandria, which had locked up a large sum of money in mortgages, had to suspend payment. It has since revived in an amalgamated shape, having allied itself with another bank. And the Bank of Genoa, having dabbled too freely in building operations, has likewise had to place itself, for a time only, in its creditors' hands. It is now once more solvent and busy. In the main, the decrease, which is very partial, is due, probably, in some degree to the ridiculously heavy taxation levied upon the banks by the State, and, moreover, to the discomfiture of some puny credit institutions which started with a wholly insufficient capital, made up of 5-lire shares, or else levying their funds from members, like our Loan and Self-Help Societies, in monthly payments. Societies organised on such lines can obviously never acquire real stability. They build, so to speak, their walls with the material which should go into the foundations. We in England see the results of such unwise policy in the rapid changes perpetually taking place in the number and strength of our Loan Societies. A Loan Society will rise up to-day, to-morrow will be suffering from a superabundance of funds, only to find all its money drawn out and itself condemned to a happy euthanasia the day after. You cannot work a bank without some fixed and **stable** capital. On the other hand, to start a *limited* liability bank with 4s. shares is obviously a risky operation. With all their merits, these Luzzatti banks will not work on very small means. **Out of ten** banks which have, on the balance, shut up shop **in** 1894, eight are small agricultural banks with such diminutive shares started **in** Piedmont. Two of these held capitals severally of £30 and £36 only. For a Raiffeisen bank that would be ample. For a Luzzatti bank it is nothing. There are diminutions also in Basilicata, Apulia, Sicilia, and the Abruzzi, all of them weak provinces, where banks are feeble. On the other hand, in Liguria, Lombardy, Venetia, Tuscany, and the Marches, there is a small increase. Business, in the sense **of** lending, has further **decreased**— from 268,736,000 lire to 243,910,000 lire. **But** deposits have grown from 357,723,000 to 372,164,388 lire.

Quite evidently the business of the co-operative banks is **not only** sound, but the soundest **that** there is in Italy. And although **their activity** has **met** with a temporary check—just as in Germany—the marked difference in comparative decline **between** them **and** other banks, telling strongly in their own favour, shows that they are destined, not only to maintain themselves satisfactorily, but to renew **their** advance as times improve. **There** is **no** more en-

<small>How the Banks spread.</small>

couraging feature about these banks than this, that one of them is never set up without calling up within very little time a family of others, clustering around it, to serve for different *clientèles*—more or less pretentious as the case may be. By the self-evidence of its advantages the business seems to propagate itself. Thus around the *Banca Popolare* of Milan have sprung up in that city alone eight new banks, as on a graduated scale; round the Bank of Bologna five; round that of Naples twenty—all of them more or less *étagées*, " ranged in tiers," suiting their requirements to their own peculiar public, and issuing shares of from 5 lire (4s.) up to 100 lire (£4). They push forward in their own peculiar way. A central bank begins by sending out *succursales;* after a time the *succursales* decide to turn themselves into independent banks; the central bank, without a suspicion of jealousy, readily helps them, and their business doubles and trebles. Thus province after province is taken possession of with a regularity of method, and a certainty of success, which remind one of the conquest of a country by a victorious army. There are cases in which the unselfish parent-bank has, like a pelican, fed its offspring on its own flesh. Thus the Bank of Cremona has four *succursales*, which do not yet pay. Indeed, three of them —Soresina, Casalmaggiore, and Piedana—among them in 1890 made a loss of 6,000 lire. Nevertheless the 5,100 members composing the five establishments, holding, in all, 42,000 shares, work together as one body, drawing precisely the same dividend throughout. The thing will right itself in time. The old Bank of Lodi has five *succursales* and eight agencies, the Bank of Novara seven, and so on. The common feature throughout is amicable co-operation, carried out on the principle which M. Luzzatti ever presses upon his banks, namely: "*Independenti sempre, isolati mai*"—union combined with decentralisation, independence, and yet general alliance—alliance extended so as to embrace also the savings banks and other similar institutions, all of which claim and are allowed their place in the periodical congresses, and study to further the cause of self-help by all means in their power. The great lending and the great borrowing or distributing institutions remain friends and allies as they have been from the beginning. By way of further development the *banche* have combined to a co-operative insurance union, *Il Popolare*, for which every *banca* acts as an agent. With so large and so dependable a *clientèle* the society is bound to do well.

Of late the proposal has been brought forward to focus the common affairs in a central bank. In view of the local centralisation which has already taken place, concentrating Lombardy business in Milan, Emilia business in Bologna, and so on, it is held questionable whether there is really room for an additional central institution.

Throughout Italy these banks have become a power for good ; and if Lord Jeffrey spoke truly when he laid it down that the greatness of a nation and the happiness of its people do not depend so much upon the increase of its military strength as upon " the spread of banks and the increase of banking facilities," Italy, with her smaller army, has no need to shrink from comparison with her more powerful military neighbours with their mighty " nations in arms "—against which she has to pit her " nation in banks." Looking at all these busy, laborious hives, in which not a drop of honey is allowed to run to waste, you cannot fail to realise that they represent a great and beneficent national possession, a richly yielding horn of plenty, and that, in M. Durand's words, " This magnificent network of institutions of popular credit, for which Italy is beholden to M. Luzzatti, may well excite the envy of Europe." " It is impossible," says M. Luzzatti, with just pride, in his presidential address of 1887, " not to acknowledge that we have delivered the small folk and the middle classes from crushing usury, that

"A Nation in Banks."

we have assisted commerce, and, lastly, that we have helped to cultivate throughout the fruitful tree of thrift on ground which previously appeared absolutely barren."

Some unsound Banks.

The large host of *banche popolari*, it is idle to deny, includes alike good, bad, and indifferent, according to the spirit prevailing among the local leaders. It would be a great mistake to look upon the system as absolutely self-regulating. Some original sin the first Italian banks inherited from their German parents. That sin has here and there blossomed into greed, dividend-hunting, a taste for speculation, carelessness; and has borne fruit in the study of large business, in big dividends, high rates of interest, and occasional collapses. As the movement has gone on, its leader has applied more and more of the purifying fire of co-operative principle, which has already cleansed away so much of the dross bequeathed by the old Adam, that some months ago M. Luzzatti could publicly boast that the "good" Italian banks distinctly surpass the best among the German in "moral" character—though he had to add the avowal that in Germany the second-rate banks in this respect excel above the Italian.

Instances of Sound Banks: The Banca Popolare of Bologna.

Fortunately there are good specimens of the Italian banks to be met with in most of the districts where they have gained a footing. I have already spoken of the great "Queen Bank" of Milan, which I desire to hold up rather as an example of success than as a model for imitation. M. Luzzatti himself awards the palm for quality among all his banks to the excellent *Banca Popolare* of Bologna, which he speaks of as undoubtedly "the first in the world." Those words were uttered at Bologna, otherwise they might appear unkind to the banks of Cremona, Bergamo, Vicenza Lodi, Pieve di Soligo, and not a few others. However, a better model certainly could not be held up for instruction and imitation than the People's Bank of Bologna, which at the close of thirty years' existence finds its paid-up capital increased from 111,756 to 1,260,540 lire, with a reserve fund of 1,292,077 lire at its back, and its turnover grown from 700,295 to 38,216,455 lire. Its annual profits have correspondingly increased from 5,469 to **149,975 lire**. In the place of the modest 696,450 lire which marked its first year's business, it now lends out annually, among its 4,971 members, 31,439,833 lire. The brilliant success secured is not, however, what either M. Luzzatti or myself would wish to hold up most conspicuously to admiration. That success has been attained by excellent management, evidenced by the careful attention given at all points to the convenience of members—but concurrently with a practical display of philanthropy and public spirit bound to attract support. The bank has shown itself largely given to good works, not only in the way of "loans of honour" and contributions to useful and charitable funds and enterprises, but also in spending freely for technical education, which is to bring profit to the Italian vine-growers, artisans, and husbandmen. Its "loans of honour" it grants, up to 100 lire, free of interest; but it insists upon prompt repayment. In interest-bearing loan business it makes it a rule to give the preference to small business. Of its loans it is interesting to note that 4,500,000 lire has gone to agriculture, and 731,000 lire to working-class borrowers. One would wish to see every People's Bank animated by the same spirit.

The People's Bank of Cremona, having nearly twice the capital of the Bank of Bologna, is as excellent a type, and is interesting more specifically on the ground of its considerable agricultural business in a district quite as much devoted to agriculture as to industry. The Bank of Lodi— *Banca Mutua Popolare Agricola*—really the oldest bank of the Luzzatti type, is another admirable bank bearing a strongly agricultural character. Of something over 7,000,000, or even maybe 8,000,000 lire, lent out annually, quite 3,000,000 lire goes to agriculturists, generally speaking of the large tenant class. Such loans are generally made in the form of cash credits, and losses are practically *nil*. As a proof of the confidence which banks like that of Lodi inspire, I may mention that an English engineer on the spot, holding an appointment in the service of the "Light Railways" of the district, informed me that he had advisedly drawn his money out of the local joint-stock bank in order to put it into this co-operative bank, "because he knew it to be safer." The Bank of Rovigo has only 2,209 members as compared with the 6,000 of Lodi, and its capital is only 337,398 lire as compared with 2,228,499 lire (in both cases including reserve funds). It is equally agricultural, but caters for a different *clièntele*—the smaller tenantry. It lent out in 1893, 9,297,896 lire on bills, in addition to more than 400,000 lire granted in cash credits. Its losses on agricultural business are likewise infinitesimal.

Rovigo.

The *Credito Agrario Bresciano* is an independent institution, but following generally Luzzatti lines. Its *clientèle* is specifically one of what in Italy counts as "medium" farmers — generally speaking freeholders. The larger farmers go by preference to the Savings Bank, which, like all Italian Savings Banks, is allowed by law to lend on personal security. The small go to the *casse rurali* of their districts, adapted "Raiffeisen" banks, of which I shall still have to speak. The Bank of Brescia is interesting as working (until recently) side by side with an industrial co-operative bank established in the same place, and in a district in which co-operative credit has not been called into being by the extortions of usury. Even without such provocation, in a district in which good cultivation makes all the difference between profitable and unprofitable husbandry—one-third of the area is under irrigation—the urgent need of ample working capital, upon which I have laid stress elsewhere, has naturally come to be recognised. The Bank of Brescia has slightly over 2,000 members, a paid-up capital

Credito Agrario Bresciano.

of 322,238 **lire, and** lends out more than 2,000,000 lire, generally (practically) for the **term of** thirty months, the principal being repayable **by** tenths, at about 6 per cent., which enables it to pay its shareholders **from 4 to 6 per** cent. in dividend. The Bank of Acqui, almost purely agri- Acqui. cultural, is interesting because it has raised itself to acknowledged strength from what was practically bankruptcy. **The** bank was formed in 1883, to serve an exclusively agricultural—that is, viticultural—district, **and** within little **time** found itself with 400,000 lire to the bad, owing in the main to depreciation of land and agricultural produce. The present manager then took charge of the establishment. Fortunately, as it happened, another bank in the neighbourhood came to grief about the same time, and people in the **district** transferred all their deposits to Acqui. Since then **the** bank has made deposits its principal source for the supply of funds. It takes bills from neighbouring smaller banks, **but rarely passes** its own on for re-discount. "A good deposit bank," so **the manager,** M. **Scotti,** puts it, "should stand in no need of credit." **To** secure itself against danger which might **arise** from a sudden withdrawal of deposits, the bank keeps a comparatively large portion **of its** funds invested in readily marketable securities, which means that, to keep itself safe, it does less lending in proportion to its money than industrial banks. It is now strong in position, and pays a good dividend. Speaking of agricultural banks, **I am** bound to mention the small banks, specifically agri- cultural, of Piedmont. Actually the smallest of these is that Spigno. of Spigno, which has little over 200 members; in 1894 there **were 228, of** whom 18 were medium cultivators, and 163, the **bulk of** the *clientèle*, decidedly small men, alike **free-** holders, tenants, and *mezzadri* (*métayers*). Thirty members were village tradesmen. Of the 228 members, 112 held only one share **of 20** lire (16s.) each. The small share capital could not **obviously** go very far, and evidently savings deposits are not very considerable. The people are very poor. The friends of the movement have come to their aid, paying in deposits and taking long-term bonds. And the local friendly society, which is really the parent of the bank, and which still provides the bulk of its members and lends its office, pays in its funds. So does the *municipio* —the parish council. By that means the little bank, holding only 11,849 lire of paid-up capital of its own, has been enabled to lend out in 1894, 179,670 lire, of which the major portion was lent in amounts under 300 lire. As much as 49,327 lire was lent out in amounts of less than 100 lire. This little bank is to me one full of interest. But what with the support which it receives on the strength of the "moral" responsibility which Cavaliere Spingardi, the President, frankly owns that men like himself—he is the "little Providence" of the bank—owe to their poorer brethren, in excess of the duty which their limited liability lays upon them, I can scarcely look upon it as a *bonâ fide* "People's Bank," however useful and beneficent it may be. And I cannot help thinking that in so small and so distinctly rural a district a Raiffeisen bank would be more in place.

The Banca Cooperativa Milanese.

In Italian towns, as in the country, to see how the *banche popolari* can do good work, it is well to step down from the level of large institutions like those of the *Banche Popolari* of Milan, Cremona, and Bologna, to a lower stratum. On a smaller scale there is quite as good work to be shown. There could not be a more co-operative bank than the *Banca Cooperativa Milanese*, which in seven years raised its profits from 38,223 lire (for seven months) to 229,874 lire, and which two years later showed a turnover of 117,404,794 lire. Its 50-lire shares sell at 75 lire. This bank, ably administered by M. Arrigo Valentini, lends most useful aid to small traders, and to other co-operative associations. It is thanks to its assistance that the *Magaz-*

THE "BANCHE POPOLARI" OF ITALY.

zini Generali del Mobilio, a productive cabinetmakers' association of originally about 400, now about 700 members, have found themselves able to defeat the "sweaters" and emancipate so large a number of working-men families, who now work for their own account and earn good wages, besides raising themselves steadily in the social scale.* In Bologna, side by side with the pretentious *Banca Popolare*, you have the modest Operatives' Bank, locally known as *La Banchina*—its correct title is *Banca Cooperativa per gli operai e la piccola industria della città e provincia di Bologna*. The bank has something over 5,000 members, spread out over a large district, and disposes of a paid-up capital (with reserve fund) of 162,173 lire. The members are all small folk with small wants in respect of loans. The majority of loans vary between 200 and 300 lire. Serving a large district, by means of local agencies, which, in conjunction with the large amount of work necessitated by the smallness of the transactions, swell the expenses and make a margin of $2\frac{1}{2}$ per cent. between lending and borrowing imperative, the bank deals out 1,864,812 lire in loans in the course of a year. Descending lower still in the scale, there is the *Cassa Cooperativa di credito della Società Operaia maschile*, which issues only 5-lire shares, thereby securing a capital of 45,790 lire, which a reserve fund of 21,983 lire has raised to 67,773 lire. Thanks to the collection of 141,834 lire in savings, it managed in 1894 to lend out to its working-men members 603,056 lire. Since New Year 1895 the number of members has further grown to 4,000, and the capital has correspondingly increased. It is really a misnomer to speak of this institution as specifically *maschile*, for there is a *Società femminile* which has joined the male Society to work the bank in common. This

La Banchina.

A Working-men's Bank.

---

* See my article, "A Defence against Sweating," in the *Economic Review* of April 1894.

little bank is really one of the triumphs of working-class self-help in Italy. It was set up in 1883, with only 464 members, subscribing 10,980 lire (£439) in share capital. For ten years its shareholders were content to do absolutely without dividend. By dint of sacrifice and pegging away the society had by the end of 1894 crept up to 2,771 members, commanding the capital quoted. From 14,670 lire its savings deposits had crept up to 116,480 lire; its credits had grown from 23,663 to 156,417 lire. And the little institution maintains itself and keeps solvent, and does an immense amount of good in dispensing relief to working folk by loans which must not in any one case exceed 150 lire (£6), if the loan be an advance, or 200 lire if it be granted by way of discount of an accepted bill. In the first twelve years of its existence it has, in all, lent out 6,190,161 lire in 7,274 loans. The interest charged is necessarily rather high, 6½ per cent., and the maximum length of time is fifteen months. No member is allowed to hold more than five shares. The whole concern is humble, and has been raised up out of palpable weakness. However, by good management it has succeeded in maintaining itself, and maintaining itself, creditably, by self-help alone.

Employees' Banks.

M. Luzzatti, in his Preface to the last Statistical Return of *Banche Popolari*, calls attention to the recent increase in the number of credit associations formed specially for the use of civil servants, railway employees, and others forming the staff of large establishments, and dependent upon salaries. There were at the close of 1894 no less than 29 such societies in existence, some of them very strong both in numbers and in capital. Among persons of such a class, of course, co-operation for credit is particularly easy, because it is to the supreme interest of every member that he should preserve a good character. Some of our own civil servants have found this out, and organised very successful societies,

THE "BANCHE POPOLARI" OF ITALY.

which are, in fact, co-operative credit associations, one among the Post Office employees, and some others among Civil Servants generally. The Italian employees' societies also include associations of school teachers, again a very suitable class, and abroad a class to whom occasional credit must be of considerable importance. We find the same kind of thing established in Germany. Railway servants are in Italy very conspicuous alike in this and in other forms of co-operation. They are answerable for no fewer than five credit associations in Italy. The employees of the Ministry of Agriculture, Industry, and Commerce have formed their own co-operative credit bank, as have also the clerks of the large Bank of Naples. Lastly, the Italian "Army and Navy Stores," an establishment smaller of course than our own in Victoria Street, but admirably conducted, the *Unione Militare*, has introduced a system of credit which is very discreetly managed, but is found useful, mainly to junior officers, when money happens to be scarce—though the sums advanced are not generally large, never exceeding £80, lent at 4 per cent.; and the entire practice really only amounts to an equivalent to credit for purchases at the particular store.

One very peculiar little association, which can scarcely be called a bank, exists at Cuglieri in Sardinia. Shares in this institution are payable, not in money, but in corn. Two hectolitres of wheat, valued at 32 lire, make a "share." The credits asked appear likewise to be given in corn. This is, in truth, a revival of a very ancient institution, the *monti frumentari*, alluded to above.

<small>A Modern monte frumentario.</small>

People's Banks having proved popular, one cannot be surprised at seeing the Church of Rome, always a good strategist in matters affecting her interests, studying to take advantage of the magnetic power of the useful institution to add one more material support or bulwark to her fabric. Denominationalism is not in itself a desirable factor

<small>"Catholic" Banks.</small>

R

to be introduced into banking, and it is to be doubted if a bank, attracting recruits by relief offered for their material needs, constitutes the best possible missionary for the Church. However, we ought to bear in mind that among purely Roman Catholic populations institutions which we should set up as generally "Christian" or "philanthropic" or "educational," as a matter of course assume the name "Catholic," under the dubbing of good men to whom "Catholic" appears identical with, if not indeed superior in expressiveness to, "Christian," or generally "good." The "Catholic" banks are in themselves sound banking institutions, and do not a little good in their purely Romanist home of Venetia, where they have already become powerful enough to act as centres to a whole network of useful, or else charitable, institutions, all of them impressed with the "Catholic" stamp, and sanctioned and headed by the bishop of the particular diocese. There are two such banks in Venetia. One—the *Banca di San Paolo*, of Brescia, founded in 1888—has a paid-up capital of 100,000 lire, and does an annual business, more particularly in bills of exchange and cash credits, amounting to 7,573,800 lire. The other is the *Piccolo Credito Bergamasco*, styled "Piccolo," to designate the character rather than the volume of its business. This bank was founded in January 1892, having 260 shareholders, who among them took up 2,034 shares of 20 lire each. The bank, designed to assist small tradesmen with credit—and, moreover, to start "Catholic" village banks of the Raiffeisen type—in three years discounted 9,732 acceptances for a total amount of 5,197,591 lire (£207,904), of which already 4,313,495 lire is repaid. It is a steady, growing business. In addition, the bank has lent upon security 355,322 lire, and by way of cash credit 2,397,205 lire, advancing in all, in three years, 7,950,115 lire (£318,004), in addition to taking 3,750,936 lire in savings deposits, of which it still holds 1,881,858 lire. Moreover, it has already sixteen Raiffeisen village banks clustered around it. This is not bad business. The paid-up capital has meanwhile grown to 245,263 lire, with a reserve fund of 20,561 lire at its back. The annual business amounts to 4,489,585 lire. The bank in truth forms the centre of a great "Catholic" social and economic propaganda, in which the "Catholic Agricultural Union," doing a large co-operative business for its members, is the foremost factor, but which comprises also a "Catholic" bakery, a "Catholic" Young Men's Provident Society, a Young Women's ditto, "Catholic" soup kitchens, a "Catholic" Working Men's Club, and some other items. There is no reason why "Catholics" should not co-operate among themselves, so long as they do not take up a position of hostility towards others. In a strongly "Catholic" province, the inscription of "Catholicism" on the co-operative banner has certainly added a potent stimulus to the co-operative movement. Among a mixed population it would work harm. And it may be pleaded that Roman Catholics, like others, might be content to accept good advice given by a high Authority, and to render unto God the things that are God's, and unto the Cæsar of economic and social work the things which are that Cæsar's.

Whatever be the merit of this specifically "Catholic" movement, and of all the other more or less independent co-operative banking, which of course one must expect to see overflowing from a vessel so rapidly filled to the brim, all that work is manifestly due to the good example set by the *banche popolari*, introduced thirty years ago by M. Luzzatti, whom, in view of the magnificent work accomplished, and still in progress of accomplishment, I accordingly have good cause for calling, as I have done in my dedication, "the benefactor of his country."

A Tribute to M. Luzzatti.

CHAPTER X.

THE "CASSE RURALI" OF ITALY.

Need in Italy of Small Village Banks.   As in the person of M. Luzzatti Italy had its own Schulze-Delitzsch, Providence so ordered it that it should have also its own Raiffeisen—not a mere mechanical imitator, but an intelligent adapter, taking into due account the peculiar circumstances of his country. There can be no doubt that the *banche popolari* do not adequately occupy all the ground which calls for cultivation. They do wonders among small trading folk with moderate means. They do very little for the large class of small agricultural cultivators, who need help very sorely.

Common Features in Rural Italy and Rural England.   The case of rural Italy ought to be interesting to us, because there are some features which link it rather strikingly with our own rural economy. In Latium, in Umbria, in the Marches, and in parts of Lombardy and Venetia, there is the same paucity of landowners, a very similar system of land tenure, even more absenteeism, and —here is a point of difference — incomparably greater harshness practised in the collection of rents. In Italy the need of the humble tenant classes is, indeed, owing to peculiar circumstances, even more accentuated than among ourselves. To the mass of the people in the country life is a perpetual struggle. Everything, of course, is backward —tillage, trade, family economy—in that little cottage which poverty has stripped bare of every comfort. The farm implements are primitive, the manure is of the scantiest, and so is the fodder given to that poor, misshapen **live stock,** which, in **nine cases** out of ten, belongs to a usurer, who **draws all** the profit out of its rearing. Rents **are** rigidly exacted, and to the **little** household, perpetually in debt, "money" **is as** much of a meaningless "expression" as "Italy" used to be geographically before the Union. Even wages offer but a slight alleviation to the cultivator's lot. **For** their scale is very low—50 **centesimi** for a woman, from 80 centesimi to 1 lira, or **at most** 1½ lira for a man.

Of course such an economical desert **must needs** bring forth its own peculiar weeds. Usury is rampant. Its practice is scarcely even held disgraceful. Indeed, the **usurer** has come to be looked upon as quite respectable. **There is** nothing on which he will **not** lay his hands. If **the poor peasant** wants money, he can have it at rates varying **from** 50 to 1,200 per cent.—often with **a** Sunday dinner thrown in as a prescriptive condition. Or he may **have it from a** bank in the town, at which, **in** consideration of a heavy fee, the usurer consents to act as surety. Should the peasant require a sack of maize—as he sometimes does— he can have that **in** kind, of inferior quality, **at** the rate **of** 24 lire for what **in** the market costs only **12** lire, but **at** three months' credit—a matter of 400 per cent. per annum. Should he require live stock, there is the same friend **in need to** provide it by **an** arrangement called *soccida,* which **throws** all the risk and cost of keeping upon the hirer, **while** securing a sure half of **the** ·profits to the lender. **Should he want** goslings for his wife to rear up and fatten for the market—as favourite an industry in Venetia **as** chicken-cramming is in Sussex—the usurer will let him have his £2 wherewith to buy fifty goslings, claiming back **as** interest, at the close of five or six months, five fat geese, representing a **value of** £1.

That has proved merry business for the usurers, but it has kept the peasantry **in** abject poverty, which was ren-

Need begets Usury. Instances.

dered more marked when hard times came, and either the earth refused to yield her fruits or the market its prices. Their condition became worse than mere poverty, for it crushed all hope and elasticity out of them. After the year 1880 had brought on the critical period of depression, there seemed scarcely anything left to work for. Cattle, implements, furniture, were all pledged to the usurer. And feed as badly, clothe himself as badly, live as badly as he would, all the peasant's toil went but to enrich his oppressor.

The Earliest Propaganda.

For such a population as this the Raiffeisen Loan Banks, with their aptitude for conjuring money out of nothing, appeared the one thing needed. Of course their fame had penetrated across the Alps, and in 1883, just before Dr Wollemborg resolved to make himself their champion in Italy, M. Luzzatti cleared one hindrance to their introduction out of the way by publicly declaring that " if the ardour of an apostle were to raise up banks similar to those of Raiffeisen, they should be welcome ; he would not in Italy renew those useless and disgraceful polemics with which these banks had been met by his friends in Germany—if they did not disdain to accept it, there he offered them his hand for alliance and help."

But, unfortunately, the fame was as yet nothing but fame. The Italians "heard the message, but they lacked the faith." No one really believed in the practicability of the thing. Signor A. Keller had championed it in speech, but gained no converts. And when Dr Wollemborg made up his mind to try his hand at a practical experiment, " everybody told me," so he himself says, "that my undertaking was 'impossible.' And I silently recalled to mind that fine saying of Carlyle's : Every noble enterprise is at its outset 'impossible.'"

Dr Leone Wollemborg.

In his own Venetian home of Loreggia Dr Wollemborg had a good district to begin upon. Loreggia is a biggish parish, with something under 3,000 inhabitants, mostly devoted to agriculture and small trade. It was at the time a typical "depressed" place because, barring Signor Wollemborg himself, none of its landlords ever came near it, contenting themselves with drawing their rents—which were heavy for land not naturally fertile and poorly developed. With a tolerably well-filled purse come to him by inheritance, Dr Wollemborg might have done a good deal by charity to relieve actual distress. But that would have been missing the best part of a good deed: the raising and educating of the people. So he decided to take his place by the side of his poorer neighbours as one of themselves, and to make every one contribute to "his own emancipation"—claiming distinction above them only in the prerogative of work. In June 1883, having secured the support of in all thirty-two members, including, of course, the *curé*, he opened his little pioneer bank. "*La date mérite d'être notée*," says M. Rostand; "*elle marquait la naissance d'une institution.*" His first work proved very uphill. There was no good fairy to stand by the bank. Every inch of ground had to be conquered. To provide the first funds, Signor Wollemborg himself opened his purse, advancing £80—besides, I presume, paying in the bulk of that £280 of deposits which the bank managed somehow to attract in its first term of business of four and a half months. Later, the public Savings Bank of Padua consented to lend £160.

<small>The First Cassa Rurale.</small>

Ever since, the Italian Savings Banks have all through stood loyally by the little *casse*—once they found them to be safe. Dr Wollemborg himself confesses that, but for their support, he would have found it difficult indeed to accomplish his purpose. The Savings Banks have not lost a penny by their confidence. And long since the *casse* have conquered for themselves a position which places them above the necessity of begging favours in any quarter.

However, I am anticipating events. When the Bank of Loreggia had been in existence three months, great was the surprise of the peasants who had become borrowers, on receiving an advice from the *ragioniere*, to the effect that they owed 1½ per cent. on their loans. One-and-a-half per cent.! Surely that must be a mistake. Incredulous, they brought their books back to the *ragioniere*; such a thing had never been heard of! When they found it to be correct all the same, the fame of their *cassa* travelled abroad as on wings. "The propaganda begun," says M. Rostand, "the diffusion worked its own way. Here, there, the author of this new institution found himself summoned, sometimes by a landlord less indifferent than the rest, sometimes by the *sindaco* or the *curé*." Now the bank numbers 128 members. It is not actually embarrassed with cash; it has to study strict economy in all things; many of its transactions seem humble and small. But it raises all the money that it wants. It has a little reserve of 2,996 lire laid up, which has grown very slowly, but promises, now that it has reached such a point, to increase more rapidly. To do them justice, the members are anxious to increase what they know must in the long run prove the backbone of their bank. At a special meeting, composed mainly of borrowers, they resolved rather to go on paying a somewhat higher interest than was absolutely necessary—that is, 6 per cent.—than stint the reserve. The bank has generally about £600 or £800 out in loans fructifying in people's farms, in the shape of cows, or pigs, or goats, or implements, or manures, or feeding stuffs; or else earning a profit in village shops in the shape of raw material which gives the tradesman employment for his labour.

Its Organisation.

In respect of organisation Dr Wollemborg has in all essential points strictly followed Raiffeisen lines. His associations are smaller than the German—generally speaking, more needy, to begin with. Strict economy, even in small things is accordingly a matter of even greater moment. Under the circumstances an active participation of each member in the work becomes more of a necessity, while at the same time its application is made easier. The members meet oftener and administer their own affairs more in common. Hence, if possible, an even more lively interest, even fuller co-operation in small things than is seen in Germany. There is not a meeting at which all members who are able do not attend. Should any fail, they are looked upon by their brethren much as were the ἰδιῶται, who would not vote on public matters, by the Athenians, and are punished accordingly—not, indeed, with the grim punishment meted out by patriotic Greeks, but with a fine of 50 centesimi, which to their thrifty notions seems quite severe enough. There is something naïvely simple, almost patriarchal, about these co-operative " parish councils," in which every member claims the exercise of his right to vote. There the members settle the instructions for the elected Council—which meets once a fortnight, to check accounts, to receive savings, and to consider applications for loans. In most banks the general meeting will limit the lending powers of the Council to 300, or 500, or 600 lire, as the case may be, per credit to any one individual; and to a larger figure for collective lending, while at the same time determining the interest to be charged on loans and allowed on deposits. At Loreggia the members began by limiting their Council's discretion to 10,000 lire, which they soon extended to 16,000 lire. At Vigonovo they began with 20,000 lire, to substitute, shortly after, 30,000. All the expenses are cut down to a minimum. The poor *cassa* of Loreggia, to state one instance, cannot afford to pay its cashier £37. 10s., as does the opulent *Darlehnskasse* of Mülheim. It allows him 40 lire (32 shillings) per annum, and all its annual expenditure totals up to only 58 lire (£2. 6s. 5d.).

One would think that with a Post Office Savings Bank always open, the villagers would for convenience prefer to deposit their savings there, rather than wait for the fortnightly meeting of the Council of the *cassa*, which allows them not a farthing more—3¼ per cent. But the vast majority bring their money by preference to the *cassa*. It is their own. It is administered by themselves and their officers. It keeps the money in their district. They take a pride in its success. For loans, of course, the villagers have no other bank open to them except the *cassa*, and they appreciate its beneficent ministrations all the more. And hence its rare educational value. In respect of personal qualifications it is strict as strict can be. A man may be as poor as a church mouse; that is no bar to his election. But he must be honest, and sober, and thrifty, and well conducted, and thoroughly trusted by his neighbours. And he must be able to write and read, at any rate rudimentarily. Under the joint influence of the *banche* and *casse*, illiteracy, which used to be as rife in Lombardy and Piedmont as ever it can be in Ireland at election time, is being rapidly stamped out. In the applications and receipts preserved by the *ragioniere* you can trace the progress of sexagenarian scholarship in elementary caligraphy, in the gradual softening and rounding of those straggling characters which stand for members' names. "The illiterate learn to write, in order to be admitted to the *cassa*," so reports M. Rostand, "because every member must be able to sign his Christian and surname. The door is closed mercilessly against those who have contracted the habit of drinking; they have mended their ways, and after that have been admitted. The rules demand guarantees of personal morality: the small field-thefts have diminished, because such or such an one has been expelled. The principle of mutual aid has grown more vivid. Conscientiousness in paying was formerly instinctive; now people have learnt to be punctual as well in their payments." The little band, in fact, realise almost to the full Signor Levi's **ideal of a** co-operative society—"an honest and industrious family," in which all members feel strongly drawn to one another, "where all gladly render gratuitous service, well knowing that in studying the common good they are at the same time furthering their own private advantage. Hence the volunteer service, willingly given, hence the love which binds all members to their bank, hence the power which enables them scrupulously to carry out all the work which they have undertaken."

Among such a constituency as this there is rarely any occasion to refuse a **loan**. The borrower **has to** state his object, as in the Raiffeisen banks. He may want to buy a heifer, or some artificial fertiliser, **or** timber for carpentering, or **some leather** for making shoes. All these items are recorded **in** the minute-book, which **shows a** surprisingly varied collection of different wants supplied. And to the object stated he must adhere.

Dr Wollemborg has not adopted the four-weeks'-notice clause, which in the Raiffeisen banks ensures conscientious employment of the loan. But he secures the same object by a different **method**, which at first sight **is** bound to appear a little roundabout and self-contradictory, but which works well in practice. For whatever term the particular loan be granted—in respect of length of time and repayment by instalments Dr Wollemborg adheres altogether to **the** Raiffeisen principle—it is actually *lent* only for three **months**. Every three months it has to be formally applied for and granted afresh. **By this** means, it seems to be held, the sense of the *conditional* character of the loan—condi**tional upon** proper employment—is more forcibly brought **home to the** borrower, and he **is** effectually put upon his good behaviour. The interest ordinarily charged upon loans is 6 per cent.—which seems a little high in comparison with **the** Raiffeisen rate, **but** may be justifiable in view of the

<small>A Slight Departure from the Raiffeisen Method.</small>

greater need in its early years of so poor a society to build up a reserve, and also of the higher bank rate prevailing. To that reserve every surplus is religiously applied. There are no salaries beyond that paid to the *ragioniere*, and there can be no dividend, because there are no shares.

Thus the whole system, though in some particulars a little differently organised, is in the main the same as in the German Raiffeisen banks: simple borrowing and lending, careful checking of everything, cheapness in service, caution in granting loans, strict avoidance of everything involving a risk. And the result has been equally happy, though not yet, of course, equally large. Unlimited liability has proved devoid of any element of danger. There have been scarcely any losses.

<small>Increase of Casse Rurali.</small> Slowly the *casse* have multiplied. Their increase was at first by nines, and eights, and sevens, till a more powerful propagating force was, as we shall see, brought into the field. There are at present 84, in addition to probably very nearly 400 of independent formation. And they have remained small, modest, humble little institutions, for the most part with a small number of members only—20, and 40, and 60. Not a few have more than 100 and there is one even with 600, and one with more than 800. But these are exceptions. None of these *casse* have shares—except the little one of Crema, which, to satisfy the whim of a crotchety local judge, has issued such to the value of 1d. Some of them do a considerable amount of business, having loans outstanding to the amount of £600, £800, £1,500, and more. Unfortunately, statistics as to their work are very few and gappy. Since the *casse* have recently united to a Federation, it may be hoped that in the future more figures will be forthcoming. M. Contini, who has the best means of knowing, calculates that 160 *casse* of which he has seen the balance-sheets have among them 1,700,000 lire outstanding in loans, which is at the rate of £425 per *cassa*;

52,000 lire amassed in their reserve funds, which is at the rate of only £13 per *cassa;* and savings deposits to the amount of 690,000 lire, which is at the rate of £172. 10s. per *cassa.* £172. 10s. collected in savings in a small village in which previously there was scarcely anything but debt and misery, £425 kept steadily employed in productive work, helping poor people to earn a living—it all looks petty and paltry to the statistician's eye. But it means a great amount of good done in the small communities. Give such a *cassa* to every agricultural village, and reckon up what the result will be! And think of the relief, the comfort, the independence, the education which such work has brought to the poor! Wherever they have gone they have done well. There is but one opinion as to their result:— *Their Success.* "*Elles sont administrées avec un enthousiasme et un dévouement*," says M. Léon Say, "*qui ne se démentent nulle part, et elles réussissent partout.*" Theirs has been the task of seeking the hundredth sheep, and sweeping the floor for the lost piece of money. They were planted on dry and thirsty land, and their fertilising work may be compared to that of the lupine, which, sown on barren sand where no other plant could live, sends down its roots feet below the surface, to draw up from the subsoil, particle by particle, the valuable mineral constituents sparsely distributed in the soil, and, with the treasure of nitrogen absorbed from the atmosphere and its own vegetable fibre added, builds up, layer by layer, a mould able to bear far more valuable crops. M. Yersin, using an equally apt simile, compares the People's Banks to a forest, which at the same time accumulates fertilising matter, dispenses shade and freshness, yields a valuable crop of timber, and improves the climate and atmospheric conditions of the district.

To see what a bank is in practice, let us go back to the pioneer bank of Loreggia. You could not find a better one to serve as a type. Nor, at Loreggia, or indeed else- *The Village Bank of Loreggia.*

where, could you have a better guide to explain to you its work than old "Corazza," in respect of age the "father" of the bank. His real name is Bernardo Pietroni; you could not tell that from his signature, which he has learned to scrawl after he was a grandfather, merely to qualify himself for admission to the bank. In the village his opinion counts for as much as that of any other six men. If he is deficient in knowledge of letters, you soon find out that he has plenty of common-sense and sound judgment, and has not allowed experience to go by without drawing profit from it. Indeed, in conversation he discovers familiarity with the principles of modern farming rather surprising in so self-taught a man. "It is the bank that has taught me that," he candidly admits. In providing him with the money which he required for his farming operations, under certain safeguards, it has made him think how he might best employ it. If you will go about his field and his yard, up to his corn-loft, and into his cow-house, you soon learn why he loves his bank. "I could not keep my farm like that formerly." His house is a large, simple and primitive, but substantial building, according to the custom of the country, affording room for his numerous family, comprising children and grandchildren, of twenty-eight, among whom he lives like a patriarch of old. Such large families are not unusual in Venetia. These twenty-eight are Corazza's "children." So far as they are capable of work, they are also his "hands." He requires no hired labour. Corazza will show you his maize-cobs, plump and bright in colour, his full-grained barley, his well-shaped potatoes. "We used not to grow them like that. It is the bank that has found the manure and the implements for good cultivation." "But could not you have saved what you wanted for that out of what you were making?" "There was nothing to save," says he. "It all went to the usurer. We never had a farthing over. Besides, if I had saved for buying imple-

The Benefits which it has assured.

ments, or manure, I must have starved the farm at some other point, where starving would have meant loss. The bank came in from outside. It gave me the additional pound or two, and never taxed me except out of the produce of that additional pound itself. It was content to wait till that had borne fruit. So I could well afford to borrow. It cost me nothing." Corazza will go on to show you his beasts. He is very proud of them. Here are two bullocks worth 1,000 lire—the ordinary price of a peasant's cow is somewhere about 200 lire. He never had a stableful like that in former times. These good beasts feed Corazza's family with milk, and they feed, what he appreciates as much, his fields with fertility. "Put into the ground as much as you can," he says, having learnt, with the bank's help, a lesson in high farming. "Our soil wants it. But it will give it you all back."

Corazza has more to tell of the benefits of the bank in other households—real cases, which will bear inquiring into. There was such and such an one in the parish, the tenant of a farm—he has it still—of about twenty acres. It was wretchedly neglected. Everything was pawned, and the only person who got anything out of it was the usurer. It was a hard case. The man joined the bank, but the bank was at a loss how much it might trust him with. It advanced him £4. That sufficed to stop a hole. He repaid the money and borrowed more. [The bank at presents lends no more than £30 to one man. But that little sum may be kept continually coming and going, earning and repaying itself, giving the poor fellow £30 perpetually to work with.] The quasi-bankrupt of ten years ago now has his farm in tolerable condition, he has six beasts of his own and £60 laid by in the Savings Bank. "Then why does he not use that instead of the bank money?" "No, no," said Corazza, "that would never do. What he borrows from the bank he knows that he must repay. So he is careful with it. He will cast over exactly what an outlay will bring him back. Aye, we have learnt to calculate. The other money is far safer where it is now. It is a good security to the bank, and the man will not fritter it away."

There was another man with a similar holding. He was miserably poor. But the bank trusted him in 1883 with £8 wherewith to buy two calves. He has borrowed again. He has put a little in here and a little there. He has now five beasts and about 1,400 lire-worth of belongings, instead of practically nothing, and is only 100 lire in debt to the bank.

Corazza has other cases to tell you of. There was that poor old widow woman, who carries fruit to Padua to sell. What with her poverty and her debts she never felt safe from day to day. The bank let her have a few pounds. That gave her the ground to stand upon. Her profits came to herself, instead of going to the usurer. She is quit of anxiety now. Her earnings benefit herself.

There was that small tradesman. He was a pauper, receiving parish relief. As such he was not eligible for the bank. But a kind friend lent him a little to get himself off the rates. The bank admitted him, gave him a few pounds to buy cheap wares with to hawk about. Now he has his little shop.

All the Benefit got is Self-earned.

Nowhere has gold dropped down in great lumps upon the people. They have not made fortunes suddenly. But they have been helped to earn fairly and to live respectably. It is this being able to get an extra pound or two to do a thing well which was formerly done badly, this power of drawing on a fund never failing at any time that an opportunity offers for employing it profitably, and this pressure put upon people to calculate what they are doing, which makes this bank so tellingly useful. The aspect of the farms whose tenants belong to the bank has been materially changed within the past decade. There is order and tidiness where there used to be the neglect inseparable from penury. "We could not then eat such good polenta," says Corazza's wife, as you stop to look at that huge mess of really appetising maize-porridge brought into the common room to serve as meal for the twenty-eight mouths, large and small. "We had to live on the inferior grain."

To see the bank at work in another aspect, come to the *municipio* to attend while the elected committee hold their sitting. There is the *sindaco* ready to bow you into the room. These village mayors know the value of a village bank. It makes government easier for them. They help it by depositing municipal moneys. Charitable and friendly societies will do the same thing—at first, it may be, to help and strengthen the little bantling, but later certainly for safe keeping. As a meeting-place the *municipio* is always open to the bank. In some parishes—as in Vigonovo—the priest will allow to the banks the use of the church. The committee meet every fortnight, or oftener, should occasion require. At Loreggia, Signor Wollemborg, as President, takes the chair. His brother, who, to save the bank expense, discharges gratuitously the functions of cashier and secretary, sits by his side. And there are the other members. It is surprising what power of following business, of mentally seizing important points, and also, in a rustic way, of expressing themselves, this bank business will infuse into these simple village folk. It is their first education in public affairs. If there are still people who believe that what village folk want to arouse their interest, and educate them to better things, is a circus and not a parish council, let them go to one of these village bank meetings, and see for themselves what a remarkably stimulating effect such council work has upon small rural folk. They take nothing for granted; they will have everything

A Committee Meeting.

out. And be the other man a squire or a day-labourer, they will argue the case with him thoroughly. At the general meetings, which are held twice or three times a year, to discuss the limits to be fixed for loans, the rates of interest to be charged or given, or any appeal from decisions of the committee, to elect the committee-men, the council-men, or whatever the business may be, there are debates which indicate real arguing power.

Elections. But the present is a committee meeting. There are candidates waiting for election. Election is no farce. Drunkards, idlers, evil-livers, and the like, the bank will not have. So, if there are any such who apply, they are rejected without much to-do. In a good many more cases than one have they come back as reformed characters to find themselves elected. Here is a market which pays value for honesty and good conduct. Job is not expected to "serve God for naught." Hence that marvellous educating power which has made priests own that the bank in their parish has done more to make good men of their parishioners than all their preaching. And that is so not at Loreggia only. Abano, Vigonovo, Crema, Faller, and whatever other places possess banks, have all similar tales to tell.

Savings. Now come the savings. Here comes in a little girl with her few centesimi; next an old woman brings a few lire. There is a lad with his bare legs still all purple from treading the grapes in true Old Testament style, in a water-tight cart from which the juice runs out by a spout. He has earned a little money, and he carries the lira or two to the bank. These people all bring their savings themselves—not as a matter of distrust towards others, but as wishing to manifest their own keen personal interest in the common institution. This is altogether a different affair from the public office work of the Post-Office Bank. This bank is to its members a living creature, whose pulse they may feel. Members do not come merely to bring their savings; they want to hear something of what is going on. They are entitled to see the balance-sheet, which is drawn up every fortnight at the close of the committee meeting, and hung up for view in the public room of the *municipio*.

After the receipt of the savings comes the consideration of applications for loans. As a rule, there is the *vacca*, or the *vitella*, or the *maiale*, to be bought—though the pig is not yet as much honoured in Italy as he deserves to be. Sometimes, in the place of a cow or a calf, there will be a goat. Or else the village wheelwright will want to buy wood, the shoemaker leather, and so on. Every case meets with careful consideration. Is the applicant trustworthy? Is his case good? Is the sum a legitimate one? Is the time proposed for repayment excessive? Are the sureties good? It may happen that the loan is refused, though such cases are not many. It may happen that the amount is reduced or the period curtailed. According as the committee decide, the applicant is advised, and then he may come with his sureties to receive the money from the cashier in exchange for a bill of exchange, which runs only for three months, for whatever period the loan be granted —two years or more—in order that he may be compelled to employ the money as was stipulated. Should he fail to do so, the bill is not renewed. Loans.

It would be ridiculous to say that our "Village Bank" has brought about the millennium in Loreggia, or anywhere else. But it has brought the local people very material and welcome help. It has sent the usurer to the right-about. He has left the place discomfited. It has taught members to bank their money instead of locking it away in a drawer or hiding it in a stocking, where it could not possibly do any one any good. It has taught them to calculate the profitableness of their enterprises, and made them fami- The Good which Village Banks have done.

liar with simple accounts. It has added a fresh stimulus to thrift. It has brought public opinion and class opinion to bear upon people in the most effective way—stimulating, checking, restraining. It has made the people better men and better neighbours. Where there used to be grudging and envying, ill-concealed delight in another's troubles, there is now fellow-feeling—because people have learned that they are bound together by a common interest, that their neighbour's hurt is their own, their neighbour's good their profit.

I will not say that to an untrained eye the difference is likely to be very striking. But any one acquainted with agriculture will be pretty sure to detect the contrast between an Italian village which has no bank, and one in which such a bank has been at work a few years. Where there is such a bank, cultivation is sure to be better. Crops look cleaner and heavier. The live stock are better kept. The buildings are in better order. There is, generally speaking, less poverty, a look of greater prosperity about both people and farms; and if any visitor has time to look into the social life of the village, he will find that there is a good deal more still to distinguish a "bank" village from an ordinary one, even apart from increased economy, sobriety, thrift, and saving. To quote M. Léon Say :—"*La petite culture se développe avec une énergie croissante et les opérations de crédit agraire du réseau des petites banques ne sont pas un des moindres encouragements donnés a cette petite culture.*"

Testimonies to their Work. "As deposits grow," so writes the parish priest of Faller, Dom Filippo Poletti, "the taverns are forsaken." Neat houses spring up where there were hovels, gardens are seen carefully trimmed, the live stock become the peasant's property, and everywhere the usurers find their occupation gone. "*Tout cela,*" writes M. Rostand, after his second visit of inspection, "*c'est bien la réalisation pratique de l'idéal coopératif au village. Il n'est pas possible que par l'union, l'esprit de la solidarité.*" "In truth," he goes on, "this second visit has satisfied us more and more that the small co-operative institutions with unlimited liability, possess, along with their practical utility manifest on the face of them, a social utility peculiarly worthy of notice. Freed from usury, the peasantry have regained courage and confidence." One more testimony I quote from Dr de Portis, the surgeon practising in Loreggia, with regard to the *cassa* in his own village :—

"The peasant who previously, helpless and forsaken, proved a ready prey to the most shameless usurer, and had no choice for himself but between extreme misery and dishonesty, has now risen to a sense of human dignity. He is proud of being a member of the Association, and of taking part in its management. In it he acquires a sense of self-respect, of independence, a love of work, of honesty, and punctuality. Usury finds its occupation gone. The usurers themselves are compelled to acknowledge the good done by the Association, though they have to leave the district. Our peasants declare, 'We mean to bring up our sons with a love of work, in order that they may take their place among the *galantuomini.*'"

Does it not make one's mouth water to read of the magician's work done by these "*attachantes institutions, dont l'humilité est la beauté*"? It is all so modest, so simple—so small, if you will. It is all purchased with personal pains, with watchfulness, care, and scrupulous thrift. There are as yet none of those millions which make M. Luzzatti's work so imposing, none of those marble palaces and masses of gold accumulated. But the persons whom the beneficent work has enriched could not possibly have been reached by any other means. The happiness diffused, the culture spread, the prosperity of which as yet really only the seeds have been sown, but sown surely, are likely to weigh as heavy in the balance of success as the much larger riches more easily accumulated, where populations are dense, and the materials of wealth lie all ready to hand. Brick upon brick, "here a little and there a little," the structure is being raised, which is likely to stand all the more enduringly, and the more securely, and to prove the better stronghold of thrift and wealth, because every inch of it was raised by an effort, and cemented with virtues and sound principles instilled.

If more Englishmen would go and study the work of these banks on the spot, as I have done at Loreggia and elsewhere, I doubt if our own villages would much longer remain without so useful an institution, which has only to be seen to be appreciated. Before the proper appreciation of its work, such as seeing would bring with it, the supposed difficulties would melt away like wax.

Adaptation of the System by the Savings Bank of Parma.

In Italy Dr Wollemborg was not allowed to wear his well-earned laurels long alone—once success had made the merits of his system plain. If savings banks could usefully help village banks by advancing them funds, why should not they take a shorter cut to the same end, and employ such banks simply as their servants or *succursales*, thus providing themselves with a sure means of investing their money, always superabundant, while at the same time performing what every Italian banker has been taught to look upon as a good work, the work of assuring credit to the small cultivator. The Savings Bank of Parma some time ago decided to venture upon the experiment. Last October it had seven such *succursales* at work in its district. Probably there are now more. The Savings Bank is ready to help with its ample funds as many as are willing to accept its terms, which are: the adoption, generally, of Wollemborg rules, with the one indispensable proviso added, that they must abstain from collecting savings. The collection of savings, it is stipulated, shall remain the *régie* or monopoly of the Savings Bank itself.

It Produces only a Second-rate Good.

There is no denying that on such lines some economic good may be done. But it is obviously only a second-rate good. It provides the use of money for poor people.

It instils into them some rudimentary notions of business. But it does not make them self-reliant, it does not tend to educate them, to make them thrifty, active in their own work, and eventually independent. It offers something of a service. It does not create a powerful bond. Accordingly, one can scarcely be surprised to find that the business done has remained comparatively trifling, and that the credit given has assumed a character not untinged with patronage, since it is as a rule not the Village Bank, but one or two well-to-do men, whose liability is accepted as security, and what is created is, therefore, really not a bank, but a bail-going association, dependent upon a few rich men. My own impression is that if the Savings Bank were to bestow as much pains as it now does upon the creation of such lending agencies, on the foundation of good, independent village banks, not only would it accomplish far more good for the benefit of the people whom it desires to help, but it would also find employment for very much more cash, and so do better both ways.

There is another propaganda in progress in Italy which has proved far more of a success. If "Catholicism" could make the Luzzatti system its own, in order to attract more faithful people to the Church with golden cords, why should not the Wollemborg system be made auxiliary in the same way? One of the distinctive causes of the success of that system has always been the marked favour everywhere shown to it by the clergy. From the starting of the Bank of Loreggia downwards, the *paroco* was as a rule the first to welcome this useful educating ally into his parish. Wherever he was favourable, the *cassa* was sure to strike root quickly and to thrive. Wherever he held back, success proved doubtful. There are many priests chairmen of Wollemborg banks. The clergy of Venetia and Lombardy, I may explain, are well in touch with their flocks in respect of their economic and social affairs, and not unpopular with

"Catholic" Village Banks

them. They take an interest in their worldly doings as in their religious. Hence their influence, and their influence, it may be added, generally for good. Why should not the ecclesiastical colouring of the banks be deepened? To the mind of Don Cerutti, the zealous and active parish priest of Gambarare, in Venetia, the banks were not multiplying nearly fast enough. Want was calling for them loudly everywhere. There was so much to be done! Here was an approved instrument handy to do it. But hands were wanting to work that instrument. A power was needed which would impart a new stimulus and fill the cylinder of the engine with propelling steam. Religion could provide such stimulus. Religion should be impressed—there is no nobler office for it than to help the poor. As it happened, religion in Italy, as in most countries, spells "denominationalism."

Their Founder.

M. Tovini and his friends had not been long at work over their "Catholic" banking at Brescia—of which I have already spoken—when Don Cerutti resolved to set the Church a-doing the same work which it had performed in the fifteenth century in Florence. His parish lies in the midst of a district not unfruitful, but neglected, backward, undeveloped. The fields and vineyards were crying out for manure, and for better cultivation. The peasants' cottages were crying out for comforts, and even for mere necessaries of life. In 1889 things looked particularly black, because, on the top of other distress, the grape crop had failed, and its failure brought ruin upon many a little household. Don Cerutti resolved to set his hand to the plough, and no doubt his ploughing has been to some purpose.

The First "Catholic" Bank.

On the 26th of February 1890 he founded his first "Catholic" bank. It did not really begin work till the 1st of July. The bank was a modest institution enough to begin with, with only twenty-six members on its roll, including three priests, the village doctor, the village chemist, three owners of tiny freeholds, an artisan, two employees, and fifty small tenants. There was not a stiver in the bank's coffers. All the money which was to be lent out had first to be borrowed. Friends put in some deposits. The Savings Bank of Venice granted a loan at a rather high rate of interest, viz., 5¼ per cent. With such help the bank managed to deal out in the first half-year, at 6 per cent. interest, about £370 in thirty-three loans. The greater portion of this money went for the purchase of stock and poultry, about £62 for farm work, £48 in loans to small tradesmen for stocking their shops, and, lastly, £20 for household purposes. The bank took 6 per cent. for its loans. At the outset it limited the borrowing powers of any one member to £20. The figure has recently been doubled. The maximum of aggregate lending allowed at one time still stands at £1,400. The whole business is small, modest, and unpretending. But the help given is sufficient for the humble purposes for which it is asked. And it is self-earned. In point of time the limit laid down for loans is three years as a maximum. But there are many short loans down to a month. By a very wise provision, borrowers repaying before the time stipulated are allowed a rebate in the interest. To make ends meet, expenses had to be kept down to a minimum, and actually not a centesimo was spent in fees or salaries to officers. Nevertheless the first year's working, very accountably, resulted in a loss—a very trifling one—somewhere about 16s. Since then there has always been a surplus, small but sure, which, lira by lira, has accumulated in three-and-a-half years to something like £36, a tiny reserve, all that the bank actually possesses, but a sum never to be shared out. It is the bank's property, and belongs to the bank alone. The next year the bank did better. Increasing success secured it more funds, more supporters, a larger business. It has now about 150 members, a reserve fund of about £40, and it does

Its Work.

Instances. business at the rate of about £1,700 a year. I will give a few instances of its work. Here are three, taken from the bank records. A poor cottager was in distress for money wherewith to pay his rent. He was £14 in arrear, and the landlord would hear of no further delay. What was the man to do? The only property on which to realise were his two cows—his very bread-winners—ill-bred beasts that our farmers would perhaps scarcely look at, but which meant very much to him. That would be draining a well to slake a moment's thirst. The bank stepped in, took security— thereby compelling the borrower to husband his means and lay by from his weekly earnings. And within four months the cows had paid off the debt, with interest, out of their milk. Another poor fellow was in a similar dilemma, with his Martinmas rent due and no money in his stocking. There were a hundred quintals of hay to sell. But the price was, in November, only 3.25 lire per quintal. If he could but tide over till Spring! He enrolled himself a member of the bank, obtained a loan at the rate of 6 per cent., and in May sold his hay at 5.25 lire the quintal, thus saving 200 lire by the transaction. Lastly, there was a poor widow who wanted to buy a pig. The village Shylock was ready to advance the money at his usual moderate rate of 5 lire per month, and the loan of 30 lire to be repaid within a year. That is at the rate of 200 per cent. Why not join the bank and borrow at 6, asked Don Cerutti? Why not, indeed? The woman took the advice, and is nearly 60 lire in pocket. These are petty savings, it may be said. But they mean a good deal to the people by whom they were made. For "little things are great to little men."*

---

* On 20th October 1894, 122 "Catholic" banks had 972,458 lire outstanding in loans. Of the money required they had raised 672,813 lire by deposits, and 386,222 lire by passing on acceptances for discount. The manner in which the funds of the little societies grow by the accumulation of the reserve fund, which is their only property, may be gathered

That is not all. All is fish that comes to Don Cerutti's net with a promise of benefiting his poor protégés by co-operation. He has started a co-operative cheese factory in his village; he has organised co-operative insurance. He is busy now endeavouring to acclimatise on the banks of the Brenta the co-operative method of pressing and selling wine which helps wine-growers so much in the valleys of the Moselle and the Ahr. *[Further Co-operation.]*

Of course his "Catholic" banks have increased in number. They have long since far outstripped the undenominational parent institutions, and are becoming a veritable host, which now, after six years, already musters, probably, at least, 400 strong.* The addition of the religious stimulus has without question proved singularly effective. But is it in place? Is it properly applied? *[Rapid Progress.]*

It is difficult to answer the question either by a plain "Yes" or "No." Unquestionably, undenominational banks *[Objections to Denominationalism and its Advantages.]* from the fact that in 1887 the reserve funds of *casse rurali* generally stood at $\frac{1}{13}$ of the collective deposits and loans; in 1895 at $\frac{1}{20}$. The following table shows the loans outstanding at Gambarare on 31st December 1894, classed according to the employment for which they were taken:—

	Loans.	Lire.
Purchase of breeding stock	155	28,890.45
Purchase of draught cattle	53	12,360.20
Seed, breadcorn, &c.	32	4,730.00
Poultry for fattening	35	1,167.36
Sulphur and vitriol for vineyards	290	5,861.81
Insurance (hail)	112	2,798.40
Purchase of land	1	800.00
Household requisites	46	6,470.85
For trading purposes	27	6,215.05
Land improvements	32	9,050.05
	783	76,044.17

* On 31st December 1895 there were 348 "Catholic Banks," of which number 191 had sprung up during the preceding twelve months.

would be better. Unquestionably, in a district with a mixed population such denominational banks would constitute a positive danger, and might work absolute harm. But, on the other hand, without the infusion of the religious idea, there would be nothing like the same number of banks, and thousands of poor folk would go without the help which they now receive. The banks are set up amid a purely Roman Catholic population, to whom "religion" means religion according to the tenets of the Church of Rome, and religious influence the influence of the priests. I do not believe that—at any rate at present—denominationalism is turned to any improper account, and that "Catholicism" is impressed in the service more than to make people who are "Catholics" already reputable, thrifty, and well conducted—perhaps a little more church-going. The rules say that a new member must "not be notoriously opposed to the Catholic Church and the existing Government (*notariamente contrario alla Chiesa Cattolica ed al Governo cistituito*)." In the bank work Catholicism is practically restricted to the opening of the proceedings with the *Actiones*, and concluding them with the *Agimus*. Moreover, it is laid down that, in the event of the society being dissolved, the reserve fund accumulated is to be applied to some Catholic work (*opera cattolica*) benefiting the parish, and that even where the society continues to exist, any overplus interest accruing from an excessive reserve shall be applied in a similar manner. That contingency appears remote. As it happens, the societies, having detected a weak point in the Italian law, seem destined to confine their life in each case to the brief period of a lustrum only, after which they rise, phœnix-like, from their own ashes as new *casse*—the object being, to evade payment of rather heavy taxes which the law imposes upon co-operative societies having lived more than five years. As banks the banks are good. They accept the Wollemborg rules *in toto*, and carry them out strictly. So long as they continue to do this, I really doubt if there is much room for any abuse of clerical influence, because the Wollemborg system is bound to make people think of themselves, and safeguard their own responsibility. It is a pity that the leaders of the movement have not proved better able to curb their tongues and pens in speaking and writing about adherents of other systems who have shown their good-will by offering them, not their friendship only, but also their support, as I myself have witnessed when Don Cerutti and I both met at M. Luzzatti's hospitable table in Padua.

What with Wollemborg banks and Catholic banks, a very considerable portion of Italy is now occupied by at any rate detachments and outposts of the co-operative army of village banks. Of course these, being for the most part "Catholic," muster strongest in the pronouncedly "Catholic" province of Venetia. The diocese of Treviso alone had at New Year 82 to show. For the whole of Venetia the figure stood at 276. Lombardy comes next with 76 banks; Piedmont ranks third with 47; and so the scale runs down to Naples and Sardinia, which have as yet only one a piece.

Doubtless the *casse rurali* are destined to increase still further—much more rapidly as time goes on. They have the same satisfactory tale to tell of success and good work, accompanied by almost an entire absence of losses, which makes the position of their prototypes so triumphant in Germany. They have shown themselves remarkably applicable to Italian habits and circumstances, and have in many a village proved a veritable godsend to the population, which under the crushing heel of usury had lost all pleasure in life and hope for earthly future. If rural Italy is to be regenerated and made prosperous once more, this evidently is the means by which it may be made so.

<small>The Casse as a Factor of National Regeneration.</small>

CHAPTER XI.

THE BELGIAN "BANQUES POPULAIRES."

Local Circumstances favour Co-operation.
BELGIUM, vigorous, pushing little country that it is, akin to ourselves in many things, and therefore often styled "the little England of the Continent," has its own history of co-operative credit, conveying several useful lessons which, in view of an admitted similarity of circumstances, may well commend themselves to our notice. In economic matters, as well as in political, its population have striven to live up to the motto which its founders aptly selected for the little kingdom: "*L'Union fait la force.*" There are no more useful supply associations than the Belgian *Vooruit* and its counterparts—of all of which unfortunately political partisanship has seized the crank, to work the serviceable machine avowedly with the object of furthering Socialism on one side, and Ultramontanism on the other. The *Unions du Crédit*, which have become most popular throughout Belgium, France, and Switzerland, with offshoots penetrating into Denmark, Germany, and Austria, are admittedly of Belgian origin. And there are other cognate organisations, all of which appear to indicate a national predisposition to co-operation. On such soil it was to be expected that the seed dropping across the frontier from the fruitful tree planted in Germany would rapidly strike root and grow up a goodly plant.

"Unions du Credit."
Of the *Unions du Crédit*, successful and surprisingly safe as they have proved to be, I have no occasion here to say very much. They are exceedingly popular. But they

apply co-operation at a point at which among ourselves its application excites little interest, and is all the less likely to do so since the method employed appears little calculated to commend itself to English tastes. It is traders—not of the richest class, but still traders doing a fair business—who combine in *Unions*, in order to make their credit go the farther. The merit of devising this type of association belongs to M. Haeck, who formed the first such society— still existing—in 1848. The idea is this:—An indefinite number of members join together, each taking up, say, one share of 200 francs. On this they pay up 20 francs each, in some cases only 10 francs. But the share entitles them to 2,000 francs of credit, on paper to which the *Union* affixes its signature, and for which the *Union* becomes responsible. Of course, in any case of default, the *Union* has its remedy against members, and of course it can also in case of need call up the full amount of the shares. But of all this outsiders know nothing. They buy *Union* paper and look to the *Union* for its redemption. In many *Unions*, more particularly in Switzerland, members are allowed to take up a number of shares, in some *Unions* as many as 200; so that, on our assumption, a man might subscribe 40,000 francs, and by payment of 4,000 francs become entitled to credit for the larger sum, for which his brother member, taking only one share, is to the extent of that share responsible, as is the 200 share member for the debt of the one share member. The whole thing is workable only on the supposition, which thus far has been verified, that the *Unions* elect their members with *extreme* caution and discrimination, so as to allow admission to scarcely any black sheep. In practice, wherever *Unions* of this type have been established they have been found remarkably successful. The very first one formed gave an earnest of this, living safely, in the very earliest period of its existence, through a crisis almost unparalleled for severity. In Switzerland, the *Union Vaudoise du Crédit* of Lausanne began in 1864 with 150 members only, and a collective credit of 24,000 francs, to increase before long both figures, the one to 1,786 and the other to 305,280, while spreading out its system over neighbouring towns. The *Crédit du Léman* and the *Crédit Yverdunois* are equally prospering associations.

<small>Need of more Popular Credit.</small>

"Mutualism" of this kind was not calculated to bring much relief to the humbler classes. But these wanted "democratised" credit fully as much as any poor folk in Germany or Italy. Belgium had its struggling small tradesman, its moneyless cultivator of a small holding, its artisan,

<small>Léon d'Andrimont, the Founder of Belgian People's Banks.</small>

its itinerant dealer in cheap wares. M. d'Andrimont tells of a hawking baker whom he found in Liége, hiring his barrow at the rate of threepence a day. A People's Bank afterwards enabled the man to purchase the barrow out and out, by instalments of the very amount which he had been paying in hire, in less than a year, and to find himself afterwards every year £4. 10s. in pocket. Of course, there are thousands of similar cases. Fortunately for the classes spoken of, M. Léon d'Andrimont, a member of an influential family, had an opportunity of witnessing in Germany the marvels which co-operative banking was there bringing forth for equally necessitous folk, under the inspiriting leadership of Schulze-Delitzsch. Impressed with the merits of the system, he resolved to put it to a practical test in his own country. He was far too devoted a disciple of the great German co-operator to so much as dream of taking liberties with his rules. He translated them word for word, desiring nothing more ardently than to reproduce on Belgian soil *exactly* the same institution which he had seen working so satisfactorily in Germany.

<small>His Early Difficulties.</small>

Facts have proved too strong for him. Unlimited liability showed itself as little acceptable to Belgians as it was to Italians. At the outset it was accepted only because its significance was not understood. When in one of the banks some years later it was proposed to limit the liability to—I think it was fifty times the value of the share—members, who had up to that time made themselves answerable for the bank up to the hilt with absolutely the *whole* of their possessions, shrank back in alarm, declaring that they could never accept so heavy a responsibility. In respect of other points no less, M. d'Andrimont's close adherence to his German model has for some time stood in the way of entire success. For a long period the movement dragged heavily. Some banks grew up rapidly, but their number and their business remained stationary, with one or two added or withdrawn every year—sixteen, seventeen, then fifteen—representing a constituency of 10,000 or 11,000, keeping very solvent, doing a fair amount of business in a very business-like way, but never really extending their sway or becoming genuinely popular, even among those teeming millions of the most populous and the busiest little country of Europe, in which Ministers and economists—like M. Graux and M. Beernaert —never weary of calling out for some popular form of credit, more especially agricultural. "How is it," plaintively asked M. d'Andrimont, as President, at the Congress held in 1888, "that, having been founded nearly twenty-five years ago, the People's Banks have not grown more numerous?" The French economist, M. Limousin, in agreement with M. Julius Schaar (Director of the *Banque Populaire* of Brussels), supplied a very plausible answer: the banks were not sufficiently "popular." "The People's Banks," so writes M. Charles M. Limousin in the *Journal des Economistes*, "become in Belgium less and less popular, that is to say, less and less useful to the poorest class of the population. Soon they will have nothing that is popular about them except the name." M. Schaar complained that "the People's Banks cannot be useful to simple artisans."

This frank judgment may have helped to lift the banks into a better position. They have always been, in the main, well—in some cases even excellently—administered. But there was something about them which seemed adverse to spreading and growth. M. d'Andrimont had placed them in his country, so to speak, as a German plant put into a Belgian pot, not, like M. Luzzatti's *banche*, as a German set planted on new soil, there to strike root and become part of an indigenous vegetation. The tree set in the new soil, in disregard of the conditions under which it had to live, for a considerable time just managed to keep alive, pushing on very little.

Eventual Success.

During the past few years things have assumed a more satisfactory aspect. It is as if the tap root had at length broken through the clay enclosure, and, drawing new nourishment from the natural soil, had become really assimilated to its surroundings. It is now spreading its branches aloft and sending out new shoots. The last annual Report of the Federation of Belgian People's Banks—which not all People's Banks actually existing have joined—counts up in all twenty-three *banques populaires* of what is still called the Schulze-Delitzsch type, of which number the returns sent in for twenty-two show a collective roll of 13,749 members, commanding a capital of 2,714,962 francs (£108,590), and doing an annual business of 261,969,728 francs (£10,478,789). These are the figures for 1895. In that year twenty-one of these banks, some of them still very young, had lent out in all 43,308,066 francs (£1,732,323). Their savings deposits amounted to 4,815,786 francs (£192,631). They paid dividends at a rate generally of from 4 to 7 per cent. (The Bank of Ghent, which is very capitalist, declared 8 per cent., and the little Bank of Jumet, likewise very capitalist, declared even 15 per cent. But these are exceptions.)

Present Strength of the Movement.

All this is not nearly as much as might have been hoped or desired. It is not even an absolute advance in respect of business. For bad times have told against People's

Banks in Belgium, **as in** Germany and in Italy. But it is unquestionably a relative advance, **and an advance** which seems likely to be maintained.

But, then, these banks **are no** more Schulze-Delitzsch banks than are the *banche popolari*. Barring two, rather essential, features, indeed, **they** much more **resemble** the latter. And they seem destined to grow more and more like them as time goes on. Although Mr Gosselin, when writing his report for our Blue-Book of 1886, **appears to** have **been** unaware of the fact, the Belgian *banques populaires* **have** long since discarded the unlimited liability recommended by Schulze—all but the **little** bank of Saint Nicolas, the business of which **is** very circumscribed. **It is true, their** limitation of liability is of a fancy character. They limit the liability of shareholders to a multiple of the **value** of the share, generally five times the amount, **in some cases more.** But notwithstanding M. d'Andrimont's persistent protests, the **feeling** in favour of further limitation, to **the actual** value **of the share, is** steadily growing, and seems destined to carry the day.

<small>Features distinguishing Belgian from German People's Banks.</small>

There are, as observed, two **features in** the main, which distinguish the Belgian banks **from** the Italian *banche popolari*. These are: **the** liability *exceeding* the share; and the comparatively *large* **figure** adopted for the share—as a rule 200 francs, to be paid up, not in ten months as in Italy, but at the member's option, in as much as 400 weeks or 100 months, at the rate of 50 centimes a week or 2 francs **a month.** Otherwise the resemblance between the two types is striking. Both **have** the Committee larger than is prescribed by Schulze-Delitzsch, **and** apply, as M. d'Andrimont has **put it,** "**the** principle of universal suffrage to purposes **of** credit." **Both** rely to a great extent upon unremunerated **labour—the** Italian paying **three officers,** the Belgian two, namely, the director (*gérant*) and the **cashier.** Both are very strict in respect **of** control and audit. Both select their members with some amount of care, although M. d'Andrimont lays down the rule that "to be admitted as member of a *banque populaire*, it is sufficient for a man to be honest and industrious; to obtain a credit, all that is required is, to comply with certain prescribed rules." Both — questionably, as I cannot help thinking — allow a fixed amount of credit in virtue of mere shareholding—the Belgian banks as a rule up to 1½ times the payments actually made towards share capital. Both allow members to hold more shares than one. Both lend for short terms. Both, I may add, are, as a rule, well administered. And I think I may say, that the Belgian bankers are less exacting in respect of dividend. Evidently they study to keep down management expenses to a minimum, and are in this respect generally successful. Obviously, also, the best of Belgian banks are distinctly more co-operative than the Italian, in respect of this point, that they confine their lending rigidly to members. They make, as a rule, new members pay 3 francs entrance fee, and 50 centimes for the book of rules, which serves at the same time as a pass-book. They have now pretty well overspread the entire little kingdom. There are banks at Liége (2), Huy, Verviers, Ghent, Namur, Saint Nicolas (Waes), Antwerp (2), Dinant, Châtelet, Malines, Andenne, Termonde, Alost, Goë Limbourg, Argenteau, Louvain, Jumet, Brussels (2), Gosselies, and Gilly. It may be well to pick out from among this number a few banks to serve as types.

The Banque Populaire of Verviers.

The *Banque Populaire* of Verviers ought to be of peculiar interest to us, not so much because in little time it has grown to be the largest People's Bank of Belgium— numbering, last midsummer, 2,995 members—as because it has set up its counter in a manufacturing town organised to all intents and purposes like a manufacturing town in Great Britain. Sceptics in this country will insist, without looking sufficiently into facts, that we could not set up co-operative credit in this kingdom, because we have "no small trade." It is the small workshops of Liége, Milan, Leipzig, so they will have it, which support these co-operative banks, and alone make it possible for them to live and thrive. In our British towns, where industry and trade are for the most part concentrated in large workshops, and the small artisan of abroad becomes the salaried "hand" or foreman, such a thing, they say, would be impossible. Well, here is a town with large workshops only. Out of its population of somewhere about 50,000, as many as 40,000 are "hands," working in those large cloth mills and yarn factories which employ 160 steam engines or more, and turn out annually above 400,000 pieces of cloth, besides yarn, clothing the entire Belgian army, and exporting at least £3,000,000 worth into the bargain. Walking in the busy streets of Verviers, you might fancy yourself in Bradford or in Leeds. Well, the *Banque Populaire* has set up its *mensa argentaria* in the midst of these shop-hands, and has gathered together more members around it than any other People's Bank in Belgium. Up to 1892 the Bank of Liége, working among a population of 160,000 inhabitants, in the very home of small trade, maintained the lead. Now Verviers has outstripped it considerably. Brussels, with its 184,000 population; Ghent, with its 152,000; Antwerp, with its 240,000; Malines, with its 52,000, all rank after it, notwithstanding that they have more small trade. It is really not the "small trade," it is the understanding and appreciating the co-operative principle which makes a co-operative bank to thrive. In its composition the Verviers Bank is thoroughly popular and "democratic." There are, it is true, among its 3,000 members, 449 "rentiers"; but most of these are, I believe, small men, retired from work or business. There are 446 small traders. There are 6 doctors, 26 proprietors of cafés, 33 small manufacturers, 188 counting-house clerks, 117 small cultivators, 76 teachers, 2 priests, 2 sacristans. All the rest may be described as working men and working women. And with such a constituency the People's Bank of Verviers does a business exceeding in volume the business of any other People's Bank of Belgium, excepting only that of Ghent, which, as I shall show, is really not a "People's" Bank at all, but a co-operative capitalists' bank. The business of Verviers amounted in 1895 to 33,707,506 francs (£1,348,300), as against 15,348,522 francs reported by the People's Bank of Liége. Its direct lending alone (in advances and discounts, without including cash credits), amounted to 6,263,545 francs (£250,541), as compared with 3,940,746 francs in Liége. And that with a paid-up capital of only 599,000 francs (£23,960). I have sometimes been asked: What do these people borrow money for? It would be difficult to say. No account is kept of that. And by far the greater portion of the lending is done by way of cash credit, which is in truth the most useful and most educating of all forms of lending. Evidently the cash credits granted have been put to good commercial use. For, in 1895, 12,705,895 francs had been drawn out and 11,636,831 francs paid in. The account is accordingly anything but "dead." And the business is so sound that, after carrying 1,941 francs to the reserve fund already standing at 70,210 francs; and 1,001 francs to the provident fund previously figuring at 116,178 francs; besides allowing 1,500 francs to the managing committee according to attendances, the bank was in a position to pay to its shareholders 38,370 francs in dividend, at the rate of 6 per cent. From an English point of view I look upon the People's Bank of Verviers as perhaps the most instructive that there is.

The Banque Populaire of Ghent.

The *Banque Populaire* of Ghent is a specimen of a totally different type. Ghent, we know, is a busy, prosperous place, in which capital is allowed free sway. Hence, as a counterpoise, that Socialist movement which has one of its chosen centres in the same city, represented by the *Vooruit*. The People's Bank of Ghent has, of all the large People's Banks of Belgium, remained, in respect of liability on shares, the most faithful to the German tradition of entire non-limitation. It issues 200 francs shares, which carry a liability of 5,000 francs. Why? The Director was perfectly frank with me on that point. There are 1,648 members—at the time of which I am speaking there were just about 1,500—with respect to 1,000 of whom the National Savings Bank of Brussels had satisfied itself—since it had their names—that they were perfectly capable of answering at any time for the amount of liability pledged, say up to 5,000,000 francs—leaving out of account altogether the remaining 500 who must after all have been "good" for something. Accordingly it allows the bank credit for practically any amount up to which it may choose to borrow. That is perfectly legitimate and perfectly safe; but it is not "democratised" or "popular" credit. In his own People's Bank of Liége, M. d'Andrimont will not allow any member to borrow more than 5,000 francs. He advisedly bids people who require more to go to the joint-stock banks. For such business they are the proper banks; they can do it, and, in all probability, in dealing with borrowers who, in truth, need no co-operative bank to make their credit marketable, they will do it quite as well.

The People's Bank of Ghent, I may add, did in 1895 a business of 113,044,500 francs,* more than one-third of all done by twenty-one People's Banks; lending out 23,083,177 francs, about one-half of the collective figure, upon the security of a share capital of only 329,240 francs, between

---

* The figure for 1895 is exceptionally large; in 1894 it was 48,916,441 francs. The figure for direct lending is equally abnormal. In 1894 it was 9,353,623 francs.

one-seventh and one-eighth of the share capital of twenty-two banks furnishing returns.

<small>The Banque Populaire of Liége.</small>   I reserve a few words for the excellent Bank of Liége, the oldest, and probably the best managed, People's Bank in Belgium. I have been permitted to sit at its Committee table and see the business transacted, with care and circumspection, and no sparing of pains. It was founded, in 1864, by M. d'Andrimont, who is still its President. The roll of its members shows, generally, a popular and democratic composition. There are small tradesmen—bakers, shoemakers, printers, tailors, plumbers; moreover teachers, male and female, clerks, also better-class artisans and small manufacturers. M. d'Andrimont intended it for a true *people's* bank, a bank not placing itself in competition with other banks, but stepping into the gap which those banks had left, and bringing down credit to those to whom it had been denied. The Bank of Liége still holds fast to liability in excess of what is paid up—five times the amount. Opinion within the bank, I believe, is favourable to contraction to the actual amount of the share, which would get rid of that inconvenient and unsafe source of credit—unpaid-up liability. However, in deference to the President, the larger, nondescript liability has been thus far retained. It is, I presume, only exaggerated regard for the opinion of Schulze-Delitzsch which leads his pupil M. d'Andrimont to insist upon this unbusinesslike margin, which Italian practice has shown to be wholly unnecessary. M. Micha is strongly favourable to a change. It is to M. Micha, who is a consistent co-operator, that the bank owes its very recent adoption of the practice of profit-sharing for the benefit of the employees. For twenty-two years M. Micha has steadily advocated this practice in vain. He carried it at the last annual meeting. The People's Bank of Liége is particularly strict in respect of its checking and auditing of accounts and transactions. Its *contrôleur spécial*, M. Fesch,

a trained banker, is pretty constantly at work in his off hours, inspecting here and auditing there, and the more he inspects, the better are the Committee pleased. With a members' roll of about 2,500, the bank pays out annually about 4,000,000 francs in advances, and declares dividends at the rate of 4 per cent. only, allowing to members the benefits of the larger margin secured.

All this is, of course, industrial business. Well as co-operative banks have succeeded in Belgium in towns, it is a standing cause of grief, alike to the leaders of the movement and to legislators and economists, that their success remains restricted to the industrial sphere. In Belgium, as in France, it has long been a favourite hobby with legislators to create a popular form of agricultural credit, designed to supply the thrifty and pushing cultivator with working capital, and get him out of the hands of the greedy "notaires," who take his money at a **low rate** of interest, **in** prosperous times, only to lend it back **to** him, when things go badly, at a truly extortionate rate. Everything, one would say, seems in Belgium to favour **some** co-operative form of agricultural credit. There is money, there are means of communication, there is knowledge of business, there are, in fact, all the elements of successful and remunerative banking present, **with** an intelligent and active class of cultivators to take advantage of them, most of them being **tenants**. Of about 5,000,000 acres under cultivation, 76.155 per cent. is in the hands **of** tenants. And most holdings are small. Only about 3,000 holdings, of tenants or owning cultivators, are estimated to exceed 125 **acres**; 35,000 holdings range from 25 to 125 acres; and the vast remainder, about 1,000,000 holdings **in all, are of less** than **25 acres.** On these it is, mainly, that Belgian labour and Belgian agricultural skill produce those heavy crops of what is really garden **produce**, which competes so embarrassingly with the fruits of our native fields, turning every favouring accident to account, down to

Agricultural Co-operative Credit continues undeveloped. Why?

Features of Belgian Agriculture.

the shale in the soil, which being fired, enables these resourceful husbandmen to supplement the solar warmth wanting in their climate for producing fruit considered the monopoly of more southern countries. For such high cultivation, above all things, money is wanted. But co-operative credit, which could give it, cheaply and conveniently, has thus far, in this particular application, as credit accessible to agriculture, remained an unrealised aspiration. Ministers have pleaded for it in Parliament. The Government has endeavoured to do its part. It has placed the practically exhaustless treasures of the National Savings Bank at the service of cultivators through the intervention of *comptoirs agricoles*, appointed in each district, and endowed with ample powers of discretion. The experiment has, however, led to scarcely any results. The simple cultivator who, as both M. Graux and M. Beernaert have pointed out, habitually shrinks from " the indignity" of borrowing, and can only be coaxed into it by having credit administered by men with familiar faces and heads which understand his case and his needs, would never take to these strange gentlemen. In 1889 there were only four *comptoirs* existing. And of those four only one, that of Genappes, showed any signs of life. Among them the four had in 1889 lent out 810,120 francs—a poor £32,404 —of which some 555,000 francs was lent in sums of 10,000 francs each and more, and could not therefore very well have gone into very " small" pockets.

In the debates of the Chambers and at the Annual Congresses of the Federation of Belgian People's Banks, stirring appeals from Ministers and the President, and resolutions passed in favour of agricultural credit, form standing dishes since a long time back. But the matter does not advance much beyond that point.

Why not? There are sufficient reasons, of course.

Belgian co-operators, when addressing themselves to the creation of co-operative credit in their own country,

[margin: The Comptoirs Agricoles.]

deliberately adopted the Schulze-Delitzsch system as the one system applicable—the Schulze-Delitzsch system in its straitest and narrowest application, it was to be. And so it would have remained, if " facts **stronger than men**" had not forcibly pushed it **out of** the " book-taught **groove.**" Those facts, which have moulded Belgian **co-operative** credit in towns, have not yet had time and opportunities for making their power felt in the country. However, men like MM. Rolin Jacquemins and Delisse have more than once **plainly** warned their brother co-operators that the present form of Belgian co-operative credit is not suited to agricultural purposes. **We** have **seen** in Germany that the Schulze-Delitzsch **system** may be made to render very useful and substantial services to agriculture, but only by a **rather marked departure from the hard** and **fast** line **originally** laid down, in respect of length of term, of amount **of shares, and of the creation** of a closer touch among **members,** corresponding to that which is in the Raiffeisen system assured by smaller districts and thoroughly **democratic** government, and even so only on the supposition that the banks attempting **to** practise agricultural credit **find** themselves particularly strong in capital, or else can issue long-term bonds in sufficient quantity, or **are in** receipt of a large quantity of steady savings. **In** Germany it is generally the savings deposits which pull the Schulze-Delitzsch banks successfully through their agricultural **business.** In Belgium the People's Banks are considerably **weaker** at this point than their sister establishments, either in Germany or in Italy. In Germany the non-co-operative savings banks are communal, **or** municipal, or provincial institutions, leaving the ground **fully** open to competing **banks.** In Italy the Government savings banks are designed—as the late Postmaster-General himself explained the matter to me—only to receive the overplus from other savings, to assist people to save who cannot place their

Some Partiality for the Schulze-Delitzsch System.

deposits elsewhere; and in point of fact they take only about a quarter of the nation's entire savings. In Belgium the National Savings Bank, strong and well established, a Government institution, absorbs the main bulk of the nation's savings. Accordingly, the problem to be solved becomes for the Belgian People's Banks a totally different one from what it is for the German or the Italian. Instead of fixing and *localising* savings in a district, they are called upon to *draw them back* into it, to become, as it were, agencies for stronger bodies providing the capital, like the *casse* of Parma. The long-term bonds issued by them do not represent a large value. And their strength in capital of their own is less considerable than what we find in Germany, as appears from the fact that in 1895 they had to make 2,714,962 francs suffice for lending out 43,308,086 francs, not counting cash credits.

<small>Why it fails in respect of Belgian Agriculture.</small>

On the other hand, the co-operators who have the ear of the public have steadily disparaged the Raiffeisen system, alike in speech and in writing. In view of about 1,000,000 holdings out of 1,038,000 being under 25 acres, and a good number, therefore, presumably very much smaller, it seems at least likely that the Raiffeisen practice, which has been found specially adapted to the use of small cultivators, would have answered the purpose aimed at very much better than the Schulze-Delitzsch system. The £8 shares of the d'Andrimont banks alone must constitute a formidable hindrance to the admission of many small cultivators. However, M. d'Andrimont would have none of the Raiffeisen system. Making himself the echo of hostile notes sounded at Berlin, he has denounced the Raiffeisen system right and left—to me, among other people—as "purely political," not meaning, of course, literally, what he said, or meaning it only in application, not to the Raiffeisen system proper (which he does not appear to have known), but to that distorted reproduction which Abbé Mellaerts had

<small>Prejudice against the Raiffeisen System.</small>

<small>Ultramontane "Caisses." Abbé Mellaerts.</small>

set up in Belgium, in the interest of the Church, which he *did* know. Those thirty odd banks, founded by Abbé Mellaerts to provide "votes, votes, votes" for the clerical party, do not appear to have done much business. However, between them M. Léon d'Andrimont and Abbé Mellaerts have certainly succeeded in affixing upon the Raiffeisen system in Belgian opinion the undeserved stigma of a doubtful reputation. The consequence has been, that for a long time, while Belgian Ministers and co-operators, M. d'Andrimont and others, still kept most dolefully bewailing the absence of co-operative agricultural credit in their country, suggesting that the agriculturists must be to blame, the very same men deliberately removed out of reach of the latter the one instrument which promised effectually to provide the credit wanted.

In addition to Abbé Mellaerts, the founder of the *Boerenbond*, Professor Francotte has been active in setting up Ultramontane credit associations of his own, in imitation of the German "Peasants' Associations." The best known of these is at Argenteau. It will probably serve as a fair type for the rest. It has *membres fondateurs* (landlords) joining for thirty years, and taking up from 1 to 5 shares each, which carry no right to borrow, but, practically, the privilege of sole management; and *membres effectifs*, who take only 1 share each—paying for it by monthly or weekly instalments, of respectively 2 francs or 50 centimes—who may withdraw, who may borrow, but who have little to say in the administration. That is patronage pure and simple, conveying the pill of social and political influence concealed under the sugar coating of financial help—patronage so pronounced that at Perck tenants become members of the association in virtue of their entry upon a tenancy without even the formality of election or payment. The whole thing is Ultramontane "primrosery," and not self-help.

Thanks to the persistent urging of M. d'Andrimont and

Professor Francotte.

Two Small Agricultural People's Banks.

his friends, two *banques populaires* have actually organised themselves as "agricultural" banks. One of these is at Goë Limbourg—the Château de Limbourg is M. d'Andrimont's country seat—the other at Argenteau. M. d'Andrimont owns himself satisfied with the results of their practice. However, Goë Limbourg has in six years managed to creep up only to 89 members, and Argenteau in five only to 42.

M. Mahillon organises a Belgian-Raiffeisen System.

M. d'Andrimont himself has now come to see that for the rural districts of Belgium different methods are required. There is money in plenty available—not money to be collected in the district in order to be kept in it, but money to be first filtered through the great National Savings Bank, which, having more than it knows what to do with, is only too willing to lend, provided that it receives adequate security. It has lately even taken the propaganda of agricultural credit associations of the Raiffeisen type into its own hands. Under a law passed in 1894, it has acquired the right of lending out part of its holdings to agricultural banks at the rate of 3 per cent. It is anxious to see that law put into practice, and accordingly last year one of its chief officers, M. Mahillon, prepared with great care a "Manual" for Raiffeisen banks which has only one fault, namely, that of being a little too complicated. It, however, provides for intending founders of village banks a very valuable *vade-mecum*, giving them much information as to the security to be given, and the steps to be taken to obtain advances. Unfortunately for Belgium, M. Mahillon died shortly after issuing his book, to the great regret of his countrymen.

Its Prospect of Success.

After so many years of hostility to Raiffeisenism, it is certainly encouraging to find M. d'Andrimont now openly pleading, so far as agricultural practice comes into account, for its two essential features, namely, the limitation of a district to *one or two parishes only*, which is wholly contrary

THE BELGIAN "BANQUES POPULAIRES"—THEIR WORK IN 1895.

(The Figures are taken from the Official Returns.)

Name of Bank.	Date of Foundation.	No. of Members 31st Dec. 1895.	Share Capital (Paid-up).	Reserve Fund.	Total Business done.	Advances and Discounts made during the Year (not counting Cash Credits).*	Savings and Deposits on 31st Dec. 1895.	Profits.	Divi. paid for 1895.
			Francs.	Francs.	Francs.	Francs.	Francs.	Francs.	Per ct.
Liége (*Banque Populaire*)	June 1, 1864	2,486	403,688.11	33,299.63	15,346,672.00	3,940,745.75	1,047,060.62	35,410.30	4
Huy	April 9, 1865	752	127,439.43	8,954.33	2,041,239.05	381,821.67	201,845.08	5,254.52	5
Verviers	May 1, 1865	2,995	599,900.00	186,388.40	33,707,505.81	6,263,545.10	1,874,986.81	38,812.39	6
Ghent	Oct. 29, 1866	1,648	329,240.00	134,797.54	113,044,499.56	23,083,117.00		103,990.09	8
Namur	Jan. 9, 1869	723	247,366.85	22,584.80	11,904,533.31	3,427,818.36	334,099.86	12,428.77	4½
St Nicolas (*Waes*)	July 5, 1869	281	55,871.36	4,692.60	1,173,229.73	791,979.39		9,795.56	5
Antwerp (*City*)	July 4, 1873	481	177,216.59	23,780.52	9,302,102.71	2,345,700.99	220,829.98	9,536.70	5
Dinant	Oct. 19, 1873	278	49,601.08	7,910.74	1,306,535.13	433,068.69		1,947.79	3
Châtelet	Dec. 10, 1873	445	88,945.45	18,295.52	3,976,542.78			8,745.	7
Malines	Feb. 16, 1874	276	53,116.56	453.38	1,230,757.60	404,657.76	86,042.98		...
Andenne	April 15, 1874	421	80,885.52	73,694.13	8,957,266.25	2,855,765.46		17,054.65	5
Termonde (*Arrondissement*)	June 15, 1875	89	21,087.18	488.09	457,890.36	67,642.48	7,314.04	297.57	0
Alost	Feb. 22, 1886	54	25,930.00	2,147.90	1,355,672.82	548,549.60		3,251.22	5
Antwerp (*Arrondissement*)	Nov. 12, 1886	1,170	146,250.00	7,384.67	17,771,062.82	3,808,222.05	837,844.72	13,970.19	4
Goé Limbourg (*Agricultural*)	Dec. 2, 1888	104	18,410.09	882.96	253,771.40	43,946.39		1,121.55	5
Argenteau (*Agricultural*)	April 23, 1889	58	6,839.15	2,220.59	325,496.54	1,235.97		703.93	4
Louvain	July 17, 1889	175	34,110.92	22,988.53	6,813,168.23	874,767.02		5,050.08	5
Jumet	July 1, 1891	96	23,850.00	24,554.81	13,393,257.31	4,611,701.66		19,496.39	15
Brussels (*Syndicat Mixte*)	Mar. 4, 1892	182	71,111.00	71,137.57	10,422,687.23	2,006,836.83	134,013.00	8,424.31	4
Gosselies (*B. P. de Crédit Mutuel*)	1892	23	10,200.00	1,489.87	1,931,932.18	625,274.67		3,001.19	6
Brussels (*Maison des Ouvriers*)†	Sept. 4, 1892	171	30,223.94	1,018.06		383,646.08		1,449.17	4
Liége (*Crédit Populaire Liégois*)	Sept. 15, 1892	841	113,578.79	4,039.95	7,342,036	774,487.12	71,749.21	6,251.18	4
Total	...	13,749	2,714,962.02	653,204.09	261,969,727.63	43,308,086.69	4,815,786.30	305,993.66	...

* The Cash Credits are in some cases much more considerable than the Advances and Discounts taken together.
† No Returns sent in.

to all that Schulze has ever taught, and the adoption of *unlimited liability*, which he himself has first rejected. Both these things he recommends on the very ground upon which Raiffeisen has insisted upon them, namely, the necessity of producing a close touch and knowledge among members, as alone qualified to make co-operative lending safe in rural districts. M. Mahillon's "Manual" and M. d'Andrimont's pleading have not yet, I believe, had time to bear fruit. I cannot doubt that they will do so in time, and I cannot but believe that among a population apparently specifically suited for it, the Raiffeisen system will yield results similar to those which it has brought forth elsewhere, and that thus the wish which Belgian legislators have so long and so fondly cherished will at length be realised, and, in addition to a strong phalanx of urban People's Banks, some of which—like those of Liége and Verviers—are very models, Belgium will have its own army to show of village credit institutions, rescuing victims from the choking grasp of usury, and dispensing to the industrious cultivators, those "sinews of husbandry" which none know better to turn to good account.

CHAPTER XII.

CO-OPERATIVE **BANKING IN** *SWITZERLAND.*

IN Switzerland money co-operation has grown **up very** Distinctive
slowly. Swiss co-operation, generally speaking, **is ex-** Character of Swiss Money
tremely "business-like." **It** studies most assiduously its Co-operation.
supporters' pecuniary interests, but does not aim at very
much beyond—except it be incidentally to promote saving
and thrift in their **aspect** of economic virtues. It may,
accordingly, perhaps be described as a little selfish. There
is none of that "Christian Socialist" nimbus about it, which
in this country seems to encircle **our** own co-operative
action as with a peculiar **halo of** virtue. 'Cheapness"
and "profit" are the watchwords—cheapness **sometimes**
even to the disregard **of** quality. **And when, by a** stroke
of good luck, **fortune** gives **to co-operators a handsome**
surplus—as it did **some time ago to** a society in Zürich,
putting £4,000 of cash unexpectedly into their pockets—
—**then** the temptation to "share out" appears to become
overpowering. The members secure their prize—in Zürich
it was £16 a-piece—and rush off each with a slice of the
common goose, trusting to a kind fate to find them **in more**
eggs, and, should that **fail,** quite content, after their lucky
"spec," to leave co-operation to take care of itself.

In spite of all this, it cannot be denied that in a co-
operative aspect Switzerland is decidedly interesting. There
is not a little genuine co-operation nestling unobtrusively
and scarcely observed in its peaceful valleys between those
giant hills. And even **where it** is only mere "business"

co-operation—a most useful agent among the factors which produce national wealth and contentment—it is marked by features—such as a business-like clearness of aim, apt organisation, and masterly management—which make it exceedingly well worth studying.

<small>Co-operative Purchase of Cattle.</small>

By the very nature of the conditions in which Providence has placed them, the Swiss are almost compelled to practise co-operation. They could scarcely make their cheese, which constitutes their most characteristic national product, except by clubbing together to form co-operative *fruitières*. Co-operation in dairying it may have been which, more particularly in the Canton of Thurgau, led, by a natural sequence of ideas, to co-operation for the purchase of cattle. There are in the Canton of Thurgau no fewer than thirty-five cattle-purchasing co-operative associations in existence, ministering to a population of 22,230, one in each parish, no matter whether that parish have but sixty inhabitants, or close upon 2,000. For more than forty years have these *Caisses Thurgoviniennes*[*] kept the inhabitants in bullocks and milch cows, rendering most useful services in their own humble way, and receiving their money back in full and punctually, with interest, which promises to enable them in course of time to extinguish the debt incurred at the outset, and put in its place a sufficient self-supporting fund. And all this has proceeded from the initiative of the parishes themselves. Only quite lately has the Cantonal Government voted subsidies, to the amount of 1,500 francs a village, not by way of necessary assistance, but as an encouragement to the extension of a useful practice. The *modus procedendi* is really very simple. The commune—that is, the parish—by a vote of its inhabitants, resolves to raise a fund by loan. Out of that fund any villager who can make out a case and show that

---

[*] For fuller information about these institutions see my article, "The Poor Man's Cow," in the *National Review*, October 1894.

he really desires to buy a beast, and has keep for it, is entitled to receive an advance. He must enter into a bond to repay **the** sum, with interest, by regular instalments, and also to buy from nobody else on credit. That done, he receives his money, and may buy wherever he chooses, paying cash. Should he fail in any of the duties undertaken, his loan is at once declared forfeited, and repayment is enforced. For the debt contracted by the parish, of course the parish is **collectively** responsible, which involves unlimited liability on the part of every parishioner up to the amount of the debt. The needs of different parishes naturally differ according to circumstances. **In** 1889 the little village of Wattenweil, having only 140 inhabitants, **lent out** 4,750 francs, the larger village of Marweil (311 population) 5,980 francs. The repayments in these two **cases** amounted to 3,980 francs and **4,597 francs respectively.** Sometimes the fund raised proves excessive, **at** other times insufficient; but the difference is never very great. The village of Tägerweilen, in the year mentioned, having a fund of 22,987 francs, found itself called upon to grant 27,000 francs in advances; in Huttlingen the demands made on a fund of 18,470 francs amounted to only 17,980 francs.

A couple of years ago, when I was in Thurgau, there was in all about 550,000 francs owing, which may have stood for 2,000 or 2,500 cows, purchased, for the most part, with borrowed money. Tägerweilen alone had about 600 **or 650 cows standing to** its credit. The *caisse* of Illnau, in Zürich, which was newly established, had already purchased 800 or 900 cows. The consequence is that, as the chairman of one of these *caisses* informed me, three cows are now kept where there used to be one. And the whole country is richer by its cultivators' **prosperity.** The funds are kept **in** a state of equilibrium **by moneys** coming back, and the **losses are** infinitesimal.

Local Substitutes for Co-operative Credit.

The reason why co-operative credit generally has been only slowly organised in Switzerland obviously is, that the country has long possessed several tolerably popular and serviceable substitutes. In no country are habits of thrift more developed. They are inculcated to children at school as part of their education. Thus it comes about that those "compulsory savings banks," which are indigenous to the country, have thriven so remarkably well on this republican soil. They apply the lesson of thrift with rigorous severity. The man who once pledges himself to lay by must lay by for the three years for which his promise runs, on pain of a fine, or, in case of repetition, of forfeiture. The monthly payments must be not less than 1 franc, nor more than 50 francs. They continue accumulating and earning compound interest till the three years are over, after which they very often go to buy a *part sociale* in the co-operative bank, which has all the time acted as cashier. For money so saved is very rarely squandered. During the process of accumulation contributors in temporary need of money may always borrow to the extent of three-fourths of what they have paid in, being charged, however, 6 per cent. interest on the loan, in the place of the 4½ per cent. which they are credited with.

For large borrowing there are other institutions ready to lend assistance. The mortgage system is in Switzerland so much developed as to some extent to cover the ground of personal credit. The legal expenses are a mere nothing. Accordingly no one who has realty to pledge hesitates to raise money for a temporary want by means of a mortgage. According to statistical returns, Switzerland is one of the most heavily mortgage-burdened countries in the world. But half its mortgages answer to what elsewhere is personal indebtedness. Mortgages for 1,000 francs (£40) are nothing uncommon, and there are mortgages even down to 150 francs (£6).

Specifically for working men there are at any rate one "Caisses Ouvrières." or two very useful People's Banks similar to that sketched by M. Ruchonnet in one of his reports to our Co-operative Congresses, taking members' contributions by fivepenny driblets, or a franc at a time, till the figure of 100 francs is reached, which constitutes a "share"; and lending out small sums on reasonable terms for ten months at a time, repaying themselves by regular instalments. These banks, though few in number, are useful so far as they go, though no doubt every now and then their well-intended zeal to support co-operation in the shape of productive co-operative societies recruited from among their own members— tin-workers, painters, plasterers, tailors, &c.— leads them into mischief. By other lending the banks rarely suffer loss. Of this class of banks the *Caisse Ouvrière d'Epargne et de Crédit Mutuel* of Geneva is a good example. From 11,275 francs with which it began work, in 1877, its capital has grown to 150,590 francs. It has taken warning by what M. Elie Reclus wrote a good many years ago, specifically with Swiss banks in his mind, about "the danger of big dividends," and has once for all limited its dividend to 5 per cent.

But the type of banks with which Swiss co-operative credit is more specifically identified is to be found in those well-managed "business" banks, of which the *Schweizerische Volksbank* may serve as an admirable example. These establishments do not look much higher in their aims than to do the best that they can for their members. To that task, however, they address themselves with most praiseworthy assiduity, and, as a rule, with much skill and success. "Our first object," in substance says the *Volksbank* in its Report issued on the occasion of its twenty years' jubilee, " is, by means of the joint action of many, to provide a credit and the requisite cash for small folk; our next, to earn a fair profit for our members; and our last, to promote

Co-operative Business Banks.

thrift, as a means of converting into a small capitalist the man who is not such already." There is very little altruism in this programme. But the object pursued—simple, purely economic, but very genuine co-operation—is thoroughly legitimate, and answers a most useful purpose in the economy of a commonwealth. Generally speaking, these banks are not very "poor" People's Banks. There are some among them which recruit their members from pretty necessitous classes—as, for instance, the *Ersparnisskasse* of Konolfingen, which has taken small men's savings for sixty-four years back and hoarded them for their benefit. The peculiarity of this bank is, that it pays no dividend whatever, but carries every surplus systematically to reserve. That has enabled it in course of time to redeem every farthing of its share capital; and now it realises the assumed ideal of a bank which confers benefits, without having cost any one a penny. All its capital is its own, earned by business. Other banks, likewise, no matter whether large or small, make no distinction between rich and poor. The working man paying his entrance fee of 5 francs, and a regular monthly instalment of 1 franc towards the purchase of his share, is as welcome as the millionaire who takes a large number of shares and pays cash down for them all. For the working man, indeed, it must be rather a hopeless business clearing his 1,000 franc share—that is the figure in the *Schweizerische Volksbank*—at the rate of 1 franc a month. But, then, his member's privileges begin — barring only the right to draw dividend—the moment that he has paid his entrance fee and his first franc. So there can be no hardship. The object which these banks aim at is, for the sake alike of custom and of security, to enlist as large an army of members as they possibly can, and to induce these men to do all their business at their counter. That is the dominating idea in all their practice, and they study its realisation in every detail.

Their Utility.

"**Keep down** your demands made upon members in respect of instalments," says M. Yersin, the Director-General of the most successful of these institutions, the *Schweizerische Volksbank* already mentioned, "make those instalments as small as possible; for the lower are your demands, the more 'popular' will be your institution, the more members will you attract. If possible, charge no **entrance fee,** because even that is likely to be felt as a 'tax.' Offer your members special advantages in the shape of a rather lower discount charged on bills, a rather higher interest allowed on deposits. Interest them in your work by every possible means; to this end make your administration thoroughly representative and democratic, allowing to each member **a** vote, and one vote only, whatever be his holding, and giving **to each** branch bank full self-government. Make people understand that you pay precisely the same attention to small business **as to large.** 'Third-class traffic' is, **in the** aggregate, **the safest, the** most remunerative, and **the most** constant. Spread out your machinery, **cover what ground** you can, multiply banking **facilities; the more** 'popular' you make your institution, the better **will** you succeed." That is M. Yersin's advice, and in his **own** bank (except that an entrance fee is taken) it **is carried out** fully in practice with unquestionable skill and indisputable success. The bank, which in 1869 began with 53 members and a capital of 2,627 francs (£105), has now a members' roll of 11,826, and a capital of 10,477,270 francs (£419,092), with a reserve of 674,314 francs (£26,972) at its back, besides a pension fund of 36,946 francs (£1,476), and does business **(counting** both sides **of** the balance-sheet) at the rate of 2,347,714,270 francs a **year** (£93,908,572), lending **out,** in 1895, 151,511,306 **francs** (£60,460,452). **These** are the returns for 1895. **Losses and law** expenses did not in that **year** between them exceed 8,**102 francs** (£324).

There are some features about this bank—which does

The "Schweizerische Volksbank."

not allow a year to pass without extending its financial sway—which make its work interesting. In the districts of Tramelan and Saignelégier it does much to encourage and support the co-operative watchmaking, which is a specialty of that country. In the Cantons of Berne and Winterthur it materially assists co-operation for agricultural purposes.

Being constituted strictly on "business" principles, the *Schweizerische Volksbank*, as a matter of course, like other Swiss banks, studies to transact every variety of profitable business, even should it lie a little beyond the limits of strictly conventional banking. Thus it undertakes to **act as stockbroker for its** members. And it also deals in silver bullion in connection with the watch trade practised very largely at Saignelégier. But its main business, as that of the other banks of its type, is, to take deposits and savings, and to raise money in other ways; and, again, to **discount** bills, grant loans, and give credit in current accounts. In one place it finds that it does more business of one sort, in another of another. Its current account (cash credit) business is now very much on the increase. In 1895 the *Schweizerische Volksbank* granted in all **3,185** cash credits of varying amounts, from 100 francs up to well beyond 10,000 francs, the aggregate sum placed at clients' disposal being 28,102,541 francs (£1,124,100). Of the 3,185 credits, 1,162 were secured only by suretyship. The bank granted six months' loans to the amount of **9,525,241** francs (£381,008), and loans for longer **terms to the amount of** 11,584,646 francs (£463,384).

For raising **money for long periods** the *Volksbank* has adopted in its own way, very successfully, the same method practised by M. Luzzatti in the issue of *buoni fruttiferi*. By means of *Kassenscheine*, running either for a period of two **years** at the rate of $3\frac{1}{4}$ and $3\frac{1}{2}$ per cent., or else for three or five years at the rate of $3\frac{3}{4}$ **and 4 per cent.,** it manages to **possess** itself of ready cash to such an amount, that at New Year 1896 there were 20,247,600 francs' worth of these bonds in circulation. There had been a notable increase in two years' bonds at 3½ per cent. interest, a corresponding decrease in bonds for longer periods at higher rates. One peculiarity about these bonds is, that they are redeemable only subject to notice to be given three months before the expiry of the period for which they are issued, failing which they run on as a matter of course for another two years, or three, or five, as the case may be. Notwithstanding the preference given to members, the value of savings deposits received from non-members amounts to about three times the sum received from members, viz., 12,758,258 francs, as compared with 4,215,184 francs—which is as conclusive a proof of the confidence reposed in the bank by the general market as could well be supplied. Most of the lending, apart from the **pledging of** shares, **is done by** discounting bills of exchange which are, as already observed, very well understood in Switzerland, and therefore involve no undue danger to borrowers, though they do occasionally bring a small loss upon the bank.

Members are admitted by election of the **Representative** Council of Administration, **from** whose decision an appeal lies to the General **Meeting of** Delegates, should ever occasion arise, which **is not** likely **to happen.** For it is to the interest of the bank to **have** as many members as it can get, whose mere admission, **as** we have seen, involves no risk. Generally speaking in Switzerland retirement is made easy. In the *Schweizerische Volksbank* members are free to retire at six months' notice. Some other banks allow members to retire at any time without notice. Some, again, require three months' notice. In the *Schweizerische Volksbank* the administration is thoroughly representative. Obviously, it would be impossible to call all the 11,826 members scattered all over Switzerland together. But each *succursale* has its own constituency, which may very well be convened from time to time. For every hundred members it is entitled to return one delegate to the central representative body; and by this means a tolerably popular representative assembly is constituted, quite large enough for practical purposes. The delegates elect a Council, and the Council in their turn nominate a **Board** of Directors, which, together with the permanent Director-General (M. Yersin), attends to the executive business. Beyond this, there is a special staff of auditors and "revisors" appointed, to check accounts.

As may be inferred from the figures given, the business of the *Schweizerische Volksbank* is a large one, and, accordingly, the permanent staff of officers and clerks stands at present at 169. The bank used to declare dividends of 6 and 7 per cent., but has come down to $4\frac{1}{2}$ and 5 per cent.—5 per cent. in the past year. The satisfactory feature about this dividend is, that its substantial amount is the result, not of high charges, but of a large business. The average interest charged to borrowers stands at less than 5 per cent.—4.984; the average interest allowed is 3.600 per cent. Thus out of the margin of 1.384 per cent., on a vast number of transactions, have expenses, losses, payments to reserve, &c., been met, leaving sufficient over to pay a reasonable dividend.

A Lesson applicable to Ourselves.

Surely there is something in all this work of which our co-operators might do well to take note. If their minds are still set, as they were twenty-three and twenty-six years ago, upon creating a banking institution which would enable them to do their own banking, to save, and beyond that to earn banker's profits, here is a pattern to work upon ready to their hand, which should recommend itself to notice, as having been found in practice equally safe and profitable. It does not educate the humble classes to the same extent as the more philanthropic types of banks; it does not take the poor cottier by the hand and teach him good morals along with good business, raising him, almost in spite of himself, from poverty to independence. But it makes the small means of those who possess a little go very much further than they otherwise would, and planes the way very effectively for their course through life. We must not, in such banks as these, look for that preponderance of small farming and working classes which we find in the Raiffeisen and Wollemborg institutions. According to the **last annual** return there are among the **11,826** members distributed over twelve districts—Berne, Zürich, Saignelégier, Fribourg, Bâle, St Gall, Wetzikon, Tramelan, Porrentruy, **Winterthur,** St Imier, and Uster (the last named opened only in 1895)—7,698 men, 4,100 women, and **28** societies. Grouped according to trades and callings there **are** : 670 independent persons engaged in agriculture and gardening, **62** employees and labourers engaged in the same calling, 719 manufacturers, engineers, &c., 1,587 artisans working for their own account, 588 factory hands, 1,382 tradesmen, 743 shopmen and shopwomen, 425 *aubergistes*, jobbing-masters and lessees of cafés, 380 railway and post-office employees, 1,694 medical men, chemists, teachers, civil servants, **notaries** and literary men, **and** 3,548 persons without **an occupation** (3,224 being women). The bank is accordingly not a genuine 'People's' Bank in **our sense ;** but it has a *clientèle* to whom its services and its profits **are** a matter of some moment, and, ministering to their wants, it unquestionably discharges highly useful functions as a national wealth-producer.

In the entire absence of official statistics it is rather difficult to speak of this class of banks in the aggregate. M. Yersin has with some pains collected statistics of his own referring to **four** years ago, which he has been good enough to place at my disposal. They give particulars of twenty different co-operative banks, including three *Unions* and one or two working-men's banks. **Throughout, there** is evidence of useful service and of steady growth. **Thus,** the *Gewerbebank* of Zürich, which began in 1867 with 500

<small>General Survey of Co-operative Banking Institutions in Switzerland.</small>

francs (£20), has raised its capital to 415,000 francs; the *Spar- und Leihkasse* of Wiedikon has increased its own funds from 98,300 to 188,510 francs; the *Spar- und Vorschussverein* of Beringen from 1,847 to 57,921 francs; the *Spar- und Leihkasse* of Morat from 8,000 to 22,500 francs; the *Spar- und Leihkasse* of Böswil from 2,500 to 33,000 francs; the **Caisse** *Ouvrière d'Epargne* of Geneva from 11,275 to 150,590 francs. All this indicates a growth of the constituency worked for as well as an extension of business. The full amount of business done by all the twenty banks in 1891 is returned as 2,224,675,778 francs (£88,987,032), which certainly points to a large volume of transactions. There is considerable variety in the organisation and rules of these twenty banks. In the main they have adopted limited liability as their principle; but in most cases it is liability under a fancy limitation, just as in Belgium, extending to twice, or three times, or whatever the multiple may be, of the amount of the share. **Some banks** allow members to take up only one share, others four, ten, fifty, up to two hundred, or else up to one-fifth of the entire share capital. Some issue shares of the value of 10 francs, others of 2,000 francs. For the most part the figure is either 100 francs or 500 francs. In nearly all these establishments the share is payable by instalments, which range from 1 franc a month to 5 francs. Only one or two of the smallest banks proportion the voting power to the number of shares taken; as a rule the principle adopted is "one man one vote." And there are very few which bind themselves absolutely to grant credit according to the amount of money paid up. That principle, which is more or less in vogue elsewhere, has proved a little dangerous in practice. As a rule, indeed, members are allowed to borrow on the strength of their holding alone, without further security than the pledging of their shares and an acceptance with their own signature, to the extent of twice their paid-up stake. But the granting or withholding of such credit rests *absolutely* with the Board **at its** own discretion ; the bank recognises no *right* whatever.

The lending upon shares opens **up rather a** troublous question in banking. The share is rather the member's bond than his asset. It constitutes him a part-proprietor in the bank. But the bank's security to its creditors **is the** share, not in its own hands, but in the member's. Therefore, by accepting **the share** as a pledge, **instead** of strengthening its **own** position, in one aspect it rather weakens **it**. For in parting with the share, **it** parts **with** potential security. Were the share to be forfeited, the bank would obviously be so much the poorer, and offer its creditors so much the less security. And if the forfeiture were often repeated, it might be left with all shares and **no funds, and** accordingly no credit. **So serious has** the danger of the withdrawal of members been felt to be, that in the *Schweizerische Volksbank* a rule **has been** passed enacting **that upon** one-fourth of **the** members giving notice of withdrawal, a general meeting shall forthwith be called, to vote upon the **question, whether** the bank is to be liquidated while the intending seceders are still members, or is to go **on without** them. **In practice** the question is not likely to arise. And even the resignation of one-fourth **of its** members would still **leave** the bank endowed with **ample** capital for all purposes. But the point **is one of** considerable importance. For it is not every **co-operative bank which can** boast of the financial strength of the ***Volksbank***. In practice, also, there has **been** found to be no danger **in lending** on members' **shares.** Indeed, it has become one of **the favourite methods of** dispensing credit. After all, it is the members' interest, *not* to forfeit their shares. That **would not exempt** them from responsibility ; for their liability **extends to twice the amount of** their **stake.** Only, M. Yersin rigidly exacts a **bill of exchange**

Danger of Lending upon Shares.

in addition to the pledged share, as giving the bank in case of need a better remedy against the defaulter.

Some Pioneer Raiffeisen Banks. Enough has been said to show that as business banks the co-operative banks of Switzerland have proved an entire success. However, from their large transactions one is not sorry to look down upon the humble, but far more philanthropic and educating work which has during the last few years been steadily carried on—for the present in the Canton of Berne only—by a few little pioneer banks of the Raiffeisen type. There are as yet only three. And the youngest of these is a very infant. One cannot help admiring their work, even though, as the foremost local champions of the system, MM. von Steiger and Jenni, admit, in the face of existing cheap credit and general prosperity, in a country in which nearly every cultivator is his own landlord, and even small holdings insure good incomes, there appears, in the more populous, and therefore the more active districts, little room for these poor men's banks. There is one at Schosshalde, close to Berne—a little beyond where the historic bears are kept—of which the local schoolmaster is cashier. It began in 1889 with little more than twenty members, and had in December 1894, when I was at Berne, crept up to sixty. For local reasons it has fixed the value of its shares considerably above what the authorities at Neuwied approve, namely, at 50 francs, in addition to which it levies 5 francs (4s.) on members by entrance fees. It is able to allow 3½ per cent. (and 3 per cent. for sums above 1,000 francs) on deposits, and to lend out at 4 per cent. Its comparatively considerable share capital, and a subsidy of 500 francs which it has received from the Government, go not a little way to enable it to work with so small a margin. I have no data as to its lending, but in December 1894 it held 21,157 francs (£847) in deposits, on 68 accounts, and it had accumulated a reserve fund of 2,400 francs (£96). It is a peculiar feature in the practice of this bank that the reserve is employed for co-operative agricultural supply, the purchase of seeds, cake, manure, and implements. The other bank is at Zimmerwald, some six or seven miles from Berne. This bank is smaller than that of Schosshalde, and issues only 30 franc (24s.) shares. Correspondingly, perhaps, it has received a subsidy of only 300 francs from the Government. Why there should be subsidies at all, I cannot quite see. They are quite unnecessary, and may be prejudicial. But in Austria, Switzerland, and France, it appears to be assumed that the population is still in the stage of childhood in which individuals have to be tempted into doing what is really the best for themselves, by the bait of a sugar-plum or some other appeal to their acquisitiveness. It is much too soon, of course, to say anything definite with respect to the success of these little pioneer banks. But, like their sister institutions elsewhere, they appear to be perseveringly plodding on, not impatient to increase the number of their members or to multiply their business, but careful above all things to admit no member who cannot be trusted, and to keep conscientiously on the safe side. Slowly they keep growing, but every day sees new friends gained by work which, though unpretending, is beneficent, and by that marvellous educational efficacy which never seems to fail institutions of this type—working on gradually but surely, and bringing out the best virtues of small labouring people. "These associations," writes the curé of Zimmerwald, Abbé Kistler, reviewing the work which they have already accomplished under his own eyes, "create a bond of brotherhood; and the moral support which they afford to their members ought not to be passed over in silence by the side of the financial support. It is a splendid thing, surely, and a matter of great importance for the agricultural classes, to have a solidarity produced between neighbours, and to see the strong support the weak, as one friend would support another, with his money and his credit, by counsel and by deed." A splendid thing it is, and while the large banks, serving for the convenience of the moderately moneyed, and earning them dividends, go on flourishing, like the *Schweizerische Volksbank*—doing useful though more or less egotistical work—one may indulge a hope that the modest beginning made in Switzerland on more philanthropic lines may prosper as well—there as elsewhere—and teach the thrifty peasant of the Alps and the Jura, who is sometimes regarded as in material matters a step-child of Nature, what marvellous resources even on his bleak mountain-side he has at his command in the treasures of combination and self-help.

CHAPTER XIII.

CO-OPERATIVE BANKING IN FRANCE.

PASSING in review, country by country, the co-operative banking done in Europe, I have advisedly left France to stand last. There is no country in which more research, and labour, and money, have been expended upon the creation of popular credit. Nevertheless when you come to look for fruit resulting from this plentiful sowing, you find, practically speaking, less than anywhere—excepting only in our own backward country. Cruelly, perhaps, but not altogether unjustly, has M. Micha summed up, with piquant brevity, the story of past achievements in respect of the most favourite form of popular credit. "The history of agricultural credit in France may be told in two words: a wish for it placed on record by the Congress of French agriculturists in 1845, and a law passed in 1888." That law, I may add, has proved disappointing. Accordingly, while Germans and Italians have long since "found salvation" in systems of their own, the French still continue seeking and groping for some satisfactory solution of the old familiar problem, with only small beginnings to encourage them in the belief that they are really finding it.

Backward State of Co-operative Banking in France.

It is odd and disappointing that this should be so. For the French were one of the first nations to direct their attention to the subject; and in other matters of co-operation they have shown no want of resource and organising capacity. It was on French soil that Gall in 1830 conceived the idea which is held to have led up to

Early History of the Movement.

the fruitful action of Schulze and his rivals. At the very least since 1837, the French Government has been working out devices for securing to the small cultivators, who make up the bulk of the nation, the benefit of cheap and ready credit. After eleven years more of careful thought and study, in 1848, M. Lefour brought forward a scheme for providing credit in a way similar to that adopted by the *Caisses Thurgoviniennes*.* The proposal, as it happened, was badly drawn, and was therefore wisely rejected. The third revolution, as a matter of course, brought forth a whole crop of new proposals, each more democratic, and more unworkable, than the other. Proudhon set up his "People's Bank," destined to live only a few weeks. Republican deputies clamoured for credit from the State, and goaded their governments into *cette grande folie*, by which 3,000,000 francs was thrown away in advances to productive associations which could not possibly live.

It may be as well to finish my record of similar failures, before proceeding to an account of more fruitful labours.

The *coup d'état* dealt a serious blow to French co-operation. The productive workshops, which had in 1849 been started with public money, were after 1851 called upon to repay their loans. They could not, of course, do so. But they could be declared bankrupt and compelled to dissolve—which was just what the Government desired. There is at the present day actually only one association of that early formation surviving. The "sixties" brought about a change for the better. Sensible of his want of popularity, the Emperor courted it by ostensibly favouring co-operation. He had but to speak the word to set a whole army of prefects at work, carrying out his behests in the wrong way. Some sound little urban co-operative societies sprung up at the same time, under the forcing warmth of

---

* See page 306.

fleeting sunshine, of which I shall still have to speak. However, the Emperor's desires were directed mainly towards assistance to be afforded to the country folk, whose votes tell most heavily in the elections. With a fair capital, he in 1860 formed the *Société du Crédit Agricole*, to deal out loans on easy terms and under proper safeguards to small cultivators. The *Société* never lost a *sou* by its agricultural lending. So M. Josseau testifies. And M. Josseau ought to know. The agricultural borrowers indeed surprised the official administrators by their honesty. However, there were not nearly enough of them. The red tape conditions for borrowing were so tightly drawn that very few indeed mustered courage to come to this distant, strange, and much too fine-looking establishment. By 1870, the *Société* managed to get into "correspondence" with about five hundred cultivators, who were probably large men. Since that did not provide anything like sufficient employment for its money, it lent a huge sum to the Khedive Ismail—and lost it. Soon after, the Empress, anxious to identify her son with a good popular work, started in his name the *Fond des Prêts de l'Enfance*. The *Fond* collapsed.

While this was going on, a plain banker, M. Giraud, gifted with common-sense, managed to score that success in the Nièvre of which I have already spoken.*

The lesson was not lost upon the banking authorities at Paris. To turn it to account, the Bank of France appointed *comptoirs d'escompte*, consisting of local gentlemen properly accredited and considered trustworthy, whom it stationed in various districts to receive applications and negotiate loans with agriculturists. However, in the majority of agricultural districts there is little wholesale fattening, and so there was no demand for comparatively short-term loans. For the small farmers these pretentiously composed

---

* See page 59.

comptoirs d'escompte proved much too fine and too strange. Thus one more promising attempt ended in failure.

For industrial lending the Emperor Napoleon III. had tried his hand unsuccessfully at a Discount Bank for Co-operative Societies. Similar ingenious experimenting was continued in the days of the Republic. Gambetta, in 1880, started a *Caisse Centrale*, to advance money to the same class of clients. The *Caisse* was to have 50,000,000 francs of capital, of which, however, only 12,000,000 was subscribed. It opened its offices with a grand flourish of trumpets, setting up "Collecting Bureaus" in various suburbs, and offering its money freely to co-operative associations. The co-operative associations—at least the solvent ones—however, would not accept the invitation, and in 1887 the *Caisse* escaped a collapse only by throwing over its original object, and converting itself into an ordinary business bank.

<small>Causes of past Failures.</small> What is the cause of all this failure? The matter is one of not purely retrospective interest, because, with a considerable mass of new experience to support past teaching, we have pretty well the same lesson still brought home to us in the present day—new experiments, new promises, new disappointments.

M. Ernest Brelay suggests that *the law* may be in fault: " It is possible that the fault lies more with our laws than with our habits." But, then, the law was even more adverse in Germany; nevertheless Schulze formed his banks and compelled the law to recognise them. The law up to 1883 absolutely *forbade* co-operative banking in Italy. Yet M. Luzzatti created a veritable army of banks. No law could possibly be more adverse, either to co-operation or to provident practices, than was our own a few decades ago. We simply snapped our fingers at it. We started our co-operative associations and friendly societies, and then got the law altered.

The law would present no insuperable hindrance if the

majority of French people were not still so hopelessly
étatiste—wanting in the power of private initiative, and by
their own choice abjectly dependent upon "the State."
They expect the State to think for them, to move them
into action, and, above all things, to *subsidise* them. It seems
as if in their opinion nothing could be done without it. I
go into a meeting of co-operative associations, which make
a boast of their independence and free initiative. There I
find a member of the Parliamentary Commission dealing
with subventions, who is present to consult with his friends
on the manner in which the annual grant in aid of co-
operation is to be appropriated. I hear of a *caisse rurale*
started, as a triumph of "self-help," in the Alpes Mari-
times. The first balance-sheet shows a Government
subvention of 500 francs, without which the *caisse* would be
hopelessly insolvent—without which, I suspect, it would
never have been started. In the Rue d'Athènes, we fight a
brilliant battle for "self-help," defeating, in the teeth of
heavy odds, the Government proposal for the creation of a
central bank endowed by the State, to advance loans to
agriculture. And immediately after, the chief spokesman
against the proposal, the chosen champion of "self-help,"
hurries to the Rue de Varenne, to claim from the Ministry
of Commerce his own share in the grant of 144,000 francs
annually set aside for Credit Associations, which he had just
before emphatically protested he would *not have subsidised*.

All this is bound to discourage one. And it seems so
much out of place. No nation has overturned its own
Government oftener than the French, and showed less
respect for it. Yet, when it comes to thinking, acting,
doing, every Frenchman looks upon the Government which
by his caprice exists for the brief period of three or else six
months—like a Schulze-Delitzsch draft—as a sort of Zeus,
by whose nod alone things are to be accomplished. Hence
that absolute want of confidence among individual French-

French Étatisme.

men in their own powers! No scheme of co-operative credit is brought forward without some little Providence being suggested which is to form the backbone to provide the funds. No scheme of urban credit is devised without a promise of support having *first* been obtained from the Bank of France, or else from some great savings bank. No scheme of agricultural credit is promulgated without due provision having been made for the creation of a class of patrons, "founders," good fairies, who are to find the money. Schulze did not ask the great banks if they were willing to patronise his institutions. Indeed he *would* not be patronised. He repudiated such fatal friendship. He created his own security, and waited for the banks to come to him. Raiffeisen did not look around for patrons. M. Durand does not create two classes of members—givers and takers. Here are the very men who write topmost upon their banner:—" Death to Socialism ! War to *les Krapotkine, les Karl Marx, les Jules Guesde!*"—perforce instilling Socialist maxims into the mass of the population, by telling them that self-help is powerless, and success hopeless without the taxing of others. Teach a man that he can help himself, teach him to stand on his own legs, and you kill the Socialist within him for ever. Make him believe that that feat is impossible, that all his help *must* come from his richer neighbours, and you make him a Socialist in spite of himself.

<small>Want of clear aim. "La Furia Francese."</small>

There is more. Want of confidence in themselves is unfortunately not the only cause to account for failure. Father de Besse talks of the *furia francese* as hindering good results by impelling Frenchmen to wish to reach their journey's end without tramping over the intervening ground. They see the walls and roof of the house, and would build one like it without studying the architecture and realising that the foundations, and the framework of beams and rafters, which are not seen, are really of very much greater importance than the brick walls and tile-roofs which are. There is still a deal of aimless, shiftless, methodless veering and tacking, just as if Schulze and Raiffeisen and Luzzatti had not laboured to prepare a trustworthy chart. It takes one's breath away to observe in what haphazard, harum-scarum way some of these would-be organisers of popular credit proceed. And every Sequah and Harness offering his specific is accepted as a teacher. M. Durand shows his countrymen how Raiffeisen banks ought to be organised. There is not a word to be said against his rules, and no one ventures to say a word against them. But he is a strong Ultramontane, and—*le cléricalisme voilà l'ennemi!* So a jurist objector gravely suggests that, although there are close upon 500 *caisses rurales* actually established on M. Durand's lines and allowed to carry on their business without shares, without any court of law so much as wagging its tongue against them, it is "open to very serious doubt whether the organisation of banks without shares is altogether legal." Nobody stops to inquire whether Raiffeisen banks are possible *with* shares—though the overwhelming majority of them do issue such. Unwilling to engage in irksome study on this point, the gentlemen of Paris cast about for some new scheme. A learned *avocat* sends to Offenbach for some prospectuses and papers. And, never having seen a Haas Bank in his life, he stands up in a Congress to deliver a study-made lecture, and announce that here is a heaven-sent system—writing, so to speak, the history of a company from its prospectus. There is no one to gainsay him, because no one knows anything about the matter. And for a brief period the general cry is for "Haas."

More instances of the kind may be quoted. Co-operative bankers of Italy, Germany, and Belgium will fully agree with me when I say that there is no prospect of sound co-operative credit being permanently established in France until Frenchmen learn, in a far greater measure than they have hitherto done, to trust to themselves, until they study with greater care the principles rather than the rules of co-operation, and address themselves to their work with patience and method as well as with zeal. The very essence of success, the pillar upon which the fabric to be raised must needs rest, is self-reliance; the only available material out of which it can be manufactured is a sense of responsibility awakened, which guards against losses far more effectually than official endowment, municipal administration, and scientifically prepared rules.

Recent History of the Movement.

We may now proceed to consider what is actually being done in the latest period of co-operative action.

The Silos of Algiers.

At the time when the cause of Schulze-Delitzsch scored its first great triumphs in Germany, about a decade after setting out upon its march to victory, co-operative banking may be said to have been dead in France. One curious institution providing popular credit had managed to survive in the African dependency, an institution tracing its origin back to those early days when Spain received its *positos*, Portugal its *celleiros*, and Italy its *monti frumentari* and *nummari*. Algiers was in those days provided by its Moorish rulers with a cognate institution termed *silos*. The *silos* were originally granaries, but in course of time became converted into credit associations. A few years ago the interesting little People's Bank of Algiers, thoroughly co-operative, but entirely local, still did good work among its own members—less than 300 in number. There were then also reported to be about sixty other little popular banks of the same type scattered over French Africa—all of them very humble institutions, small and unpretending, but thoroughly useful and genuinely co-operative—descendants, it may be, of the ancient Moorish *silos*—lending out among them about 3,000,000 francs annually to their members.

Apart from some modest little associations, resembling rather our Slate Clubs than genuine People's Banks, that small cluster of *silos* was probably all of its kind existing under the shadow of the tricolor, when the pæans of triumph raised by Schulze's friends sent their echoes across the Rhine. Among a population so quick to seize upon new ideas, and standing so much in need of popular credit, those sounds were bound to touch a responsive chord, and to stimulate to emulation. Buchez, the father of French co-operation, who had devised for co-operation the well-known motto which republicanism has since appropriated to itself—" Liberty, Equality, Brotherhood "—had already familiarised his countrymen with the idea of "credit to labour," proclaiming in words which seemed to anticipate Sir R. Morier's dictum already quoted—" *Il faut créer le crédit du travail, comme on a créé le crédit foncier, le crédit mobilier, &c.*" Beluze, taking up the idea thirteen years later, made it his ambition to acclimatise Schulze's creation in France, as about the same time it was being acclimatised in Italy and Belgium. The French laws were until lately, as we already know from M. Brelay, distinctly adverse to such enterprise. However, Beluze knew how to turn the difficulty. In 1863 he started an institution which has become historic—his well-known *Crédit au Travail*—a co-operative banking society, formed *en commandite*, without shares. Such organisation, he judged, would enable members to pay in an indefinite amount of cash by instalments, as they pleased, and at the same time it would protect the association against being taken possession of by a few greedy capitalist shareholders. On two rather important points Beluze deviated from his master's ideal. For administrative purposes he directed the election of a committee larger than Schulze's; and, moreover, he gave the *Commission de Contrôle* power of its own authority to remove officers. Both these things to my mind repre-

[margin: Buchez.]

[margin: The "Crédit au Travail."]

sent improvements. On the 27th September 1863, when the society was called together, formally to pass the rules, and legally to constitute itself, there were 172 members, subscribing among them a capital of 20,100 francs. However, only 4,082 francs was actually paid in by 1st October, when the *Crédit* opened its doors for business. The work to be taken in hand was very similar to that of the Schulze-Delitzsch associations. The *Crédit* was to collect savings and deposits, issue long-term bonds at 6 per cent. interest for terms not exceeding five years, cash and discount bills, grant loans, and all the rest of it. Its success was not very brilliant, but it *was* a success; and it is all the more to be regretted that untoward circumstances, more particularly the locking up of too much money in loans not readily recoverable—followed up by the disastrous war which, along with the empire, swept away a good many things which were much better worth preserving—brought this particular phase of French credit co-operation to a close. Because, if French co-operators had been permitted to proceed upon such indigenous lines, thoroughly congenial to themselves, it is likely that they would have produced some distinct and specifically *French* form of co-operative banking, instead of simply borrowing from abroad, as they are now doing, entirely foreign systems. While it lasted, the *Crédit au Travail* kept indisputably solvent, and did very good work. Its losses were trifling. It should be borne in mind that it was carrying on its business under a Government which, though outwardly coquetting with co-operation, was in spirit so hostile that in the very year in which the *Crédit au Travail* first became really strong—that is, in 1867—the Emperor would not allow Schulze to come to Paris to take part in a co-operative congress at which he was expected as the hero of the occasion. By February 1867 the *Crédit au Travail* had increased the number of its members to 1,500, and its capital to 250,000 francs. Its annual business exceeded 10,500,000 francs. The smaller tradesmen and manufacturers speedily learnt to appreciate the advantages which it offered, and gladly availed themselves of them. So did—unfortunately, as it happened—the productive co-operative societies, not all of them sound. It was they who brought the institution to grief by failing to repay loans. So successful, in fact, was the *Crédit au Travail* held to be, and so much satisfying a genuine want, that similar institutions, moulded upon the same model, sprang up in considerable number in various industrial towns of the empire—Lyons, Lille, Nîmes, Strasbourg, Colmar, Bordeaux, Mulhouse, and elsewhere—though the Paris institution itself did a great deal of provincial business. The Lyons *Crédit au Travail*, founded in April 1865, with 50,000 francs capital subscribed in 500 francs shares, did exceedingly good business at a minimum of cost. The *Crédit au Travail* of Lille had 389 members, and a capital of 105,700 francs; the Saint Etienne *Crédit* had 292 members and 32,000 francs. In Paris, as a rival institution, the *Caisse d'Escompte des Associations Populaires*, rose up, fathered by M. Léon Say, besides a *Caisse des Sociétés Coopératives*, which were supported by philanthropy rather than by *bonâ fide* co-operation.

But concurrently with these more or less pretentious institutions there grew up in France an entire little host of small co-operative credit associations, formed by working men for working men, in the humblest of ways, but on genuinely co-operative lines, and answering well in their own modest sphere. I will not say much of the infinitesimally small *"groupes à deux sous"* of Lyons, in which working men, never exceeding twenty, clubbed together to subscribe their penny a week in order to be able to borrow tiny sums up to 20 francs, repayable at the rate of 2 francs a month. That is not banking. But there was the *Société Mère* of Paris, with its family of children, some seventy or

"Groupes à deux sous."

The "Société Mère" and its Offspring.

eighty in and around Paris, plenty more in the Provinces—in Lille, and Saint Etienne, and Valence, and Lyons, and other places—the *Sociétés du Crédit Mutuel.* They were all small, modest, in their way obscure. They had from twenty-five to fifty members each, meeting once a week or once a month in a private workshop, administering their own funds, doing their own work gratuitously. The same man would sometimes be president, cashier, and secretary all in one. In the year 1866 France possessed no less than about 300 such modest societies, all doing well, all supplying in a humble way a real want, readily and easily, at small cost to any one. They levied their weekly or monthly subscriptions, of from 50 centimes to 5 francs, and dealt with the money so provided—not exactly cheaply for borrowers, for they charged interest at the rate of from 6 to 10 per cent., but beneficially. None of them disposed of large funds. The richest held a capital of 31,712 francs, with 750 francs of reserve, in all £1,300. The majority had very much less. Yet they did a large amount of lending, and lost almost literally nothing. The *Société Mère* had in 1866 lent out 252,223 francs and lost only 5 francs. One of the most pretentious societies of this sort, established in the Faubourg Saint Antoine, had in six years' business, upon loans which amounted to about 6,000,000 francs, only two small losses to record. It was the very humility of the thing, the lively sense of responsibility, the rigour of "self-help," which made these small societies flourish and answer their purpose, while the millionaire enterprises of an emperor, of republics, and of capitalist associations failed. "The smallness of the losses," reports Mr Egerton in our Blue-Book, "proceeded from the members being well acquainted with each other; for the societies were small though numerous. . . . Their main strength was in the mutual confidence from *mutual knowledge of each other of their members.*"

All this useful work was put a stop to by the war of

1870, which, entered into "with a light heart," ended by leaving millions of very heavy ones, tearing associations asunder, breaking up circles and unions, and replacing union by isolation. It is a thousand pities that the good work of these little societies was not taken up afresh when times changed for the better. But by that time Frenchmen had forgotten the things that were behind, and were reaching forward to others which were before, more ambitious, and, may be, destined to become more useful. *Effect of the Franco-German War.*

The first seed of this new crop, wafted across from the fruitful soil cultivated by M. Luzzatti, took root and ripened under the forcing sun of the Mediterranean littoral. The French Riviera had worn the blue tricolor instead of the green for thirty-six years, but the character of its population was not essentially changed when Providence selected it, no doubt in virtue of inherited aptnesses and old links with Italy, for the birthplace of an economic movement new to France, and destined to become of considerable benefit. One little experiment was first made on soil which had been French before, but it failed. In 1875, Francesco Viganò, the "father" of Italian co-operation, took in hand the formation of a co-operative bank at Cannes. Cannes wanted such a bank, and wants one still, and, please God, will soon have one once more. The bank founded by Viganò—he had first thought of Antibes—grew up well, but after little time became a profit-mongering joint-stock undertaking, which in fact it was, without anything that could be called "co-operative" about it, at the time when Mr Egerton sent to Downing Street that glowing report about its success which figures in our Blue-Book of 1886. The lesson taught is an old and familiar one. It is not enough to found a People's Bank. You must watch and look after it. *Influence of the Italian Example.* *Viganò's First People's Bank at Cannes.*

More satisfactory work was in store for Mentone. Whatever French annexation may have done for that little settle- *The Banque Populaire of Mentone.*

ment, its conquest by the English has certainly made a more prosperous place of it. It used to be a quiet country town, living upon the produce of the surrounding olive gardens, and lemon groves, and flower beds. The advent of English visitors put new life into the place, and practically turned nearly every one among the 9,000 population into a speculator, building hotels and houses for them to live in, and laying out terraces and roads and gardens, for which nothing but credit could provide the funds. In 1882, one of the six joint-stock banks existing in the town, having lent out its money too recklessly, failed with 200,000 francs of deficit. The little community found itself thrown into a state of consternation. Nobody knew whom to trust, or to whom to turn for credit. M. Palmaro and a few more of the older residents kept cool heads upon their shoulders, and at once summoned a town's meeting to consider the condition of affairs. A proposal was made to form a People's Bank, after the example of the Italian *banche popolari*. It was agreed that the thing should be done if £800 was subscribed. People had learnt so painful a lesson of joint-stock banking that every one jumped at the proposal. By the 18th February 1883, 150,000 francs was subscribed. According to the resolutions adopted, only 100,000 francs could be allotted. On 9th April accordingly the new bank opened its office doors, in the most modest of ways. Its office was a little room, taken at a half-yearly rent of £8. The furniture was of the scantiest and the cheapest. The management expenses were kept down to £25 a month. But the bank buckled to its work in good workmanlike style, and, to create confidence, posted its balance-sheet outside its door every evening. Before the year was out business had assumed such considerable proportions that it became necessary to double the capital. At the present time the capital of the bank stands at 350,200 francs, with 54,850 francs of reserve fund laid up; the annual business figures at 41,648,798 francs; and the bank is without exception the strongest and busiest bank in the town. It has lived through two or three more crises—more crashes, seasons of cholera, earthquakes, &c.—and has come out the stronger from every one of them.

The *Banque Populaire* of Mentone is to **all intents and** purposes a bank of the Luzzatti type, and engages in precisely the same class of business. It has 100 francs shares, for paying up which in exceptional cases it allows longer time than M. Luzzatti.* And in consideration of the reserve **fund** it issues its shares at a premium, which now **stands at 15** per cent. Generally speaking **it is** " Luzzatti " **to the core.**

Its director has shown so much propagandist ability and such sympathetic regard **for the** poorer among the population, that I feel justified in anticipating that, as the bank **has** already succeeded in planting offshoots in Marseilles, Nice, Bordeaux, Cognac, and other places†—about **a** score in all, all of the same type, in addition to **starting** a little cluster of useful *caisses rurales* of the Wollemborg type all around—it will end by becoming **the centre of** a well-developed federation **of** People's Banks, making available to French trade and commerce and agriculture the **same** facilities which have proved of such inestimable advantage in Italy.

<small>Its Propagandist Work.</small>

Nevertheless, I feel bound to insist that these banks, **even the** parent Bank of Mentone, are **not in** the highest sense co-operative, as we understand that term. The Bank **of** Mentone limits its dividend to 5 per cent., it dispenses as much as it can in **" loans of honour "** to the poor, **it** works for education, propaganda, **charities.** But look at its

<small>Its Defects.</small>

---

* I have heard of only one such case, in which twenty months was allowed.

† There is now a propagandist society at work **at Oran, in** Algeria, which has, according to M. Rostand, founded one bank.

members! There are 39 proprietors of hotels, cafés, and restaurants, including the richest and most thriving hotel-keepers in Mentone. Among 427 members there are, in fact, only 84 artisans working for their own account—jobbing operatives—97 small tradesmen, and 11 shopmen. It is no wonder that poor people are shy of going into this fine establishment, as I know from their own statements. They would be made heartily welcome and receive every consideration. But do you see people of the same class go freely into our great Joint-Stock Banks, or into the Army and Navy Stores? Their money is as good as that of the rich folk. But they have a shyness which wants to be propitiated. The Mentone Bank scarcely does this sufficiently. And look at its office! The first thing which meets your eye is a notice put up in English, French, German, and Italian, to the effect that circular notes are cashed and every kind of banking business is done. The bank, in fact, has, for the convenience of visitors, a branch office at Monaco, which has given the Monagasque concessionaire, Mr Smith, not a little trouble. There is, moreover, a reading room for visitors, as in Paris at the *Crédit Lyonnais*. There is a money-changer's table. All these things can scarcely be called " co-operative." This outside trading is of course designed to benefit the members, reducing for them the terms of their own credit. But it does so, not by co-operative work, but by trading for profit. Some People's Banks, I admit, are compelled to resort to business with non-members, in order to secure them sufficient work to keep them going. Thus I find it to be at Marseilles, where there is a People's Bank formed after the model of Mentone. But that is a second-best, a reserve to fall back upon only in case of need. And the People's Bank of Mentone is scarcely in a position to plead in excuse the reason of need. Its advocates point in justification to the outside trading done by our British Co-operative **Stores.** But that is a different affair altogether. That is advisedly and avowedly done *to enable members who are*, **not** too rich, but *too poor*, **to take shares,** *to qualify for membership* by accumulating their half-bonuses in the cash-box of the store.

On the **other hand, the** People's Bank **of Mentone, and** its director, **M. Rayneri, show themselves thoroughly co-**operative **in the zeal and goodwill with which they have thrown themselves into the work of forming in** all the country round smaller **People's** Banks, and more especially, village **banks** of the Wollemborg type — instructing the local people, advising them, and advancing them funds, or else taking their surpluses **on** deposit. There are seven such Wollemborg *caisses* in **the** neighbourhood of Mentone already—at Castellar, La **Turbie,** Cagnes, Saint Laurent du **Var,** Sainte **Agnès,** Cabbé-Roquebrune, **and** Gorbio. I could wish that the item of " subvention from the State " did not figure so prominently in their accounts. It is unnecessary, and it corrupts the principle at the very starting. But, once started, these banks appear sound. And M. Rayneri encourages other **forms of** co-operation. At Castellar, **the** country of particularly good olives, **we are** promised an olive-pressing co-operative **society—we have a** co-operative **society already for** combined pressing **of the refuse.** M. Rayneri is indeed full of energy and **full of resource.** At Cagnes the *caisse rurale* does little **business.** People do not take to **the particular form of organisation, dreading unlimited** liability, with **which at** present they **con**siderately saddle the patient **secretary, who takes it** all upon his own shoulders. So in that place he proposes to set up a limited liability **bank to see which of the two will thrive best.**

The **little cluster of banks** springing up under the instigation of **M. Rayneri and his** eloquent ally M. Rostand, has gathered **some additional** strength from a **junction of** forces with a small **group of** banks, the formation of which

M. Rayneri's "Caisses Rurales."

Père Ludovic and his "Catholic" Banks.

was begun about the same period, but on entirely different lines, and with totally different objects in view. The People's Bank of Mentone was formed with *business* aims. It was to assure to its members, alike rich and poor, cheap and safe banking. It has done so. Father Ludovic de Besse, a Capuchin friar, when, a second Barnabas of Terni, he resolved to combine the work of an economic reformer with that of a chosen preacher of the gospel, distinctly spurned the idea of business and profit. The study of financial gain was not for him. Warmly compassionate for the poor, he felt a sensitive spot in his heart touched by the present Pope's famous encyclical upon the condition of the working classes. "*Il faut adapter les corporations aux conditions nouvelles.*" That was to him what the "Tolle, lege" had been to S. Augustine. Forthwith he addressed himself to his work. Be it M. Rayneri's task to "serve tables"; he would go forth preaching economic glad tidings to the poor. His aim was to *moraliser les affaires*, to infuse a Christian spirit into business, to make honesty take the place of fraud, to come to the rescue of the needy, gathering the *élite* of the working men around his banner, and steadily adding to his host by attracting new recruits—all this avowedly not as *une affaire*, but as *une œuvre*, not as a piece of economic business to bear profit, but as a noble work to be requited hereafter. Nobody that has seen or heard Father Ludovic can withhold from him hearty sympathy, affection, esteem. His sincerity is perfectly manifest. And his eloquence is a true propagandist power. So far from being narrow-minded or a bigot, he is, in fact, so large-hearted as to have incurred the serious displeasure of the ultra-orthodox, who deem it unmeet for the creature to imitate the example of his Creator in letting the sun of his favour, and effort at improvement, shine alike upon just and unjust, upon orthodox and heretic. But unfortunately the Father is very little of a banker. When at Bordeaux I heard him lament in the simplicity and the sincerity of his heart the "dangers" (*écueils*) which he had found besetting co-operative banking in the shape of wicked men, who, while professing intentions of honest business, seek to defraud the bank, I was bound to be prepared for the catastrophe which happened only a few weeks after—the collapse of his bank, the *Crédit Mutuel* of Paris. Full to overflowing of good principle, Father de Besse entered upon his work without any very clear idea of a consistent method. His own "system" appears a medley of scraps, incongruous and incompatible among themselves, borrowed from other systems. At heart, of course, he is a devoted Raiffeisenist, altruistic to a degree. But pure Raiffeisenism for some reason or other would not serve his purpose. Accordingly he preaches "self-help"—and yet makes an impassioned appeal to the *hommes riches* to come to his aid with money for which they are to expect no return.* He adopts unlimited liability, lending on personal security only, to the poor, in consideration of the employment of the loan—and yet makes his districts so large that that instinctive and automatic watching and checking which in the Raiffeisen banks ensures safety without causing invidiousness, becomes impossible, and he has to urge his members to undertake the repulsive task of playing the spy upon one another as a matter of "Christian duty." He is anxious to produce the close touch and community of interest of the Raiffeisen associations—and yet he deliberately divides his members into two distinct classes, rich and poor—*fondateurs*, who take up shares of 50 francs each, the more the merrier, but paying no interest; and *sociétaires*, who pay only an entrance fee of 5 francs. In addition there are to be *patrons chrétiens*. One cannot be surprised to find the results as M. Hubert Valleroux has called them, "poor" (*faible*).

The "Catholic Banks" have accomplished a certain Their Work.

---

* See his articles in the *Union économique*.

amount of good. With what military men would call a skeleton army they have occupied a capacious territory, but their transactions are not imposingly large. The first bank was formed at Angers, Père Ludovic's own city, under the auspices of the "Society of S. Joseph." It began with only thirty members—ten *fondateurs* and twenty *sociétaires*. In 1889 it commanded a capital of 68,750 francs, which had, however, by 1890 attracted deposits only to the amount of 16,316 francs. That is very much less than what is usual in ordinary banking. Its *portefeuille* at the close of 1890 held bills worth 35,955 francs; the current accounts amounted to 15,261 francs; and the transactions balanced at 91,870 francs. That does not indicate a very active business. The *Crédit Mutuel* of Paris, the principal establishment of this group, according to Father de Besse's own account, in 1888 had a turnover of 2,000,000 francs, on which there was 1,244 francs of loss. The "Catholic Bank" of Saint Chamond — a bank of this connection, but managed independently—according to M. Courtois, discounts bills annually at the rate of 1,800,000 francs. There are, or were, other such banks—at Arras, Cette, Limoges, Toulouse, and Rennes. At best all these institutions can be looked upon only as pioneers. They may be useful as preparing the ground. They cannot be regarded seriously as banks. Accordingly nobody who knows what co-operative banking should be will regard with regret the alliance struck up between these banks and the more businesslike institutions of M. Rostand and M. Rayneri, which has probably by this time already materially improved the "Catholic Banks," while setting the eloquent father free from the humdrum routine of office supervision for work for which he is very much better adapted, and fully liberating his powerful tongue for the oratorical advocacy of co-operative banking, for which no more effective pleader could be found. So officered, the *Centre fédératif du Crédit Populaire* seems

CO-OPERATIVE BANKING IN FRANCE. 341

destined to become in truth the centre of the co-operative banking movement of France.

There is since some years another most fruitful centre of propaganda in France, for the benefit specifically of the country districts. If M. Rayneri drew his knowledge from his native country of Italy, M. Durand, of Lyons, learnt a lesson of a different kind at the feet of the Gamaliel of the Rhine. He is Raiffeisenist to his finger tips. He has studied the system, and—like most who have studied it carefully—has become enamoured of its principles and enthusiastic for its diffusion. For a brief period he was content to work in union with M. Rostand, P. de Besse, and M. Rayneri. However, his highly religious aims, strongly tinged with Romanism of the most pronounced type, soon drove him on a different path. With the personal differences which have arisen between the two parties I have here no concern. They have, unfortunately, grown fierce and bitter. Be M. Durand's charity towards his dissenting fellow-workers what it will, his Raiffeisen rules are absolutely orthodox. His banks act less than one would wish to see them do as local savings banks. But that is not because M. Durand disapproves of such action, but simply because the French law imposes a tax upon savings, which makes it wasteful to deposit very small sums outside the recognised savings banks. These village banks have not been at work long enough to enable one to pronounce a definite judgment upon their merits. However, from the reports and balance-sheets which I have seen, I am bound to believe them to be good. And they have multiplied as co-operative banks have never multiplied before. M. Durand seems to stamp them out of the earth, as Pompey did legions. Under his zealous advocacy the difficulty which has in France so long stood in the way of Raiffeisen credit, in the shape of an assumed unwillingness on the part of the French peasantry to accept unlimited liability, wholly

M. Durand's Caisses Rurales.

disappears. "*Une chose même m'étonne; c'est la facilité avec laquelle nos paysans français acceptent l'idée de la solidarité; on les a beaucoup calomniés en les réprésentant comme refractaires à toute idée de progrès et à tout sentiment d'association.*" It is true, M. Durand has the Church working for him. His banks are not "Catholic" in name, like Don Cerutti's, but they are evidently so in fact. The very first year saw about 200 grow up in swarms. There are now close upon 500, and although enemies disapproving of their "Catholicism" are raising up obstacles which have made the rate of progress to slacken, the cause still keeps advancing. I could wish it to be less specifically "Catholic." But no one could improve upon M. Durand's rules.

Thus in two of the three great propagating centres of co-operative banking in France we have the two foreign systems faithfully reproduced in their entirety, with no modification except that of language.

The Syndicats Agricoles.

The third great centre has a character altogether of its own, but that character is for the present little more than chaos. Ordering, regulating, developing forces are at work, but without any distinct aim or unity of purpose. Those who guide them are evidently anxious "to do something," but as to the "what to do," they cannot yet make up their mind. The agricultural syndicates of France, including the pick of the agricultural population of the country, have long since inscribed "agricultural credit" upon their programme. They could not do without it. All symptoms apparent in the diseased agricultural body plainly call for it. There has never been a force at work in France more serviceable to agriculture or attaining more rapid success than those agricultural syndicates. We may for our purpose consider them simply as co-operative societies, formed, generally, to promote all legitimate interests of farmers. When Professor Tanviray started the first institution of this kind at Blois, he did not think of the championship of distinctive class interests in the arena of politics—such as has afterwards been here and there foisted into the programme—but simply of co-operative selling and buying, and a diffusion of instruction, to meet, on the one hand, the frauds and extortions of dealers, and, on the other, to lift a great national calling, peculiarly favoured by nature—in respect of climate, soil, surroundings, and general condition of things—out of the hopeless slough, not of depression, so much, as of ruinous backwardness, in which it lay embedded. He found French agriculture, in the graphic words of Count Rocquigny—*routinière, arriérée, pauvre*. "Backward, did you say," replied to me three years ago Professor Carrère, representing the Ministry of Agriculture, at Toulouse, when I remarked upon the lamentably undeveloped state of agriculture in that original "Pays de Cocagne," the sunny, fertile, Lauraguais; "we are still living in the era of the old Roman plough." Education in their trade was what French cultivators wanted, and facilities for taking advantage of all opportunities favouring cheaper production. Professor Tanviray started his agricultural syndicate at Blois in 1883; and within a decade the number of such syndicates in France grew to somewhere about 1,500. Every department now has some. United—that is, for the most part, united—they have become a power strong enough successfully to insist on redress of some of the most crying of agricultural grievances. They spread information and instruction. They have revolutionised the market, "democratising" the use of feeding stuffs and artificial manures. The quantity applied has been more than trebled, the quality improved, and the price at the same time lowered by 20, 30, and in some cases even 40 and 50 per cent. Cultivators have learnt to perform certain kinds of work in common, to thresh in common, to some extent to sell in common. In the *Société des Agriculteurs* the syndicates have become the ruling power.

They inscribe Co-operative Banking on their Programme.

Fully to take advantage of all their opportunities, to carry consistently through the progress intended, the leaders of the syndicates soon came to realise, they must with all this useful activity combine the creation of convenient "popular" credit. The difficulty was, how to do it. None of the methods thus far, very empirically, adopted, can be described as approaching to perfection. The first idea was to "give"—to open the purses of the rich for the necessities of the poor. There is some other banking. From the first, the Bank of France was willing to lend its support. If an agricultural syndicate would form, affording sufficient security, the Bank declared itself prepared to discount its paper, provided that there were, in all, three acceptable signatures. Acting on this offer in the most elementary manner, the Agricultural Syndicate of the Indre-et-Loire organised a system of agricultural credit which simply requires the applicant, being an elected member, to find one surety to endorse his acceptance, and the syndicate, adding its own, passes the paper on to the Bank of France. Some inquiries are, of course, made. But, in general, the security relied upon is that of the unlimited liability of all members. A., it is assumed, will not back B.'s bill unless he knows B. to be good. And B.'s neighbours, asked for information, will not give him a good character unless they feel sure that he deserves it. They might have to pay for their complaisance. Thus far—or at any rate up to a short time ago, when I saw the President, M. Bossebœuf, at Tours— this very rudimentary system had proved perfectly safe. However, as a rule, in the Agricultural Syndicates dealing in credit, care is taken to provide *some* stock of money, or some distinctly apparent security in the shape of the

Objections to their Practice.

liability of wealthy men. In most cases there are two classes of members—*fondateurs*, who take up comparatively large shares, act as patrons, do not borrow, but provide the security; and *sociétaires* or *membres effectifs*, who come to the society as to a little Providence, which gives them what their self-help has not produced—being required to take a small, often a merely nominal, share, being entitled to borrow and also to bank their savings, but having no voice, or as good as no voice, in the management. Although this system has made fair sums of money available for small cultivators, on which practically no losses are reported, it must be quite evident that in itself it is not good. I have the less occasion to criticise it since the gentleman most identified with the practice in by far the strongest syndicate of the kind, the Syndicate of Poligny, has frankly written to me that in his opinion the Raiffeisen system is preferable, and since I understand that the syndicate referred to is being gradually transformed into a cluster of Raiffeisen banks.*

Instances.
In many cases there is some rich man who helps with his money or his securities. Thus in the syndicate just spoken of, M. Bouvet, a rich timber-merchant, not only found money in shares, and induced some of his well-to-do friends to take up other shares, in order to provide the working capital required, but in addition he allowed the syndicate the use of his office and the service of his clerks free of charge, and undertook to pay interest—at first it was at the rate of 4 per cent.—on all deposits lodged. At Genlis, in Burgundy, Count Lejéas, likewise a very philanthropic large landowner, has placed a certain sum in marketable effects (close upon £500) at the disposal of his syndicate, which the latter is authorised to pledge to the bankers giving credit.

---

* The *Bulletin Mensuel de l' Union des Caisses Rurales et Ouvrières* of last April announces that the *Crédit Mutuel* of Poligny has formally joined the *Union des Caisses Rurales*, the Union of Lyons, founded by my friend M. Durand, and constituted itself a central bank for the district embracing the departments of the Jura, Haute-Saône, and Doubs. It opens a credit of 600 francs (£24) to any *caisse* forming under approved rules, and takes its money on deposit, or else makes advances at the same rate, viz., 3 per cent.

He secures himself by a general control of affairs, being one of the Council of the Syndicate, and by the right reserved to withdraw his effects in the event of the reserve fund of the syndicate dropping below a stipulated figure. How he could, under French law, withdraw what is actually pledged to the bankers, I cannot say. However, Count Lejéas assures me that he is fully secured, and satisfied that he incurs no risk. I have no precise particulars about M. Duport's experimental *Crédit Agricole* of Belleville, but I believe it to be likewise founded on the "rich help the poor" principle. M. Méline's *Crédit Agricole* of Remiremont likewise has *membres fondateurs*. M. Josseau—presumably in virtue of his official position—has managed to secure for his own *Syndicat Agricole* of Coulommiers a Government subvention of 6,000 francs (£240), which no doubt would give a good start to any such society. Moreover, he provides 30,500 francs—to be increased to 200,000 francs—in shares taken up by rich *fondateurs*, who may patronise but must not borrow. There are many similar methods, all more or less marked by the same defect.

All this is not really co-operation. It is not self-help. It does not educate. It teaches small folk to look for favours. There is an unmistakable want of "trust in the people" and trust in self-help, a halting and half-heartedness in it all, naturally bound to impair the success. The system fails to evoke that most necessary foundation of all self-help, a sense of responsibility, which is only to be awakened by a full share in the management and liability. It seems a matter of gift and condescension, a deliberate keeping of classes apart, instead of drawing them together. The whole thing presents itself as a palpable miss of a good aim. The best that can be said of it is, in M. Levasseur's words, that it represents "the infant germ" (*molécule germinative*) of sound agricultural credit.

Practically the same thing is done in *caisses* in which,

not rich patrons, but large financial firms, such as the Savings Bank of Lyons, come to the support of poor cultivators. The foundation upon which the system of the Agricultural Credit Bank of Bessenay, organised by the Lyons Savings Bank, practically rests is this, that for every franc raised in share capital by the society, the Savings Bank is willing—subject to the adoption of prescribed rules—to advance two, considering the one franc self-raised adequate cover.

M. de Fontgalland has in the Drôme adopted yet another practice, which carries down the support given to fractional figures. Really it amounts to the employment of funds accumulated in the slender reserve fund of the syndicate to lending purposes.

All this is mere tentative scouting, mere haphazard exploring of a country needlessly unknown, since experience elsewhere has provided sufficiently clear and trustworthy charts. At best it is only pioneer work, and pioneer work calculated to do as much harm as good in teaching people to look to crutches when they should be looking to their own legs. In course of time, no doubt, out of this chaos of dim and hazy notions will be evolved some clear and sound system calculated to bring relief in an educating way. The current of opinion appears generally to have set in the direction of Raiffeisenism. In some modification or other presumably that will be adopted. And in course of time probably it will be supplemented in larger and more populous areas by the system of MM. Luzzatti and Ferraris, of the good effects of which in Italy I have already spoken. The French have thus far closed their eyes with curious persistency to the methods adopted for applying this practice specifically to agriculture. The "model rules" prepared by the late Italian Postmaster-General, M. Ferraris, ought to be distinctly useful for this purpose.

The Bank of Co-operative Productive Associations.

To return to co-operative banking in towns, there is an instructive speciality to be seen profitably at work at Paris, which ought to interest our co-operative associations, since the wants of co-operative associations are sure to be more or less alike all the world over. Like our own productive associations, the French are, for the most part, not over-strong in capital. In their isolated condition the credit of every one of them has not proved sufficient to purchase for it much in the way of goods, or to help it to obtain contracts for which known solvency is needed. It occurred to the intelligent leaders of the co-operative productive movement, that they would be placing themselves in a very much better position if their associations were to join together to become their own bankers. The result has fully justified their expectations. The *Banque de l'Union des Associations Ouvrières* in the Boulevard St Martin has already rendered admirable services, and promises to render such even more largely. It is composed of productive co-operative societies only, who take shares and elect the Committee of Management. Liability is, of course, limited. Of course, also, no association which has a good case for borrowing to show, hesitates to apply for a loan. Equally of course, no association in the opposite position dares to do so. As a last "of course," associations, under such circumstances, repay honestly and punctually. The bank is by its rules restricted entirely to business with its own members. Beginning with a modest share capital of only £2,000, it found that even so it could make the united resources of the individual associations go considerably farther than they would without union. Being stronger than each of them severally, it could obtain credit elsewhere, and thereby multiply their small funds for working purposes. A happy accident substantially increased its power for work. M. Moigneu, a wealthy philanthropist, much interested in co-operation, read of its useful doings, and handed over to it, in various instalments, a sum of £20,000, as a gift, to form part of its capital. Thus endowed, the *Banque* has not only found itself strong enough to extend materially its useful ministrations to its shareholder associations; it has also been enabled to put the *Verrerie aux Verriers* of St Etienne, taken over as the result of a strike by the trade unions interested in the glass trade, on a sound business footing, advancing to it funds for keeping up work in slack times, to sell produce in brisk. And, lastly, it has actually proved the salvation—unfortunately, only for a time—of the Wholesale Stores of Charenton. Those stores, weak in capital, were entirely dependent for their work upon credit given to them by dealers, who took bills which joint-stock banks discounted. The stores redeemed the bills when the money for the goods distributed to local societies came in. At the instigation of discontented traders, one day, the banks declined to discount further Charenton paper. Bankruptcy stared the Wholesale Stores in the face. By the letter of its rules the Productive Associations' Bank was not empowered to step in to help, but its members agreed that they would be fully carrying out their spirit by doing so. They did. They discounted the Wholesale acceptances. Being themselves strong, they could pass them on to other banks. Nobody was one penny the worse. The traders' trick had failed, and the Wholesale Society was saved.* The management of the *Banque de l'Union des Associations Ouvrières*, I may add, is very good and businesslike, and its practice deserves to be recommended for consideration to our Productive Federation, which is trying to arrive at the same end by means which appear to me more hand-to-mouth.

---

* The salvation effected was unfortunately, as observed, only temporary. The Wholesale Society had started too weak in capital, and has since gone into liquidation.

The Crédit Coopératif de Lorraine.

There are two more French forms of co-operative credit, for which I must find space. The first of these really lies geographically outside present France. But in its essence it is French to such a degree that probably no one except ultra-patriotic Germans will object to my classing M. Prével's *Crédit Coopératif de Lorraine* under my present head. The *Crédit Coopératif de Lorraine* is in essence a Schulze-Delitzsch bank with *limited* liability—and accordingly with rather substantial shares, viz., of £10 each, payable by instalments of not less than 3s. a month. In respect of organisation M. Prével has departed from Schulze-Delitzsch traditions. He has made his Council or Committee larger, viz., consisting of six unsalaried members and the two salaried officers; and has, on the other hand, kept the controlling body small, consisting of three *réviseurs* only. The organisation has amply approved itself in practice, and the rapid growth and expansion of the *Crédit* shows how much such an institution was wanted, though the need was at first distinctly denied. It began in 1892 with only 90 members and £7,000 share capital. At the close of the year 1895 it had 1,143 members,* and £35,860 share capital, of which £15,721 was paid up. It had in the twelvemonth lent out, to members only, £375,395, for the most part by cash credits, to supply which amount it had not found it necessary to pass on more than £13,378 of its bills for discount. The entire business of the year amounted to £635,959, just about twice as much as had been done in 1894. The *Crédit* held £26,287 in savings. The annual expense did not amount to more than £694. In fact the bank is growing so strong that the question of the hour has come to be

---

* By the middle of March the number of members had further increased to 1,255, holding 1,992 shares. Of the 1,143 members enrolled at New Year, 407 were tradesmen, 28 small manufacturers, 219 farmers, 125 *rentiers*, 115 public employees, 137 surgeons, teachers, &c., 25 persons employed in the military service, and 87 unclassified.

how to keep down the capital. Like their German forerunners, these Lorrain Schulzists have failed rightly to estimate the abundance of their resources, and have been over-greedy in seeking to attract share capital. [The German law appears to be adverse to the application of a corrective found very useful elsewhere, viz., the issue of shares of a smaller denomination concurrently with the larger.] The *Crédit Coopératif* has already begun starting branch offices. Its development and business are most encouraging, and the losses have proved insignificant.

The last place in this chapter I have reserved for a modest little institution which to my mind is the most genuine People's Bank of all in France. What is the object for which People's Banks are formed? Surely not to save banking expenses to the rich and swell the ranks of capitalist institutions, but to provide easy and cheap credit for the poor, to whom by other means it is inaccessible. Striking out a different path altogether from that taken by the flourishing business banks of Mentone, and Nice, and Marseilles—with which he does not wish his own bank to be placed on a level—M. H. Rouzès, when starting his humble little *Banque Populaire du Cinquième Arondissement* at Paris, decided to confine himself to the business of *small* people, to follow truly co-operative lines in making his members give that which they could in exchange for that which they wanted. Their right to credit could only be rendered effective by close touch, community of interest, frequent meeting, and sufficient knowledge of one another. They must become more than a bank. They must be a society. It was in accordance with these principles that he laid down his rules. Liability must be limited, of course. But election must be careful and searching. The value of the share was fixed at 50 francs, payable by instalments. There were to be three officers, as in the Schulze-Delitzsch banks. But the real administrative body must be the

The Paris People's Bank of M. Rouzès.

Council, consisting of from five to fifteen unsalaried members, thoroughly representative, giving up much time to the work, and reinforced by two trustworthy *commissaires de surveillance*. And the members generally must be brought together at least once a quarter. Still further to maintain touch and knowledge among members, M. Rouzès proposed that the names of all shareholders should be posted up in the office of the bank, where in fact the list may now always be seen. The result has fully proved the wisdom of such organisation. The bank formally constituted itself on 23rd December 1890, with only sixteen members, all selected, taking up among them 31 shares, which gave the bank a "guarantee capital" of £62, but only £6. 4s. in cash. That was insufficient for beginning work upon. The bank must wait until at least 100 shares were taken up. This was done by 1st July 1891, and on that day the bank opened its office. Its business has throughout been small. There is none of that tossing gold about by the shovelful which may be witnessed, figuratively speaking, in some banks in Italy and the Riviera. And there are no rich hotelkeepers to bring their substantial accounts to its counter. It is a *poor* man's bank. Accordingly it has to be circumspect and particularly prudent. In the first three months of its practice it discounted 262 acceptances to the value of 24,453 francs—only about £3. 15s. apiece. But it lost nothing. In the second quarter the figures rose to 445 and 29,857 respectively, which is actually a diminution of average amount, viz., to not quite 54s. per loan. So the figures kept growing, slowly but steadily. On 31st December last the bank numbered 190 members. It held 60,100 francs in paid-up capital, besides 1,601 francs in the reserve fund. In the course of the year it had lent out 627,478 francs in 5,258 loans, averaging only 119.34 francs (£4. 15s.) apiece. Its annual expenses amount to somewhere about £190. It was enabled to declare a dividend at the rate of 4 per cent.—it is true with the help of a subvention of 500 francs ($\frac{5}{8}$ per cent. on the capital) awarded by the State. In France, it seems, even into what is otherwise a model little bank the State must needs intrude its corrupting aid, to weaken the power of self-help. All the business has proved safe. And the members feel drawn together as if by ties of a family. They canvass for membership among their own friends, carefully avoiding to admit doubtful characters. The frequent meetings of members are very largely accountable for this effect. Nobody keeps away from such who can attend. "It is at these gatherings that the prosperous condition of our bank has been made clear ; it is thanks to them and to the publication of the figures, showing a steady increase, that confidence in the future of the society has been confirmed. The first members have become ardent advocates of our work ; they bring their friends to us, they invite their dealers to become members. If we had facilities for rediscount we should grow rapidly, but we do not complain of the want of that. We have all along made it our study to be prudent, and we adhere to that rule." So says M. Rouzès.

Obviously these are the lines upon which people's banking should be carried on. "I should wish to see France covered with such little banks," so M. Rouzès remarked to me ; "every arrondissement should have one, serving it alone, but serving it effectively. And then, among them, these local institutions should form a strong central bank all their own." I heartily echo that wish, and would carry its realisation far beyond France. The success of People's Banks should not be measured by "business" and riches. That is a false standard altogether. As it happens, there is a very forbidding "Tom Idle" to be instructively placed by the side of M. Rouzès' exemplary "Frank Goodchild." M. Rouzès founded a second bank in Paris, on precisely the same lines, in the Third Arrondissement. Of course he could not officer the two. M. Thouvenin was supposed to be an able manager. He took charge of the bank. He pushed it on. His aim was, to rival the big banks of the South. In little time he had in outward appearance distanced the older bank of the Boulevard de Saint Germain. But a few months ago his body was found in the Seine. He had landed his bank in a deficit of nearly 60,000 francs, and had in consequence committed suicide. I earnestly commend his fate to the attention of those in this country who are more anxious to "get on" and make a show of many banks started, than to proceed on safe lines and start none but good ones.

<small>Hopeful Prospects of the Movement in France.</small>

It is the profit-hunting of the big People's Banks, it is the glowing talk of successes and the counting up of colossal sums at People's Banks Congresses which is answerable for such results as M. Thouvenin's death. Once you make "business" the standard, everybody as a matter of course strains after it. But the object for which People's Banks are formed, I repeat it, is *not* business. It is the filling up of a gap which requires filling. You cannot do *people's* banking well without minute care, without inquiry into small cases, which inquiry requires minute machinery penetrating into small nooks and corners. The poor man's distinctive friend, the man to whom he opens his heart and confides his troubles, is not the bishop in his gilded coach who preaches an eloquent charity sermon, nor the Lord Mayor who acts as chairman to a charity fund, but the visiting curate who looks up the sick and needy in their hovels, who judges from his own observation what sufferer deserves and requires help, and dispenses it, and the distributing officer who proceeds with similar discrimination in dealing out the fund to which the Lord Mayor's appeal has attracted subscriptions. People's Banks want to help the poor. They can do it only by adopting machinery, homely and humble, qualified to answer such purpose, and by giving themselves up thoroughly to that service. To my mind the People's Bank of M. Rouzès, with its modest lendings and its slender dividend, is as a People's Bank as vastly preferable to all those flourishing business establishments whose success is paraded in periodicals, as was the poor widow with her two mites to the rich alms-givers of the Gospel. It does its work and it keeps itself safe. Its money chest is small. But, to quote M. Luzzatti—"*La cooperazione è un affare sorretto da un' idea morale. Tanto vale l' affare quanto splende quella idea.*"

France has in the last few years made very considerable progress in the extension of co-operative banking. It looks as if my hope expressed when I wrote the first edition of this book were to be realised, and on the foundation built up by the sinking of so much costly and well-intended rubbish in an apparently insatiable "Chat Moss" were to rise up a substantial and enduring fabric. The architectural lines have been laid down, and there is ample material to complete the structure. If Frenchmen will but break with their timid want of faith in themselves and in their own powers, and learn to trust to what they themselves can do, rather than to the State with its subventions and the rich with their "founders' shares" and patron management, and go to the bottom of the principle, thinking of that rather than of mere technical rules—with their remarkable aptitude for common work, their quick wit, and ready ingenuity, they can scarcely fail to make the desideratum of at least fifty years a reality, and provide for their small tradesmen, their humble cultivators, their artisans seeking for freedom and independence in co-operative workshops, a source of financial support proving as widely useful as M. Luzzatti's work has proved in Italy, and Schulze's and Raiffeisen's in Germany.

CHAPTER XIV.

CONCLUSION.

<small>A Summary of what has been told.</small>

SLIGHT and sketchy as must of necessity be the drawing which, within the compass of a moderate-sized book, I have been able to present of the fruitful new economic force rendered available for practical service by the labours of Schulze and Raiffeisen and their pupils, I think that I must have said enough to show that the praises bestowed upon it by such competent observers as MM. Léon Say, E. de Laveleye, Held, and Von Dobransky are in no way overstrained, and that here in truth is a power raised up capable of accomplishing an inestimable amount of good, alike economic and educational, the story of whose past work I have by no means misdescribed in terming it, on my title-page, "A Record of Social and Economic Success," or in comparing it in respect of its potency to steam. Reckon up the mere volume of money which this co-operative mint has drawn from the capitalist market, to place it at the service of small producers—cultivators, traders, and wage-earners —distributing it judiciously at the very points at which there was greatest need for it and at which it promised to prove most productive, dividing it according to the requirements of each case, watching over its employment, and then, after having given bread to the eater and seed to the sower, gathering it all up again with scarcely any loss and with adequate interest! That sum, we know, must now tell up to many hundreds of millions. We have not, unfortunately, very full statistics of what has been done. But we

<small>The Economic Result.</small>

know quite enough to be able to say that an estimate of £150,000,000 a year—of money, I should wish to be understood, not created, but made available by credit for productive purposes—must be very well within the mark. In the various chapters relating to different countries I have given figures taken from authoritative sources, which bring the total, absolutely certain, very near to the point named, and leaving a wide margin to make up the balance. And thus M. Jules Simon's words have been made true to the very letter, and "the greatest banker of the world" has been proved to be he "who disposes of the mite of the poor." And, as well as the greatest, he has also proved the *safest* —the man to whom rich and poor alike may without fear of loss intrust their deposits, well assured that, since he has no inducement to incur risk, he will incur none.

That is not the result in the creative work accomplished upon which I should wish to lay greatest stress. I should be disposed to set an even higher value upon the *quality*, than upon the mere quantity of the work done—upon the reaching down to the very humblest and necessitous, whom nothing else would help, and raising him by education and by training to business ways, in addition to providing him with means for turning such ways to account. To the application of this power it appears, moreover, in truth impossible to set any limit. Its raw material abounds wherever there is opportunity for work. Its opportunity for converting that material into money's worth, by the specific expedient of making it men's interest to be businesslike and honest, exists wherever there is need. To my mind there has never been a more prolific source of potential temporal good placed at the disposal of those who are dependent upon labour. For to them co-operative banking means, if they choose to profit by its gifts, not democratisation of credit only, but, by the help of democratised credit, the *democratisation of production* also, the securing to the

The Moral Result.

toiler of the full reward for his labour—and emancipation! Do not let us quarrel over the legitimacy of such a change! It will never do away with capitalist enterprise. It will never bring about the establishment of an economic ochlocracy. But it may open a fair field for capacity and industry, and the proverbial "career" to "talent" in the very poorest. It would unbuckle the knapsack of the soldier in the great industrial army, in which, according to tradition, lies concealed the marshal's bâton. To a nation it must mean much more. It means—or at any rate, it may mean—concurrently with democratisation, an indefinite *increase of production*, a wholesale mobilisation of productive forces, fuller satisfaction to the toiler without additional taxation of any one, diminution of want, a diffusion of prosperity, to a very great extent the disappearance of economic strife, education, elevation, the making the entire community richer, happier, better.

Before proceeding to consider whether this beneficent agency, which has already rendered such invaluable services elsewhere, has any gift in store for ourselves, it may be well very briefly to sum up the lesson which Continental experience has taught us, and try to arrive at its gist.

The Underlying Principle.

If I have done anything like what I desired to do, I have shown that at bottom the force at work in co-operative banking is *all one*, and that at any rate among the best of the systems reviewed—I will not now speak of any other—there is no fundamental difference of principle. There are differences of application. Necessarily so. You cannot serve a densely populated district as you would a country parish. You cannot provide for a tradesman trained to business in precisely the same way in which you provide for an untrained rustic. Again, there are differences of the spirit in which the principle is applied. There are those whose aim ends in the pocket, who would, so to speak, take their ticket in co-operation as they take it in a railway train, which runs for many, but in which every one travels for his own profit.

There are those, again, who through the pocket wish to reach the heart, who co-operate as do joint-settlers in a new colony, in which each has his own gift to bring to the common stock for his own, but at the same time also for the common, good.

I feel bound here to interpolate a general caution, begging students of co-operative banking not to take for gospel all the charges which they may hear advanced by champions of different systems against one another. All those indictments have their home in Germany, where recent experience, of which we have been the victims, must have made us aware that nicely weighed scruples about the truth of an accusation do not necessarily stand in the way of its being made, when the opponent is considered deserving of castigation, which a rival is sure to be. I take a special interest in these charges. I like to hear of supposed weak points in a system—not from any malice or ἐπιχαιρεκακία, but simply because, obviously, it is by its weak points that to a great extent a system ought to be judged. It is its weak points which are most instructive, determining its strength, as the weakest link determines the strength of a chain. I have investigated all those charges. Most of them are pointed against the Raiffeisen system—by men who appear never so much as to have seen a Raiffeisen bank, but to take their evidence at second-hand, and who pass it on without adding Swift's saving clause, "If it is a lie, I have it as cheap as you." So far as these charges apply to systems—as distinct from specific cases of maladministration—I have found them all unfounded. I will not enter into them now. I would sooner efface all record of them. If my tale of what has been done teaches anything as it ought, it teaches that there is good in *all* the principal systems applied—that, in fact, "system" is of very much smaller account in this matter than "principle"; and that the good done by any system is precisely proportioned in degree to the fidelity with which it is made to adhere to the co-operative rule of self-help, vigilance, strictness in enforcing engagements, abstention from profit-seeking, from over-taxing the borrower for the profit of the lender, to the rule of subordinating every other consideration to that of providing, without after-thought or by-end, the cheapest possible and the most accessible credit to all.

<small>Strength and Weakness of the Several Systems.</small>
Each system is good in its own sphere, and subject to the observance of its own proper safeguards. No other system has produced equally large, equally truly imposing results as that of Schulze-Delitzsch. And provided that sufficient touch can be maintained among members, and that conscientious and capable officers can be secured, none, I may add, is more "co-operative." Among populations less submissive than the Germans to unlimited liability, and practically to the oligarchic rule of three officers, the Italian system of M. Luzzatti and the cognate adaptation of Schulze-Delitzschism, which has found a home in Belgium, supply in the more businesslike strata all that is required—always supposing that their principle be kept pure. For the very poor and the dispersed in the country there is absolutely no system to place into competition with that of Raiffeisen. There is a peculiar charm attaching to that system, which makes those who become thoroughly acquainted with it prize and love it like none other. It stoops so low. It helps so much with the heart as well as with the hand. "Our *banche* cannot attempt to do for the poor what the Raiffeisen *casse* do." This is what the Marchese Scati, himself a *sindaco* of an excellent Luzzatti bank, admitted to me at Turin. "They look after their members as a shepherd looks after his sheep, they watch over them, they check them, they educate them." However, though no other system accords to the moral educating element the same prominence in its programme, it is an entire mistake to suppose that the Raiffeisen banks possess

a monopoly of kind feeling. It is impossible to assert this —to state one instance—after the resolution adopted at the last meeting of Austrian Schulze-Delitzsch associations, on the motion of Herr Siegl. "It is true," so Herr Siegl remarked to me some weeks before, "that we have neglected the philanthropic, educating side of co-operation. We *can* cultivate it as well as the Raiffeisen co-operators, and we *must* cultivate it." His motion, giving effect to that desire, was adopted at Gablonz by acclamation, without a dissentient voice.

Indeed, the various systems are drawing nearer and nearer together every year, and M. Luzzatti's recent declaration in favour of a direct union of systems, calling upon the *banche popolari* to raise up around them clusters of *casse rurali*, and support such with their funds, is nothing more than the logical outcome from a gradual mutual approach which shows itself, among other things, in the practice becoming more and more common in the *banche* of inquiring into the employment of loans asked. M. Luzzatti himself, with his warm heart beating for every one who is in need, goes—in respect of that "philanthropy" which rigid economists at Berlin affect to deride—even beyond Raiffeisen, and, indeed, beyond co-operation—as is evidenced by his suggestion that the huge reserve funds accumulating in the coffers of excessively prosperous Italian banks, should be employed to buy up the share capital, and create, so to speak, impersonal corporations, disposing of money to which no individual has a claim, and which is to be dispensed in loans to the poor. It is the peculiarly good practice of the great Italian Savings Banks which has suggested this unfortunate idea. But what jobbery there would be in England under such a system! Loans would be distributed, like official patronage, according to party favour. Every redeemed bank would in fact become a *Legs Rampal*. That proposal starts from a wrong principle altogether, and

Co-operation and Philanthropy.

shoots far ahead of co-operation, which does not aim at setting up Little Providences to make exertion unnecessary, which does not mean the taxing of the present generation of members for the creation of an "unearned increment" to benefit their children; but the provision of machinery enabling the poor to place themselves, by an effort made in combination, for certain purposes on an equality with the rich—earning, working for all that they get, and securing for themselves—collectively it may be, but still *for themselves*— whatever they do earn.

Abuses.

In truth, the proposal put forward places in bold relief a gross abuse practised—one of those abuses that co-operative banking is liable to, and which we ought to take into consideration—amounting to a distinct deviation from the co-operative path, only less reprehensible than the payment of those huge dividends of 40 and 56 per cent. which used to be declared in Germany. Italian banks have in some instances entirely perverted the use of reserve funds, making that which ought to be a means the end, and neglecting the tree for the sake of its prop. A reserve fund is, as its name implies, not intended to take the place of the share capital, but to stand as a support behind it. There *ought* to be no such huge reserve funds at all, as M. Luzzatti points to—more especially while dividends are declared at the rate of 10, 12, and 14 per cent. These things mean, that the banks which accumulate such funds and declare such dividends, lose sight of the co-operative principle; that they do not study the cheapening of credit, for which they were created, but profit; that they overtax the borrower, for whose sake they were in fact set up. Excess profits in co-operative banks clearly belong to the borrower, just as in co-operative supply societies they belong to the purchaser.

There is no word of protest too strong which can be employed against those unconscionable dividends which are doing a terrible amount of mischief, and acting as a very dangerous example. M. Luzzatti has frankly owned to me that he did not at the outset limit the dividend, simply because he did not anticipate that there would be much profit to divide. We know at present what co-operative banking has it in its power to accomplish, and we should be careful to avoid falling into the same error into which, to his own great present regret, M. Luzzatti has allowed his older banks to stray. Those large dividends mean the letting in of the corrupting principle of greed and self-seeking. Those huge reserve funds, which embody the same gain-hunting principle only in another form, mean a premium upon shares, which makes the supposed poor man's friend and helper difficult of access to the poor. Very rightly now is M. Luzzatti exerting all his authority and influence to induce co-operative banks in Italy strictly to limit dividend. And in somewhat fainter tones, though evidently intended to be equally earnest, is Dr Schenck insisting upon the same thing in Germany. It is for us ἐπίγονοι to learn from our forerunners' mistakes.

There are other abuses which this aping of joint-stock trading has unfortunately brought in its train, and such new founders of People's Banks ought accordingly to study to steer clear of. The small attendances at general meetings in Schulze-Delitzsch and Luzzatti banks, where out of 1,000 or 17,000, only 150 or 250 members put in an appearance, betoken a want of interest, and unquestionably represent a peril. What is, for instance, to prevent the 100 employees of the *Banca Popolare* of Milan—who are all required to be shareholders—from constituting themselves a Prætorian guard, electing their "emperors," not according to the best interests of the bank, but according to their own particular convenience?

Every system has, in fact, along with its peculiar elements of strength, also its own peculiar besetting weaknesses. The Raiffeisen banks, being small, strictly local, giving very wide scope to personal influences, are no doubt liable to abuse for personal or partisan ends, which only *strict adherence* to the sound principle originally laid down, enlisting the *general* interest of members against possible encroachments by *individuals*, can successfully keep out. That is why relaxed or adulterated Raiffeisenism—such as I have had occasion to speak of in some connections, and such as some of our English advocates of co-operative credit, ignorant, from inexperience, of the danger with which it is beset, are calling upon their neighbours to adopt—should be most carefully avoided. It is much easier credit to start, I grant, but experience has shown that it has no soundness or stability in it.

<small>Necessity of Strict Adherence to the Co-operative Principle in its Purity.</small>

Gathering up once more the lesson to be learnt from the failures and abuses alluded to, we come back to the point which I have thought it necessary so often to insist upon, that it is of *imperative* importance that the co-operative principle accepted should in all applications of the banking system be adhered to in its *absolute* purity, with unbending fidelity. Every deviation, every relaxation, must mean peril. And it is better to have no bank at all than a bad one. There should be strict enforcement of rules, merciless discipline, and rigid maintenance of the safeguards required, so as to keep the institution entirely true to self-help, avoiding adventitious supports, rejecting speculative gains, evoking vigilance, interest, control, responsibility, keeping the association true to the "one for all and all for one."

<small>Is there Room for Co-operative Banking among Ourselves?</small>

It is time now to consider the question which naturally suggests itself—Has this richly creative institution, which has proved so abundantly useful abroad, no gift for ourselves? I consider that there can be no doubt that it has. It has been disputed. It has been objected that the thing is "foreign." It is exactly as "foreign" as was capitalist banking before it was introduced here from precisely the same regions, **more** particularly from Lombardy and Venetia. But, then, it is contended that we have no "small trade," and the question seems never to be asked whether democratised credit has proved useful to anything besides "small trade." **We have** seen how useful it has shown itself in rural districts, among working men generally, and among factory hands—one may say of the English type—at Verviers. **In** truth, however, **we have** more "small trade" than **many** people are **aware of; and we** have plenty of underpaid labour which, **for want of** capital, cannot **rise** to the dignity of "small **trade."** We have the "**sweated**" artisan, who would be only too thankful **to raise himself to** the status of a small trader. **We have the co-operative** workshop which now **seeks** the **financial support which there is no** People's Bank to lend, **in the** deposit **department of the** less efficient "Productive Federation,"* as it has **previously** sought it in the questionable assistance given by the "Aid Association" of the "Wholesale Society," happily defunct. It is not everywhere **that** co-operative producers find the stores of their **own locality ready** to help them in **their** struggles. **As a rule, our** productive associations **have** had to raise themselves **to** prosperity before they could successfully **appeal for the help** which had at that stage of their life become almost unnecessary. There are plenty more workmen who would like **to** enrol themselves **in** productive societies did they see their way to **obtaining the means.** People's Banks could provide such. **We have,** moreover, the costermonger and his **class-mates of** precarious itinerant trades, among **whom small credit on usurious** terms **is a** valued, **but** still only insufficiently developed, institution. There is many a hundred pounds now lent out in this small way, the use of which coster-

Arguments on the Affirmative Side.

---

* I **have tried to** make clear this point in *Labour Co-partnership* of April 1895.

mongers are so thankful to buy, even at a high price, that they have been known to give complimentary suppers to small money-lenders retiring from business, as if they had been public benefactors. A grade higher there is the small householder, who purchases a good many things "through the nose" on the hire-purchase system from dealers who would willingly sell their goods more cheaply for cash. We should not have our Civil Service Share Purchase Advance and Investment Societies if there were no want of credit even among our salaried fellow-citizens. In one of these societies I have heard of loans asked, on the security of well-known railway shares, which a joint-stock bank offered to grant at an exorbitant rate, but which were afterwards obtained through the society, on *precisely the same security*, at the ordinary bank charge. It was co-operation which secured the reduction. One well-known bank, formed on a quasi-co-operative basis, avowedly for the use of small folk who cannot afford an ordinary banking account, regularly charges 10 per cent. for advances even on first-class securities. That is, to my mind, an abuse under which those are made to suffer who can least afford it, and which, if it be at all possible, should be remedied. Then look around in our country districts! We are trying to increase the number of allotment holders. What are they to do with their bare land, let, as a rule, at a very high rental? They must have their cow, their pig, their implements, their manure, their seed, and all else. With the help of these things they can make their allotments pay. In my book "Agricultural Banks" I have quoted the case of a tenant of the famous "three acres" who, with the help of money rendered available, kept, not one cow, but seven, and made them pay. Give the men the means for turning their land to account, and Mr Collings's reproach of "£38,000,000 sent abroad every year" for produce, which we might well raise at home, will become a by-word without a meaning.

But the men cannot raise tomatoes and peas with their hands only, nor buy without money that cow which, once got, will easily repay its value out of its milk. I have already spoken elsewhere of the needs of larger agriculture,* so need not here repeat my argument. But is there no call for the extension of other **co-operative** practices such as co-operative banking would facilitate—co-operative purchase, co-operative dairying, co-operative sale of produce? Abroad these things have "grown out of" co-operative banking, as a matter of course, in thousands of establishments, against which we have only dozens to show. **Without co-operative** banking they would have been impossible. **I have already** related the barren result **of an** attempt which I myself made in this direction in Sussex.† And is **there not Ireland with** its "gombeen man" and **its starvation alike of soil and of body?** And is there not India, to quote M. Léon Say's words, " literally devoured **by usury,"** with its famished ryots **who** pledge their children **unborn** to the usurer, and cultivate the **land, which the usurer** has practically seized, **at starvation** wages for **his sole** benefit? And, all the empire over, is there not **the poor,** not only the occasional poor, who **annoys** other people **with** requests for a loan to get him out of some temporary difficulty—which loan **a** People's Bank could grant more easily **and to** much better purpose—but the genuinely poor whom **we are** told that **we** shall have with us always—the unemployed, **clamorous, or** else submissively silent, who sighs **for** labour **which without** money to pay his muscles is **not to be obtained; and** the helpless poor whom we quarter **upon** our workhouses? "Whoever sets **up** Raiffeisen banks," so says a German couplet, **"pulls down** workhouses."‡ He makes them superfluous.

---

* Chapter V.   † See page 64.
‡ "Wer Raiffeisenvereine baut
   Reisst Armenhäuser nieder."

368   PEOPLE'S BANKS.

Evidence in Support.

Surely there can be no disputing the existence of a want of people's credit? The whole ground is crying out for it.

Our Cognate Rudimentary Institutions.

Else, what keeps our pawnshops and our usurers busy? What has called our Slate Clubs, and Funding Clubs, and Money Clubs, and Loan Societies, and Self-help Societies, and Civil Service Share and Purchase Societies into being? What has led so many of our Friendly Societies to avail themselves of the power given them of lending to members? What has prompted the Irish to set up their "Loan Boards," which in their elementary way are doing not a little good? Here we have the proof of a need and a demand actually evidenced in the existence of rudimentary institutions which supply it in a more or less inefficient way. For the most part these institutions are very insecure, often avowedly temporary institutions, which minister to need in a hand-to-mouth fashion. As a rule they have no funds of their own. They deal out the money which comes in by subscriptions, and which may be withdrawn to the last farthing any day. Hence their instability. They can grant no long loans, which are the most useful loans for men who, let us say, wish to set up in business, to purchase articles for agricultural use, or to pay off an old debt. When money is flush, everybody pays in, and the societies are at a loss how to invest their funds. I have known £500 and £900 accumulated in the hands of a single society, whose officers were at their wits' end how to lay it out. When money is scarce, everybody draws out, and the society perishes—just when its help is most needed.

Let us very briefly look at the best known of these institutions.

Slate Clubs.
Loan Societies.

The Slate Clubs are, of course, very insignificant and merely temporary concerns, but widely diffused. The Loan Societies, I am glad to say, are going altogether out of favour, and their number is rapidly dwindling. Last year only six new societies of this order were registered. The Act under which they are formed is a very inconvenient Act, and deservedly unpopular, alike with the Treasury and with the magistrates, whose assistance is appealed to to call in bad debts. They are so organised as to create no touch or mutual control among members. No borrower wishes it to be known that he has borrowed. As a matter of fact, nearly the entire management is committed to the Secretary, who in many cases draws a substantial salary. Rates of interest are high, though disguised in the shape of commissions and special contributions tacked on to the usual 5 per cent. for forty weeks, equal to $6\frac{1}{4}$ per cent. per annum, payable in advance. There are still about 350 of these societies in the kingdom, and it ought to be pointed out that they are composed of *just the class of men* who abroad group themselves together to much better purpose in People's Banks. As they die out, their places are taken by "specially authorised" societies, formed under the Friendly Societies Act, which are at any rate rather better organised, and by "Lending Societies" constituted under the Industrial and Provident Societies Act. There are about 245 of the former, and a very much smaller number (but doing a comparatively larger business) of the latter. The number of both is increasing. At best, these institutions are imperfect. Their prototypes, the original Loan Societies, formed under the Act of 1840, were authorised as "Friend of Labour Loan Societies." However, since their rules do not, like the rules of People's Banks, prescribe a supervision over the employment of the loan, and money is accordingly generally borrowed for improvident purposes, which leads the borrower into enduring mischief, they richly deserve the nickname, by which in fact they have become known, as "Enemy of Labour Loan Societies." Under their faulty organisation very much money has to be called in by legal proceedings.

"Lending Societies."

2 A

In 1890 there were no fewer than 3,052 summonses issued.

"Self-Help Societies."

The Self-Help Societies, which are as yet peculiar to Middlesex, are very much better institutions, but mainly so, because there is in them more democratic management, and an approach in respect of organisation to People's Banks. Members are elected. Applications for loans are more openly dealt with than in the Loan Societies, and members are to a larger extent put upon their responsibility. These useful little societies teach us two lessons very valuable for our present purpose. In the first place, they make it clear that there is no insuperable aversion, such as has been sometimes assumed to exist among our smaller folk, to "going bail" for one another. Money is, as a rule, lent on personal security only, supported by two sureties, which to a man known as honest are always forthcoming. In the second place, they show what very trustworthy borrowers labouring folk are, here as elsewhere. The Self-Help Society of St Pancras, being composed mainly of costermongers, railway hands, and other small folk, in 6½ years lent out £8,462, and lost, in all, only 7s. The Self-Help Society of Ealing lent out in six years £5,028, and did not lose a penny. It is true that in respect of not quite £11 the sureties had to be called upon to make good their principals' default. But of that sum £6 was guaranteed by the Vicar, who is considered fair game for robbing, and who has in consequence very properly been disqualified for serving as surety again. I take it that these are very satisfactory results. And even in this elementary form the resort to self-government and quickened responsibility is found to have a directly educating effect. One member borrowed £2 from the Vicar, which he apparently never thought of repaying. He joined the Self-Help Society, borrowed from it, and paid punctually. "How is it that you don't think of repaying me?" one day asked the Vicar. "Ah, you're the Vicar, you don't want it," was the reply. That shows the difference between private lending and co-operative lending, as it were, in a nutshell. And here, in this society, obviously, we have all the elements of a People's Bank in germ, and a People's Bank, I hope, the Self-Help Society will one day become.

The "Share Purchase Advance and Investment Societies" are more fully developed institutions, which deserve to be better known than they are. Their good management and satisfactory results are of course in part owing to the fact that they have a peculiarly trustworthy constituency to deal with in the persons of civil servants, who could not afford to fail in their duty to the society. Ostensibly, their primary object is, to purchase shares and other investments for members. But the societies are really, I believe, to a much larger extent credit banks, making advances on security which elsewhere would involve a much higher rate of interest. The United Service Share Purchase Society in 1894 lent out as much as £9,488; the Civil Service Society, having a paid-up share capital of £23,742, in the same year advanced £17,296. These societies raise funds by the issue of shares of varying amounts, generally speaking from £5 to £20, the value of which may be paid up by instalments of 10s., but not the whole of which need be accepted by the Society, should it not be required. Loans are granted at moderate rates, for varying terms, generally up to three years, repayable by instalments.

Share Purchase and Advance Societies.

Scotland possesses a far more democratic Co-operative Credit Institution in its "People's Bank" of Edinburgh, a very useful society, formed to enable working folk to purchase their own "flats." Hence the security which is pledged, generally speaking, consists of realty—though the Society has taken power to lend on personal security also, and to a very small extent avails itself of that power. It

The Edinburgh "People's Bank."

raises its money by £1 shares, payable at the holder's option by half-crown instalments. Beginning its work in a very modest way in 1889, it has in six years crept up to a share capital subscribed of £2,604 (only £1,348 paid up), with a reserve fund of £150. On 31st December last it had £12,598. 11s. 8½d. outstanding in advances to members, besides £886. 19s. 11d. on overdrafts, and £71. 1s. 10d. advanced on bills, therefore £13,536. 13s. 5½d. lent out in all. Its lending is done at varying rates, ranging now from 3½ to 5 per cent., according to the quality of the security given. The business has proved steady and safe, and unquestionably a convenience to the members who apply for loans. A fact particularly deserving of notice is this, that, according to the testimony of the Secretary, the whole of the money advanced was lent out to people "*who would not have approached the larger banks, which are generally looked upon as aristocratic institutions.*" This makes thoroughly good what *Chambers's Journal* wrote in 1883 :—

"There is a great blank or want of intermediate banks between the large Joint-Stock Banks and the Savings Banks. We have no banks to correspond with the People's Banks of Germany, or the moderate-sized National Banks of the United States. There is a large, industrious, and respectable class of small-farmers, tradesmen, shopkeepers, and others who are left out in the cold. There should be popular banks and banking facilities provided for the numerous class of small customers who require a bank to deposit their savings in, and at the same time to turn their little money to the best account ; also, on the other hand, to accommodate those who may want to borrow small sums occasionally for stocking their farms or their shops."

There *should* be such banks. The instances quoted conclusively prove the want of them, and they also show that Nature, making its bidding heard through the unerring voice of instinct, leads those among us, who are in want of money, to seek relief, in principle, by precisely the same methods by which foreigners have found it. Every one of the societies described may be considered a People's Bank in embryo—a People's Bank in the rough, hewn out of the same material, but not yet properly squared and put together, answering its purpose as does a log-hut as compared with a well-constructed building—in a partial, elementary, and temporary way.

All things considered, it can scarcely occasion surprise that in our gropings for a remedy we have thus far failed fully to seize the idea of co-operative banking. For our own co-operation runs all the other way. It is co-operation which begins with the possession of money or earnings; not co-operation which, like people's banking, leads up to these things. One may be said to begin where the other ends. They are cast on different lines, though the principle at bottom is identical. Slaves to habit and fixed rules, we have adhered to our traditional notion that "co-operation" must needs mean "stores," and that "credit" must needs be objectionable as meaning the illegitimate, improvident credit, which is just what People's Banks are intended to stamp out. What our neighbours are doing ought to open our minds to wider views. Why our Co-operators have not sought to remedy an admitted want.

I think it is beginning to do so. I have more telling evidence than I have yet put forward to quote in support of the applicableness of People's Banks to our circumstances. We have them actually among us now, and, in their humble way, they are thriving. I must confess that three or four years ago, when I first set my hand to the work, I did not look for anything like such rapid results. I am now able to point to them in support of my pleading. Before I do so, however, perhaps it may be well to explain our exact position in the matter, on what points our peculiar circumstances—differing in many respects from those of our neighbours—assist the work, on what points they hinder it.

There is no denying that the more limited amount of small trade and small cultivation which we possess—though I hold the proportion of the difference in respect of the Our Hindrances.

former to be generally exaggerated—more or less adversely affects our recruiting ground. Moreover, the populations of our rural parishes are, as a rule, smaller and more scattered. Again, the more vigorous among our working populations appear to have their minds far more set upon *fighting*, than upon creating and *acquiring*, capital, as a means of bettering the condition of their class. In addition, it is said that our working population are more improvident. But that remains to be proved. I dispute it as a general proposition. We have some working men, no doubt, who compare unfavourably in respect of thrift and forethought with their classmates abroad. But we have a good many others who could serve as excellent examples in any part of the globe.

Our Advantages.

These are the *cons*. We have some *pros*, fortunately, to pit against them. If our organised working classes are more pugnacious than foreigners, they undoubtedly also know their own mind very much better, they are more practical and businesslike, and much better accustomed to combined action. Once they take up a matter, they are sure to go on with it in a practical spirit, without losing sight of their main aim. "You compliment us upon our co-operative production," so said to me a year or two ago the Chairman of one of the Parisian Productive Associations, who has worked a long time in London; "were your countrymen to take up the same method of united action, they would succeed very much better. For they are more businesslike. They respect the decision of the majority, and abide by resolutions once passed. Our men are perpetually reopening old questions, always trying to upset what has been settled, restlessly shifting and changing about." Moreover, we have friendly and provident societies—such as have in Italy proved the very parents of People's Banks—better organised, stronger, larger, more numerous than anywhere. We certainly have more and very much cheaper money than our neighbours, circulating far more freely in channels which are always open. We have a much more fully developed banking system, into which co-operative banking could very well be made to fit in as an auxiliary and supplement, and a more diffused knowledge of banking and business. And, in the last place, we have more men of the leisured, and even the busy class, willing to devote time, labour, and, if need be, money, to the service of their fellow-men.

Thus far, therefore, circumstances cannot by any means be said to be unfavourable. And I think I may add that our law likewise lends itself fairly enough, if not altogether readily, to the proposed practice, at any rate so far as is required for a beginning. For co-operative banks to be formed with *limited liability* only—banks, that is, to carry on their business in towns and among medium and larger farmers, people who can take up fairly substantial shares— we have an Act, the Industrial and Provident Societies Act, which is really more liberal than any foreign co-operative law now in force. It allows us to do actually anything that we are at all likely to desire to do—bank, discount, take deposits from any one ; *only*, we must not issue withdrawable shares. That restriction certainly appears to me a matter for regret. For, from a co-operative point of view, withdrawable shares are decidedly preferable to non-withdrawable, and they would go some way towards warding off the "un-co-operative" practice, always apt to creep in, of levying toll upon incoming members, at a progressive ratio, in the shape of a premium upon shares. The beau-ideal of shares in a co-operative concern is what the French call *parts sociales*, fixed contributions, which do not vary in issue value. On this point, without a doubt, the associations of Schulze-Delitzsch have remained truer to the "co-operative" ideal than the banks set up by his disciples. However, the restriction is not fatal. We can manage without withdrawable shares, and the successful provision made against the

Our Law is not unfavourable.

sale of shares at a premium in some of our best co-operative associations—for instance, in that of Hebden Bridge—shows that, even as our law stands, shares may be kept at an unvarying level.

In respect of limited liability banks, really, our established banking *custom* is productive of more inconvenience —I will not call it worse—than our law. No doubt the method universally adopted abroad by banks of this description, of making the bill of exchange or "acceptance" the recognised medium of loan transactions, offers many advantages.* There is no *law* to prevent our doing just the same thing. We may, if we so choose, employ bills of exchange or promissory notes in exactly the same way. The legal provisions with respect to the two are precisely the same, except in respect of one or two trifling particulars.† Promissory notes are fully as "negotiable" as bills of exchange; and there is no reason why bills of exchange should not be used for the purchase of cash as they are for the purchase of goods. However, we are not in the habit of employing these instruments in such a manner. We are not in the habit of discounting promissory notes or of taking bills of exchange for money. Possibly our banking market may adapt itself to the new requirements. Otherwise we shall have to, and we *can*, do without the more convenient practice. A sound bank ought always to be in a position to secure a sufficient overdraft. And after some time, probably, as security for such, ordinary banks will be content to take acceptances and promissory notes as pledges, even if they decline to discount them. In any case, the Industrial and Provident Societies Act enables us to proceed at the outset with sufficient freedom.

---

* See page 202.

† See M. D. Chalmers, "A Digest of the Law of Bills of Exchange," Fourth Edition, 1891.

There are more serious hindrances to be faced in proceeding with the formation of banks which do not limit the liability of members, such as are those of the Raiffeisen type. For in this work we are compelled to fall back upon the rather inconvenient Friendly Societies Act, which limits the power of societies forming under it far more narrowly—because that is the only Act available which permits unlimited liability. Even so, the hindrances presenting themselves are not actually insuperable, or nearly as great as some would-be pioneers, who have not taken the trouble to study either co-operative banking or Provident Society legislation, choose to give out.

I will begin by dealing with two objections which have been raised without any good reason. In the first place, there is the law of "distress," which has staggered some of our novices. Well, no doubt the law of "distress" constitutes a hindrance to credit of any kind, in any case in which the proposed borrower is a tenant. But it is *least* so, by a long way, in the case of co-operative banks, because such banks rely on different and very much more effective means, both for informing themselves upon their borrowers' title to credit and for enforcing repayment, than other credit institutions. Their strength lies in the mutual knowledge of and influence upon one another maintained among members, which have been found a good deal more efficacious than any pledge or writ. It is their business to find out before granting a loan, whether a distress is to be apprehended. If it is, and if they lend all the same, or if they do not take care to ascertain, they richly deserve to lose their money. "Distress" has proved no hindrance abroad. There is a law of "distress" in force in Italy, every bit as stringent as our own, and more rigorously enforced. It does not stand in the way of co-operative banking. In some cases, as I have shown, landlords are appealed to, and consent to waive their preferential right in respect of a par-

The Bogie of "Distress."

ticular loan. Otherwise banks take the trouble of finding out about their applicants, and secure themselves accordingly, and no inconvenience whatever has been found to result.

The Taking of Deposits.

In the second place, it is made a complaint that under the Friendly Societies Act our Village Banks *must not take deposits from persons who are not members.* That is so, undoubtedly. And unquestionably it constitutes a drawback—a drawback mitigated, possibly, by the fact that if Village Banks were, nevertheless, to collect deposits from outsiders, probably very little would be heard about their violation of a legal precept which, in Bishop Butler's terminology, is "positive" only, and not "moral." The complainants to set the law in motion against offending Village Banks are the local bankers. Are they likely to do so? The amounts taken are not likely to be very large.

People's Banks as Savings Banks.

The question of taking savings from the general public is, I am ready to admit, a matter of very considerable importance, and calculated very materially to affect the utility of People's Banks in this country. It is by no means least as convenient receptacles for people's savings that I expect to see People's Banks showing themselves deserving of public favour. In the matter of arrangements for collecting public savings we appear to be approaching something of a crisis. Requirements and appliances evidently no longer fit into and fully answer one another. The child for which in 1861 we made what then seemed adequate provision has outgrown its narrow cradle, and those who are appointed to watch over it are becoming seriously alarmed, and appear not unwilling, like a second Procrustes, to lop off the limbs embarrassingly protruding—which they themselves have deliberately stimulated into growth, without apparently realising what remarkable

A Flaw in our Savings Bank System.

fecundity there is in thrift. "Certain it is," says the *Times* of 21st April, "that they (Consols) are at famine price, and that continued purchases on account of the Government must tend still further to reduce the available supply. The purchases for the Post Office are the largest and most important factor. We hope that the contemplated reduction of interest on the savings bank deposits will tend to diminish them." What does that mean but that the *Times* and those for whom it speaks indulge the hope that, since poor people's thrift is—by our own fault—growing troublesome to us, who have constituted ourselves the sole authorised custodians of its fruits—not, we shall make more ample provision for collecting those incoming savings, the welcome sign of prosperity, but that our poor will reduce their economies, and lay by less, out of consideration for us, because we have not sufficient Consols to sell. For thirty-five years we have been priding ourselves upon our admirable savings banks system. Even now the *Times* takes credit for a "loss to the State"*—the existence of which the Post Office authorities deny, with which we are said magnanimously to be burdening ourselves in our generous effort to stimulate poor folks' thrift. However, that system is not proving equal to the strain put upon it. Our model baby of 1861 now proves something of a Frankenstein, and we are haunted by the fear to which, very rightly, and the first statesman of note to do so in England, Mr Goschen, gave expression some sessions ago, when in effect he said—"Here you have £120,000,000 of other people's money, every farthing of which is withdrawable at the depositor's pleasure." By the present time the sum has grown to nearly £150,000,000. That is the spectre which is causing us such grave misgivings, and driving us into all sorts of inconsistent practices, at once stimulating and restricting, encouraging and forbidding. Our boasted system, it is now found, is far less perfect than has been

---

* *Times*, 13th April 1896.

assumed. If there are, on the one hand, all the advantages to be got out of it for the State in the shape of a constraint, which to all intents and purposes raises a forced loan of unfixed amount from our savers—adding to our credit, driving up the price of Consols to an unheard-of figure—there is, on the other, as a dangerous set-off, the risk of sudden and large withdrawals, which we could not forbid, but which would be most embarrassing. Hence those clamours for reduction of interest, hence that limit to deposits, only slightly relaxed three years ago—with a provision added which undoes much of the good unquestionably effected.*

---

* I refer to the "Automatic Investment Clauses" insisted upon by the Treasury, which provide that whenever a deposit grows so as to exceed the maximum limit allowed of £200 by any sum not less than £5, unless the depositor directs otherwise, the excess shall be invested in Government Stock. This provision has led to the withdrawal of a large number of what are to the Savings Banks the most profitable accounts. Poor folk do not like Consols, which may vary in price. They do not want more than their £1 back for £1 deposited. But they will not run the risk of receiving *less*. Accordingly very little use indeed has been made of the power given to depositors to accumulate £500 in Consols in addition to £200 which they may accumulate in deposits. The Inspection Committee, in its Official Report for 1896, expresses itself as follows on the "Automatic Investment Clauses":—

"It is reported to us that the feeling of the banks is adverse to the provisions which the Regulations were framed to give effect to. Written communications to depositors respecting the state of their accounts are said to be opposed to the traditions and practice of Trustee Savings Banks, and to be liable to cause domestic trouble. Instances have occurred where the notices sent to the depositors under the Regulations, calling on them to deal with sums in excess of £200, have *led to withdrawals of large sums* and even *to the entire closing of some of the large accounts*, which, being more remunerative to the banks, meet in part the cost of the smaller accounts. The Regulations further affect the income account of the banks by bringing about the withdrawal of the amounts in excess of £200. On these amounts the trustees receive interest and pay none, owing to the statutory provisions by which balances bear interest only up to the amount of £200. This

The object of the limit, it is said, is, to keep out depositors of classes for whom the savings banks were not intended. The danger of such persons taking advantage in any considerable number of the facilities given for depositing is really not serious. In the Post Office Savings Banks it may be difficult to classify depositors. In our Trustee Savings Banks, on the other hand, we have adequate means of ascertaining to what classes depositors belong, and our books show that the number of accounts opened to persons who might be considered illegitimate depositors is very small. It is sheer nonsense to assert that for genuine working men the limit of £100 in all would be sufficient. We have many accounts of larger amounts standing to the credit of thoroughly *bonâ fide* working men, the fruits of twenty, thirty, forty, even sixty years' savings.* It is at these, the very men whom we ought to wish to see increasing in number, that the restriction advocated by the *Times* would strike. I will tell the *Times* and its friends how, to my knowledge, that "limit," so plausibly insisted upon by people out of touch with working men, has acted in practice. In the Trustee Bank of which I have just been speaking,

---

provision is no doubt sufficient to guard the limit of £200 from any considerable infringement. The sums in excess of £200, *though small in themselves, have been sufficient in the aggregate to act as a material set-off against the uninvested balance necessarily retained in hand to meet current requirements.* The clerical labour involved is a further ground of complaint, and one that also applies to the trouble of crediting stock dividends to depositors' accounts quarterly instead of yearly only, as is usually the case with interest credited by the banks to depositors."

* I can speak positively with regard to one Trustee Bank in which the average of deposit accounts stands at about £35, which is a high figure. In that bank there were, at New Year, out of 2,050 accounts of individuals, 238 exceeding £100 (102 exceeding £150 and 21 exceeding £200), nearly every one of which stands to the credit of a genuine working man.

and of which I myself was for a time one of the "Managers," established in a town of 12,000 inhabitants, we held about £100,000 in deposits. But for the "limit," we might have held £300,000. Where did the balance of £200,000 go to? For the most part it went into the Balfour companies and other similar specious concerns whose promoters knew how to take advantage of the Government restrictions on saving—where it was lost, to the severe distress of the poor people.

That is the result of a law which says:—Up to a certain, very moderate, figure we will "paternally" take your savings out of your hands. You shall not be educated into knowing how to employ them yourselves. We insist upon receiving them. Beyond that sum you may gamble, speculate, trade, do whatever you like and whatever, in view of your want of training for the business, you are likely to do; but you shall not "save." Is that a desirable state of things?

Obviously, if we really wish to benefit the poor people in whom, as we say, we desire to stimulate thrift—if we are really thinking more of the community, which is sure to be benefited by an extension of saving, than of the Treasury anxious to keep its credit abnormally high, the proper remedy for the predicament into which we have got is, not to prohibit further saving, but to make more liberal and more convenient provision for the receipt of savings, since the old receptacle has "grown too strait" for them.

There was very much to be said for the arrangement which we came to when passing the Savings Bank Act—at a time when our working classes were a totally different set of people from what they are now—less educated, less independent, less capable of managing their own affairs. And up to a certain point unquestionably it is right that the State should provide means for the safe keeping of popular savings, at a low rate of interest, but absolutely secure. However, depositors and those who administer their moneys for them should be given a choice. In Italy the great corporate bodies not interfered with by the State do not complain of inconveniently large receipts. They dispose of their moneys as they choose—on mortgages, on acceptances, on improvement loans. And they make no losses. Their excellent administration and the safety with which they conduct their business excite the admiration of economists who visit them.* For those who do not care to go to these institutions, there are the Post Office Savings Banks, the same as here, but doing only about one-fourth of the collective business. In Germany, the communal, district, and provincial savings banks do not propose a limit on savings. They have proved absolutely safe. And so far from bringing about an embarrassing accumulation of money, such as alarms the *Times*, thanks to the freedom of employment allowed to them, they are providing the means for materially *counteracting the mischievous hoarding* which is going on under the Old Age Pensions Law. They borrow the money from the Pension Offices and deal it out in loans to the public. Surely we do not now want forced loans to raise our credit! We have more useful employment for the over-abundant money resulting from savings, than by a method which creates a plethora in one place balanced by anæmia elsewhere. And we have administrators as efficient as any that Italy or Germany, or—in its "autonomous" banks—France can find, for the custody of savings.

There is more than this. The Post Office Savings Bank is a safe money-box. But to the poor it is nothing more. To them it is a brick building with a slot in its wall to receive their pennies—and a bit of blue paper sent out to

---

* I commend more particularly the great Savings Banks of Milan and Bologna, and the Monte dei Paschi of Siena, to the notice of students of this question.

tell, often enough to the wrong people, who the depositors are. The Trustee Bank has ears, as well, with which to listen to questions, and a mouth wherewith to give advice, and in many cases also a heart to make that advice more than judicious, to make it kind. The fact that deposits average very much higher in Trustee Banks than they do in Post Office Banks—generally speaking about £26 to less than £15—proves that of the two kinds they are the more popular. However, they are not in official favour, and, under the application of modern legislation, under the effects of control which they find irksome, and interference which debars them from rendering as good service as some of them otherwise might render to the public, both their number and their business are declining.

<small>People's Banks to fill the gap.</small>

Here is an opening into which it appears to me that People's Banks are peculiarly well fitted to step in. Experience shows them to be safe; experience shows them to be popular. As I have been able to state, in Prussia law courts allow trust moneys to be deposited into their keeping. As I have likewise explained, in the words of M. Rostand and other witnesses, in Italy the counters of the Post Office Savings Banks stand decidedly second in public favour to those of People's and Village Banks, officered by men of the depositors' own choice, and therefore trusted by them—local popular institutions, in which each inhabitant knows that he has a direct interest, and of which he is jealous and proud. It might be the same thing among ourselves. And in all probability People's Banks would be able to allow a higher interest than the Post Office, and, under its dictation, the Trustee Banks. Under the Industrial and Provident Societies Act we can take what savings we please, and all that is wanted is to convince the public of the safety of the People's Banks to be created. In rural parishes, where there is really much greater call for such a supplementary institution, we cannot yet, under the Friendly

Societies Acts, do the same thing. Very probably before very long we shall be permitted to. Meanwhile, so far as the interest of village banks themselves comes into question, we can very well do without the right which we covet. In France, as I have shown, under a similar legal disqualification, many village banks take as good as no savings (as distinguished from larger deposits). In Parma, the village banks take no savings at all. No more does the little bank of Belleville. And there is many a village bank in Germany which actually takes no savings, or only very few, but nevertheless does well. As an instance to pit against the case of a village bank in England, which ignorant wiseacres have prevented from doing any work for just eighteen months on the ground of its assumed inability to procure sufficient funds for successful work without the taking of savings—though it had £250 guaranteed to it in a drawing credit—I should wish to state what was done at Metzels in Saxe-Meiningen, a poverty-stricken little village, on high, barren ground, overlooking that castle of Landsberg which was built when the Saxe-Meiningen Princess Adelaide was our queen. The poor peasantry are such as Lady Verney was in the habit of portraying with apparent gusto when writing down peasant properties. In the summer of 1893 eighteen of these poor men clubbed together, with the minister for nineteenth, to start their Raiffeisen Loan Bank, with only a few shillings coming in as first instalments on the small shares of, I believe, 5s. each. There was no man of any means to lend his help. The cash available at starting was, accordingly, practically nothing at all. However, the minister scraped together £12. 10s. to advance to the bank, with which money the latter acquired a £50 share in the Central Bank of Neuwied, the managers of which opened to it a drawing credit for £250. In respect of initial resources the two cases were accordingly almost exactly on a par. In the course of the eighteen months during which our English bank did nothing, the Metzels bank lent out to its members £155 in money, and purchased for them £439 worth of goods—a service very much appreciated—laying up meanwhile a reserve fund of £6. 2s. 5d., and increasing the number of its members to fifty-seven—all without the collection of any savings to speak of, either from outsiders or from members.

<small>Difficulties in the Law.</small>

There are really provisions a great deal more inconvenient for our present purpose than the prohibition of taking savings from non-members—for members are free to make deposits—in the Friendly Societies Act.

One is, that we cannot make the Reserve Fund indivisible *after the dissolution* of the society, as the Raiffeisen principle in its purity demands. That defect we must simply put up with until there is a likelihood of our Act being amended. For some time to come no inconvenience is likely to arise. Meanwhile we may effect by understanding what we cannot assure by law.

The other drawback is more serious. Our object is to lend, without having any money of our own, and to accumulate our own fund out of the profits accruing from the lending. However, the Friendly Societies Act lays it down that we must positively not lend out £3 without having at least £1 of our own to include in the sum. I have got over this difficulty by introducing a new feature, cash credit to be guaranteed on behalf of the bank by some acceptable sureties. That gives us precisely what the credit at the Central Bank gave to the little village bank of Metzels, and gives to other banks in Germany. It is quite sufficient for our purpose, and the authorities allow it to serve in substitution of funds. But care should be taken to make absolutely sure that it is advanced only as a loan, to be scrupulously repaid, and meanwhile to be steadily reduced as the fund belonging to the bank itself grows **up.** Not under any circumstances should it become a gift.*

Generally speaking, then, circumstances are not **un**favourable ; and even **the** task of convincing bankers that we do not come into the field as their rivals, and the work of bringing home to the public interested that here **is** an institution offered deserving of adoption and encouragement, have proved very much lighter than I had any reason to expect when four years ago I addressed myself to propagandist work. My first article, written in 1892, I had to hawk about from *Review* to *Review*. The subject, I **was** told, **was** bound to fall flat. It has *not* fallen flat. My book was sold out in little time. I have been asked **to** explain the principle of co-operative banking be,fore a gathering of members of Parliament at Westminster, before **two** Royal Commissions, before Chambers of Agriculture, before **so** representative **a** body as **the** Irish Agricultural Organisation Society**, which** is **now actively turning** that explanation to account, and elsewhere. **I have not** wanted for encouraging messages from persons **of** accepted judgment. One banker has **written to** say that what I am trying to do really existing **banks** should have done, but have not, from pure selfishness. **The** Duke of Argyll has written to say that "your system of strict payments and watching the loan is admirable." I have even had that sincerest of all compliments paid me :—counterfeit People's Banks and a counterfeit Raiffeisen Association have sprung **up to turn** what was becoming a popular cause to account

---

* Unfortunately **our** authorities will **not** allow us **to** say anything whatever about this in our rules. Both in the short—the original, not the present—rules which I drew up for the Agricultural Banks Association, and in the fuller rules which I prepared afterwards for publication, the clauses which I put in relating to guarantors and their safeguards have been mercilessly struck out by the Chief Registrar.

in a way for which it was certainly not intended—just as has happened in Germany, in Belgium, in Italy.

Our Pioneer Banks.

Beyond all this, we have now some pioneer banks at work, the story of whose first experiences may be worth the telling.

Newport.

And first, for town banks—co-operative banks of the system of Commendatore Luzzatti, with small shares and limited liability. We have two such. The first, at Newport in Monmouthshire, was started in November 1894. Mr Thomas Jones, who had read my book, asked me to go down and explain the system. I found both Mr Jones and his active ally, Mr Charles L. Barfoot—severally subsequently the chairman and the unpaid secretary of the bank—very zealous in the matter. And the people whom they had invited to hear me manifested unmistakable interest. The bank did not really begin business until April 1895. Work at first proved very uphill. By the 1st of May, seventy members had been enrolled, subscribing among them £387 in £1 shares. But only £147 was paid up. Only two men had applied for and received loans, of respectively £20 and £30. However, a local "Discount Company," alarmed at the appearance of its new, popular, competitor on the scene, had discreetly taken warning and shut up shop. For a little while the bank was rather embarrassed with a plethora of cash. A little time after, when its advantages came to be understood, and loans were rather freely applied for, its embarrassment proved the other way. The borrowers' promissory notes, which abroad are employed as a means of raising cash by being discounted, could not be so passed on, because they were made repayable by instalments. However—

"you will be glad to hear," so Mr Barfoot wrote to me on 8th June, "that we have got hold of the right class of borrowers. Two of the £30 loans have been to assist members in starting in business on their own account, and £30 to assist a working man to extend his small business,"—

CONCLUSION.

and so on. Eventually money came in in the shape of deposits, and then a local bank accorded an overdraft. By the end of the year (April to December) the number of members had risen to a hundred, holding collectively 425 shares. Four non-members had deposited £295. 10s. The bank had advanced in all £624. 17s. in twenty-eight loans, ranging from £1. 10s. to £70. The committee, in their annual report, confess themselves thoroughly convinced that the bank is satisfactorily meeting a real existing want, and that it promises to prove of great utility to the poorer population in the town, and can be worked on sound businesslike principles. Among the loans granted was one of £50, to get a man out of the clutches of a Bristol usurer, who was on that amount bleeding his victim to the tune of £30 a year. Unfortunately, owing to a forgery (which might have been guarded against, and which, under proper safeguards, is not likely to be repeated), the first year's working closed with a loss. That does not, however, touch the principle of the system, which is now so well appreciated that business has grown considerably brisker (between 1st January and 25th February about £200 was granted in loans). The committee is now very properly proposing to extend its work by including cash credit to members among its operations.* The founders and managers of that bank may well take credit for having set a bright example in their pioneer institution, which is sure to serve as a good teacher to others.

Our second urban bank is more modest. It was started at Finsbury Park, a suburb of London, on 23rd February 1895. But some time elapsed before it got really to work. At New Year it numbered thirty-five members, holding among them eighty-three £1 shares, upon which £62. 1s.

_{Finsbury Park.}

---

* This has, meanwhile, I understand, been satisfactorily provided for.

had been paid up. Payment on such shares may be made at the easy rate of 6d. per week, which renders the bank accessible to every working man. Some small deposits made had enabled the bank to lend out in ten months £79. 17s. in forty loans, which are being steadily repaid, some by instalments of 6d. a week. In all, at New Year £41. 11s. 6d. had been thus recovered. As in the Newport Bank, borrowers are found to observe their repayment terms well. The loans are all considered to have been rightly placed, and to have done good.

"One was to get a member out of difficulties in a County Court case. This has been repaid. Another, to assist a coster to buy his donkey—£5. Another, £10, to buy a greengrocer his horse, for which he had been paying ten shillings a week on hire. Another, to a small painter and decorator, to enable him to proceed with a contract he took with a loan in view, but which he could not otherwise have undertaken."

All this I consider to be very satisfactory work, upon which the founder, Mr J. E. Carver, may well congratulate himself.

Our Village Banks.

The record of our village banks is, on the whole, at least as encouraging. We have, as might almost have been expected, thus far fared best in Ireland. There is greatest need there, also much greater quickness of apprehension in respect of new ideas, than in England. And in addition the task of forming banks has there fallen to unquestionably capable men.

Doneraile.

The pioneer bank in Ireland, in Doneraile, has already shown itself distinctly useful and businesslike. It was founded on the personal initiative of the Hon. H. Plunkett, M.P. It was opened early in 1895. On the 1st of August, Mr Anderson, Secretary of the Irish Agricultural Organisation Society, wrote to me as follows :—

"You will be glad to hear that the Doneraile bank is doing very well indeed, and we are so much encouraged by the experiment, that we are determined to push the system wherever we find an opening for it."

CONCLUSION. 391

By the end of the year there were fifty members (there were fifty-six by the end of February), taking no shares, but subscribing only their liability, and paying an entrance fee of 6d. each. Deposits had been received to the amount of £75, and thirty-seven loans had been granted, to the amount of £174, collectively, at 6 per cent. interest. The money is being repaid by instalments, with scrupulous promptitude. And notwithstanding the fact that the first year's transactions were burdened with the initial expenses, account balances with a surplus of 11s. 0½d. Experience has, indeed, shown things to be so satisfactory, that in future the committee propose to allow 4 per cent. instead of 3 on deposits.

"The business done by the Doneraile bank is likely to increase very largely in the near future," so wrote to me Mr Anderson, on the 12th of February, "as both the loans to the bank and the applications for loans from it have increased very considerably since the end of the year."

"The borrowers," says the report, "especially those of small sums, expressed satisfaction at the low rates at which they could obtain loans."

"Your bank," so writes the public auditor, Mr Thomas Scott, in his report, "has made its way amongst the people without solicitation or advertisement. It was an experiment. Your proceedings were of necessity of a tentative character, and I am bound to say they have been conducted with marked intelligence. Your pioneer bank can now be taken as an example over the country. It illustrates clearly the unspeakable benefit which may be conferred on the honest poor by co-operative banks. Without them co-operation is to hundreds of thousands of the people an impossible thing. It is therefore not extravagant to say, that the modest and unpretentious co-operative village bank ought to be regarded as the mainspring of the whole movement."

"There are many noticeable good results already," wrote to me the secretary, Mr D. Lascelles Roche, on the 24th of February, "among the borrowers, and members generally; some have borrowed who possessed small savings, but, as they stated by way of explanation, were afraid to disturb the money, fearing inability to replace it again, and by borrowing and repaying in small instalments to the bank they succeeded in obtaining property which otherwise they would not have done. I have this year received £1 deposit from a labourer who was a borrower last year; and in a case where the widow and her little family were partly dependent on charity, she was enabled to purchase a donkey and cart and earn a living by drawing water. In one or two cases horses have been purchased by carriers, and small public contracts have been taken and completed by tradesmen, who could not have done so except for the money they obtained from the bank. Houses which were very unfit for human habitation have been made comfortable. Labourers have been enabled to provide manure and seed for potato gardens, and farmers purchased pigs, sheep, cattle, &c."

"I am sure," so the same correspondent has written me since, "that Agricultural Credit Societies will grow up quickly in this country after the system has stood the practical test in a few districts. I have had letters and applications from almost every county in Ireland on the subject."

And, again, on 22nd April :—" The more I see of the movement, the more I am convinced of its adaptability to this country."

It is not surprising that the system is spreading. There are five village banks now established in Ireland—at Doneraile, Kyle, Urlingford, Belmullet, and Johnstown. And the number promises to increase.

Scawby.

In England we have not gone on quite so fast, but we have some good beginnings to show. Our first English village bank was formed at Scawby, in Lincolnshire, in June 1894, at the instance of the squire of the parish, Mr R. N. Sutton Nelthorpe, a devoted champion of the idea of co-operative banking. However, owing to bad advice, for which others than Mr Nelthorpe and myself are responsible, the bank did not actually begin business till October 1895. It promptly took some deposits and lent out two loans. One of £30 was to a small tenant of 53 acres, simply to provide him with working capital for his farm, which he wanted. Without the bank to do this, he says that he would have had no choice but to sell his lambs, which, in fact, he sold in spring for so much more money as to leave him, as I understand, about £20 in pocket. And for that loan he paid 23s. The second loan was one of £20 to the village blacksmith, to enable him to buy stock with, when he had keep and stock was cheap. Without the bank he would have had to let his keep run to waste or else wait till he had money, by which time stock would have been dear. He is likewise satisfied with his bargain. Unfortunately the members of the bank insisted upon the money being lent out at 5 per cent. instead of 6 per cent. Accordingly the transactions of 1895 have resulted in a loss of 18s. 7d. That is not a very serious deficiency, and if it teaches members of such banks that in any case a sufficient margin is absolutely necessary in their dealings, it will not represent money wasted.

Next, we have a good little bank at Pembury, in Kent, started in the autumn of 1894, with only a dozen members, by Mr Walter Malden, the medical man in the parish. He had read my book, and, upon the basis of what he had there learnt, so he writes to me, he had quite independently formed his organisation on true Raiffeisen lines, asking for no shares (but taking an entrance fee of 5s.), selecting his members with care, and insisting upon very rigid checking of the committee's work by the council. The bank has only recently been registered. Its work has been humble, but extremely useful and encouraging. There were in March thirty-one members (twenty-eight men and three women). Within a little more than a twelvemonth £170 had been lent out in loans varying from £4 to £50— *Pembury.*

"for purchase of cows, manure, seed potatoes, &c. We have made it a rule that all stock bought with borrowed money must be insured. At present we are dealing with a large London company, but we hope to start an insurance branch of our own before long. Up to the present time we have had every instalment paid on the day it was due. It is rather early to be able to trace any distinct results ; but the borrowers all speak of the immense convenience of being able to command necessary cash on such easy terms. At present we have not taken any deposits, but we hope to do so during the present year."

The bank started with a loan interest rate of 5 per cent., but has had to increase it to 6 per cent. to cover working expenses. Like the Doneraile bank, the village bank of Pembury closes its year's work with a small balance on the right side.

"Personally," writes Mr Malden, "I am convinced that in time our bank will do a larger and more useful work; also that the principle is sound, and only requires to be more widely known to be largely adopted in agricultural villages."

Co-operation begets co-operation.

"We are working out a scheme for dealing with produce, dairy, poultry, fruit, and vegetables. It will, I think, take the form of an association as a limited company, with a depot in the village for collection of all produce, and perhaps a shop in Tunbridge Wells."

The society has already taken up a farm of 120 acres, and divided it into seven small holdings. "We hope to develop a Producers' Association in connection with this." I think this result, which is again traceable to the zealous initiative and judicious guidance of one good worker, who readily finds people to range themselves under his lead, is distinctly satisfactory.

Laxfield.

There is the young bank of Laxfield, in Suffolk, started in the same way by the active local doctor, Mr Charles W. Biden, upon the ground of what he had read in my book. Laxfield is rather a large parish, almost entirely agricultural, with a population slightly exceeding 900—in Dr Biden's words, "just the place where a bank could do much good." However, there is that ingrained suspiciousness to hinder the work, of farmers on the one hand, and labourers on the other, each apprehensive that they may be put to use for the other's benefit. I have found in many parishes that the farmers look upon village banks as nothing more than a preparative for the expropriation of their best bits of land by the parish councils, to be parcelled out in allotments. Without money, the farmers clearly see, these allotments could do the labourers no good. And so they argue that these banks are designed specially for the purpose of providing an excuse for cutting the little bits of Goshen out of their own holdings for the benefit of labourers —at the farmer's expense. It is not the *banks* that the farmers oppose, but the *ulterior use* to which they persuade themselves that the banks are intended to be put. One farmer in Lincolnshire plainly admitted this. Mr Biden could at the outset find only eight men to join him. In his rules he disallows shares, and limits the entrance fee, which is to provide the funds for initial expenses, to 2s. The number of members now stands at eleven ; and some useful loans have already been granted—one to enable a hawker to buy a pony, another to help a man to buy a cow, a third to enable a man to keep his litter of pigs and rear and fatten them for sale. The beginnings are small, but Mr Biden hopes for an early development.

Lastly, there is the village bank of Grandborough, in Warwickshire, started in May 1895, with only eight members, by that indefatigable co-operator, Mr Bolton King, who, like Mr Plunkett, has thoroughly grasped the idea of co-operative village banking. It is too early still to say anything very definite about this bank, but Mr King writes that he is "very hopeful of its future." Thus far it has "done well." Grandborough.

I understand that there are some other banks for the good practice of which I can in no wise answer, and about which I am all the more wishful to say little, since there seems at the present time reason for hoping that what has indisputably, and very unfortunately, been done amiss, will after all be set right. At one or two places in this book I have had occasion to refer to some most unsound, absolutely mischievous, rules, and to some very bad practices, which have found their way into the work of an association of which I was one of the founders, but Other Banks.

from which, in consequence of the errors committed, I have, like some other members, felt it my duty to retire. The temptation to such deviation from the right path, as has been indicated, is strong on new ground and among persons used to politics. The mischief sure to result is equally great— so great that no pains ought to be spared to avoid it.

Generally, Prospects are promising.

Otherwise things are certainly progressing favourably, and we may make sure that in the end the good principle will triumph, as it has triumphed elsewhere. Generally speaking, interest has been awakened, the principle is being every day more widely approved and appreciated. We are making headway in Ireland, we have encouraging promises in England. Before long, please God, we shall set up our banks in the overcrowded, famished, "sweated" poor folks' quarters in our great cities. Sir John Brunner is having my rules translated into Welsh, with a view to spreading co-operative banking in Wales, as it is becoming diffused in Ireland. And there is promise of good work being done in India, where the want of Raiffeisen banks is acknowledged, among others, by Mr F. A. Nicholson, who concludes the preface of his excellent official report with the two words, which he says sum up all that he has to say, "Find Raiffeisen."*

The Outlook in England. Ireland.

Wales.

India.

Australia.

New Zealand.

Australia, likewise, is to have its People's Banks—probably of the Luzzatti type — to guard against a repetition of calamitous bank crashes. And even from New Zealand I have had inquiries.

The work is going on, then, and promises to prosper.

---

* Many influential men in India, to whom I have explained the system, appear strongly favourable to its adoption, and disposed to assist such with their support or countenance. The Salvation Army has taken the work practically in hand, with every promise of success, of supplying the oppressed ryots with a network of Raiffeisen Banks. Colonel Langercrantz, late of the Swedish, now of the Salvation Army, has recently gone out to direct operations. From his energy and ability good results may be expected.

Once we take it up in earnest, I believe that we shall succeed with it even better than our neighbours, for we are made of more businesslike stuff. God speed its progress! There is no work, in my opinion, which is likely to prove more helpful to our poor, and even to those who are not altogether poor in the conventional sense of the term, but still in want of that support which combination can secure.

I ought not, however, to conclude without just one word of warning which, unfortunately, appears needed. I am far from recommending co-operative banks as a panacea. Wherever they are required they may do much good. Where there is no call for them, it would be folly to set them up. Where there is use for them, if they are to do any good they must be good themselves, and they must be of the system suited for their particular work. A bad bank, badly organised, in which the co-operative principle is corrupted or diluted, can only do mischief—not very serious mischief, perhaps, but work which is bound to end in disappointment and to discredit a good institution. Therefore it is of the utmost importance that we should hold fast by the sound principle. The introduction, for instance, of politics—such as has actually been tried—or else attempts to make the banks instruments for securing to one class of members undue influence over others, ought to be most carefully avoided, as bound to result in fatal mischief. We ought also to be careful to make clear to ourselves exactly what we intend a bank to do. I find that there is still a great confusion of ideas on this score. I find, moreover, that commonly far too great importance is attached to *rules* as a matter of specific regulations. I want to point out that rules, however desirable it is that they should be good—for bad rules cannot fail to prove mischievous—really rank only second in significance. We are addressing ourselves to the work of applying a principle amply approved elsewhere on new and untried ground. Our

A Word of Warning.

circumstances differ in many particulars from the circumstances of those whom we are proposing to imitate. Accordingly it is only by practical experience that we can ascertain precisely what rules are best suited to our case. I have, with the kind help of the Chief Registrar of Friendly Societies, prepared rules which I think contain all that is wanted, and which I believe certain to work well.* However, I shall be the last to grumble at their modification in points of purely practical application, wherever circumstances appear to demand such treatment, so long as the principle is loyally maintained. Master the principle, adopt it loyally, and you may allow the rules to take care of themselves. That principle is—that the institution should be *absolutely* based upon *self-help*, that its *government* should be *democratic*, that the quality of its work should be assured by a *quickening of the sense of responsibility*, by checking, and union, and control. No gift from "honorary members" such as I have had to refer to, no patronage can have a place in these banks. Every dallying with greed, every yielding to the spirit of patronage, foreign experience has shown, adds a toe of clay to the huge brazen Colossus, and thereby threatens to overthrow it in spite of its size. And the thing must grow up from out of its own self, from the bottom to the top. None of the systems which have succeeded abroad have been organised from above. They have all risen from below. Nowhere, moreover, has this work been "good fairy" work. Every shilling's worth of success has been purchased by unremitting application, by economy, gratuitous labour (so far as gratuitous labour was possible), zeal, and caution. And experience has shown that it is not otherwise to be obtained. There may be hindrances,

---

* 1. "Village Banks or Agricultural Credit Societies: How to Start them, &c." P. S. King & Son. 6d.
2. "A People's Bank Manual." P. S. King & Son. 6d.

and progress may at first appear slow, but in the end the work is bound to succeed wherever there is call for it.

I must warn founders of co-operative banks, no matter of what kind, that in the first year they may very likely find themselves working at a loss. There will be outlay which business may not at once be sufficient to cover. If there is shown to be want of a bank in the locality, if it be found to develop healthily, that deficit ought not to frighten any one; it will soon be wiped out. But, generally speaking, if we address ourselves to the work in the right spirit, it is bound to succeed among ourselves as it has succeeded among Teutons, Slavs, Latins, and Turanians, under every variety of European sky, under the most diverse conditions, bringing good wherever it has taken root, raising the poor where other educating methods have failed, teaching habits of business, thrift, sobriety—making the drunkard sober, the spendthrift saving, the ne'er-do-weel well-conducted, turning the illiterate into a penman—and at the same time stimulating, with its magic wand, as M. Léon Say has put it, commerce, industry, and small husbandry, substituting plenty for want and happiness for misery, raising, enriching, emancipating the working classes, and flooding the whole country, economically speaking, like the waters of the Nile, with fertilising influences. Here is a work, in view of the magnificent results attainable by it, for the benefit of millions of fellow-countrymen, which ought to have attractions for statesmen, philanthropists, and ministers of religion. Please God, we shall some day see a rich crop growing up from the seed now being sown, and our country the richer, the happier, and the more contented for its growth. For, applying the words of M. Ernest Brelay, we may truly say—I think my narrative must have shown that—that the resources of this beneficent creative power are "illimitable."

A Prize worth striving for.

Printed at THE DARIEN PRESS, Edinburgh.

www.ingramcontent.com/pod-product-compliance
Lightning Source LLC
Chambersburg PA
CBHW030555300426
44111CB00009B/995